THE MARK OF THE SWORD

The MARK of the SWORD

A narrative history of

THE CUTLERS' COMPANY

1189–1975

TOM GIRTIN

HUTCHINSON BENHAM, LONDON

Hutchinson Benham Ltd
3 Fitzroy Square, London W1

An imprint of the Hutchinson Group

London Melbourne Sydney Auckland
Wellington Johannesburg and agencies
throughout the world

First published 1975
© Cutlers' Company 1975

Set in Monotype Spectrum

Printed in Great Britain by The Anchor Press Ltd
and bound by Wm Brendon & Son Ltd
both of Tiptree, Essex

ISBN 0 09 124790 X

Contents

Contents

Illustrations

Foreword

In an earlier age of more spacious and leisured days it was customary to write history at considerable length and in great detail. Such a *History of the Cutlers' Company of London* was compiled by Charles Welch and published in 1916. That was the first volume covering 'From Early Times to the Year 1500'. It contained 372 pages, beautifully printed on splendid paper. The second volume, bringing the History down to modern times, appeared in 1923, adding a further 410 pages. This is a life-work of marvellous devotion and diligence. Not only was its author Master of the Company (1907–8) but he was also the Librarian at Guildhall.

The time has now come for a more popular history. Few men have had more experience of research into the City Livery Companies than Mr. Tom Girtin, who has already acquired a reputation for his scholarly yet readable books in this field. The Cutlers' Company was very fortunate to find him willing to undertake this task with his usual thoroughness and good humour. I am confident that this book will bring pleasure and pride, amusement and enlightenment, to Cutlers and to many others who delight in the City of London, its traditions and institutions.

Strictly speaking the title should have been *The Mark of the Dagger* since this was the mark of the London Cutlers. But this might have sounded like a thriller, and in a generation weary of violence it was felt that the sword, also made by Cutlers and associated with ceremonial, with uniform, and indeed with the preservation of peace, might be a more appropriate symbol in the title.

The publication of this History comes just sixty years after its predecessor. During that period much has happened and the climate of the times is one in which many questions are asked about the Livery Companies and the great City that gave them birth. It is hoped that this book will provide some of the answers.

March 1975   Douglas Webster, *Master*

Preface

THE Narrow Seas – that evocative name for the English Channel –
were, in the opening years of the fifteenth century, more than
usually dangerous. English privateers, operating principally from
Cornwall, were causing havoc as they seized great numbers of
foreign merchant ships and made themselves feared and hated
from Danzig to Finisterre. Officially their activities, which made
them local heroes, were discouraged. The King himself wrote
frequently from France demanding that stern measures be taken
to suppress them. For the actions of the privateers led to reprisals:
not only did rival buccaneers of various nationalities install themselves in bases along the coast of Brittany, threatening the vital
trade routes, but English merchant communities on the Continent
were subjected to persecution. In October 1413 an Anglo-Flemish
treaty was signed 'to investigate charges of piracy and to restore
goods to their lawful owners.'[1]

And, in addition to the dangers to English merchant-ships
from privateers, there were all the normal trading hazards and
difficulties inherent in a war with France which had been dragging
on since 1368.

It was, no doubt, this situation that led the Cutlers' Company, in
petitioning the Crown for a Charter, to proclaim in the preamble
to the Grant:

Know ye that since many men of the Mistery of Cutlers of our City of London
in times past by misfortune at sea and other unfortunate chances have reached
so great poverty and need that they have not means of livelihood except from
the alms of Christ's faithful people coming to their help. . . .

The merchant cutlers may well have lost cargoes of ivory imported for knife-handles or shipments of imported or exported cutlery but it is very likely that this plea *ad misericordiam* was overstated. Certainly it was customary, in any circumstances, when drafting a petition to anyone in authority, to exaggerate considerably the gravity of the situation. But in any case, it was not, as we shall see, the only, or even the most important, reason for requiring a Charter. This was urgently needed so that they might deal with the property in Watling Street which for eight years had been held in trust for them. It was needed, too, for purposes of status in the ever denser and more dangerous trade jungle.

As England had slowly evolved from a comparatively primitive and unsophisticated society so the organization of towns in general and London in particular had evolved. And to understand the nature of the problems of the Cutlers' Company which led to their requesting, and receiving, their first Charter in 1416 it is necessary to consider the whole gild system in which they had their being.

Five centuries of Anglo-Saxon history had seen the transition of society from a number of tribes to a national jurisdiction. Society had created the State 'as an instrument of self-preservation and inward order'. Then, when the State had grown too powerful, when the instrument had become stronger than the user, Society had reacted instinctively, adopting forms of feudalism with which to fight feudalism.[2] The necessary organizations for the struggle had been there from the very earliest days in the shape of those gilds in which for common protection and comfort men had banded together. By the end of the twelfth century the gilds had become 'collective lordships' with which to control the State. The term is not an extravagant one for the ruling bodies of the gilds wielded an actual jurisdiction over their members, punishing them with the same punishments that a feudal lord imposed upon his serfs.

The gilds were of three kinds of which the religious gild was the oldest. Dedicated to Christ, or to his holy mother, or to a saint, or to some Christian concept such as the Holy Trinity, the members were usually composed of those worshipping in the same church. And since most of the workers in any particular craft usually lived in the same parish it was inevitable that the craft would be prominent in that gild. The primary purpose of the organization, or fraternity, was to have masses said for dead members and to provide funerals that were both socially and religiously appropriate. The brethren, who wore a distinctively coloured livery – a gown and hood – made at the discretion of the wardens and paid for at cost,[3] elected their own officers who exercised the normal administrative duties. The religious gilds usually owned property, the revenue from which was applied to maintaining one or more chaplains about their business.

This form of organization provided the model for the next category – the gilds merchant – associations of important traders which were found in very close relationship with the municipal authorities of the towns in which they had their being. Though there seems never to have been a gild merchant in London they formed an important part of the administrative machinery of the provincial boroughs subordinate to the local magistrates but having, in their general supervision over the crafts in the town and their inspection of all manufactured goods sold there, far more autonomy than has any modern department of local government. They had some kinship with the old religious gilds and, especially in their concern with the care of sick and needy members of the trades, they had kinship with the later craft gilds, organizations which, in a sense, were subsidiary and 'designed to discharge more completely and adequately powers which required a detailed knowledge (or mistery) of the craft not readily acquired by outsiders.'[4]

These voluntary organizations fulfilled the social and sociable needs of man in an increasingly complex and potentially hostile environment. Unity was strength, and with that strength there was the comforting security of a standard of behaviour and a rule of law administered – on the whole justly – in a country with no centralized system of law and order. If a man were wronged, his gild would protect him; if he were in need he would be helped; if in dispute with his master or his servant, or even his wife, he could seek arbitration. He had, too, the sense of belonging that, with the increasing sophistication of civilization, became ever more desirable. The gild provided a limited but well organized social life: there were periodical meetings and feastings and churchgoings and the psychological pleasures of belonging to a secret society – the taking of oaths of obedience and the paying of dues, the electing of leaders and the keeping of the secrets of the gild. There was everything a man, or woman, needed in order to have the sense of being an insider. Communal duties were undertaken compulsorily within the voluntary organization and it was here, in that same voluntary organization – 'the life blood of modern society' as it has been called[5] – that the political liberty of the country was secured. For, with their power over their trades and their members, the gilds became 'strong enough to control the State and yet flexible enough to be constantly remoulded by the free forces of change. . . . It was in the gild that voluntary association first came into relation with political power.'[6]

As the pressure of the business of government increased the King's representatives, who at first controlled the trades, were forced to appoint deputies. Gradually, the deputies found that their powers were being usurped by the trades themselves. The Weavers' and the Fishmongers' Companies, for instance, did so quite openly and paid a yearly sum to the Exchequer for the privilege of holding their own Courts. Others, known as 'adulterine gilds' – there were at least eighteen of them – who exercised the same powers without official sanction were, in 1180, fined for their presumption. But the display of general dissatisfaction with the official forms of government which led to the grant by the Crown to the London Commune had shewn the power of the gilds to organize civic opinion and to use it to their own advantage. In London, those trades that were in the ascendancy in times of crisis played a really striking part in the history of the City.

It has been shown that the religious gilds tended to contain a majority of members of the same occupation. It was therefore inevitable that the religious and the craft gilds should contain a large proportion of the same members. From there it was by an easy and natural step that the 'religious and industrial organizations of craftsmen frequently became one society rather than two parallel organizations of the same persons. To that extent a fraternal element crept into the craft organizations but it would be an exaggeration to suppose that the craft gild was in general a kind of fraternity ... they were different organizations of the same group of men.'[7]

Different organizations they might be but they became ultimately so intermingled that by the time the granting of the first Charter to the Cutlers' Company is reached no attempt will be made here to distinguish between the different aspects of the association.

By that time there was, however, one sphere of operations in which the gilds found themselves at a disadvantage. By the laws of mortmain they were unable to deal in property: land could be held only by individuals. Fortunately an ancient custom of London permitted freemen to bequeath lands in the City to be held by associations in spite of mortmain. This loophole enabled gilds to vest their property in some aged member whose death, in the due course of nature, could not be too long deferred and who, holding it as trustee, at last bequeathed it to the company. Then in 1391, after a Royal enquiry, it became necessary to obtain a licence to hold land in mortmain. The growth of any gild was greatly restricted if it did not obtain the special privileges which only the King could grant, for these special privileges allowed it, *inter alia*, to hold property in its corporate capacity. From henceforth any gild which had any property was virtually compelled to apply – and pay – for a charter to enable it to stay in existence.[8] This then, perhaps more than actual poverty, more than the dependence for their very existence on the alms of good Christian Londoners, was the reason that the Cutlers' Company had applied and, on that fourth day of December in the fourth year of the reign of King Henry the Fifth after the Conquest, had obtained their Grant to have henceforth one perpetual Commonalty, permitted to elect its own Master and two wardens and, by the King's 'more abundant grace' to acquire lands, tenements and rents in the City and suburbs to the value of twenty pounds a year.

The Mark of the Sword

1

A Matter of Politics

1189-1369

THE Cutlers' Company were proud of their charter. A century later they were boasting that the date of their incorporation made them the tenth oldest Company in the City. The figures they gave were doubtful[9] and, in any case, irrelevant: the date of incorporation – even if accurate – of any Company gave no indication of its actual age. In the absence of any records there is in fact no knowing when, in some London parish, the cutlers in the congregation first banded themselves together, under the protecting wing of the Church, to form their fraternity against the outside world.

That, even in the fifteenth century, it had all happened long, long ago, is certain. It has, in fact, been asserted that 'London Cutlers were associated with some kind of fraternity or society as early as 1154–1189.'[10]

It was in this latter year that the rich aldermen had been powerful enough to persuade John, in the absence of Richard at the Third Crusade, to grant to London the rights of a commune. For all the connotations of the word, the City continued to be ruled by an oligarchy and although, since cutlery was a staple trade, it is likely that there were cutlers among the merchants there seems little direct evidence of a Cutlers' gild, probable though its existence may be. Records in the last decade of the twelfth century of such personages as Adam the Cutler and Thomas le Cutiller are, of themselves, no direct evidence of any association of those in the trade. But it is clear that the political influence of the gilds was already beginning to be felt by government. In 1256, about the time of the Feast of the Conversion of St. Paul, news was brought to King

Henry III that the 'citie of London was nought trewly nor in due manner gowerned.'[11] An enquiry comprised of twenty-six men from every ward was set up and since by this date the first of many cutlers prominent in the City and in the wards have begun to appear in the records it is certain that they must have been represented in the enquiry. It was claimed by one who 'tolde the tale for all the companye' that the Mayor, who had been in power for five years, should be deprived of his office together with a Sheriff and seven of the aldermen. Here, indeed was a concerted attempt by the gilds to influence the course of City politics. Although the result of the hearing is not stated an inference may be drawn that the increasing complexity of business was becoming too great for the City authorities to handle themselves from the fact that in 1262 the mayor

had all the populace of the City summoned, telling them that the men of each craft must make such provisions as should be to their own advantage and he himself would have the same proclaimed throughout the City and strictly observed. Accordingly after this from day to day individuals of every craft of themselves made new statutes and provisions – or, rather, what might be styled 'abominations' and that solely for their own advantage and to the intolerable loss of all merchants coming to London and visiting the fairs of England and the exceeding injury of all persons of the realm.[12]

There spake the true voice of mediaeval reaction but it is possible that this highly significant devolution of power was in part hastened by the effects of the Civil War. For in London, although the aldermen and some of the principal citizens sided with the King, the Mayor and the people openly declared themselves for the barons. The everyday routine of trade control by a central authority would clearly have been virtually impossible to maintain.

Be this as it may, the oligarchy was beginning to crack.

As it happened the gilds did not for long enjoy their new autonomy for only three years later, with a changing shift of power, their revolutionary privileges were snatched from them.

But things could never again be quite the same. The crafts had become aware of their potential strength and in 1271 they actually succeeded in their opposition to the aldermanic candidate for Mayor. They shouted at the tops of their voices 'We are the Commune. We ought to elect the Mayor. We want Hervey to be Mayor. Hervey is our man.' Hervey was elected.[13]

The gilds had taken a vast step forward. And it is not long afterwards that in 1285 there occurs what appears to be the very first reference to the Cutlers' Company as such when a 'house of the Cutlers' is mentioned.[14] It stood on the north side of West Cheap, opposite the conduit into which water from Tyburn had that year been piped. On or near the site of the present Mercers' Hall, it was there that the rulers of the Cutlers conducted their business, in the heart of the area known as the Cutlery.

London at that time still resembled in many respects a county town. The country came right up to the walls, there were still thatched houses and gardens to be found in the City and pigs scavenged in the filthy streets. It was a populous place containing more than 30,000 inhabitants and the general standards of comfort were not high.

The poor had to crowd their families into single rooms in alley tenements that rented for a few shillings a year, carrying on their crafts there, if they were domestic workers, as best they could. Sanitation, ventilation, light and cooking facilities were of the worst. The shopkeepers were better off, having a separate place in which to work, but the majority had probably only one living room, built either behind their shop or as an attic, or solar, above it. The smaller shops, wedged into corners or huddled against the great merchants' warehouses, measured as little as five or six feet by ten. The larger ones were built in long rows with solars above them, identical in design. The street frontage was ten or twelve feet and the depth about twenty feet; sometimes there was a garden of equal length at the back where craftsmen could take the more cumbrous or noxious processes of their work.[15]

The merchants' houses might have the same amount of frontage with a shop on the ground floor and warehouse space behind it. On the first floor was the hall, or main room, with kitchen, larder and butlery adjoining. Above that were the somewhat limited sleeping quarters in which, since privacy was not then much esteemed, the merchant, his wife and his children might well sleep in one room.[16]

Such was the living and working background of the mediaeval cutlers. Their so-called Cutlers' House must have been a large one for the rental was £12 a year.

At the time that it is first mentioned, in 1285, the tenants were the Brethren of the Hospital of St. Thomas of Acon but whether the Cutlers' Company had altogether moved out or whether they occupied part of the premises as sub-tenants is not known. At any rate their business had at some time been conducted there.

It was a many-sided business, defined as the making of 'swords, daggers, rapiers, hangers, wood-knives, pen-knives, razors, surgeons' instruments, skeynes, hilts, pommels, battle-axes, halberds, etc. . . .'[17] – but it was not so straightforward as that. There were, in fact, several different crafts involved in the manufacture of cutlery, some of them, in the early days, having their own organizations and ordinances and lines of demarcation: the bladesmith, or knife-smith, made the blades, the hafter made the handles, and the sheathers the scabbards or sheaths. It was the trade of the cutler to put the various parts together and to sell them. The hafter was the artist among the craftsmen, particularly in the days when the hilts of swords and daggers and the handles of knives might be made of ivory, of gold or of silver, and embellished with precious stones. Yet, although hafters were clearly a highly-skilled and important class of workman, they were never a mistery independent of the Cutlers' Company.

The Sheathers, on the other hand, were a more numerous body who at one time had a separate organization and ranked as one of the misteries of the City.[18] Most important of all were the blade-smiths: they began by being a separate mistery from the Cutlers and long remained so. Subdivided into swordsmiths and knife-smiths the majority of the latter seem to have come under the control of the cutlers while the swordsmiths continued under the rule of the bladesmiths.

There were, in addition, two subsidiary trades which from time to time were of concern to the Cutlers' Company. The Furbours' craft consisted in refurbishing and repairing old weapons and armour; their mistery was common to both armourers and cutlers. The Grinders – perhaps the lowliest of all the trades involved with cutlery – were also concerned with the Shearmen and the Drapers. It will be obvious that at a time when the newly powerful gilds were jockeying for positions in the struggle for power, there was great scope for disputes and quarrels and unfraternal behaviour. In fact, so great was the violence of political feeling in the City that Edward I suspended the mayoralty for thirteen years and restored the City liberties in 1299 only upon promises of future good behaviour. For the Master and the two Wardens of the Cutlers' Company, assisted though they were by the 'ancients' of the gild, it meant much hard, unpaid, often thankless and even dangerous work.

For the times were indeed difficult. There was war with Scotland; the barons were restive; there were uprisings and alarms. On the Thursday before Christmas in 1294 the precept came that a special watch – additional to the usual watch maintained by the wards – was to be kept each night throughout the City and Salomon le Cotiller, an alderman and one of the great men of the Company, rode with five colleagues to keep the peace. There was heavy taxation and there were special levies; first, one thousand pounds to be raised from London as 'courtesy' to Edward I, and then 2000 marks for restoring the City liberties. This had involved a petition to the King, a long ride away in Scotland, and to obtain 'pardon and abatement of the King's wrath lately conceived against the City' the deputation had taken with them, to add substance to their plea, one hundred pounds in silver as a present to him. And when they were successful, to raise the 2000 marks that Edward demanded, even the servant boys were assessed as well as the masters.[19]

But, with the confirmation of London's ancient Charters, liberties and customs the gilds stood poised to renew the pursuit of power.

In about the year 1307 – very probably the accession of a new King prompted new action – the Cutlers sought freedom for self-rule. Although only the Weavers had achieved the status of Incorporation, there were others who had already acquired the rights of autonomy.

The Cutlers therefore petitioned

that they may have their franchise as the other Crafts of the same City have, so that no craft meddle with them or their trade, but that they may be ruled by certain people of the same Mistery such as are loyal and amenable to our lord the King and to all people, so that if any foreigner or other come within the same City with false Cutlery as before these times they have done and do from day to day, to the great prejudice of the said Mistery and damage to the King and deceit of all the people, that they may be corrected by those same certain and loyal people of the said Mistery and their false cutlery be forfeited if for such they be convicted.[20]

They also requested that if any of their own number made false cutlery they might be tried by a Court of their own. They ended the petition with a request for the same franchise over other towns throughout the country.

They were to a certain extent successful. The document was endorsed:

Let there be done in London what is asked by this Petition . . . save that which concerns gold and silver the which article has been made by the goldsmiths. . . . And as to the other good towns of England the King will make ordinance in the same manner.

It was a decision that foreshadowed a long dispute between the Cutlers and the Goldsmiths and although it appears that they failed to gain control over anywhere other than the City and its suburbs they were, at any rate, empowered to deal with the 'foreigner'.

When it is remembered that a 'foreigner' was not simply an alien but anyone, Londoner or otherwise, who was not free of the City – a freedom gained through membership of a mistery – the extent of their power to control the trade will be appreciated.

There were many country cutlers, men like Adam of Thaxted or Robert of Ipswich, who, having learned their trade in their native town, wished to settle in the capital. Before they could set up in business and open a shop they had to purchase their freedom from the Cutlers' Company. To wield such power with the official consent of the Crown was clearly a great step forward.

Edward II was not a strong ruler and he had inherited a difficult situation in which many of the barons were continually in opposition to the Crown. The uneasy atmosphere affected the man in the London streets. It was necessary to order that

no one shall be so daring on the day of the Coronation as to carry sword, or knife with point, or misericorde, [a short dagger], mace or club, or any other arm on pain of imprisonment for a year and a day.[21]

Any man who struck another was to lose his hand. Even brandishing a weapon 'to do evil therewith' was to be punished by being pierced through the hand – probably with the spike of a mace.

The general anarchic atmosphere was reflected in the politics of the City. Succeeding Mayors were of a mind for reform. And when Edward II hurried northwards in an attempt to save his favourite, Gaveston, and the City was left to defend itself, the popular party took the opportunity to secure changes: no alien was to be admitted to the freedom, no obligations were to be undertaken by the aldermen without the consent of the Commonalty who to make quite sure were to guard three out of the six keys of the chest in which was kept the City Seal. One set of demands led to another. In 1312, the crafts took the next logical step: a deputation represesnting the rank and file of all the misteries in London demanded, *inter alia*, that

the statutes and ordinances regulating the various trades be duly enrolled in a register and that once or twice a year they be read in public assembly and copies be delivered to such as desire them. Also forasmuch as the City ought always to be governed by the aid of men engaged in trades and handicrafts, and whereas it was anciently accustomed that no stranger, native or foreign, whose position and character were unknown, should be admitted to the freedom of the city until the merchants and craftsmen whose business he wished to enter, had previously certified the Mayor and Aldermen of his condition and trustworthiness, the whole Commonalty pray that such observance be strictly kept for the future as regards the wholesale trades and handicrafts.[22]

This general demand arose, of course, from a particular incident: a mercer had been admitted 'by the favour of great men and contrary to the will of the good men of the Mistery.'[23] As a result of the agitation the offending mercer, together with his 'valet', came forward and 'willingly' disclaimed the Freedom. But the general outcome of the reformers' petition is unknown. The issues were, in any case, for a while obscured in the general turmoil of national politics. Gaveston had been executed by the King's opponents and Edward became thereby irreconcilably in conflict with his murderers. Yet neither side was strong enough to crush the other and the indecisive struggle between Edward and his cousin, Thomas of Lancaster, paralysed the government of the country and of the city.[24]

During this time it was noted that, already unsettled by the warring of their social superiors, 'the common people and plebeians are conspiring among themselves and holding clandestine meetings in private places and have of their own accord, without being summoned, thrust themselves into the election of the Mayor.'[25]

Such indecent behaviour was carried on at a time when the plebeians had other matters to distract them. 1316 was a year of famine; there had been 'an orible moreyn of beestes...and the poure peple eten for hunger cattes and hors and houndes and stal children and eten themme and thanne anon after there fille a gret pestilence among the peple.'[26] Famine and plague were intermittently recurring factors in their lives; government was with them always and the political manoeuvring continued almost unabated.

In 1319 the City received – at the cost of £1000 – its new charter which embodied all the concessions made to the Commonalty in the preceding years. The charter was obtained for the City by the Mayor and aldermen in spite of their opposition to what it contained. They had, most significantly, become the instruments – and in this case the unwilling instruments – of the popular will. Here was, indeed, a change in the political power structure, a change which if all the clauses had been enforced would have revolutionized the government of the City. But, of course, all the clauses were not enforced and the revolution was less complete than it might have been. Nonetheless, the really operative part of the constitution was, in fact, observed: no man of English birth, and especially no English merchant who followed any specific mistery or craft, was to be admitted to the freedom of the City except on the security of six reputable men of that mistery or craft. This article, taken in conjunction with the complementary one which each craft subsequently caused to be inserted in its own ordinances – that no one should exercise that craft unless he were free of the City – served not only to give the crafts as a whole a hold on the constitution but also to give each craft the power of drawing all who exercised the trade in question into its ranks and thus placing that trade under its control. On this power all the later political achievements of the crafts were based.[27]

Feudalism in 1319, in that first flush of popular success and re-forming zeal, seemed a thing of the past. A new era of civic life was felt to be opening. 'In this year swords were forbidden...by reason of which many swords were taken and hung up beneath Ludgate within and without. At this time many of the people of the trades of London were arrayed in Livery and a good time was about to begin.'[28]

It may be doubted whether the long-cutlers – those who made the forbidden swords – were convinced of the coming of better days and, unless the chronicler was indulging in irony he was curiously blind to the situation. A good time was not about to begin. The end of the war with Scotland, already twenty-three years a-fighting, was still four years away, and the defeat of the English in Swaledale held out no great hopes of a successful out-come. The independence of some of the barons brought a turbulent element into the national scene and there was soon to be what was, if not actually a fully-fledged civil war at any rate large-scale localized fighting in 1322 between the Royalists and the followers of the Duke of Lancaster.

And from the point of view of the Companies there was the uncomfortable fact that the City authorities decided to fight back to recover some of the power that had been wrested from them.

'At this time many of the people of the trades of London were arrayed in Livery. . . .'[28], the Chronicler had written and this must have been one of the notes of warning that sounded direly in the ears of the City fathers. Livery had always been the mark of the followers of a feudal lord; worn by the members of a gild it gave a clear warning of the new feudalism. Livery worn at the more-or-less secret – or at any rate private – occasions of a fraternity was one thing; worn openly and on all occasions in the streets of London was another. Six hundred years later the effect of rival bands of citizens flaunting in allegiance the colours of their favourite football team gave rise to violence that every week erupted to the annoyance and danger of those less sporting.

In the no less unruly and disturbed atmosphere of the early fourteenth century the daily wearing of partisan colours by gilds already – many of them – sufficiently hostile to one another, the dangers were obvious. The City, which had lost much ground to the Livery Companies – as they must from henceforth be called – tried in 1321 to regain a little. They petitioned the King for authority 'to govern the Misteries and redress faults therein, according to ancient usage' and the subsequent summons to the rulers of the Companies to be sworn at Guildhall was one of the first steps in the attempt to obtain a more effective control.[29]

The details become lost in the further disintegration of national stability. Supporters of Isabella, Edward II's estranged Queen, arrived in East Anglia and the countryside rose to support them with Sir Roger Mortimer leading them. The Queen addressed a letter to the City, who had just sent one hundred men to the King at Porchester, asking the commonalty for their help. She got no reply. London was full of the King's favourites, the Despencers, and their attendant lords, and the citizens, as they might well be, were frightened.

An order was made for all employers to report all cases of rebellion among their servants and apprentices for punishment, and the following year wardens of misteries were made responsible for keeping men at work and for reporting all cases of disobedience to the Mayor.[30]

But at last the Despencers, together with the King, fled to Wales. The City became the storm-centre of the Queen's revolution. The unfortunate Bishop of Exeter, left to govern the City, was led to the standard in Cheapside near the Cutlery and there executed. His head they set in his right hand.[31]

And, as though seeking assurance that the rule of law still meant something in the protection of their own closed world, still existed in their own affairs, the Sheathers – a mistery not yet merged with the Cutlers – produced a new set of Ordinances.

In 1327 Edward II was deposed and murdered and Edward III came to the throne as a minor. Because the Mayor had been a partisan of the Queen, the City received its charter within a few months of the accession: the constitutional power remained vested in the wards and in the aldermen, a body who were far from relishing the idea of the continually warring crafts, many of them financially small-fry, exercising a share of government.

The Cutlers' Company were amongst those who were in dispute: the Goldsmiths were complaining that some of the decorative work effected by the cutlers, for which, since it was made of precious metals, they felt responsible, was defective. They first accused the cutlers of covering

tin and silver so subtly and with such sleight that the same cannot be severed from the tin, and by that means they sell the tin so covered as fine silver to the great damage and deceit of us and our people.

Soon they claimed the right of search over all cutlery on which gold and silver was worked.[32]

The dispute, as will be seen, was to continue for many years: its immediate effects are not recorded.

The following year, the King confirmed the franchises of the City. Under the reaffirmed powers of the aldermen, officers for the government and instruction of the Companies were called to be sworn before the Mayor. There were twenty-eight Companies thus summoned – the Cutlers amongst them – and since the turn of the century there had been ninety-eight trades recorded in London it is clear that a large number had still not yet been organized. The charter of the City included several articles which had, or were soon to have, a hollow ring: the liberties and franchises for example should never, for any cause, be taken into the King's hand; citizens should not be constrained to go out of London to any war. Citizens had always been at the mercy of precepts and the mediaeval equivalent of the press gang. A cutler had only recently, in 1314, been sent to Berwick as an arbalester against the Scots. Cutlers, in the company of all their fellow citizens of all their sister misteries, would always be dragged at a moment's notice from their families and their homes and their livelihoods to be flung into some vainglorious and, generally, inefficient campaign.

Among other distractions of that year of 1328 when the power of the aldermen was re-established there were two moons seen in the firmament at once and there were two popes and a highly un-popular peace with Scotland. For sixteen years the Cutlers' Company disappears altogether from the records while life in the City continued to weave the normal patterns to which, although they are no longer visible, the Cutlers inevitably contributed: renewed war with Scotland and with France – in 1337 the country drifted into the Hundred Years War – and heavy taxation to pay for both victory and defeat. In 1340 the King demanded the vast sum of £20,000 from the City. In the atmosphere of almost oriental bargaining that was such a feature of the relations of mediaeval men with the Exchequer the City offered 5000 marks. It was scornfully rejected and the King threateningly demanded a list of the names of all the wealthy citizens who might be assessed to raise the full amount. A meeting took place, hastily and before sunrise. The City raised its offer to £5000. It was accepted.

Meanwhile, in the historical obscurity into which they had temporarily disappeared, the rulers of the Cutlers were at work planning and organizing. If they and the Livery Companies generally had suffered a momentary setback in the power game they could at any rate tighten their control over their trade.

In 1344, on the Friday after the Decollation of St. John the Baptist, the new Articles of the Cutlers were read before the Mayor, John Hamond, and some of the aldermen.[33]

The first article was simple enough. The Mayor and aldermen were to select some of the cutlers, approved by the Company, to search and assay all cutlery, at home or in the shops 'sparing no man for favour, and grieving no person for hate.' All false work was to be taken before the Mayor and aldermen to be judged by them. A scale of fines from 3s. 4d to 10/- was set for the first three offences. Anyone rash enough to offend a fourth time was to be 'forsworn the trade.'

Secondly, no Master or Warden was to support 'any person of whatsoever condition he might be against the folks of the said trade whereby they might be in any point injured or damnified.'

Thirdly, no cutler was to make any common sale on Sundays – a prohibition arising, rather unexpectedly, less from moral grounds than from practical considerations 'seeing that their journeymen and apprentices have wasted and purloined the property of their masters while they have been attending at their parish churches, or elsewhere.'

Next came articles about apprentices: no one might keep an apprentice, or, for that matter, open a shop, unless he were a freeman and no terms of apprenticeship might be for less than seven years. An apprentice might not be enticed away or employed by anyone other than his master until his time had been served.

Then there was an article forbidding all work at night. The reason given was that it was almost impossible for the Wardens of the Company to assay such work which was then 'sent privily to sell in divers counties of the realm, in deceit, and to the loss of the common people and to the prejudice and scandal of the folks of the said trade.'[34] It has been suggested that the reason went deeper than the difficulty of overseeing. The Sheathers, in their Ordinance forbidding night-work, had made a different claim: work done by night was not so profitable or so good as that done by day. It is possible that, in both Companies, the reason for the ban was, in fact, partly due to trade jealousy and was intended to limit the output of the more enterprising craftsmen.[35]

Finally, and importantly from a tactical point of view, there was the proviso that those not wishing to submit to the Master and Wardens could ask for the Mayor and aldermen to adjudicate.

All the Articles were to be 'confirmed in such manner that they cannot another time be contradicted.'

It will be observed that, so far as autonomy was concerned, the Cutlers' Company had achieved something less than total control – their officials had to be approved by the City and their powers of adjudication could be by-passed, a serious limitation that was done away with in the ordinances of 1380. But, for the meantime, there was reason for a modest satisfaction on the part of the eight signatories to the articles.

Within five years all of them were dead. The Black Death, starting from India, reached England in 1348 and found a fertile breeding ground. London 'the flower of cities all' was growing upon a midden. It had been observed in 1345 that the Thames at Dowgate had become so corrupted by dung and filth thrown into it that the carters who carried water were no longer able to serve the commonalty.[36]

For many years, while the plague abated or increased, there were similar reports. In 1355 the Chronicler wrote that the moat around the Fleet Prison, which should have been 10 feet wide and so full of water as to float easily a 1-ton boat, was so choked with rubbish thrown into it with filth from latrines – eleven necessary houses had been built illegally above it – from sewers and from three tanneries that it no longer surrounded the prison. Do-gooders even feared for the safety of those detained there such was the infection of the air. There was talk of the abominable stench and grievous maladies. Two years later the King, passing along the Thames, had noted from his barge 'dung and laystalls and other filth accumulated in divers places in the said City, upon the bank of the river aforesaid. . . .' He had 'also perceived the fumes and other abominable stenches arising therefrom.' He ordered that the City be immediately cleaned, and that the 'boxes, empty tuns, and other articles, lying and placed in the streets and lanes, before the doors of divers folks. . .be taken away': it was, he added sharply, to be thrown neither into the Thames nor the Fleet, nor into any of the moats. The street cleaners or the dung-boats were to take it all away.

Picking their way among the detritus, such cutlers as escaped the plague went about their business. The Furbishers amongst them had in 1350 enrolled their ordinances. Pommels and sword hilts must be of good steel and scabbards of good calf-leather; broken swords were not to be made up again 'by greed or subtlety' with intent to deceive.

The economic and social difficulties were immense. Exaggerated figures are given for the number of deaths from the plague in London but it seems probable that throughout England one third of the population was wiped out. The result was a crippling shortage of labour – particularly as it was the overcrowded poor of the towns and cities who suffered most. The shortage led to wages and prices being frozen. The Mayor and aldermen were given powers to punish all demands for higher wages with imprisonment.[37] Each Ward of the City was to provide overseers to ensure that the regulations were observed. There were, naturally, workmen who were unwilling to abide by the rules and left the City. It was ordered that those who did so should, if they returned, be flung into prison for three months, forfeit all their chattels, if they had any, and give surety for their future good behaviour. If they did not return to the City to face their punishment they were to be banished for ever.

It is to be remarked that in the negotiations for price-standstill the Cutlers were not mentioned.

The war with France had all this time been pursuing the normal pattern for such wars. A prestige victory at Crécy brought Edward III no strategic gains; a year's siege of Calais ended in the capture of the town and its settlement by Englishmen. The battle of Poitiers was fought and won. It was all very expensive and there were frequent 'presents' to the King. The Cutlers' share of the London levy in 1363 was four pounds. Times were hard and business was bad. For the cutlers the general slump was intensified by the fact that they were affected by one of the sumptuary laws that the Crown periodically imposed, possibly to conserve precious materials but, more generally, to cut down to size some presumptuous section of society. This time it was the artisans, their wives and their children: they were forbidden to wear cutlery adorned with gold or silver.

If this order reads strangely today we must remind ourselves that in the Middle Ages 'cutlery' – that long list of instruments, mostly lethal, which has already been noted – did not include table ware. 'Only great princes and nobles had special knives for cutting up their food, and these they not only used in their homes but also

c

took with them on their journeys. The ordinary citizen carried at his girdle a knife which served all purposes and could be used equally well for carving his food or cutting his enemy's throat.'[38] The point of the knife, or his fingers, served for a fork. Now for the artisan this knife was to be of the simplest. The artisans were the subject of further control in 1364 when ordinances were passed for the governance of the misteries. Every one of them was to 'choose each his own Mistery before Candlemas and having so chosen it to use no other.' The misteries were to be truly governed 'each in its degree in due manner, so that no falseness, no false work, nor deceit be found in any manner.' As many persons as the mistery required to control the workers should be elected and given full powers by the Mayor. 'And if any person shall be rebellious, contradictory or disturbing ... he shall remain in prison the first time ten days and shall pay to the Commonalty ten shillings for the contempt.'[39] The punishment for further offences was reckoned on a sliding scale.

For the merchants in the Company it was different. They could avail themselves of the custom of London that every freeman of the City might cross the seas with any merchandise he liked and bring back to the City any merchandise he liked as long as he only acted as a wholesaler: retail sales were restricted to the product of his mistery.

It was about this time too that it became the legal duty of every cutler to strike his mark, duly registered with the Company, upon every piece he made. In theory it should thus have been possible to identify all London-made blades. But, unfortunately, the Cutlers' Company had not achieved the same degree of influence at this period as, for example, had the fishmongers. Influence went hand in hand with wealth. And the cutlers were still far from rich – indeed, on one occasion the Master excused himself from attending the Mayor upon Election Day on the grounds of poverty and the anonymous writer of a pamphlet called *A Touchstone for Cutlers' Wares*, published in 1680, asserts that for all the ordinances very few cutlers then belonged to the Company which was quite unable to check the importation of quantities of blades of inferior quality which were sold at low prices.[40]

Though the Livery Companies of London as a whole had gained much ground in the long political and constitutional struggle, the Cutlers' Company – though they sent two representatives to the Committee of Common Council – were still in a position of personal weakness and, therefore, of some danger, in a City which in the forthcoming decade was to be disastrously rent by the violence of warring factions.

2

The Dangerous City

1369–1382

WE have seen how the fraternities had come into being as mutual protection societies against times of trouble and how they had become intermingled and confused with the craft misteries on the upward road of evolution towards becoming Livery Companies. Somewhere along that road the cutlers had evidently altogether abandoned their fraternity for suddenly in 1370, it was reported that

in honour of our Lord Jesus Christ and of His sweet Mother and of all saints certain of the good folks of the Mistery of Cutlers of London have begun a Fraternity among themselves in support of two tapers to burn before the image of our Lady in the Church of the Annunciation of our Lady called the Charter-house, West Smithfield. . . .

The Brethren were to be of good report and bearing; they were not to be contentious and they were expressly forbidden to get involved in riots in which they might get hurt. The manuscript containing the articles of association is defective but the inference is that if a Brother got hurt as the result of contention he could not expect any sick-benefit. Nor, if he were complained against under the laws of the land, could he expect to be bailed by the Fraternity. On the other hand sufferers from storm, fire or theft, or other mischance by visitation of God, were to receive ten pence a week so long as the mischance lasted.

There were many rules that bound the Brethren together: there were to be quarterly meetings to pay 6d to support the ever-burning tapers; there was to be an annual attendance at mass, wearing livery, on the Feast of the Annunciation; all must give a penny to the collection and then, on the first Sunday after Trinity meet at some appointed place to eat and drink together; fines were to be inflicted for non-attendance. There were rules, too, that belonged more properly to the mistery: apprentices and servants for example were not to be enticed.[41]

It is tempting to see in this surprising reversion to a fraternity an instinctive back-to-the-womb drawing of the livery hood around the face and retreating from the dangerous outside world into the comforting moral and physical protection of a closed society: London was becoming daily a more dangerous world in which the mistery of the Cutlers was impoverished and lacking power. There-fore they would revive the fraternity in a desperate attempt to avoid personal disaster. In fact, the forming of a fraternity was the mark of a Company in which master-craftsmen and journeymen, feeling themselves excluded from the benefits of the gild by the mercantile element, sought security in an association of their own. The first of the perils that confronted them was external. In August 1370 it was reported that galleys filled with armed men (presumably French) were lying off the North Foreland and that an attack upon the City must be expected. A nightly watch was kept between the Tower and Billingsgate to protect both London and the King's ships which were lying in the Thames at the hamlet of Ratcliffe. Forty men and sixty archers were supplied on a rota by seventeen Livery Companies: the Cutlers shared the Sunday watch with the Armourers and the Ironmongers.

But far more dangerous than any immediate threat of arms to the City was the disastrous national disunity which affected the country. With the end of victories in France came the end of the old King's popularity. Within the Royal family there were factions as John of Gaunt, the King's fourth son, organized a successful opposition to his father's ministers but failed to secure better results with his own. In every aspect of affairs discontent was almost universal. There was a split between the ruling oligarchy and the citizens – aldermen who had been elected for one year only were holding office for life and a proclamation that no one might take part in the election of Mayor and Sheriffs unless he were 'of the better sort' and specially summoned[41] did nothing to calm those who felt themselves deprived.

There was opposition of interest between importers and exporters and between those with a national interest and those with a purely local interest.

The reform movement was weak because the 'liberties' of the City depended upon the King being persuaded that London could govern itself without friction. There were indications that he was in some doubt when he summoned the Mayor, Sheriffs, Recorder and aldermen to Guildford ordering them to bring with them the leading commoners from every mistery.[42]

In the City itself there was such unease that in 1372 the carrying of weapons was prohibited except by the servants of lords or by knights carrying their masters' swords. Every inn-keeper had to warn his guests on arrival that they must lay aside their arms.

The death, at a wrestling match at Black Heath, of a mercer caused what was euphemistically described as 'great dissension and debate' among the Companies. The state of moral disorder in the City was symbolized by the obstinate neglect of all the King's orders to carry out a physical cleansing. Near Baynard's Castle, for example, entrails and offal from the shambles of St. Nicholas were carried through the streets, filling the gutters with putrifying blood, before being thrown into the Thames. There were complaints from the Crown of the abominable sights, the stenches, the corruption and filth. There were orders that slaughtering of great beasts should take place at such places as Knightsbridge instead of within the City. Nothing was done. All orders were simply disregarded.[43]

It was in this unruly and explosive situation that the so-called Good Parliament sitting in 1376 produced the revelation that approximately half the aldermen of London were corrupt. The scandal had an immediate effect. The reformers led by John of Northampton, an eminent draper, acted quickly.

At the beginning of August forty-one crafts assembled in a spirit of reformist indignation, deposed the delinquent aldermen, and laid down the principle that reason demanded more participation by citizens in the government of the City; nothing should be done by the Mayor and aldermen in secret; Common Councils should be held for mayoral and shrieval elections; aldermen must retire each year and serve but once; they must summon the Common Council regularly and act upon its advice.[44] The debate upon such impious proposals became so heated that the King threatened to intervene and, rather than risk losing the privileges of the City, the Mayor capitulated and a charter was given to the City embodying the new and apparently democratic order. A Common Council upon which the Cutlers had two representatives – some of the greater Companies had six – was elected and the King was told that the crisis was ended. As matters turned out, however, it was very far from ended.

It would be a mistake to think that the reformers were democrats. John of Northampton had skilfully exploited the latent opposition between artisans and merchants and with a handful of associates amongst the drapers and mercers he built up a party among the lesser crafts. The reformers were in fact progressives, anti-clerical, manufacturing free-traders, democratic more by theory than by social sympathy. Temperamentally they were aristocrats – but aristocrats who were forced to appeal to popular support. This they used, as long as was necessary and no longer.[45] For example the ruling that aldermen might serve but once and for one year only would have meant, if it had been observed, that the wastage would have been so great that sooner or later members of minor Companies would hold office. Perhaps, even, the unthinkable might occur and the City would find itself with aldermen who were artisans. Even John of Northampton demurred at that. A meeting of the merchants in March the following year took a conservative interpretation of the rules: aldermen, unless convicted of misbehaviour, might after one year's interval stand for re-election. In the meantime the reformers revised the Ordinances of the City upon popular lines and entered them in the so-called 'Jubilee Book.' John of Northampton had let it be known that he was on the side of consumer-protection and intended to control the cost of living by controlling the victualling trades, whose intended monopoly of the import of foodstuffs he regarded as inflationary. The cry of 'Cheap Food' has always been popular but

when it became clear to the public that the intention of the reformers was in fact to manipulate the new constitution to their
own advantage their power began very rapidly to fade.[46]

At this juncture the civic crisis became intermingled with a
national crisis. In 1373 Edward III died and was succeeded by his
ten-year-old grandson Richard II. The country was divided in
loyalty between the young King and his uncle, John of Gaunt the
Duke of Lancaster: in London the reformers supported the Duke,
the anti-reformist victuallers and the merchants supported the
King.

Violence, never very far away from the London mob, erupted. A
large body of anti-reformist citizens set upon the servants of the
Earl of Buckingham in Cornhill 'and beat and wounded them and
pursued them, when flying to his hostel, and broke and hewed
down the door of the same with axes and other arms, the said Earl
being then within and lying in his bed, and by reason thereof no
little alarmed.'[48]

Led by Nicholas Brembre, the victuallers contrived to obtain a
majority among the aldermen. After only one year of reformist
rule and with only half the votes, they gained control of the City
by means of a royal writ to depose the Mayor and put Brembre in
his place. In return, a loan of £5000, secured on the royal jewels and
plate, was made to the King. If it were not repaid by the following
Lady Day the City might take its profit.

The rallying point of Brembre's party, the platform upon which
he sought public support, was, as it has always been, almost as
popular as the control of food prices: he appealed to the eternal,
deep-seated anti-alien emotions of the English. At that moment
xenophobia was going through one of its more virulent phases,
much to the embarrassment of the Crown which depended greatly
for trade upon the foreign merchants. But as long as Brembre and
the City supported the King with readily forthcoming loans there
was little that the Crown could do about it.

The Royal jewels were carried to and fro between the City and
Westminster as pledges for money lent. In 1379, for example, the
sum was five thousand pounds, in 1380 it was two thousand pounds.
It was noticeable that, in the inventories of the jewels, the same

items constantly recurred like the staple pledges of the common man weekly visiting the pawnshop.

And, in exchange, the free citizens were granted a charter which gave them a monopoly of the retail trades at the same time as it put restraints upon foreign trades and merchant strangers.

The Duke's party were not, however, resigned to the loss of power in London for the pressure of the merchants in the city Government was causing embarrassment to the national Government: In 1379 John of Gaunt discreetly removed the Parliament to Gloucester and from this safe distance he annulled the so-recently granted charter of monopoly. The consternation that was instantly manifested in the City was more immediately concerned with the enormous loss of trade that ensued when Parliament, with all its hangers-on, was not sitting at Westminster. The reaction was typical of the age. £350 was quickly raised from the Londoners – the Mayor himself contributed £10 – and expended on presents for carefully chosen Lords. 'Thanks be to God' it was noted 'a good accord was effected between the lords of the realm and the City.' The money had been well spent: the next two Parliaments were held at Westminster.[47]

In the meantime the normal day-to-day business of earning a living had to go on. There must have been a fairly steady trade in abselards – a kind of dagger – for there was a positive epidemic of thefts by cutting them from their owners' girdles. Robert Spryg actually lost his baselard at the Mayor's house but on this occasion the thief was taken both with the dagger and with the knife he had used for cutting it away. He was sentenced to the pillory and to banishment from the City.

In 1375 the Sheathers had revised their ordinances, complaining that the old ones had not been observed. It was noteworthy that they asked to be allowed to work at night because, they said, the cutlers worked at night. Now the Cutlers themselves started to compile a new set of rules to bring some kind of personal order into the disordered life of the City.

Anti-alien feeling was at its height. In 1379 there came a sudden rumour that the Government was planning to overcome the practical disadvantages of London's xenophobia by removing trade

to another port. It was said that a Genoese merchant had offered
to defray the expense of making Southampton the greatest port
in England. Whether the rumour was true or false made no difference to the chauvinist Londoners. The Genoese merchant was
openly and in cold blood murdered. The rule of law might mean
little, the King's peace might be nothing more than a phrase, but
this was an offence which could not be tolerated. In 1380, Parliament
removed discreetly to Northampton, where the murderer was
executed. The anger of the King's party was intense: they had lost
their charter, the aliens were still in business, the man who had
struck a blow for their liberties had been executed and John of
Gaunt, the leader of the Government and the man responsible,
was still in power.

Simmering with rage, they awaited their opportunity. And, very
shortly before the storm broke, the Cutlers presented their new
Ordinances for the Mayor's approval. They were needed because
the great merchant-cutlers had made a dead-letter of the old
Ordinances of 1344. New rules were necessary for the conduct of
trade 'in amendment and correction of many faults which have
been customary.' They were fairly comprehensive. To provide
against demands for excessive wages no journeyman who was not
a freeman of the City, or who had not been apprenticed for the
full term, was to be admitted to work unless he had been tested by
overseers who were to fix the wages commensurate with his skill.
When the overseers had fixed his wage 'according to their consciences, employers must pay the man not less than that rate and
not more until he shall have learned to deserve more.' Silver work
on the cutlery had to be of sterling alloy; wooden handles (other
than those of boxwood) were not to be coloured. No cutlery was
to be taken out of the City until it had been inspected by a master:
if the master did not come readily to a viewing the worker would
be excused if he exported the cutlery unexamined. Goods were
not to be taken to, or sold at 'Evechepynges' (that is to say at
markets held at night) or in hostelries; they were to be sold in the
cutler's shop 'save and except, however, where some great lord or
reputable man shall send after such cutlery for his own use, to be
brought to his place or to his hostel, to see whether it pleases him

or not.' There was to be no Sunday trading and, no matter what the sheathers had alleged, no night shifts either. If there were a dispute about faulty goods the Mayor was to set up a panel of four to arbitrate – if the panel decided that the goods were not, after all, faulty, the master involved was to pay not only the fines that would have been levied but also damages to the worker. There were many other rules, including the fixing of fees for those who searched for faulty work, for annual meetings, and for fines for non-attendance. More important perhaps was the proviso that none might carry on the trade unless he agreed to the ordinances, and accepted the rule of the overseers.

It will be noted that, as befitted the ordinances of good reformers, there was quite a liberal air about these regulations – there were several points at which the masters had quite carefully to watch their behaviour towards their workmen.

The reforming zeal of the Cutlers was not echoed in the City government. The previous year the elected City Council had been 'weighted' by the arbitrary addition of 'others of the more powerful and discreet citizens.'[49] Almost all the hard-won reforms were swept away. No longer was the City Council to be elected by the misteries. Power was to be once more to the strong although in 1380 a compromise was reached by which the election of the Council was made partly from the Livery Companies and partly from the Wards. The anti-reformers were, in fact, rapidly moving into a position of great strength. Still smarting from the events which had followed the murder of the Genoese merchant, which they had instigated, they were waiting only the moment to strike. It came, quickly enough, in 1381. The unpopularity of an unsuccessful war had made it difficult for the Crown to raise the usual loans from the City. A poll-tax was, therefore, imposed which, though it involved every member of the population, was felt most hardly by the poorer classes. Twenty-eight counties rose up in revolt. In June, when the men of Essex and Kent attacked the City, the gates were treacherously opened and they came swarming in.

It might have been expected that the reformers would have been the culprits; they were, after all, theoretically on the side of the masses. But, in fact, it was the victuallers of the anti-reform party, the supporters of the King, who had betrayed London: they no doubt thought as the mob of rebels swept in through the gates that a short time of unrest – at the end of which they would emerge as the young King's advisers – was worth the opportunity of paying off old scores and getting rid of their enemies for ever. Old scores were certainly settled. John of Gaunt's palace was burnt to the ground; the Chancellor and the Archbishop of Canterbury were seized and executed; envious artisans murdered their foreign rivals unhindered; lawyers who might draft laws against the mob were particularly marked down for slaughter; in the general panic that filled the ruling classes the impregnable fortress of the Tower was surrendered; many men, eminent in all walks of life, were murdered. In contemporary records it was known as the 'hurling-time'.

What happened to the more eminent members of the Cutler's Company, who were known to have supported the reformers, is unrecorded, but it is a virtual certainty that many of them, in the general holocaust, lost their properties and their lives.

It was the young King Richard II who put an end to the shameful business by riding forth to meet Wat Tyler at Mile End. The somewhat equivocal circumstances in which William Walworth, who, after all, as a victualler was one of the party who had opened the gates to the rebels, struck down the rebel leader are sufficiently well-known. The fact that he and Brembre were both knighted on the field should, with its implied recognition of the supremacy of his party, have set the seal on the success of the anti-reformists. But their triumph was short-lived. A year later the action of the victuallers in delivering up the City to the orgy of destruction, to the vast loss of life and property and trade was held against them. The reformers swept back into power and the Livery Companies for two years regained their political functions, Northampton being elected for a second term as Mayor. It is pleasant to see this as the natural and highly moral outcome of an unedifying incident. The Cutlers were naturally delighted by the turn of events. But their pleasure was not to last long. The exercise by the reformers of their regained powers has been described as having a revolutionary character which did not offer any prospect of permanence.[50] In the two years that Northampton ruled the City he was tireless in the enforcement of price regulation; he attacked profiteers and, so his enemies – fearful of a social revolution – alleged, inflamed the poor by saying that he would put out of town all but the worthiest, expelling all usurers.[51]

This clearly was not a situation that the merchants could for long tolerate. What happened next when Northampton in 1382 summoned the freemen to the mayoral election, is best described in the Cutlers' own words.[52]

> Master Nicholas (Brembre) with his accomplices, the same day, with intent to destroy the good government of the said City, arrayed certain evil-doers of his following, armed for that day to elect the said Master Nicholas as Mayor of that City against the crown of the King our said lord and the franchise of the said City. And some of his following who were there present with him, beat and dragged certain folks, so that the good folks who were there for duly making the election of their Mayor durst not tarry for dread of their lives, so that the said Master Nicholas was elected in his first year, at the which time he took upon him Royal power against the crown of the King . . .

Nor was this all. The Royal charter to the City had granted the right of the election of the Mayor to the commonalty. Yet at the next election, if the Cutlers and their allies were to be believed, Brembre proclaimed throughout the City that 'on penalty of imprisonment and on pain of offending against the King none should be so bold as to be at the said election save those who were summoned.' He then summoned none but those who were of his party. The Guildhall was packed with armed men (strangers as well as denizens) who would have put to death anyone who had not been summoned. As a further show of power, Brembre, so the Cutlers alleged:

> came into Cheap with a great multitude of people of his own accord, armed to the great dread of the good people of the said City, and several people . . . were imprisoned to the great dread of their lives and great loss of their goods and hurt of their persons without relief.

They made further allegation that Brembre and his accomplices

> conspired and devised to have put to death several good people of London and because they could not do that thing without any cause they conspired to

indite them of felony and they put on the inquests of indictment those who were of affinity and accord with Master Nicholas and who were of evil fame....

However exaggerated the case may have been there clearly existed a state of local government which was not by later standards acceptable. A state, too, which appears to have been in direct contravention of an order by Richard II by which no victualler should hold judicial office unless he gave up his trade.

This violent clash between the two Livery Company factions must have given even greater uneasiness to those who were already worried by the growth of the new feudalism. It was no doubt responsible for the order, when in 1382 the Companies rode out to meet the new Queen, Anne of Bohemia, that all should be dressed alike in the same livery. Although the order was obeyed, nonetheless they managed to make their allegiances clear by the wearing of 'divers cognizances.'

On this occasion there was no trouble but news continually filtered through to Brembre that the reformers were plotting against his supremacy. The situation was intolerable. Brembre appealed to the King, and Northampton was bound over to keep the peace. The dramatic incident that followed the King's order epitomizes the lawless and savage atmosphere of fourteenth-century London.

Brembre was sitting at home when a messenger burst in to tell him that John of Northampton was approaching, marching at the head of a large band of his followers, through the City streets. Master Nicholas was forced to act swiftly and courageously. With a handful of his servants he placed himself in Northampton's path and bade him, under penalty, retire. Without a word, without a gesture, the private army advanced. Brembre retreated before them, repeatedly calling upon the sinister, silent marchers to halt. But halt they would not. They passed with grim determination through the streets – to attend, as they had all the time intended to do, mass.[53]

It was a gesture on the grand scale. But this open humiliation of the Mayor by one who, as a citizen, was under oath to obey him, was going too far. John of Northampton was arrested, and 'dampned unto the Tower to be drawn and hanged.' His sentence was commuted to ten years' imprisonment in the Castle of Tintagel – a prison no doubt selected as being as far from London as it was possible to be. And although he was released after only two years it was upon the condition that he did not approach within eighty miles of London.

The Cutlers, though their champion was no longer in the field, were not deterred from continuing the fight against Brembre. In 1386 they, together with the Bowyers, Fletchers, Spurriers and Bladesmiths, presented a petition to the King against Nicholas Brembre. In it they recited the outrageous behaviour which has already been noted. In complaining of the plot to bring false charges of felony against innocent citizens they alleged that if Nicholas Exton, the Mayor at that time, were ordered to produce all his records, it would be quite clear how badly the citizens had been wronged. The petitioners themselves had been, and still were, in danger from Brembre and his colleagues who had several times made a great assembly,

and there conspired among them how they might maintain their villainy which they had begun, to destroy the present complainants, and all others who were indicted by their false device and conspiracy, and it was ordained by their common accord to take ... for that villainy large sums of money ... the which wrongful taking of money has been continued from the time that John of Northampton was thrust from his office.

The cutlers and their allies begged, 'for God and as a work of charity', that the King would have the offenders punished and Nicholas Exton removed from his post: not only had he been illegally elected, but he had also burnt the Jubilee Book in which were entered all the articles that he was sworn to uphold for the good government of the City. The Recorder, too, should be discharged and so should the Sheriff of London.

In retrospect the petition appears to be an act of almost foolhardy daring. In the event it was unsuccessful but there is no record of individual cutlers having been further endangered.

For five years the anti-reformers ruled the City; the Livery Companies lost their rights of election to the Council; power returned to the Wards; the charters of many of the companies had to be submitted to the Mayor in an act of submission; political assemblies at the Halls were forbidden. They might have ruled London for many years to come had not, once again, national unrest caused repercussions in the City. Richard's policy for peace in a war in which victory had not been won led in 1388 to armed conflict in which the doves were overthrown by the hawks. The King's party was decisively defeated in armed conflict and its leaders exiled, imprisoned, or executed. Among those put to death was Master Nicholas Brembre. He was outlived for ten years by his arch enemy John of Northampton who died, peacefully, in what is described – with, possibly, theological inaccuracy – as 'the odour of sanctity.' With the non-victualling trades – it would be misleading to continue to refer to them as 'reformers' – in a pre-eminent position, peace came to the City.

3

Evolution and Demarkation

1382–1439

IN the background of these stirring events the ordinary routine
continued as best it might. There had been an order to all the companies to supply men for the Midsummer watches at the end of
June on St. John's Eve and on the Feast of SS. Peter and Paul. A
suggested explanation is that they were instituted for the prevention of conflagrations at what was normally a dry season of the
year, a time when London would be especially in danger from the
St. John's Fires and from the fact that every house was decorated,
by order, with a burning lantern. The Watch went on their way
carrying cressets and lances – the latter hung with streamers in the
colours of the Wards that provided them: white streamers powder-
ed with red stars, black streamers with white stars, streamers
wreathed in scarlet and so on. Always it seems there was the need
for self-identification, for the display of partisanship and of association: even when no violence immediately threatened there was
the manifest desire for the same exclusiveness that regulated the
misteries.

We have seen how those country craftsmen wishing to set up in
business in London had first to seek entry to the appropriate Livery
Company. There were, then as now, City sophisticates waiting to
batten on the credulous provincial. In 1382, for example,

William Warde, cutler, of the City of York, of late came to London and
requested one John Foxtone to assist him in being admitted and becoming
freeman of the trade of Cutlers in London and the same John Foxtone promised
him so to do; but afterwards, he deceitfully caused him to be admitted into
another trade, and not that of the cutlers, the trade namely of the Bladers. . . .

D

(Here the commentator interpolates: 'he supposing, probably, that *bladers* meant *bladesmiths* whereas a blader was in fact a corndealer.')

. . . in deceit both of the City aforesaid and of the said William and of the trade of Cutlers as well, and against the ordinance of the city aforesaid: for doing which, he received of the said William about 6 marks, alleging that he had given half a mark to a certain Alderman and half a mark to a certain clerk that they might help him in being admitted to the freedom aforesaid; and had also paid sixty shillings to the Chamberlain of the City for obtaining the same; whereas he had paid no more than twenty shillings . . . and had so deceived the said Chamberlain's Court; seeing that according to his means the said William would have had to pay sixty shillings.[54]

When challenged to name the alderman and the clerk who had been bribed Foxtone admitted sheepishly that, in fact, he had not bribed anyone and had simply pocketed the extra mark. The Court was outraged. If any of the aldermen had heard the story they might each have suspected the other. Therefore – and because Foxtone had deceived the Court, the City, the Cutlers and William – he must pay 60/– to the Chamberlain, 18/– to the simple William and spend forty days in gaol.

During this period too there are signs that the old trouble with the Goldsmiths was working away, fermenting beneath the surface. In 1386 the Goldsmiths went so far as to spend 12d to search the Cutlers' ordinances, 'a high-handed action' that is said to have caused much offence[55] though – since the ordinances were enrolled at Guildhall for all to see – the rulers of the Cutlers are shewn in a somewhat unreasonable light.

Now with the end of the immediate troubles in the City the dangers to the nation of London being the battle-ground for warring commercial barons began to be comprehended. There was a feeling that the larger communities – the City and the nation – should assert their rights over the interests of trade or class who should henceforth subordinate themselves to the rule of a common authority. The nation started in fact to take stock of the 'social forces that had begun by building it up and might end by tearing it asunder.'[56]

As part of this stock-taking the king, in 1388, ordered all the gilds and fraternities of London to submit a full account in writing of the manner and nature of their foundations, together with their rules and ordinances, and an account of all their lands, goods, and chattels, under pain of having their grants revoked or annulled.

Government officials, in fact, nervously regarded every such society as a potentially criminal or revolutionary organization. They believed that conspiracies to raise prices and wages were spreading and it was known that some of the lesser crafts of London had made use of oaths for these purposes.[60]

The enquiry revealed, after the charters had been inspected, that the majority were quite illegally holding landed possessions. Thus it was that, sooner or later, all the Companies were forced to apply for a Royal Charter[57] and of course to become, by this action, subordinate to the Crown.

Moreover, because the times were so unsettled and the people so little governable the aldermen and chief men of the City were compelled by Parliament to subscribe to an oath that they would not allow the Acts passed at that time ever to be repealed. Among the 490 signatories in the City there were several cutlers.[58]

Faction could not, however, be laid aside by the stroke of a pen. The events of the 'hurling-time' had been too vicious and too bitter to be quickly forgotten. London was still divided, trade against trade and person against person, between the partisans of Brembre and Northampton, so much so, in fact, that in 1391 an order was made that for the general good 'no man, great or small, of whatever estate or condition he be, shall speak from henceforth, or agitate upon any of the opinions of either of them. . . .'[59]

The penalty for free speech was imprisonment for a year and a day.

This order was characteristic of the authoritarian attitude of the Crown – an attitude that was to lead to more trouble. By 1397, the King had managed to raise a private army of his own to oppose the private armies of his magnates and he felt strong enough to make a move against them.

Such nobles as Gloucester, Arundel and Warwick were arrested and accused of treason. From his stronghold at Shrewsbury the King declared all the Acts of the previous Parliament illegal. His Cheshire supporters came to London, made a great fray in Friday

Street, and got beaten up for their pains. From the City the King demanded sealed blank charters which he could later fill in as he pleased if the citizens offended him.[61]

All the men of every craft 'as well allowes and servants as the masters were charged to come to the Guildhall to set their seals to the said blank charters'[62] for the privilege of which they had to pay one thousand pounds.

But Richard's reliance on the divine right of his royal prerogative proved as fatal to him as it proved to other rulers. His dispossession of Henry of Lancaster from his estates when the old Duke John of Gaunt died unsettled all those with property. If great magnates like the Lancasters could lose everything to the Crown nobody was safe. The magnates rose against the King; in 1399 Richard, a prisoner in the Tower, abdicated and died. Henry of Lancaster ruled in his stead and at his coronation procession Cheapside had seven fountains running with red and white wine.[63]

For the ordinary citizen, when the fountains ceased to flow, a change of rule meant little difference in the uncertainties of his daily life. Once again the cutlers found themselves the worse for a sumptuary law by which no one was allowed to wear a baselard or dagger mounted with silver unless he owned houses, rents or lands worth £20 a year or goods and chattels valued at £200.

Some cutlers, in common with other artificers, in order to meet the demand for cheap finery, had coated their copper sword pommels with gold or silver – a malpractice which brought the whole Company into a new phase of the continuing struggle against the Goldsmiths.

At the beginning of 1404 the Goldsmiths petitioned Parliament. They cited their immemorial right to search and assay all gold and silver work and referred to the dispute of 1327 when members of the Cutlers' Company had been accused of fraudulent workmanship. At that time, said the Goldsmiths, they had been specifically granted the right to search for all such faulty work. Now, they alleged, cutlers were up to new tricks: they were

wont to work in gold and silver in a different manner from what they did in the time aforesaid; whereby through the defaults and subtleties in the work of the said cutlers, great scandals and drawbacks will come. . . .[64]

The petitioners requested that cutlers, and others, be forbidden to engage in any other work in gold and silver than they did in 1327; they demanded, too, that they should have the search and assay of all such workmanship.

The Cutlers reacted strongly. They had, they said, always worked gold and silver on baselards and daggers and had four Wardens, sworn before the Mayor, to oversee the work. Now the Goldsmiths had made a 'false suggestion' with the intention of getting control over the Cutlers 'which would be utter destruction and ruin' of the petitioners. They begged Parliament to preserve their franchises.[65]

The two petitions were considered by the Government and referred to the Mayor for an opinion upon which the King might act. The representatives of both Companies were called before him: he inspected all their old charters, grants and the like, and heard their arguments. Then he reported back to Parliament that it seemed to him that the cutlers

have from ancient time used to work in gold and silver within the Liberty of the City as their times and their ability were then wont to require, and the same cutlers still work in gold and silver in the said City as the times and their ability, according to the change of time require and demand.

The goldsmiths for their part had always had the search and assay of gold and silver work done by the cutlers.

Armed with this information the King confirmed the goldsmiths' ancient right to assay the cutlers' gold and silver work.

It was, presumably, against this grant – a grant confirmed in the Goldsmiths' new charter – that the Cutlers again petitioned King and Parliament. Their rivals had been given the general right to control all gold and silver work in the City and to punish and correct any faults they might find 'whereas the punishment and correction of the faults found in the said craft of the Cutlers always belonged, and ought to belong, to the Mayor . . . by presentment made to him by the four Wardens of the said craft.'

It was this sort of thing, declared the indignant Cutlers, that would destroy the privileges of the City; it would also, incidentally, ruin their Company 'and would be the cause of great trouble between the said Crafts and irreparable damages might arise which God forbid.'[66]

The reply to this petition is unrecorded, but the incident shows that many of the Livery Companies were still far from autonomous – discipline was still vested in the Mayor.

The question of search was always a sensitive one.

In August 1408 a number of masters, and other reputable cutlers, appeared before the Mayor

> shewing . . . with all due urgency, how that they and their predecessors, cutlers of the said City, were wont to sell knives fully prepared and decorated, to all buyers whatsoever; but that every knife is prepared separately by three different crafts, first the blade by smiths called 'Bladesmiths', the handle and the other fitting work by the cutlers, and the sheath by the sheathers; and that if the article is good commendation is the result, but if bad, then blame and scandal falls and is charged upon the said trade of the Cutlers. And . . . that for any default of the sheaths, being not properly made, no little blame and scandal falls upon the said trade of Cutlers, and manifest damage ensues therefrom, as well to the whole realm as to the community of the City aforesaid.[67]

Many sheathers, and cutlers too, it was alleged, had been making sheaths without any inspection and with no presentation of the finished work before the Chamberlain 'to the common loss and manifest scandal' of the trade of the Cutlers.

The Mayor and aldermen sent for representatives of the sheathers and put the matter to them. It was determined that in future two of the masters of the Cutlers should at due and fitting times warn two of the masters of the Sheathers to make a joint scrutiny of sheaths made by the members of either Company – or by anyone in the Kingdom if their goods were put on sale in London – and to take any defaulters before the City Chamberlain.

Gradually the spheres of influence, the lines of demarcation, were settled. In October that same year the Cutlers and Blade-smiths made a joint petition demonstrating how 'foreign folk from divers parts of England' were selling to London cutlers faulty blades and knives marked in such a manner as to resemble the marks of bladesmiths who were free of the City. 'May it therefore please your very wise discreetnesses,' they begged, to decree that no cutler may buy such goods. The Bladesmiths undertook, at the same time, not to raise their prices except by agreement with the Cutlers.

Later that month the Bladesmiths – still a separate and rival Company – presented a petition of their own for the regulation of trade. It appeared that bladesmiths, both freemen and foreigners 'who dwell in foreign lanes' were – because their goods were faulty – selling their products in some secret place. Articles were proposed that no one should be allowed to carry false work for sale through the streets; sales should be made only from their shops or openly at Gracechurch or on the pavement near St. Nicholas Flesshambles or near the Tun at Cornhill.

Tools and weapons must have sufficiently hard edges and points to pass an assay; all work must bear its maker's mark; masters were not to teach the secret of the trade to journeymen as if they were apprentices. With these and other rules – frequently more to be found in the breach than in the observance – the Companies established their respective positions. And, as we have already seen, in 1416, the Cutlers scored a signal advantage by securing a Royal charter.

The years immediately before this great achievement were still turbulent. Henry IV had defeated conspiracies at home, had put down rebellions by the Welsh, and had been victorious over the Scots. But the position of anyone seizing power, as Henry had done, with but faint claims to legitimate succession, was always in danger from resentful barons.

There was unease in the City. In 1405, for instance, the Mayor ordered that a watch be kept every night during the solemn feast of Christmas 'and that no persons shall go in the said City, or in the suburbs thereof with visors or false faces. . . .' Every house in the main streets was to have a lantern with a candle to burn so long as it might last. The feeling that the Livery Companies were becoming too 'pompous' persisted. They were prone, it was alleged, to an excess of display, particularly in their attendances upon the Mayor. In future no minstrels were to ride before any of the Companies but only before the Mayor – and then only in three groups.

There was a suspicion, too, that Companies were unduly using their influence on the officers of local government. The City officials – at a time when everyone was inclined to think the worst of his neighbour – must be above suspicion. In 1415 the order went forth

Seeing that the exigencies of sound government, and the happiness that results therefrom, even when the advantages thereof have been well weighed, hardly seem to allay the singular impressions and the tendency to obloquy on the part of some people; so it is that at the present day even, there is no old usage, sanctioned though it be by the path of laudable prescription, but that the same path is so choked up by the dust of obloquy that it is prejudiced, contrary to all expectation, by having the worse construction put upon it instead of the better.

This apologetic preamble was leading to the abolition of the long-established custom of giving livery hoods and clothing to the City Officers – a custom 'hardly able now to get a good word even said on its behalf.'

But, that same year, there were other distractions that took men's minds temporarily away from such mutual suspicion and rivalry and for an all too brief moment united the nation. France had been invaded by the young King Henry V and there had been a victory at Harfleur. An imperialist war on French soil was greatly to the nation's liking. The City had willingly lent the King 10,000 marks on the security of his great Collar of gold and precious stones. Then, quite suddenly, came the dreadful news: there had been a crushing defeat at Agincourt. The procession planned to be on horseback for the Lord Mayor's Day was changed to one on foot. The Mayor's Day, October 29, dawned in an atmosphere of gloom. But

the same day, early in the morning came tidings to London while that men were in their beds, that the King had fought and had the battle and the field aforesaid. And anon as they had the tidings thereof they went to all the churches in the City of London and rang all the bells of every church; and solemnly all the priests of every church and other men that were lettered sang *Te Deum Laudamus &c.* And against ix of the bell were warned all the orders of religious men of the City of London for to go in procession from St. Paul's unto St. Edward's shrine at Westminster. And the new mayor and his aldermen with all the crafts of London, and the queen, with all her lords also went from St. Paul's unto Westminster and offered at St. Edward's shrine aforesaid before the mayor took his charge; and when the mayor had taken his charge every man came riding home from Westminster on horseback, and were joyful and glad for the good tidings that they had of the King and thanked our Lord Jesus Christ, his mother St. Mary, and St. George and all the holy company of heaven and said *Hic est dies quam fecit Dominus.*[68]

On November 15 the King returned from France and eight days later

The mayor of London and all the aldermen with all the crafts of London rode, every man in red with hoods red and white and met with the King on Blackheath coming from Elthamwards towards his City of London; and against his coming was ordained much royalty in London, that was to wait at London Bridge, at the conduit in Cornhill, at the great conduit in Cheap; and at the cross in Cheap was made a royal castle with angels and virgins singing therein; and so the King and his prisoners of Frenchmen rode through London to Westminster to meat and there the King abode still. And on the morrow after, it was Sunday and the 24th day of November, the mayor and all the aldermen with two hundred of the best commoners of London went to Westminster to the king and presented him with a £1000 in two basins of gold worth £500. . . .[69]

Those were great days to stir the blood in that year before the Cutlers achieved their first charter.

In 1416 the King went again to France where he remained with the army during September and part of October. Seven weeks after his return, on December 4, he put his signature to the Cutlers' charter.

Apart from the advantage, which has already been noted, of being able to hold lands in Mortmain to the value of twenty pounds a year, the mere fact of incorporation, ensuring as it did a continuous and permanent existence, enhanced the prestige of any organization and thus indirectly endowed it with more political influence.[70] But the immediate effects must not be over-estimated – it was only later, as the Companies became more and more independent, that the charters were seen to be really valuable.

But there were not many immediately tangible changes in the image of the Cutlers' Company. Only the rule of the mistery was slightly altered: whereas there had formerly been four Wardens of equal rank who acted, it has been suggested,[71] like an executive committee, the commonalty was now to elect each year a Master and two Wardens. Otherwise the status quo prevailed.

The properties in Watling Street for which they had required their licence in Mortmain now came into the Company's corporate hands. Henceforth much of their time would be increasingly devoted to leases and rents and all the aspects of property management which provided some sort of security, and, ultimately, prosperity for a Livery Company.

With an increase in the business of governing a Corporation it was inevitable that those who were richer – and usually older too – were most able to devote their freely-given time to these matters. The power in any Company thus tended to fall into the hands of such men. It is possible that the whole of the lengthy process of acquiring the Cutlers charter' had been the work of a few of the leading members of the Company, who having secured the grant, secured for themselves the complete direction of the corporate affairs. There was probably among the commonalty a fairly general apathy – arising partly from a preoccupation with the harsh facts of earning a living – about the way the Company was run. By the arrears of quarterage which were always to be collected it appears that a failure to attend the assemblies of the Company was by no means uncommon. In the event of widespread disinterest, it was a natural consequence that those who attended regularly to the business should elect and re-elect one another to the offices of Master and Wardens.

This might be accepted by the rank and file so long as the administration was felt to be both honest and equitable. But in July 1420, less than four years after their incorporation, there was internal dissension in the Company: the commonalty appealed to Richard Whittington, the Mayor.

At the enquiry that followed it was reported that one of the chief complaints lay in the fact that the Master and Wardens were elected by six or eight members of the mistery without the knowledge or consent of the rest of the commonalty. Worse still, an audit shewed that the officers who had collected the rents and fines and so on and who should have paid them into the corporate fund were in arrears by more than thirty-four pounds. The Mayor appointed a date by which these arrears should be paid, claiming part of them for the City, and he ordered that all 'unreasonable' ordinances contained in the rule book of the Company which had not been sanctioned by the aldermen should be annulled. It is clear from this that the early Masters and Wardens were less than scrupulous in their behaviour – not only were they displaying a dubious financial honesty but had introduced their own harsh code of laws into the Company books. For the peaceable choice of future officers the Mayor decreed that the election should take place yearly 'without murmurings' about the Feast of the Holy Trinity – a clear indication of the Dedication of the Mistery – and that those so chosen should be presented to the Court of Aldermen to take their oath. In the meantime an election was to take place in October, under supervision. Accordingly the whole Company came together at 'Marners Inn' and peacefully elected their new Master and Wardens for the rest of the year until Trinity Sunday. They were duly sworn before the Mayor and aldermen and the constitutional crisis, though it was to re-occur at intervals in the centuries to come, was for the moment ended.

The new Master and Wardens submitted some new articles for the approval of the Mayor: no one should be elected to office unless he were a freeman by birth or by apprenticeship served in the City; once he had been elected and had served he could not be re-elected for five years except in the case of a Warden being promoted to Master; the Master and Wardens should have the power to summon before them all members of the Company 'whether they be of the livery and clothing of the mistery or not' and demand that they observe the ordinances approved by the Mayor – those who failed to answer the summons speedily, men or women, should be fined twelve pence. There was a further article, promulgated under the recent Statute of Apprentices, that has a curious 'Boys-Own-Paper' ring about it: 'no one of the Mistery shall take any apprentice that is not of free birth and condition, handsome in stature, having straight and proper limbs. . . .'[72]

It is interesting but unprofitable to speculate upon the reason for an order, common to all companies, that tended to deprive the City at a time of labour shortage, of the services of young crippled geniuses.

It may have been observed that among the Articles there is an indication that the evolution of the Company was proceeding along the same path as it did in other Companies. Already the members had become divided into two classes – those within the Livery or Clothing and those without. All were free but some were more free than others. It was part of the natural social and economic development. The more enterprising members of a craft who either specialized in finer goods or who had a wider market or a more extensive circle of clients (perhaps through sending their goods to country markets such as Stourbridge Fair) employed the poorer members or, even, 'foreigns' in some of the manufacturing processes – often in the finishing of the goods. The Cutlers' Company are among those who are known to have done this.[73] Those who worked for the richer members as journeymen or servingmen lived for a term of years in their masters' houses. They were known as the Yeomanry or, alternatively, since in their masters' houses they remained unmarried, as the Bachelors. The masters were granted the Livery of the Company and the Yeomanry were not – although, as will be later seen, it was possible to pass from the lower ranks to the upper. Gradually the Yeomanry became organized on the same lines as their betters in a position subordinate to them: they had their own officers, their own meeting place and they collected their own fines and quarterage which was administered for them by the Livery. It was the Livery from whom the rulers of the Company were chosen but the choice of Master and Wardens was in the hands of the whole body of the Freemen, Livery and Yeomanry alike. Then as later, the Livery was sometimes given to prominent persons and public officials who had been useful to the Company – but this practice had been somewhat discouraged by the order of 1415 which we have already noted.

The two organizations, survived in varying degrees of discontent, the one with the other, for many years to come. It was not until the middle of the seventeenth century that, in common with the Drapers' Company, the Cutlers lost all patience with the workers and disbanded them. It is to be regretted that in none of the Livery Companies do any of the Yeomanry records appear to have survived. Their views of the state of the nation might have shewn a slightly different countenance to that to be reconstructed from the Livery records.

In 1422 King Henry V, in France, succumbed to dysentery. The funeral of one who had died in the prime of life and at the apparent summit of success called for proper arrangements to be carefully made.

From Eastcheap to the Southwark side of London Bridge the streets should be lined with substantial people of the Wards carrying lighted torches. All the chaplains of churches and chapels along the route were to stand at their doorways in their best and richest vestments, bearing in their hands gold and silver censers and chanting solemnly and antiphonally the Venite and suitable Dirges.

The streets were to be cleaned – a sure mark of a special occasion – and the Mayor, the Sheriffs, the Recorder and the aldermen, and all the officers,

and the more sufficient persons of the whole Commonalty, clad in black vestments, together with three hundred torches borne by three hundred persons clothed in white gowns and hoods, shall proceed on foot up to St. George's Bar and there tenderly salute the corpse, following it the first day to St. Paul's Church where they shall attend the funeral solemnities, and the next day to Westminster. . . .

The City provided the gowns and hoods of the torchbearers and the Livery Companies provided the torches. Pieces of torch remaining after the funeral were the property of the Company that provided them. The Cutlers' share was four torches.

Henry V had, in fact, in the timing of his death been fortunate. The renown of his success was untarnished by the bitter aftermath of his policies. His infant son, Henry VI, succeeded to a disastrous legacy of national bankruptcy incurred in the endlessly mounting expenditure of war. The gold coinage was devalued and silver became so scarce that it was often impossible to get small change. The long period of the new King's minority provided the great magnates with an unrivalled opportunity for consolidating their powers without interference from the Crown. The Council became the seat of all real power in the realm. It was irremovable and self-perpetuating. Attendance at its meetings was vastly lucrative. Soon the members of the Council were quarrelling over the pickings, their individual claims being supported by their private armies which had been reinforced by the bullies and brawling soldiers returned from France. As always, it was the man in the street who suffered from the effects of such lawless rival factions as those of Humphrey, Duke of Gloucester, and Henry Beaufort, Bishop of Winchester who now became the greatest source of danger to the City.

In 1425, during the Mayor's Day Dinner, Gloucester – 'the good Duke Humphrey' as he was known in the City – sent for the Mayor and aldermen and commanded them to keep a good watch that night. This they did and it was not until the next morning the Bishop's men attempted to enter the City in great numbers. They were prevented from doing so and at once mounted a full-scale assault against the gates. In common cause with their fellow citizens the cutlers closed their shops and rushed to man the barriers. It seemed as if bloodshed on a large scale was inevitable. The Mayor and aldermen hurried about trying to keep the peace. The Archbishop of Canterbury and, oddly, the Prince of Portugal who happened to be in England, rode eight times between the opposing forces to prevent combat being joined. At last the danger was averted and although no physical damage was done the continuing social disorder in the City and throughout the country was causing irreparable harm to the mental outlook of every class of citizen.

Under the new regime the Cutlers had received a charter confirming the one granted to them only six years previously. They seem at this time to have been keeping what in twentieth-century jargon was to become known as a 'low-profile' – there is little record of their activities and it seems that they still had no home of their own: in 1422 there is some reference to the Cutlers as being among those to whom the Brewers lent their Hall that year.

Their subsidiaries, the Grinders, made a momentary appearance when the Court of Aldermen laid down rules for the better governance of the Sheargrinders – a tiny cell of two or three men only, within the larger body. They dealt exclusively with the Shearmen and the Drapers and they had been charging from day to day 'so excessiflich for their occupation . . . that it is shame and dole for to here.'

Their wages were now to be controlled; the Shearmen were to provide two men to turn the stone for the Grinder and if repairs were necessary the grinders were to go to the Shearmen's house and carry out the work there.

There is evidence, too, that the Cutlers, in spite of the ruling made that the Goldsmiths were to have the search and assay of faulty work in gold and silver, were making themselves responsible for this. Between 10 December 1428 and 11 January 1429 they made no less than three prosecutions before the Mayor of John Hooke – he had first been found with a baselard worked with silver of a false alloy, then he was caught with two bars of low grade silver with which he was preparing to harness a girdle, and, finally, he had in his possession two false silver lockets for harnessing a baselard. Each time he cheerfully admitted his guilt and was fined on the rising scale laid down by the ordinances.[74]

Had he offended a fourth time he would have been 'forsworn the Mistery.'

In thus taking upon themselves some of the Goldsmith's powers it is probable that the Cutlers were displaying the confidence that their charter gave them. Formerly their rivals had been in the superior position of having been incorporated for at least forty years. Now they could be faced on a basis – if mere riches were discounted – of approximate equality.

Incorporation by charter had, by this time, become the estab-

lished rule among the greater Companies and an object of legitimate ambition to all the rest.[75] The fact that a charter was obtained
from the Crown and for its continuance ultimately depended
upon the goodwill of the Crown tended to detract from the
authority of any city where a mistery existed and municipal
authorities in general felt bound to act before too great a diminution of their influence should have taken place. They secured in
1437 an Act of Parliament to reassert their status. The preamble
read, in part,

> that masters, wardens, and people of gilds and fraternities and other companies
> corporate . . . often times by colour of rule and governance and other terms in
> general words to them granted . . . by charters . . . of divers kings, made amongst
> themselves many unlawful and unreasonable ordinances as well in prices of
> wares and other things for their own singular profit.

The Act demanded that all should bring in their charters to be
registered by their municipal leaders. The City of London had
been the moving spirit in obtaining the legislation and began at
once to put it into action. Disputes about the validity of royal
charters seem to have formed the basis of city politics at this period.
And in 1439 – a year of great dearth, 'the second Dear Year,' when
people made bread from bean or vetch or fern-root flour – the
Cutlers enrolled their charter in the City books.

4

Business as Usual

1439-1463

IN the middle ages the Hall of a Company was second home to the citizen. He lived and worked close by, and at the Hall he met his friends, discussed trade and public affairs, and sometimes took with him his womenfolk.[76] As befitted the new feudalism the Halls often resembled the houses of great nobles. Sometimes a Hall had actually been the house of some great noble.[77]

The question of the Cutlers' Hall is one of some obscurity. We have seen that there had once been the Cutlers' House opposite the conduit in Cheapside; we have seen, too, that afterwards they appear to have been without a Hall of their own: the disputed election of 1420 had been held at a hostelry and in 1422 they had borrowed Brewers' Hall. Yet, by 1442, when the first domestic records of the Company begin, they were apparently already occupying, without paying any rent, the Hall in Cloak Lane that was not conveyed to them officially until 1451.

The Hall was on the south side of the Lane – which was at this time called Horseshoe Bridge Street – and near the Walbrook, a stream then still navigable as far as Bucklersbury. From the earliest accounts it is possible to build up a sketchy impression of their home. The whole frontage extended some 130 ft: there was a great Hall and chamber, a parlour and a little parlour, a counting house, a kitchen and a storehouse. Among the complex of buildings was the almshouse and a house for the Beadle. Later, as the Company evolved, there was a Yeomanry hall, associated offices and, even, a tenement to let. There was a garden where vines grew and a well.

A feature of the Hall was the great bay window behind the dais.

E

Heating came from a fire in the centre of the room – a hundred 'faggots' were bought each year – the smoke escaping, more or less, from a lantern in the roof. The floor was tiled and strewn with rushes, the walls hung with arras or painted cloths.

There were two somewhat striking features of the decorations of the Hall: an Angel in the bay window and another hanging from a beam in the high-pitched roof. It has been rather improbably suggested that each was representational of the Holy Trinity:[78] iconographically it seems likely that they both belonged to, and represented the dedication of, the Cutlers' Fraternity of the Annunciation, which the good folks of the mistery had established in 1370. Now, the mistery seemed to have adopted the responsibilities of the fraternity for it was from the wardens' accounts that the waxchandler was paid for the lights in the Charterhouse, that a clerk was paid for keeping the light and scouring the candlesticks. So, too, the wardens paid for restoring and repainting the Angels.

In this Hall, where the names of the brethren were painted upon a board, the Company held the 'Coney Feast' at Christmas with players to entertain the company which included the Clerk of St. Martin's, the Clerk of Whittington College and three of the almsmen. It was a Hall that from time to time they hired out, together with all their pewter plate, to other Livery Companies such as the Fullers and the Smiths and it was a Hall where they carried out such mysterious activities as, at the cost of one penny, 'making a hole in a post for a brake.'[79]

It was an old building and much in need of repair. The retiling of the roof in 1443 took two tilers each with his men twenty-four days and sixteen days respectively.

From the accounts, scanty though they are, it is also possible to draw other statistics. The wardens in 1442–3 collected 56/- in quarterage which suggests that the total number of members, both in and out of the Livery, amounted to perhaps sixty-five. There were thirty apprentices and five almsfolk two of whom received 10d, the remainder 4d each.

The Cutlers drew rents from twelve properties in Walbrook, in the parish of Paternoster Church and in Watling Street. Their rent roll amounted to £25. 16s. 8d.

The system of accounting was, and remained for some centuries, a simple one. There were two accounts, one kept by the Renter who collected rents and paid for repairs to the property and was allowed money towards a potation with the tenants and the other kept by the Wardens who collected quarterage and fines and paid for all the running expenses of the Company. At the end of the year the Renter and the Wardens either handed over any surplus money in their hands or were paid the deficit from the Company treasury.

The accounts for the year 1443–1444 shewed a debit balance of £4. 12s. 9d. on the wardens' account and a credit of £10. 6s. 0d. on the Renter's account. The Company were thus able to put £5. 13s. 3d. into the great, iron communal chest.

As long as there remained a small but sufficient balance each year the Company might well have been content. But once again the outside world broke in with yet another terrifying display of violence.

The war in France was proving a disaster. And with the loss of Normandy in 1450 there was lost all faith in the Government. The debts of the Crown amounted to nearly £400,000. The King's income was only £5000 a year yet his household expenses amounted to £24,000.[80] Protesting against the incompetence of their rulers and the penal taxation they imposed, the Kentishmen rose in revolt and marched on London. Their leader was Jack Cade, 'a ribald and Irishman', and at first the City, as a whole, supported him. On July 3 some of the leading citizens gave him the keys and he and the rabble swarmed through the gates. Those who had thus surrendered London were quick to have regrets. The mob fell to looting and robbing. From the dark alleys came bitter men with old scores still to settle. There was another orgy of the killing and the violence which had by now become part of the natural way of life to many Londoners. Lord Say was on his way to trial at Guildhall when the mob took the law into its own hands and beheaded him in Cheapside and his body was drawn naked along the cobbles 'so that the flesh cleave to the stones from Cheap to Southwark.'

William Crowmere was seized and beheaded at Mile End and his head was paraded with that of Lord Say on poles through the City. As the mob proceeded they continually brought the poles together so that the heads kissed one another.[81] Jack Cade rode about, amid the scenes of death and destruction, 'bearing a naked sword in his hand, armed in a pair of brigandines, wearing a pair of gilt spurs and a gilt sallet, and a gown of blue velvet as he had been a lord or knight – and yet he was but a knave – and had his sword borne before him.'[82]

After three days, the Londoners had had enough. Cade's popularity had received a severe set-back and when it became known that he had robbed the house to which he had been invited the turning point was reached. During the night the citizens 'laid hands on them that were disparbled about . . . and beat them and drove them out of the city and shut the gates.'

In spite of Cade's desperate attempts to break in again he was opposed the whole night with great steadfastness. Eventually he was defeated and slain. The immediate danger was ended but the unrest inside the City continued for some time. There was a spate of fly-posting of political posters; there were robberies in the streets; the Duke of Somerset was openly set upon by a gang, and barely escaped with his life.

Worse, it seemed, was to follow. Richard Duke of York, the heir-presumptive to the throne, returned unexpectedly from quasi-exile in Ireland and in a very short time clashed with Somerset who had his own ambitions towards the throne.

In 1452 York and his allies 'gathered a great people in destruction of their enemies that were about the King; and sent by a herald to London praying that they might pass with their people through the City.'[83]

The City authorities refused permission: whatever their feelings might be, they were preserving for the moment a strict neutrality. The first skirmishes of the Wars of the Roses were at hand. The merchant aristocracy – mercers, grocers and drapers for the most part – who ruled the capital 'wisely resisted the temptation to take an active part in the struggle of the rival families for the Crown. . . . But they compelled the armies of the White and

Red Roses to respect London's liberties and commerce. . . .'[84]

So for a time, while the countryside of England provided a series of battlefields, the Cutlers' records – such as they are – tell of nothing but domestic minutiae.

One of the more important details was the official acquisition in 1451 of the Hall in which they had for some considerable time been installed. Yet already, during the earlier years of occupation when there is no record of any rental having been paid for the building, they had made extensions to the premises: there were receipts for rent of the tenement 'within the place of craft'; an oven had been built in the Hall and a baker appears for the first time on the regular payroll of the Company. But, at last, came the official taking-possession of the premises by two beadles; deeds were drawn up by one Belgrave who was treated to supper at the King's Head, in Cheapside, as well as being given a knife. It was one of the earliest recorded occasions on which the Company presented a knife or knives as rewards – or encouragements – for services rendered or hoped for.

When a bill was presented to the Mayor against one Henry Ottley three pairs of knives were given to three of the Mayor's clerks, at a total cost of three shillings.

With the official acquisition of the Hall came also the public responsibilities of ownership: they were served with an indictment against the nuisance of their dunghill outside the Hall door.

Water was being laid on. There was a pipe provided to the Hall and cisterns were installed, both there and in other of their pro-perties. Sister-companies made use of the refurbished and re-decorated building – the Smiths, the Scriveners and the Glovers all regularly rented the place for their business. In addition to the specific obits for their special benefactors a general obit was now held each year at Whittington College for all the deceased brothers and sisters of the craft.

Women were, in fact, well in evidence in the early days of the Company: there were women cutlers who enrolled apprentices and there were freewomen and, of course, there were the widows of members of the freedom to be cared for in times of need.

On the day the Company rode with the Mayor to Westminster a

horse was regularly hired for the Beadle, the chief officer of the
Company with a house of his own attached to the Hall and a salary
greater than that of the Clerk. When riding to Westminster became
in 1453 – and remained for very many years – a thing of the past and
the procession took to the Thames, the Cutlers hired a barge for
the occasion and paid for rushes for the deck and meat and drink
for the oarsmen. That was the year when the English lost all their
possessions in France with the exception of Calais, the King became
for a while insane and York claimed the Regency. And although he
recognized the child who was born that year to the Queen as the
rightful heir, Margaret's fear of his intentions led, when the King
recovered his health, to the first great encounter, at St. Albans in
1455, of the Wars of the Roses. Although the Lancastrians were
defeated, York treated the King with respect and, claiming that he
intended no disloyalty to the Crown, he accompanied Henry VI
back to London. For four years an uneasy peace persisted: while, in
the background, the two sides manoeuvred and plotted for position and advantage, the Government lost all semblance of
authority over the country.

In London, during this sinister calm, there were riots and
disputes. 1456 was marked by 'wanton rule by the Mayor and
Mercers of London against the Lombards who were driven out
of the City.'[85] The next year there were further anti-Italian riots:
an Italian had walked down Cheapside with a dagger hanging at
his girdle and an outraged mercer, who had been forbidden to go
armed, attacked him. The fracas spread and the mob fell to looting
aliens' houses. The Government, powerless to punish the offenders,
faced a threat by Florentine, Genoese and Venetian merchants to
remove their business to Winchester: already the great Venetian
merchant fleet was using Southampton, to the decay of the port
and trade of London.

In 1458 the fortunes of war with France had sunk so low that the
French were actually able to carry out a raid on Sandwich. A great
watch was kept in London on all the gates, with two aldermen on
duty every night.

Though they shewed a neutral approach to the situation, the
Londoners were still bound by the principles of loyalty to the

Crown. In 1459 they had raised money for the King but a commission for raising men-at-arms and archers was refused on the grounds that such a demand was derogatory to the City's franchise and liberties.

By 1460 the claims of the rival factions had become so bitter that a meeting was called to settle the grievances between the two parties. During January and February the protagonists moved into London for the conference: the Duke of York lodged at Barnard's Castle, the Earl of Salisbury at the Herber, Somerset and Exeter without Temple Bar. In the suburbs, Northumberland, Egremond and Clifford found accommodation. Finally, Warwick arrived at Grey Friars and the King and Queen moved into the Bishop of London's palace. Each was accompanied by retainers and men at arms varying in numbers from four hundred to six hundred. The situation must have seemed appallingly dangerous to the Londoners. The Mayor rose to the occasion and raised a watch of five thousand citizens; three thousand of them, led by three aldermen, rode about the City each night until seven o'clock in the morning to see that any trouble that might break out should be restrained. 'Thus good order was kept and there was no attempt whatsoever to break the King's peace.'[86]

The Yorkist Lords retired to Calais and there awaited their moment.

In June Salisbury, Warwick and March landed once more in England and marched, unopposed, towards London. On June 27 the Livery Companies agreed to defend the gates; anyone wishing to enter had first to give a good account of himself; a strict check was made of strangers already within the walls; the Mayor and sheriffs patrolled with armed men; a deputation was sent to the rebels requesting them not to try to enter the City.

Yet, for all this display of strength there were other influences at work. Only three days later, on June 30, there were signs that the City's allegiance was beginning to waver. The aldermen had been sent, and – contrary to their previous decisions – had accepted a message from the earls. What the message said is not recorded but on July 2 the rebels were admitted to the City and Salisbury was declared 'ruler and governor of London.'

This unexpected *volte face* was not entirely unopposed.

Lord Scales and Lord Somerford had themselves sought control of the City: they had been rejected by the citizens who had said they were quite capable of ruling themselves. Now these lords retired indignantly with a large number of followers into the Tower. They were besieged by land and blockaded from the river. At length, after they had caused much damage and injury by firing wildly and indiscriminately into the City, a bombardment across the Thames from the South Bank breached the walls and the Tower surrendered. In October, York arrived in London and claimed the throne; only two months later he was killed at the Battle of Wakefield and Queen Margaret advanced towards London, sending ahead of her knights bearing demands for supplies. The Mayor ordered that bread and victuals be sent to her but when the Londoners learned the destination of the supply carts they seized them and refused to let them leave the City[87] – a refusal that they no doubt remembered uncomfortably when, after Margaret's supporters had won the second Battle of St. Albans, the report reached the City that the Welsh and the northern levies had been granted the looting of London as part of their wages. There was great unease as the Lancastrians drew near but, at the very last moment London was saved in a lightning campaign by the Earl of March.

'Then all the City was fain and thanked God and said "Let us walk in a new vineyard and let us make a gay garden in the month of March with this fair white rose and herb the Earl of March" '[88] – the sort of remark that does not normally trip very easily from London tongues.

In 1461, on March 4, Edward IV was hailed at Westminster as King.

The Cutlers' own garden with its vinery was clearly in good order. It had been necessary to spend no more than eightpence on it the previous year. The Company seem to have been suffering the sort of slight decline that might be expected if there had been casualties among the members: less quarterage was collected and there were far fewer apprentices. But they were indulging in what appears to have been a new activity – that of buying ivory and selling it to their members at advantageous prices. To help the less wealthy they would lend money for the purchase of ivory – it was sixpence a pound in 1461 – and accept a gradual and protracted repayment as and when the finished goods were sold. There were five such sales recorded that year, the amount ranging in weight from one pound to nearly twenty-five pounds. It was a useful service but it continued for no more than about a dozen years. It is possible that the fluctuations in price – at one shilling a pound when a Thaxted cutler bought a whole tusk weighing 53 pounds the cost had doubled in one year – made the operation too risky for the Company; with the money repaid to them they could buy but half the amount of ivory needed to restock their store. Such matters were clearly better left to such merchants as dealt in ivory.

The routine of their normal activities continued unchanged by war. Sometimes they employed City officers to act for them: a sergeant summoned the Bladesmiths for their combined search; a sergeant searched St. Bartholomew's Fair; on two occasions an officer summoned the representatives of the Pinners Company (in the course of some now forgotten dispute) before the Chamberlain.

The provision of funerals for decayed brethren continued: 13s. 7d. was spent on a winding sheet, torches, torchbearers, and the services of the necessary clergy for the burial of one Thomas Raymond. Coal was for the first time added to faggots for heating the Hall – and soon allowances of coal were being made to the almsfolk.

A new regulation was entered in the register – 'no person of the said Craft shall at any time have any work in his chamber nor in any close or secret place but to work openly by the street side. . . .'

Expenses were allowed to certain members to ride to meet the King coming for his coronation.

Banners and buckram were bought to provide decorations for the occasion. There was new pewter and the salt-cellars were pounced. The Company shewed its charter to the Recorder with, presumably, the intention of having it renewed by the young King. 'Business as usual' had, by now, become the *sine qua non* of survival in the City and the Cutlers were looking, too, to the future. There were certain matters put before Parliament 'for the weal and profit of the Company,' and £5. 5s. 8d. was paid 'to divers persons for to shew their good wills and to be friendly and solicitous in the same matter.' What these matters may have been is not known but the activities of the Company, who were to play a leading part in the important legislation enacted by Edward IV, clearly impressed the Pewterers. They, too, had been ambitious to secure a charter but their incorporation had been hampered by the Civil War. Now they sought advice on matters of procedure. They sent a deputation, armed with eightpence to spend on drinks, to consult the officers at Cutlers' Hall.[89] At some time during the interview they were informed – no doubt with great tact and with no more than the most fleeting of glances at the humble potation – that it was really a very expensive business and that before applying for a charter they ought to have more financial reserves.

The Bladesmiths, for their part – still a separate mistery from the Cutlers – in 1463 registered new ordinances which recited grievances of their trade: they were, certainly, grievances that the Cutlers shared. 'Foreign' bladesmiths from towns all over England as well as from the suburbs of London were coming to the City and selling their goods – often fraudulently stamped with London marks – at inns and at other private and unlawful places. They should sell, openly and on market days only at Leadenhall. Many a good blade was being ruined by unskilful Grinders: 'foreigners' should be restrained from engaging in such work until they had been tested and then enfranchised. Untrue and unserviceable goods were not to be sold for 'light cheap' in secret places: nothing should be sold until it had been inspected by the officers of the craft and London smiths should not mark country blades with their own marks. All these requests the Bladesmiths made to 'their right sad and wise discretions' the Mayor and aldermen and in due course they were granted.

The Bladesmiths and those in the cutlery trades might be trying to confine sales by non-freemen to Leadenhall but there was also a general move by the City to segregate all such shopkeepers into one area, near Mark Lane, called Blancheappleton.[90]

But the enfranchised traders of London were not the only craftsmen to be discontented. Artificers all over England and Wales had

piteously shewed and complained how that all they in general, and every of them, be greatly impoverished and much hindered and prejudiced of their worldly increase and daily living by the great multitudes of divers commodities and Wares pertaining to their Misteries and Occupations, being fully wrought and ready made to sale, as well by the hands of Strangers being the King's Enemies as other in this Realm and Wales, fetched and brought from beyond the Sea, as well by Merchant Strangers as Denizens, whereof the greatest part in substance is deceitful and nothing worth . . .[91]

The result, they claimed, was unemployment, poverty, misery and need – all of which led to grave inconveniences.

The King returned, about this time, to London from the North after his decisive victory over the Lancastrians at Towton. Some 350 horsemen from thirty-nine of the Livery Companies together with the Mayor and aldermen, clothed all in scarlet, were ordered to ride to meet him. The Cutlers, seventeenth in order of precedence, nominated six riders. They and all the commonalty were robed in sanguine gowns with hoods and black liripipes. Then suddenly, at a day's notice, the programme was entirely altered. The King, they were told, now intended to approach Westminster from his palace at Sheen by water. The City made hasty arrangements to hire the necessary barges to accompany him down the river and in due course he was worthily installed in his City.

One of his first actions, in reply to the petitions of the artisans, was to assent to an Act which, with a view to encouraging native industries, placed import restrictions on a wide range of commodities, including knives, daggers, scissors and razors. By the only exception to the Act it was, however, still possible to sell proscribed articles which had been 'genuinely and without collusion' – a necessary stipulation – taken at sea by force of arms or salvaged from wrecks. To the Master and Wardens of each craft was given the right to search for all such articles both in their own Companies and in other Companies where such goods were offered for sale.

It was a policy that was strongly supported by the Cutlers' Company. They had taken a leading part in securing the passage of the Act – perhaps it was for that they had paid out more than five pounds for those in high places to be solicitous for them – and they had been backed by the contributions of such lesser crafts as the Pinners and the Card-makers. Those Companies had each paid ten shillings to obtain what they called an 'exemplification of the Act' in the form of a mandate demanding that the Mayor enforce it. A copy of this they deposited for safe-keeping at Cutlers' Hall.

There then followed a period of some twenty years when it seems that the Cutlers' Company were able to settle back into a cosy domesticity. The outside world – although undoubtedly there were moments of excitement, of excursions and alarms – hardly breaks in upon them. After the greater storms which they had already safely weathered they were able to consolidate in comparative calm.

5

The Pursuit of Domesticity

1463–1509

THE trade depression of the mid-fifteenth century was ending. With the accession of Edward IV there came a great commercial revival and, of all the flourishing cities of the realm, London, with its multiplicity of trades, became the most prosperous. As it became, too, ever-increasingly the centre of expanding government departments, it became the fashion for the great magnates of the land to have houses in London and Westminster and they, with their retinues of servants, all swelled the trade of the City. As the Cutlers' Company evolved and as it became increasingly consolidated so the records of the outside world become increasingly scarce: their tale was all of domesticity. The routine was becoming well-established. They now had three regular festive occasions each year. The first of these, the Coney Feast, held during the Christmas season, was the most elaborate. The brethren paid for their own dinners – and for those of their wives – and the Company paid for such official guests as the Master and the Clerk of Whittington College and some, or all, of the almsfolk. The fact that, on one occasion, it was noted that Mistress Langwych was provided with a 'whole service' at the Coney Feast implies, perhaps, that the almsfolk and lesser guests were supplied with a less copious dinner than those who were richer and more important.

On these occasions the Company provided players to make an entertainment and the Hall was decorated with evergreen oak and ivy, and rushes were strewn upon the floor.

Then, in summer, at the Feast of the Trinity, in a Hall decorated with garlands and bows, they held their election: as far as food was concerned it was a modest affair of bread, or buns, and ale.

Finally there was the dinner when the Master and wardens took their oaths and were installed in office.

In addition to these regular functions that marked their own calendar there were recurring City functions that were celebrated – when the Mayor went by river to Westminster, meat and drink were provided for those of the Company who went with him.

When the Company were ordered to man the rails to celebrate the arrival or departure of royalty – as it might be the coronation of Edward's Queen, Margaret, when the Company were twentieth in order of precedence, or the restoration of Henry VI – refreshments were provided at the Hall for those taking part. And, of course, there were simple potations to celebrate any number of domestic occasions – the collection of the rents or that red-letter day in 1465 'when the rubbish was carried out of the Hall'.

The pewter vessels used on these occasions they were prepared to hire to others, such as the Blacksmiths, who from time to time might be accommodated at the Hall. They were properly established and comfortably settled. They bought a new bucket for the well at the Hall but the water they drew out, collecting together as it did from a catchment area of dung-hills and cesspits – a new pit was to be dug for the Company's necessary house – could never, it may be thought, have made very good or safe drinking. They shewed themselves brotherly to one another and to their Company. Master John Amell – already the donor of a splendid standing mazer – was making his will: they sent him little gifts – a pickerel on one occasion, together with bread and ale. Another time they gave him a gurnard and a chine of fresh salmon.

In 1470 one Agnes Carter, in sisterly goodwill, bequeathed to the Company a contingent legacy of her Houndsditch estate, then known more descriptively as 'The Woolpack Tavern and the grounds adjoining thereto'.

Less magnificently but no less lovingly the wife of a member presented the Company with a fine cloth for the high table – an indication that napery was becoming a normal refinement.

All unrecorded by the Company, life outside the Hall went roaring by. Edward IV fled to the Netherlands; Henry VI reigned; Edward returned to England; the Bastard Falconbridge besieged the City and actually broke through at Aldgate before the citizens rallied and threw the rebels back; the Battles of Barnet and Tewkesbury secured the throne for Edward; Henry was deposed; the Wars of the Roses came to an end; Caxton introduced the art of printing; two new, and deadly, diseases broke out – a new flux and the 'styche'. In the Company fines for various offences began to play a more pervasive part in the accounts.

It is clear that, at this period, many cutlers were in a very small way of business; one of them who had somewhat overreached himself in taking three apprentices paid for their registration in kind – producing to the Court a brass pot, a charger, seven plates, three dishes and a round pottle pot of pewter.

But the Company as a whole must have been one of a certain influence, for in 1476 they received a distinction that was still comparatively rare among the Livery Companies: the Grant of Arms. To men of the Middle Ages, the coat of arms was, it has been said,[93] more than a matter of vanity or of genealogical interest. Whole complexes of pride and ambition, of loyalty and devotion, were condensed in the symbols which marked and expressed intricate mental contexts by means of an image. This distinction – the complete expression of the new feudalism – provided a reason for great, and legitimate, pride and rejoicing when, on 7 May, Thomas Holme, Clarenceux King of Arms, gave the Cutlers for their Seal 'Gules, three pairs of swords in saltire argent, hilts and pommels or. Crest: an elephant's head couped gules, armed or'. Their motto was 'Parvenir a bonne foy'.

The Company's choice of the elephant – a symbol unusual in heraldry – is generally supposed to stem from the use of ivory in the trade, small though the proportion of the material employed might be. Certainly the attachment of the Cutlers to the elephant was of long standing: as early as 1411 there are records of a house in the Cutlery bearing the sign of the elephant. It made, in any case, an unusual and rather jolly 'mascot' even though it was not always easy, artistically speaking, to employ it with success.

In a heraldic menagerie of mermaids, griffins – pelleted or otherwise – camels and goats, it was at any rate unique and a legitimate
object of affectionate pride.

The cherished arms were set up in the Hall and repairs were
carried out in the kitchen. The work, which consisted largely of
paving, included the placing of a great stone that cost the not
inconsiderable sum of 5d to bring by water so large was it.

The Company provided the paviours with four pounds of cotton
candles so that they could carry on with the work at night. The
windows of the Great Parlour were mended – seven feet of new
glass was needed there. In 1480 they rented for 2/- a year a Garden,
on the otherwise vacant land at the back of the Hall, from the
Steward of Clerkenwell. After the troublous times it was all very
peaceful and domesticated.

Edward IV at last sat firmly on his throne. He was solvent and
independent. There were no costly campaigns to drain his exchequer and many dangerously 'over-mighty subjects' had died in
the wars. The country therefore in general and London in particular was calm. There was peace and prosperity. The King
summoned only one Parliament, between 1475 and 1482, and even
then he asked it for no grants. He did, however, in 1481, ask for very
considerable loans from the citizens of London who, after much
discussion, agreed to lend him 5000 marks. But the money was
repaid the following year and, considering the trade revival, the
loan can have caused no great hardship.[94]

The situation was one that, as experience might have suggested,
could not last.

In the first place, in 1483, the statute, which twenty years earlier
the Cutlers had been so instrumental in obtaining, expired and
large amounts of foreign cutlery, as well as other goods, flooded
into the country. Then Edward died, untimely, at the age of
forty and was succeeded by his twelve-year-old son. The citizens,
clothed all in violet, met the Regent, Richard Duke of Gloucester, at Hornsey. A month later there was a reception by the
City for the young Edward V: the Cutlers, now fifteenth in order
of precedence, were clothed in murrey. But the coronation never
took place. Richard confined the young king to the Tower and,

sometime between July and September, caused him to be murdered. In spite of the country's distaste for a further outbreak of civil war this was more than could be borne. Rebellion broke out. Watches in the City were frequent. From seven in the morning until seven at night some 220 men were on guard in Cheapside and Cornhill. Sixty-six misteries were involved supplying various numbers of men from one dozen down to a single representative. The Cutlers, in their middling position, provided three.

Richard, in an attempt to gain popular support, enacted laws to do away with corruption and forced loans, and to encourage English trade. Great unemployment had arisen because of the import, by aliens, of various goods which used to employ many English workmen: in the very first year of his short reign, Richard – virtually reviving the statute of 1463 – decreed, through Parliament, that a wide range of artefacts which included knives, hangers, scissors and the like should again be proscribed from import. But his murder of the Princes in the Tower had outraged a public opinion not then notable for squeamishness and had assured for Richard a niche among the propagandist bogey-men of history.

Two years later he lay dead on Bosworth Field and another of the convenient but artificial milestones for historians had been reached.

The Cutlers at this time were, as a company, making financial ends meet – but only just. On the Master's account – after taking into consideration sundry debtors – they were £1. 15s. 5d. out of pocket but this was more than counterbalanced by a credit balance of above £17 on the Rent account. They took their obligations as landlords seriously enough. In the houses of two tenants the privies were cleaned and, in an operation lasting two nights, 16 tuns of excrement were carried away before the floorboards were again nailed down over the stinking vaults. It was all an added expense at a time when trade had been thrown out of gear by the renewal of civil strife and by the momentary flooding of the market with imported cutlery. It was such import trade, no doubt, that lay behind the report by the Mercers' Company[95] that, at a General Court of Adventurers, the grievances of the Cutlers' Company, 'for buying of wares in the town of Antwerp' were considered. Merchants, it will be recalled, were by the custom of London permitted to deal wholesale in any manner of goods regardless of their company affiliations and we must suppose that merchant members of the Mercers had been indulging in the import of cutlery. The meeting with the Adventurers proved worse than useless for the cutlers being 'of ungoodly demeanour and unfitting in their language . . . so uncourteously and unadvisedly spoken to such great displeasure of all the Court' that 'they all departed without any other or further communication in the premises. . . .'

The trouble lay in the fact that many of the cutlers were 'simple' people – an adjective that in the fifteenth century was synonymous with small, in the sense of a negative capacity in goods or understanding.[96] Simple people, faced with negotiators very far from simple, are apt, in a fit of feeling inferior, to behave ungoodly. The Cutlers' officers themselves were quick to complain to the Court of aldermen of the 'simplicity' of those members of the Livery who took a greater number of apprentices than they could 'sustain' and then turned them over, at a profit, to other simple people who did not possess the skill to teach them their craft. As a result of this behaviour many apprentices found themselves without employment and temporarily left the City in order to teach the secrets of the trade in other places. Other apprentices, perhaps three or four of them, would band themselves together as partners and, setting up shop in some secret place, worked there night and day, on the Vigils of Saint's days, and on Saturday afternoons, in defiance of the Company's ordinances. Furthermore, to avoid the hazards of the search of goods displayed for sale they farmed out work to 'foreigns' and sent it away to be done outside the jurisdiction of the City. Thus, in turn, cutlers who had properly served their apprenticeships were deprived of work and 'for lack of occupation became idle and vagabonds and have none occupation whereby they may get their living.'

This complaint to the aldermen led to the formulation of new ordinances. The number of apprentices that any person might take was to be limited, their transfer to other masters strictly controlled. The prescribed hours of work were to be strictly observed and no work other than 'Furbing and glasing' was to be done by candle-light. All the points of complaint were, in fact, covered by the new ordinances, and partners ('parting fellows') were forbidden without licence: 'all such persons, forasmuch as they be not of hability to take house and shop of themselves . . . to be put into service until such time as they be of Power to take house or shop upon themselves'. As for anyone who left the City to teach the craft elsewhere – he was, if he returned, to be treated as a 'foreign'.

The ordinances were approved by the Mayor and aldermen. They were entered in a parchment roll and placed among the Company records. The arms of the Company were confirmed and a copy of the confirmation bought. The members contributed towards the cost of new banners, buying silk and fringing and gold thread. Cloth of Arras was bought for the high dais of the Hall. There were other new hangings and cushions and benches were bought or made. It was almost as if, after the slighting way they had felt themselves to be treated by the Mercers, they were asserting their personalities and flaunting the distinction of their arms.

Six of the Company rode with the Mayor to greet the new King as he came to his City from Bosworth. The Company dressed them for the occasion and gave them bread and ale. Those who kept watch, only five days after Henry VII came to the throne, for fear of disturbances in the City, were similarly regaled.

This display of their status proved to be staggeringly expensive. The Master's account was more than £23 overspent with scarcely a debtor outstanding to offset the amount. And the Renter's account, which could usually be relied upon to provide an overall credit balance to be put in the great iron chest, provided in 1486 no more than forty-five shillings. And the following year the total receipts on the Master's account amounted to a beggarly £6. 6s. 7d. with expenses almost double that figure.

There had by now been so many upheavals within living memory that there was no great confidence that Henry VII would long survive. There were, in fact, two immediate risings against him –

first under Lord Lovell and then under Lambert Simnell – but both were suppressed and for the Londoners a period of some uneventfulness ensued.

The City authorities, however, were still keeping a jealous watch over the powers of the Livery Companies and in 1488 they ordered an inspection of the ordinances of the various misteries. On 18 July the Master and Wardens of the Cutlers brought their Book of Ordinances before the Mayor and aldermen. These had not yet been authorized and the Cutlers 'prayed that they might have and enjoy the same by authority of the Court (of Aldermen) like as they had used and enjoyed them by their own authority and common assent'.

Here was an admission that they had been acting beyond their legal authority but the Mayor and aldermen granted the application without apparent demur. The ordinances in question concerned quarterly payments by the freedom, for the cost of the searches and, more importantly, restrictions on the activities of workmen.

Every allowe or covenant servant of any of the Fellowship who withdraws himself from his master's service, by night or day, or lies out of his master's house without licence, shall pay to the Master and Wardens for the time being the value of a week's wages towards the maintenance of the poor men of the Craft; and every master who permits a servant to leave his house and fails to report the matter shall pay 3s. 4d, one half to the use of the Chamber and the other for the maintenance of poor craftsmen.

The following year the scale of fines was laid down: there were flat rates of 20d 'for working on a Saturday after 3 a clock at afternoon' and of 6s. 8d. for working out of the City of London. For living out of his master's house the fines varied between 8d. and 3s. 4d. And if these restrictions on the personal liberties of the workers seem today to be oppressive they must be viewed against the background of a society in which serfdom, or slavery, still existed and in which for another two hundred years it would still be possible to have a runaway serf branded on the forehead. Much must have depended upon the degree of complaisance of the individual employer but, for all the apparent lack of order in the City, and the constant outbreaks of ungovernable behaviour, liberty of action, as it was later to be understood, was a commodity in very short supply.

In October 1491 the King departed on a journey to France. A great 'benevolence' was raised for him. Every alderman gave, *nolens volens,* two hundred pounds and the commoners raised nearly £9700. The Cutlers' contribution is not stated but nearly three years earlier when £740 was raised for the King they had been cessed at £26 and, presumably, their gift was now in the same proportion.

There were, naturally, many complaints of the incidence of taxation. The contribution by the misteries to the repairs to the walls of London in 1492 was by no means enthusiastically subscribed: those who were paying local taxation in their Wards were not eager to pay further taxation for the same project in their Companies[97] and, in fact, fifty-one Livery Companies (including the Cutlers) failed to pay.

An atmosphere of unease was again beginning to be felt. The imposture of Perkin Warbeck was attracting adherents and it became necessary, perhaps for that reason, to remind people of their due stations in life. On 1 December the Mayor and aldermen summoned the Masters and wardens of all the misteries to Guildhall. There they were commanded 'to see that good Rule be kept among their fellowships'. They were to call their Companies together and 'shew them the same Commandment charging them that they keep a due order for them and their servants'.[98]

It was not until 1499, with the execution of Warbeck, that the King could again feel reasonably secure.

And, as the surviving account rolls of the Cutlers' Company come to an end in 1497, leaving a regrettable gap of nearly ninety years in the records, the note of cosy domesticity at the Hall, more or less untroubled by the outside world, returned. Seventeen stone of feathers were used to make sixteen more cushions for the greater comfort of the Livery; the players who ever since the records began, more than fifty years earlier, had been performing at Feasts for the same fee of seven shillings for the whole group, were now given the additional perquisite of a mess of meat; the best cloth in the Hall was taken down each Bartholomewtide – but whether for cleaning or for fear of rowdyism at so lively a season is not apparent.

There was, it is true, one discordant note in the shape of a dispute with the Blacksmiths (who had been fraternally renting the Hall as part-time tenants[99]): a bill was received from the Mayor's Court and a bill was sent back in answer; the rules in the Blacksmith's book of ordinances were searched and noted. But the reasons for the quarrel have gone the way of the other contemporary records. They have been consumed by time as completely as the buns and bastard were consumed each Trinity Eve, as the 'saltfish and two great Plaice' on the day 'when the stuff belonging to the Hall' was received, as the bread and ale were consumed by the cutlers when they served upon the general watch.

For always, as the Middle Ages came to an end, the City kept watch.

The Mayor and aldermen had already shewn their suspicion of the Livery Companies and desired to control the way in which they were governed. The Crown was hardly less concerned. Changes were taking place in the social fabric of the nation. The families of the old magnates who had died in the Wars of the Roses, whose estates had been forfeited and who could no longer afford the great liveried retinues which were obligatory to their standing, were making matrimonial alliances with trade: a new breed of City magnate was emerging in the influential positions in the misteries. A Bill, placed before Parliament in 1504, complained of 'unreasonable ordinances as to the prices of wares' which were to be found among the gilds. The Statute was enacted that henceforth no one 'should take upon them to make any acts or ordinances . . . made in disinheritance or diminution of the King's prerogative . . . nor against the common profit of the people unless the same acts and ordinances be examined and approved by the Chancellor, the Treasurer of England, the Chief Justice of either Bench, or three of them. . . .'.

This examination was additional to the scrutiny and approval of the Mayor and aldermen and by it the Crown gave clear notice of its intention to control the trade and industry of the country.

The old system by which the national economy was based upon a municipal authority, usually representative of mercantile interests, was about to disappear for ever.[100] Henceforth the State would decide what was in the national interest. (But, as we shall see, this did not prevent the gilds from developing along their own unique lines of influence and power.)

In the meantime the King, in 1505, demanded five thousand marks for his confirmation of the City's liberties. The Companies paid him – by instalments – and accompanied him on 23 April to St. Paul's 'where was shewed a leg of St. George, closed in silver, which was newly sent to the King.'[101]

But, with the coming of a new reign, even that comparatively harmless superstitious pleasure was soon to be denied them. The sixteenth century, a century of splendour so much admired in retrospect – the century of Bluff King Hal and Good Queen Bess, the Swan of Avon and Merrie England – a century as atrocious in its bloody persecutions, its treachery, and its appalling cruelty, as any they had yet endured, had begun.

6

Of Faith and Morals

1509–1558

ON 22 April 1509, Henry VIII came to the throne and in due course, in June, the City received his state visit for the coronation. The Cutlers' Company took their place on the rails which each Gild had to provide for itself. There were twenty-four members in the Livery at the time, the numbers in other Companies ranging from eighty-four to two. For themselves and for those of the Company out of the Livery – the 'yeomanry' as they were soon to be generally known – for their apprentices and servants and almsfolk they needed twelve yards of rails. The chief Company that year was the Merchant Taylors who occupied a stand on the south of Cheapside, a little from the old 'Change end of the street, and the other misteries were ranged eastwards towards the Tower in an order of precedence which, strangely, and without apparent consistency, changed each year: in 1509 the Cutlers were twenty-second out of forty-six.[102]

In the brilliant extrovert young eighteen-year-old, endowed with so many attributes and graces, it is unlikely that the cheering crowds could recognize a character so insecure in the establishment of his dynasty that all his actions were to be coloured by the necessity to beget a male heir to secure the Tudor succession. Later, they submitted to his arbitrary actions and accepted his instability because they wanted no return to the days of Civil War. They needed security and prosperity.

The Cutlers in particular, having duly received from the Crown the confirmation of their Charter, were greatly exercised by matters of status that amounted virtually to a fight for their very existence as an independent mistery.

It was the Bladesmiths who were to blame. Many of them, particularly the knifesmiths amongst them, had been incorporated in the Cutlers' Company in 1416. The swordsmiths had, on the whole, remained faithful to the Bladesmiths' Company. Separate ordinances had in 1463 been granted to them[103] and they had continued as an independent craft.

Now, quite suddenly in 1515, the Master and wardens of the Bladesmiths petitioned to be amalgamated with the Armourers. New ordinances to cope with the situation were drawn up by that Company and submitted to the Court of Aldermen. On 25 September the Bladesmiths' Company ceased to exist.[104]

It is clear that some bladesmiths were unwilling thus incontinently to become Armourers. It was found necessary to decree enormous penalties to be exacted from any new member who indulged in secret efforts to be translated to another craft. All search of bladesmiths' work was to lie with the wardens of the Armourers. This was bad enough but, under the new ordinances approved by the Mayor and aldermen and, no doubt, soon to be approved by the Crown if no action were taken, all makers of 'edge-tools' were to be under the control of the Armourers. As the Cutlers' whole occupation was the manufacture of 'edge-tools' the ruling amounted to what was virtually a total absorption of their own craft by the Armourers. It looked, in those first black moments, as if they had been defeated in the inter-Company struggle. But they refused to submit to the take-over, they refused to give in. Disputes broke out and in 1517 matters came to a head. Three bladesmiths refused to submit to being searched by the Armourers: they were taken before the Court of Aldermen, who, faced by what was clearly a matter of great constitutional importance, asked the Recorder to look into the old precedents. While he was still engaged on this task it became apparent that there were other bladesmiths who had no wish to become members of the Armourers' Company and refused to be searched by their wardens. They, very naturally, regarded the Cutlers' Company as their champions and supported them against the City authorities.

On 11 March 1518 the Court of Aldermen gave a judgement that to all intents and purposes annulled the merger of Armourers and Bladesmiths: any of the latter who wished to 'depart unto the Fellowship of the Cutlers' were entitled to do so upon payment of the usual fee for translation from one Company to another. Those who wished to remain with the Armourers were permitted to do so without any further payment. The day had been saved although, of course, the repercussions rumbled on. It was only in 1520, the year of the Field of the Cloth of Gold, that the Cutlers, by obtaining from the Court of Aldermen a grant which allowed them fully to control the bladesmiths among them by assigning and controlling their trade Marks, brought an end to the dispute. It was the beginning of a truce between the two Companies which lasted some fifty years.

While this struggle for survival had been fought there had been further disorder in the City: once again xenophobia – one of the less attractive aspects of the English character – was behind it. In 1514 there was a petition by the craftsmen of London against the freedom allowed to aliens; two years later handbills, posted in the City, accused King and Council of ruining England by favouring foreigners; finally came the 'Evil May Day' of 1517. Certainly the number of aliens had greatly increased and a further imbalance in the trading order of things had followed the tendency of freemen in a small way of business to leave the City and live and trade in the suburbs and elsewhere. The Common Council of the City had attempted to persuade them and their families to return under the threat of removing their franchises. They had tried in vain. The aliens, who employed alien apprentices and journeymen were accused, in what have become familiar terms, of taking the bread out of the mouths of honest English workers. Ministers of religion preached inflammatory sermons. The mob was roused and on May Day the apprentices, who were always eagerly on the look-out for trouble, raced through the streets, launching viciously violent attacks upon aliens. The riots were, as it happened, soon suppressed. As part of the policy of demonstrating to the City that the Crown was now, and intended to continue, in command, Wolsey at the height of his personal power as Cardinal and Lord Chancellor – although he had done little to anticipate the trouble – acted with great firmness. Twelve apprentices were hanged outside the doors of their masters' shops and another four hundred actually had a rope around their necks before a pardon was granted them. The Masters and Wardens of Livery Companies were summoned to Westminster, were notified officially of the King's displeasure and then graciously granted a royal pardon for having permitted such things to be. The occasion was humiliating and the lesson was learned. If the Cutlers were like other Companies – and in the absence of records it is possible only to speculate – there ensued a great preoccupation with the maintenance of interior discipline.

But, as sometimes happens, the Crown, having shewn its power, applied it to rectifying the causes of grievance which the revolt had demonstrated. A great tightening up of controls over aliens was put under way. The Mayor and aldermen instigated the process with a Bill before Parliament in 1519 to promote trade. They recited in the preamble that

there is within this city a great number of simple persons which be both subtle, crafty and false, as well aliens and foreigners as other freemen of the said city, that without any licence or admission . . . take upon them as brokers and daily make many corrupt and unlawful bargains, as well of usury as otherwise, not only to the displeasure of Almighty God, dishonour and slander unto this noble city . . . but also to the hurt of lawful merchants.

The ensuing Act decreed that brokers should only be appointed by the Mayor and aldermen from among the members of the gilds.

Moreover, no alien should be allowed to engage in retail trade, for, if things were allowed to continue in the way they were going, with strangers keeping open warehouses all over London, the whole trade of the City would end in foreign hands.

The better to supervise their subtle behaviour, the aliens were to be compelled to lodge only in the houses of Englishmen – in the interests of commerce the native born had to put up with some inconvenience – to declare to their hosts all the goods they had imported and to sell them, wholesale, within four months of their arrival in the country.

The screw was further tightened in 1523 when it was enacted that aliens must no longer keep alien apprentices, must contribute to taxes paid by the City Companies, must pay quarterage to the Company of their trade, must swear allegiance to the Sovereign at the Hall, must assemble when summoned by the Beadle and must not assemble anywhere else.

These were notable increments to the personal authority of the very gilds whose powers the authorities were, in various ways, attempting to control.[105]

It was a time of plague and of great scarcity. The price of corn was very high and in 1521 the first of the municipal loans, for purchasing corn in time of plenty and storing it in the Bridge-house, to be sold later without profit in times of scarcity, was levied 'in all goodly haste from the fellowships of sundry misteries and crafts'. In later years this admirable system was modified: the Companies themselves had to buy the grain, at the best price they could, and arrange for its storage. They were assessed according to their means and this assessment was used as a handy basis for calculating all kinds of other loans and imposts.

Then the Mayor called for a report on the Plate and cash in hand of all the Companies and a tax was levied on the total value. Next the King demanded from the City an eight months' loan of twenty thousand pounds towards which the Cutlers must have paid their share.

To add to these difficulties there was a preliminary manipulation of the currency – all coins except pence and foreign gold were changed into 'new nobles' – the amount of the depreciation was very small but it added to a general atmosphere of uncertainty. In such times property was the most desirable commodity and it was now, in 1522, that John Monk bequeathed his Aldersgate property to the Company. Of the Cutlers' actual state there is no remaining record. Of their activities and of their obligations at this period no more may be adduced than can be seen in the common activities and obligations of other well-documented Companies. In 1527, for example, as the news of the King's intention to seek a divorce from Katherine – who had failed to produce the essential male heir to the throne – and to marry Anne Boleyn, began to spread amongst the citizens, all the Companies received a warning not to indulge in idle talk. That same year, too, the Mayor promulgated rules that further controlled apprenticeship: those who permitted apprentices to serve for less than seven years and presented them, illegally, for admission to the Freedom, those who took married apprentices, those who paid them wages or who allowed them to earn money on their own account, those buying from or selling to apprentices without the consent of their masters – all these offenders, both masters and apprentices, were to be forever disfranchised.

These are the sort of scraps of information that may be garnered from the City records and from the records of other Companies.[106] But, on the wider national issues there is little to be learned: wider national issues are not, on the whole, to be found among the papers of the gilds. If this lack should seem surprising, on consideration it is perhaps only to be expected: the gilds were trade organizations who, whatever they might think about the course of events outside the closed circle of each Company, had occasion to record them only when they impinged directly upon their own administration. Thus, of all the stirring events that heralded the shattering changes of the Reformation little appears. In May 1527 Wolsey passes through the City in great pomp and ceremony on his way to France, there to conclude an alliance against the Emperor; French ambassadors and noblemen coming to London in the train of this treaty are met by riders from the Livery Companies; in April 1533, when the long drawn out affair of the divorce of Catherine is coming to its head, the Mayor advises the members of every Company 'to be well ware what conversation thay had, or should have, of the marriage that the King's Highness intended to conclude with the Lady Anne that no word escaped them or any of them, concerning the said matter' in order that they might avoid 'the King's high displeasure and extreme punishment that were like to ensue unto the offenders in that behalf'. The citizens had, no doubt, been speculating rather too openly upon the increasingly apparent pregnancy of Anne – who had, in fact, been secretly married to the King four months before this warning was given. In June, amidst considerable civic pageantry, she was crowned – a member of the nouveau riche aristocracy, the great-granddaughter of a merchant, one of a class that earlier could never have aspired to such rank.[107] In September her child was born – it was a girl, the Princess Elizabeth.

The Livery Companies were assembled at their Halls 'and there sworn on a book to be true to Queen Anne and to believe and take her for the lawful wife of the King and rightful Queen of England and utterly to think the Lady Marie, daughter to the King by Queen Katherine, but as a bastard and thus to do without any scrupulosity of conscience'. The extant minutes of other gilds shew, in 1535, the new style of Henry as 'Supreme Head of the Church of England' and in October 1536, after the execution of Anne and her supplanting by Jane Seymour – which are un-noticed – there are records of the King's demand, through the Mayor, for two hundred and fifty men to be sent against the rebels in the North who had risen in support of the old Church order. All were to be well harnessed with boots and spurs. Some were to be mounted on good horses, some to carry bows and sheafs of arrows, others were to be halbardiers. They were ordered to muster before the Mayor the very next day. It is not clear from what sources the Companies on these occasions, which were to become increasingly frequent, recruited their men: whether they were volunteers from among the freemen or whether they were raised from among the unemployed of the City does not appear. The fact that in other Companies they not infrequently, when they were eventually discharged, decamped with the Company equipment suggests that they did not normally stand in a relationship of obedience to the Master and Wardens.

The Cutlers at this period had twenty-nine Liverymen – eleven were on the Court – and thirty-six Yeomanry: demands on their manpower would not have been great. In addition to these demands, however, the Crown was becoming insatiable for money. The monasteries had been dissolved and their revenues and treasures – even the lead upon their roofs – had been forfeited to the Crown. To the Livery Companies came demands 'as it were for quit rents', the Clerk to the Drapers noted with outrage, for the obits pre-viously kept. Money was also demanded to pay pensions to the displaced clergy and, although this was an act of charity it was not one that the Company carried out with any enthusiasm.

So great an upset in the established order of things must have enjoyed popular support, or, perhaps, general public disinterest: it could never have been carried through with such speedy ruthlessness if it had been against the active will of the majority. It was inevitably reflected in social unrest among the people as a whole. The Mayor complained about the state of affairs to be found amongst the citizens.

... there is divers and many obstinate and misruled and riotous Journeymen and Servants, and also apprentices ... the which Journeymen at their own wills and pleasures at divers times will not work without they may be hired for a certain time but will rather sit in Ale houses and haunt ill company, and also play at unlawful games, the which is great hurt and hindrance and an undoing to all young men and an ill example for many servants ...

It was therefore decreed that:

if any master hath need of a Journeyman and knows where that he is, and if the said Journeyman will not work without he may be hired for a certain time, take him and set him to work as long as your work will last and it be for one day or two. And that if there be any Journeyman that will not work after this Rate but had rather play and go up and down like a Vagabond let all such be sent into prison and there to tarry ... a day or twain for the first fault. And for the second like fault to be in prison five days. And at the third to be tied at a cart's Arse and beaten naked through the City like a vagabond. And to be banished from the City for seven years and a day by my Lord Mayor's commandment, and this to be used without favour ... Furthermore there be divers and many house holders the which receiveth and taketh apprentices to be bound unto them and, within short space after, they do let the said Apprentices have so much of their will that they run abroad and in conclusion their masters cannot rule and order them. Wherefore all such masters that have any 'prentices, or hereafter shall have any, the said masters shall charge and give in commandment unto their 'prentices that on holidays they shall truly wait upon their master or masters to the church and there to serve God.

And after, to wait upon their master and masters at dinner and supper. And in no wise to go from their master's house or door without the licence of their master. And that their master shall give no licence to no apprentice to go forth to no place without he know whither he goeth, and in what company he goeth in, that he haunt neither tavern no alehouse nor bowling alley nor none other suspicious place.

And if the said 'prentice do, the charge to be laid to the said master and (he) to be punished for the said 'prentice. Also and if any master hath any apprentices that keepeth any ill rule (such) as haunting of whores or any other unlawful games and cannot Rule the said 'prentice, nor by punishment neither by fair words, that then the said master shall complain unto the Master and Wardens and bring him to the Hall . . . and there shall punish him according unto his offences openly in the Hall. . . .[108]

The next year, perhaps to work off some of the surplus energy of the Londoners and to encourage them in some kind of healthy military training, the citizens were, in May 1539, 'mustered all in bright harness & coats of white silk, with white cloth and chains of gold, in iii great battles to the great wonder of strangers'.[109]

It may be speculated just how much the average Londoner enjoyed this form of compulsory self-entertainment. No doubt, if the weather was fine, it provided an acceptable change from a working life of considerable restriction – like taking part in the Military Tournament or the Edinburgh Tattoo, perhaps – but the repeated interference of the State in their lives was seldom as marginally agreeable.

In 1540, for example, the City authorities organized another means-test for the Companies: once again the value of their plate, of the capital in their iron treasuries, of their revenue from lands, all had to be declared to provide the basis for an assessment to raise the subsidy that Parliament had granted to the King. Internal evidence suggests that in some Companies, the declarations erred on the side of modesty.

Jane Seymour had died three years earlier and now the citizens were summoned to greet her successor Anne of Cleves. The marriage took place on Twelfth Night and the annulment – which brought about the downfall of Thomas Cromwell – almost exactly six months later.

But among the introverted City Companies it was the new set of orders from the Mayor – it was about this date that he began to be called Lord Mayor – that was noted: all householders who kept apprentices and journeymen were again urged to see that they were of honest behaviour and, further, they were to ensure that they were 'indoors before ten at night and not out before four o'clock in the morning as they would answer at their uttermost perils'.

The social unrest that such orders were intended to contain within controllable bounds must certainly have been increased by a great rise in the cost of living. As the Clerk to the Drapers observed, in 1541, 'for every groat in the past we now pay five'. The inflationary policies of Henry VIII did, in fact, increase, during his lifetime, the cost of living by one quarter. The expenses of raising and fitting-out troops in 1544 'billmen and bowmen equipped for the King's wars, with swords, daggers, white kersey caps etc,' became increasingly difficult to collect on top of all the other forms of taxation, the precepts for corn and so on. The payment of soldiers was not then the small-beer it was later to become: press-money alone was 2s. 6d. a head which was not returnable if the man turned out to be unfit: his replacement also must be paid for being pressed. Simply to raise, say, thirty soldiers could cost a Company the then considerable amount of thirty-five pounds. That July in 1544 it was money ill-spent: 'the said soldiers went no further than Gravesend and came home again' and, at any rate in the case of the Drapers' Company, made away with their arms and equipment.

The very next year saw a 'benevolence' to the King; hardly had some proportion of one year's Wheat Money been recovered – if it was recovered at all – than the next year's contribution became due; the City was called upon to raise a regiment of one thousand men. The times were difficult indeed. And at this critical moment in the financial affairs of almost every citizen of London there came, in 1545, the first of the Chantries Acts.

A chantry was, in the words of the Oxford English Dictionary, 'an endowment for the maintenance of priests to sing masses, usually for the soul of the founder' and the first of the acts against this pious activity did not, in fact, condemn the principle of the system. It was aimed, instead, so it was claimed, at the abuse of such endowments in practice – a distinction of some delicacy but one that cleared the way for the confiscation of the chantries in the same

G

way that the dissolution of the monasteries had been prepared by a pretended investigation into the morality of their inmates. The Crown appointed Commissioners to investigate the administration of the chantries by their trustees.

In due course the Livery Companies were visited in turn with demands for a report to be made of all chantry lands and stipendiary priests. Each reacted in its own particular manner: many of them were then requested to think again and put in returns 'more at large.'[110]

Before, however, the full effects of the Act could be appreciated the Defender of the Faith, on 28 January, was 'deceased to God', dirges and requiems were sung in the 112 parish churches of the City and a dole of a groat a head was given to every man, woman and child 'for the Soul of the most excellent and of most famous memory Henry the Eighth.'

In the inventory of his effects there were no less than four pages of items of interest to the cutlers, including twenty-three sets of cutlery with handles of precious metals. Of these the most splendid was described as

One woman of silver and gilt being a case for knives garnished with sundry emeralds and pearls and rubies about the neck and divers amethysts, jacynths and balases upon the foot thereof furnished with knives having diamonds at the ends of them.[111]

Edward the Sixth, the young and rather sickly heir to all such splendours, passed triumphantly on 19 February through the City streets, lined with the Livery Companies, to his crowning at Westminster, and to a reign in which during the first years the Lord Protector Somerset was the power behind the throne.

Somerset was one of the reformers who felt that the time had come for the dogma of the Church to be changed as drastically as church administration had already been. But, because he was a man who shrank from the tyrannical violence that later reformers were to display, there followed a period of some religious confusion among the Companies – sometimes an obit would be held, sometimes an obit would be cancelled because no mass or dirge 'as in times past used' was permitted. Preachers were forbidden to give sermons until they had received new commissions from the

Crown, and the Liverymen of the City were warned that neither they nor their families, upon pain of imprisonment, should attend sermons, either at St. Paul's or elsewhere, until such commissions had been granted.

A second Chantries Act was passed. The preamble recited that 'a great part of superstition and errors in Christian religion' had been brought about 'by devising and phantasing vain opinions of Purgatory and Masses satisfactory to be done for them which be departed.' The funds bequeathed for such purposes would be better employed for financing schools and ministering to the poor and needy – a class who, it may be noted, had formerly been cared for by the proscribed religious foundations. The Act, therefore, declared all chantries, hospitals, free chapels, fraternities and gilds, with their lands and revenues, to be henceforth in the possession of the King.

It looked, at first sight, as if the intention of the Crown was to do away with the gilds at whose growth it had for so long shewn unease. But the next clause in the Act put the matter in its true perspective: the bodies concerned were to pay to the Crown the rent-charges arising from 'superstitious uses.' In cases where the sum involved arose partly from superstition and partly in the course of a purely secular trust only the superstitious element was to be forefeit to the Crown – a division which was to cause the Livery Companies, with their inheritance of complicated trusts, the greatest difficulties of interpretation.

It has been estimated[112] that the Crown at first received no more than a total income of £1000 a year from the chantries of the London craft gilds and, indeed, it can be reasonably argued that there was little or no element of confiscation in the Act – the revenues went to the Crown instead of the chantries and the Livery Companies were materially none the poorer. It was only, as will be shewn, in later years that the situation came to be exploited with extortion.

Religious upheaval, the overthrow of traditional values and observances, was echoed in another outburst of social unrest. In addition to the predictable risings of outraged religionists there were rebellions by those who wanted agrarian reforms. There was a Cornish rebellion in the West, and Robert Ket's rebellion in Norfolk. The latter was a most decorous and well-behaved affair; it was more of a gigantic sit-down strike, in a camp run on communistic lines, on the outskirts of Norwich, where the rebels remained immobile. Yet the comparative nearness of the dissidents to London caused the usual alarms in the City where the gates 'were warded by certain of the ancient citizens in harness.'[113]

On 3 July 1549 the Lord Mayor warned all householders 'that they look to their whole families or men servants that they suffer none of them to be abroad out of their houses at nine of the clock in the evening till five of the clock in the morning nor upon the holy days to wander at liberty or absent themselves from their said houses without their consent or their commandments but that they and every of them be of honest rule and behaviour during this time of unquietness.'

Twelve days later orders came from the Mayor to prepare 'good and substantial harness' for every Company's proportion of 'able and tall men and good and substantial habilments of war. . . . bows and sheafs of arrows, hagbutters or handguns, and bills.'

Five days after that, each Company was ordered to send 'sad and discreet persons' to guard the gates from five in the morning until eight at night, stopping and examining everybody who came in and out and whom they might suspect of being 'parties or adherents to any of the congregations or unlawful assemblies of the people at this present commotion.' Those with whom they should find fault, or whom they suspected, they were to commit to the ward. They were to allow 'neither any number of armed or harnessed men or unharnessed to enter or issue into this our Sovreign Lord's city, or any manner of guns or gunpowder, harness, weapons or any habilments of war to be carried or conveyed out of the city. . . .'

Among the more obvious military effects that came under this export ban were shooting-gloves, Scots caps, and black skull-caps.

The defence preparations looked even further ahead: all householders who could do so were ordered to lay in a month's supply of victuals – there was no bias, there, against 'hoarding' – and the Companies sent parties to work on the fortifications: the town ditches which had once been dug 'for the great surety, defence and

safeguard of the City and namely in time of War and Rebellion'
were 'at this present dangerous time' either foul or actually filled-
in, to make gardens. By the end of August, however, the rebellions
had been put down – with the help of Italian and German
mercenaries on their way to the Scottish war – and the defenders
of London were allowed to stand-down.

Hardly had they done so than there was fresh trouble. Somerset
had proved himself too lenient a tyrant to survive in the ruthless
Tudor political underworld. The City authorities received orders
from members of the Council to ignore the Protector's commands:
they were to keep the City in a state of alert. There were those who
were mindful of the dangers of taking sides in such political power
games but, none the less, the Lord Mayor decided to again mount
watch over the City gates. He issued the Companies with a precept
for bowmen, gunners and billmen: on 11 October they were
mustered in all their military splendour in Moorfields. Here they
were told the crisis was ended. Somerset had been arrested, they
could return to their Halls, hand in their arms and go home. The
atmosphere must have been not unlike that prevailing at some of
the military manoeuvres of the Second World War. The abortive
proceedings cost the Companies money that they could ill afford.

For the country was experiencing a period of equally extensive
economic revolution. The financially disastrous wars of Henry VIII
had been paid for by direct taxation (which had been more than
doubled), by confiscation (the religious lands if properly administered should have spelt financial independence to the Crown),
and by devaluation (£400,000 of silver coin had been melted down
and reminted as £526,000).

The growth of London was providing a dangerous imbalance to
the country: every year more and more arable land was swallowed
up while the City demanded more and more crops to feed its evergrowing population. The spiral of inflation continued: the sum
demanded for Wheat Money had trebled; in July 1551 the value of
the shilling was fixed at ninepence and of the groat at threepence.
'In the month of August following was another proclamation for
the like so that the piece of nine pennies was but six pennies, the
piece of three pennies was but two pennies, the piece of two

pennies was but a penny and the piece of a penny but half a penny.'
With the penny halved and the three penny piece becoming two
pence there must have been ample scope for the sort of financial
manipulation so much enjoyed by traders during the process of
decimalization four centuries later.

The Crown, ever eager for more money, suggested to the Livery
Companies that they might buy back 'if they so desired . . . all such
quit-rents as they now pay . . . for obits, lights and chantry priests'
stipends.' Eventually the City paid, in all, nearly £19,000.

The money was difficult to raise for, in the familiar cycle of trade,
the boom had been succeeded by a slump. In an attempt to stimu-
late business in the City, the import of certain items, including
cutlery, was again forbidden.[114]

To add to the discontent of the Londoners there was another
outbreak of plague and the town was swarming, too, with the
hated and despised aliens. Peace with France had been concluded
and there were Frenchmen everywhere – some Companies could
not even carry on their normal activities due to being 'disturbed
by strangers to their great damage.'

The Mayor found it necessary to issue a precept against racism
'that no man do or suffer their family or servants in any wise to
mock, scoff or give any occasion of dissension unto any Frenchman
or stranger.'

And while all this was going on the ardent reformers, under the
villainous Duke of Northumberland – 'one of England's worst
rulers'[115] – were replacing Somerset's mild government with the
more characteristically brutal intolerance of Tudor bigotry. Smoke
from the fires of martyrdom, relit with relish in Smithfield, drifted
again across the City. It must have been at about this time – for
there had been, in 1550, an act for the destruction of Images – that
the Cutlers' Angels of the Annunciation, together with the other
well-loved symbols of their faith, were discreetly removed from
the Hall.

In October 1551, Somerset, who had for some time been a free
man and restored to his membership of the Council, was re-
arrested. The Cutlers, in common with other Companies, were
called together and warned 'not to murmur or grudge at the

Imprisonment of the Duke of Somerset and others now put into the Tower. For most worthily have they deserved the same which hereafter shall be known. . . .' Once again there was the fear of trouble in the City; once again the Liverymen mounted watch over the gates.

In the first month of 1552 Somerset was beheaded and, for a little while, a fearful silence fell upon the Londoners. They had been warned to watch both their speech and their behaviour and little comment occurs in City records of Northumberland's short-lived attempt the following year, when the ailing Edward VI died, to secure the throne for Lady Jane Dudley, his daughter-in-law.

Once again the various Companies were summoned to their Halls and warned to keep their servants from unlawful assemblies and not to discuss the affairs of the Privy Council who in July had proclaimed the new Queen. The Council, in fact, were soon in the sort of difficulties that were only too eagerly discussed: having marched under Northumberland against the forces of Mary at Framlingham they found themselves faced with 'the greatest mass-demonstration of loyalty ever accorded to a Tudor.'[116] Without a battle, Northumberland retreated to Cambridge where the news reached him that London had declared for Queen Mary. At this the Council reversed its decision and proclaimed as Queen of England her who had, so few years before, been publicly proclaimed a bastard. Such a *volte face* not unnaturally made it necessary for the Council to warn those in the gilds and misteries 'that every man should take good heed unto their [sic] apprentices and servants and give them monition to beware of their talk and to take example by one who lost both his ears yesterday in Cheapside.' It was necessary, too, yet again, to guard the City gates.

Yet there were, at first, comparatively few dangers against which to guard the gates. The 'denationalization' of religion, in London was accompanied by but little immediate disorder. The City granted the new Queen a gift of money to which all the Companies contributed and when Mary came by water from Westminster they were all out, upon the river, in their barges worthily to accompany her.

They were ordered to 'strictly charge and oversee their servants that they misuse not themselves towards priests . . . upon pain of imprisoning and straight punishing.'

Mary, in fact, at first shewed signs of a dogmatic liberalism – she wished, she said, that people would observe the old religion but, none the less, everyone ought to be able to worship as he thought best, without criticism from his neighbours. Images were restored to their places. In December the sacrifice of the Mass was restored – an opportunity for a few outbursts of sectarian feeling which led to the Mayor issuing a precept that 'no person should mock or scorn any priests passing by the streets neither do them any bodily hurt or suffer their servants or any of their families so to do as in throwing at them CRABS or other unlawful things as they will avoid the Queen's Majesty's high indignation.'

None of this was very serious. Boys had always been boys in the London mob, and the mocking of passers-by, whether priests or foreigners, and the pelting of them with anything at hand, had always been part of their expected though severely punished behaviour. But there were greater dangers apparent, immediately ahead, with Mary's expressed intention, against the advice of all her ministers, to marry Philip of Spain.

A male heir was as necessary to Mary as it had been to her father. A male heir had secured the Protestant Reformation and only a male heir could now achieve, by preventing Elizabeth from succeeding to the throne, the Catholic Restoration. As a husband, Philip of Spain was both eligible and staunchly Catholic. Unfortunately for the Queen he was utterly unacceptable to the English people. Their hatred and fear of foreigners had for the most part been directed against Frenchmen, with the Germans and Italians close runners-up. Now that the attention of traders was being directed, with the collapse of traditional markets in Europe, towards the New World, Englishmen were increasingly falling foul of Spaniards and Spanish sea-power. Englishmen lay in Spanish dungeons. The Spaniards were as readily detestable as any other aliens. It was not a propitious moment for the Queen to seek a marriage with the Spanish King.

There were spontaneous risings throughout the country and

although they were, generally speaking, quickly and without difficulty suppressed, that led by Sir Thomas Wyatt in Kent constituted a serious threat to the Tudor dynasty. It began on 15 January 1554[117] and 'pretended to defend the realm from the Spaniards and other strangers.' By the end of the month Wyatt had gathered 4000 followers at Rochester – a force which included a number of Londoners, who, sent against the rebels, had defected to them. Within the walls there were preparations to defend the City. On 26 January 'the ancient citizens and their servants' guarded the gates and three days later the Lord Mayor issued a precept which stated that 'The Kentish men threat to come to London to spoil Strangers' an announcement which, it might be thought, would not have inspired the Londoners with any particular desire to oppose them. However, they obeyed the Mayor's orders:

'Every man to get himself weapons and harness.
Every man to govern his servants in order not to suffer them to go abroad nor to flock together in councils nor to go but only to church and about their masters' business and not to go to play and a-walking on Shrove Monday nor on Shrove Tuesday for every man shall answer for his servants.
That all men be obedient to go and stand harnessed and to serve in such manner and form as the Mayor and Aldermen shall appoint them.
That ye cause those persons that ye do appoint to ward at the gates to continue there and not depart until the Constable come with his watch at night.'

Two days later the Companies received another precept for 'harnessed men being householders and citizens to serve within the same City and not elsewhere.' While these 'Home Guards' were standing-to, the Queen came, on 1 February, to Guildhall, 'scepter in hand as a token of peace, with a goodly train of ladies, and there shewed her mind concerning marriage to the Mayor and the whole City.' As a gesture it was highly successful: London became the rock upon which the wave of rebellion split. Wyatt, finding the bridge at Southwark too resolutely held, carried out a flanking movement by Kingston and on 7 February approached the City from the West. It was Ash Wednesday. He passed along Fleet Street and at the Belle Sauvage, soon to become the Cutlers' property, he found Ludgate was locked and as securely held as the bridge had been. He turned back and found himself hemmed in by the Earl of Pembroke and his men. Wyatt surrendered at Temple Bar.

Two months later he was executed: with him died many another notable including Queen Jane and her husband whose continued existence as possible rivals for the throne Mary could no longer tolerate. From gallows at the City gates swung the bodies of humbler offenders – the first victims of the frightfulness of the Marian persecutions which now began – persecutions that, with the race-memories they induced, put paid to the Catholic cause in England not only for centuries but probably for ever.

The emergency had ended, officially, on 26 February but three weeks later the Companies were called upon to provide money 'for the maintenance of a garrison which her highness intendeth to keep this summer' near the City 'as well for the surety of Her Highness' Royal person as also for the safeguard of the said City.'

The Londoners were suspicious. The garrison, under Lord Clinton, was too near the City for their comfort. There was evidently a considerable amount of disaffected talk. On 10 May the Cutlers with all the other Companies were summoned to Guildhall 'where was declared unto them by Master Recorder that a letter of sedition was let fall about the Parliament House and whosoever could bring the party forth should be rewarded for his labour. And further they were there admonished also to beware of their talk concerning the Queen's Majesty and the Prince of Spain and of other evil talk. And not to say the Queen loveth not the City for her Grace sayeth she loveth the City. And where some report that my Lord Clinton should govern the City Her Grace's pleasure is not so but that he shall lie within 20 miles of the City to aid the City if any need should be. And this they were commanded to publish and declare to their whole Companies at their Halls.'

On 20 July Philip arrived at Southampton. His marriage to Mary had already taken place by proxy a month after the suppression of Wyatt's rebellion. Now he was to claim his bride in person with a royal wedding on 25 July at Winchester. He rode from Southampton with a great crowd of notables 'but ye daie was a rainie daie so that the journey was sum what the lesse plesaunt.'[118]

In the middle of August the King and Queen came to London. They were 'by the grace of God, King and Queen of England, France, Naples, Jerusalem and Ireland, defenders of the faith, princes of Spain and Sicily, Archdukes of Austria, Dukes of Milan, Burgundy and Brabant, Counts of Hapsburg, Flanders and Tyrol.' The citizens were admonished 'that they and their families should gently entertain all Spaniards and to afford to them honest pennyworths of wares and victuals.' The City had been richly hung about with cloths of arras and tapestry. At every conduit there were gorgeous pageants of divers stories in praise and commendations of the King and Queen.

Amongst the people such commendations were not universal. Although many of the human sacrifices at Smithfield were intended to serve, also, as a discouragement to disloyalty there was still muttering among the populace.

In December 1555 the Mayor was instructed to address a serious enquiry to all members of Livery Companies 'touching a Seditious Book called *A Warning for England*' – an anonymous pamphlet which described 'the horrible practices of the King of Spain in the Kingdom of Naples'.

The wardens of the Cutlers were ordered, as were the officers of other Companies, to ask all their members whether they had seen any copies of the book; whether they had heard of any and, if so, where; did they know of anybody who had recently come to London from abroad – especially from such Protestant strongholds as Zürich; was there anybody that they did 'know or suspect vehemently to be common carriers of letters or money thither and from thence.' If they subsequently discovered any seditious books they were instantly to hand them in to the Lord Mayor. Before the year was ended another warning was given them 'to beware of pernicious books let fall abroad' – an indication that offending pamphlets were being scattered in the streets.

In this unhealthy, uneasy atmosphere of intrigue and discontent the plague raged from 1555 until the autumn of the following year. There was unemployment and a general distress in which preoccupation about the observance of the employment regulations naturally became paramount.

There was a spate of complaints to the City authorities. The Cutlers, for example, complained against a lorimer called Richard Dicher who employed 'foreigners' in the art of cutlery and refused to be searched by the wardens of the Cutlers. The Court of Aldermen ordered him to submit and emphasized the Act of Common Council which expressly forbade any citizen, with certain exceptions, to employ any but freemen under a penalty of £5. It became necessary to make a regulation that a trader must not lure away from a competitor's shop any chapman who was trying to strike a bargain: there must be no 'plucking him or them by the garments or by any other enticement till he or they of their own minds depart from the other's shop not being agreed of their bargain clearly.' For the really poor and unemployed a house of correction was to be built in which they could be usefully set to work: the Livery Companies were taxed to provide it.

Of the financial state of the Cutlers' Company at this moment it is impossible to do more than speculate: the majority of the City Companies had suffered a severe decay in numbers and in financial status. Many of them shewed an increase only in the numbers of apprentices – a sure indication that members were ignoring the rules and taking more apprentices than were permitted – a procedure that resulted in much unemployment and, subsequently, discontent and disorder. An order of the Common Council in 1556 restricted the number of apprentices who might be employed in various trades which included that of the Cutlers. The period of Servitude was extended up to the age of twenty-four 'chiefly as a remedy against hasty marriages.'[119] One of the reasons alleged for the increase of poverty in the City lay in the fact that young people came out of apprenticeship at an early age and set up households with insufficient means.[120] Now admission to the Freedom of the City was forbidden until the age of twenty-four had been reached: the term of years of apprenticeships had to be so arranged to coincide with attaining that age.

This in itself became a cause of much discontent: the general mood of the City was far from calm. It was found necessary to issue a Royal proclamation against brawls and riots in churches, churchyards and other places of public resort; swords and rapiers, too, of excessive length were forbidden to be manufactured.[121]

Amongst the other discontents that faced them in 1567 was the involvement of the country, once again, in war with France.

In January King Philip, who had long-since abandoned all pretence that his marriage to Mary was anything but political, hurred back from Spain to his deserted Queen in order to embroil her country in the Hapsburg struggle against the French.

He was greeted as he entered London with all the conventionally enforced expressions of loyalty by the Livery Companies occupying their usual places along the rails of Cheapside. And, when he appealed to Parliament, an opportunely discovered plot, hatched by the French King against the English Crown, overcame the reluctance of the Members. In June war was declared and soon the City Companies found themselves ordered to provide fighting men. Sometimes they were able to raise the forces from among the unemployed: at other times their own members were called-up, hastily, and not without confusion, equipped and posted overseas. One contingent was raised in the first days of July; another demand – this time for 'good, sad, apt and able men to be arquebusmen, or bowmen or pikemen or bill men' – came at the beginning of August. They were to be equipped for the general defence of the King, Queen and City, against whatever malicious attempts might be made by any enemies: they were to be ready in one week's time and they were thereafter to be maintained on twenty-four hours' notice to go wherever they might be sent. This raising of a standing troop was an expensive business and there must have been considerable relief among the Masters and wardens – if not amongst the soldiers – when they were despatched to France and became the financial responsibility of the Crown.

The course of the war went disastrously. In January 1558 Calais was in imminent danger and further reinforcements were demanded from the Companies – bowmen were to be preferred. It was too late. Calais fell and the English were quick to note that, after all, the place had been more of a liability than an asset. Nonetheless, the humiliating manner of its loss and the way in which no attempt was made to recapture it caused further muttering among the people: their readiness to contribute to forced loans was less enthusiastic than ever. In March the City was ordered to produce £20,000. The sum was, admittedly, demanded for one year only and at the then very reasonable rate of twelve per cent but there was little feeling of patriotic enthusiasm behind the raising of it.

It was not Mary who would repay the loan. Sunk in a melancholy not far removed from insanity, it was soon apparent that she was dying. Deserted by her husband, hated by her people, surrounded with ministers upon whom she could not depend and served by a divided Council, in everything that she had most desired she had utterly failed: failed to bear a child, failed to preserve her marriage, failed to win back the nation to her ancient Faith, failed in war. For a little while, with nothing to live for, with nothing any more to hope for, she lingered and the leaderless nation drifted aimlessly. In November 1558 she died and in her place Elizabeth was Queen.

7

The Great Days of Elizabeth I

1558-1587

THE auspices for Elizabeth's reign were not, on the whole, good. She had inherited a bankrupt economy. Her people were disordered and demoralized. Her right to the throne was challenged by the French to whom Mary Stuart, Queen of Scots, was the rightful monarch. On the credit side, however, Elizabeth had the support of Philip of Spain who, devout Catholic though he was, had made no bones about proposing to marry his deceased wife's sister – a degree of consanguinity then frowned upon. Elizabeth was thus able to use the rivalry between France and Spain to her own ends – an advantage which she was to exploit with a superb skill.

In January 1559 there were vast celebrations in the City to mark the Queen's accession. She was 'triumphantly greeted with much cost and pageants.'[122] The Companies had subscribed to a purse containing 1000 marks in gold: when it was presented to her she said, 'I thank my Lord Mayor, his brethren and you all. And whereas your request is that I should continue your good lady and queen be sure that I will be as good unto you as ever was queen to her people. No will in me can lack, neither, do I trust, there shall be any lack of power; and persuade yourselves that, for the safety of you all, I will not spare, if need be, to spend my blood.'

This, felicitous speech was greeted by a 'marvellous shout' and much rejoicing. And as the procession went down towards Fleet Street one of Her Majesty's court observed to her 'that there was no expense spared' in the City's welcome. To which 'her Grace answered that she did well consider the same and that it should be remembered. An honourable answer worthy of a noble Prince.'

In April peace was made between England, France, and Spain, and the demands upon the persons of the Londoners to provide troops was to decline. There were, in fact, three such precepts during 1560 for soldiers to go on an expedition to Scotland but these were the last for nearly twenty years. The country was, in any case, in no financial condition to go to war. The constant rise in the cost of living was accentuated by 'a great dearth and scarcity of all things.' Wheat Money, which had not been demanded for several years, was once again levied – the scarcity of provisions was, it was thought, likely to get worse because of the 'abundance of rain and the unseasonable weather which it has pleased Almighty God to send within this realm.' Such loans were now made in a more peremptory fashion and in terms of varying severity. The Companies were told 'Fail not as ye will answer to the contrary at your peril' – an exhortation which, when they failed, was amended to 'your uttermost peril.'

The Crown was determined to establish a stable economy and this demanded a stable currency. There had been several devaluations and there was now some confusion as to what was, and what was not, the lawful coin of the realm. In September the old currency was called in: the Crown would bear the expenses of reminting it. There was a good deal of fairly essential bureaucracy: it was necessary to know how much debased coinage was in circulation and all the Companies had to make weekly reports of the amounts of money, and in what coin, they had, in the previous week, paid to Merchant Strangers. Some foreign coins in circulation were devalued. Unfortunately the beneficial effect on the cost of living was by no means immediately apparent: the mercers and grocers failed signally to lower their prices and the butchers and fishmongers were believed actually to have raised them. But nonetheless, confidence in the coinage was gradually re-established.

A stable currency was not the sole necessity for a stable economy. The 'looseness of the times' called for discipline. And discipline the country got. To deal with unemployment and vagabondage the collection of poor-relief was made compulsory; to help fishermen who were the chief source of supply for recruitment to the Navy, meatless days, in addition to those determined by religion, were ordained; the importation of foreign luxuries was forbidden.

'The Girdlers, Cutlers, Saddlers, Glovers, Point-makers and such-like Handicraftsmen' had already complained about this import trade. In the past they had been

> greatly set on work as well for the sustenation of themselves, their wives and families as for a good education of a great part of the Youth in this Realm in good Art and laudable Exercise. . . .

Quite apart from this, their employment had meant that

> by reason of their Knowledge, Inventions, and continual Travel . . . Manifold benefits daily and universally came to the whole estate of the Commonwealth of the said Realm.

Now, owing to the flood of imports from Flanders and the Low Countries, their artificers were less employed and, therefore, more impoverished; Youth went untrained; faculties decayed; the realm was damaged and other countries enriched 'to the great discouragement of skilful workmen of this Realm, being in very deed nothing inferior to any Stranger in the faculties aforesaid.' So, once again, there were restrictions made – until the end of the next Parliament – on the import of a wide range of goods which included rapiers, daggers, knives, hilts, pommels, lockets, chapes, dagger-blades, handles, scabbards and sheaths for knives.

It will be observed that, in this list, there is no mention of sword-blades in the making of which there was to be for many years a strong dissent to the claim that English workmen were as skilful as strangers. But these restrictions, important though they undeniably were, would not have sufficed to restore the country to economic stability: that was intended to be brought about by an Act of 1563 – the Statute of Artificers.

The Statute of Artificers 'was unquestionably the most notable embodiment of the policies that dominated industrial life until the Industrial Revolution was well advanced. It was, in a measure, a codification of older statutes which had been imperfectly administered.'[123] Its main purpose was not so much to introduce innova-

H

tions as to prevent change: it was intended to halt the decline of the corporate towns, provide better training for industrial artisans, assure a better supply of agricultural labourers and to try to create 'a living wage' by balancing wages with price rises which had taken place.

With its programme of 'full employment' and priorities and wage-controls it was the very model of State planning and control: it was not what later generations, sentimentalizing about free enterprise in the great freebooting Elizabethan days, would have believed possible. The Act has been compared, not unreasonably, with the National Service Act of the Second World War: the principle underlying it was that of the universal obligation – except for property-owners, gentle folk and scholars – to work. Everybody else was obliged to choose a definite profession or calling: he must choose between the sea, the crafts, the land. There was a determined attempt to direct the workers into appropriate callings in a strict order of priority in which agriculture and its ancillary trades came first and the professions came last: in official favour the husband-man was the most, and the lawyer the least, socially useful citizen. Unfortunately, the Elizabethan man-in-the-street adopted the same obstinate attitude towards this state of affairs as did his descendant in the days of the second Queen Elizabeth. Not for him the arduous tilling of the soil for fifteen hours a day. He sought a better paid, 'black-coated', job in trade, industry or the professions. There came an increased pressure to enter the less back-breaking and more profitable occupations. Regulations were made to relieve the pressure by creating residential or property qualifications. Mobility among the workers had to be severely limited: no one might leave the parish where he had been employed unless he obtained a formal testimonial from the appropriate authorities or from two householders certifying that he was at liberty to take new employment.[124] Seven years' apprenticeship became universal; in certain trades – that of the Cutlers among them – employment was no longer by the day, week, or month but by the year.

The wages of workmen in these trades were fixed 'by the year with meat and drink' a proviso which itself acted as a safeguard for the employee against rises in the cost of living. Among the cutlers the top wage for workman, journeyman or hired servant was £4. 6s. 8d. a year.

The Act worked well enough in the country but in complex urban societies it proved less successful and, indeed, in London where individual enterprise was at a premium, exemptions were made to some of the provisions of the Act: a person there who was 'free' of one trade was at liberty to follow another. It was probably wrily noted by the provincials that, as usual, Londoners always seemed to do things differently.

But, undoubtedly, London was already a very special case.

In the meantime the Cutlers were once again engaged in dispute with their old rivals, the Armourers.

It had begun with a royal proclamation, in 1562, limiting the length of swords and other weapons.[125] Both Companies were summoned before the Lord Mayor and exhorted to see that the law was observed but it was to the wardens of the Cutlers that, two years later, on 1 September 1564, orders were given that they must see to it that none of their Company, nor of any other of which they had the search, should make any weapon beyond the permitted length. By January 1566 it is clear that trouble had arisen: the Cutlers were petitioning the Court of Aldermen with grievances which resulted in the Court specifically granting them search 'of all swords, daggers, knives, and such other wares as properly pertain to their art and occupation in whose hands soever they shall find the same.'

This unlimited authority soon brought them into an open conflict with the Armourers, which was temporarily settled pending an Aldermanic enquiry, by a decree of 1566 which granted the Cutlers search of all manner of cutlery, except among the armourers.[126] There, for the moment, the matter rested.

And when the Queen, that same year, issued another proclamation for 'the reform of the abuse of great hose, swords, daggers, and other disorderly apparel' it was the wardens of the Cutlers' Company who were ordered to break and cut off the points of weapons which they had seized as being too long.

Later in the year they were to find themselves restrained from 'the bearing of swords or dagger-blades naked in the streets.' This was a tiresome restriction. During the processes of manufacture, and particularly in assembling cutlery, it was necessary to carry the goods from one workman to another. Now they were summoned before the Court of Aldermen to show how the dangers inherent in this practice could be avoided. There was some hurried contriving and improvising and testing. Within nine days the wardens produced to the aldermen 'the pattern of a case of leather with a little Board fashioned to the bottom thereof for to carry abroad their sword and dagger blades unto their workmen. . . .' and this the Court approved.

The Cutlers, in common with other Companies, were very jealous in guarding their privileges: in that same year of 1566, they set before Parliament a Bill to prevent cutlers who were not free of the Company practising their trade within three miles of the City. The reaction was immediate; twenty cutlers in Westminster appealed to Sir William Cecil. The Company's action was, they claimed, contrary to the Patent which gave them control over the trade within the City only.[129] No more is heard of this complaint: the Cutlers certainly seem to have continued to enforce the rights of search 'within the City and suburbs.'

While these external disputes were being waged the Cutlers were much involved with internal reorganization. In 1566, the Yeomanry of the Company were given new rules and ordinances for their control, and it is convenient at this moment to consider the whole question of these members outside the Livery – the 'young men' or 'the Bachelors' of earlier days.

As in other Companies there were many members of the Freedom who, by their youth or by their lack of means, were unable to set up house or shop. They were Cutlers, with all the partisan feelings that membership evoked, but for various reasons they were outside the charmed circle. It was by natural evolution that they organized themselves into a body modelled almost exactly upon the Livery. They were ruled by wardens, appointed with the approval of the Court of the Cutlers, and by a Court of Assistants of their own. They had rules and ordinances and a certain limited degree of autonomy: the Yeomanry officials submitted their accounts to the Junior Warden of the Livery, collected quarterage and taxes from their members and, even, inflicted small fines for breaches of the ordinances. They had their own 'Hall' on the Company's property where from time to time they held their own functions. Membership of the Yeomanry organization could lead to admission to the Livery: those who had served as wardens or assistants of the Yeomanry were admitted to the Livery at a reduced scale of fees. And every one – no matter what his social station – was supposed to spend at least a year in the Yeomanry, after ending his apprenticeship, before he could be admitted to the Livery.

Inevitably the junior organization often found itself at variance with its seniors – either over the choice of its officers or, more usually, over some matter of trade. They were, on the whole, the workers of the trade – or, at the highest, masters in a very small way of business; the Livery were, on the whole, the masters.

The Yeomanry, feeling the shoe where it pinched the most, were usually those who created disturbances for the righting of wrongs and abuses in the trades; they were the action-groups who stimulated the legislation which the Livery were then, sometimes, apt to ignore. They were the 'young rebels.' As the numbers of workers in London increased with the growing population, so the number of working members in the Yeomanry grew – while the numbers of the Livery, restricted by the ordinances, remained the same. There was thus a larger body – sometimes ten times the size of the Livery – to become dissatisfied with its governance. Furthermore, many small masters, unable in times of economic crises to pay their way, were forced to become journeymen to earn a living. (Ironically, as the proportion of surviving small masters waiting in the Yeomanry for vacancies on the Livery increased so the journeymen – the real working-classes of the Companies – sank lower and lower in the social scale and they were soon complaining about the misgovernance not only of the Court of Assistants and Livery but of their own officers and assistants.) There was ample scope for discontent and disorder. And in many Companies the Yeomanry provided a continual source of uneasiness to, if not of actual revolt against, the Livery.

Each Company in which such disturbances occurred dealt with them according to their greater or lesser enlightenment: at some time the organized Yeomanry of the Cutlers' Company had actually been disbanded for bad behaviour. This drastic action had occurred during the period of which there remain no records of the Cutlers – perhaps in the 1540s when there was unrest in other Companies – and the Yeomanry had remained a disorganized body of the under-privileged. Now, however, in 1566, it was thought safe, with a new set of regulations for their control, to allow them the privileges – and duties – of association. Once again the Cutlers exhibited a complete example of a Livery Company in all its social ranks and orders. They were, in everything, entirely characteristic of the society of which they were a part.

Under the disciplined government of Elizabeth the reputation of homemade wares seems to have been increasing. According to Stow[130] – a chronicler apparently unaware of the earlier fine work of the London cutlers – 'it was about this time that fine knives and knife hafts were being made in London . . . Richard Matthew at Fleetbridge was the first Englishman that attained to the Skill of making fine Knives and Knife-hafts.' It was he, Stow alleged, who had been responsible for the prohibition of 1563 'against all Strangers and others from bringing Knives into England from beyond Seas; which until that time were brought in by Ship loads from Flanders, and other places.'

Certainly it was Richard Matthew who in 1563 presented to the City a Sword of State 'a very fair and goodly sword, well and workmanly wrought and gilded, and a scabbard of crimson velvet for the same, very well garnished and trimmed.' He shewed that he was aware that gifts to those in high places might be miscon-strued for he made it clear that he gave the sword 'freely to the City desiring only the reasonable favour of this Court (of Aldermen) in such his honest suits as he by any just occasion shall hereafter have cause to make to the same and nothing else.'

The point, expressed with admirable discreetness, was no doubt taken.

The sword is said to have survived and to be the present Sword of Justice 'constantly fixed over the senior judge's seat in the Central Criminal Court at the Old Bailey. Its blade is of no great antiquity, but the pommel and quillons, which are of copper-gilt and handsomely wrought, belong to the sixteenth century.... The scabbard is covered with purple velvet, and retains its original six lockets and chape of copper-gilt with intermediate devices of recent date. . . .'[131]

In 1565 the Companies received a precept for building the Royal Exchange. Many individual contributions, apart from those raised collectively by the Companies, were received and, towards this long delayed project the flourishing Richard Matthew subscribed twenty shillings.

It was a time for the Cutlers' Company, too, to begin to flourish: they received at this period some valuable legacies of properties from members who had greatly loved the Company. There came to them in 1567 Thomas Buck's properties in Fleet Street, Fleet Lane and Ludgate Hill; they received under the same will the 141-year residue of a lease of the Catherine Wheel Estate in Egham. Comprising fifty-three acres, with eight holdings upon them, it provided the very respectable rent-roll of more than £64. The view day upon which the Cutlers annually inspected their City properties could not include such distant lands. Henceforth there must be a special expedition on horseback to Egham – it occupied two or three days, with the viewers assembling at a tavern in Knightsbridge, and having their breakfast on the way. On the return journey there was a potation with a contribution to the poor. Finally when they reached the City in safety they would celebrate their return with supper at some tavern. The expenses of such an outing with horse-hire and tips to the servants at the Catherine Wheel were considerable – more than £6, or a tenth of the rent-roll – but it was a pleasant, if exhausting, occasion and in those early days there seem to have been no complaints about the cost: it was only eighty years later that the viewers were expected to pay the costs of providing their horses.

Then, within two years, in 1569, the Estate of John Craythorne (he had been Master in 1560 when the Company received their

Inspeximus Charter from the Queen) came to the Company: it
consisted of Belle Sauvage Yard, Naked Boy Court and a house
and rooms over a gateway in Ludgate Hill. It was a handsome
bequest which was later to prove of even greater value to the
Company, although it was encumbered to a considerable extent
with trusts to support two scholars at the Universities of Oxford
and Cambridge, the relief of poor prisoners and the like.

If the times had been more financially stable and if there had been
less scarcity and unemployment the Cutlers' Company would
have seemed fairly set upon a course of prosperity and security.

But the times were still far from stable. Until 1569, while Europe
was the scene of religious wars and revolts, England with its less
enthusiastic approach to religion, had accepted the re-nationaliza-
tion of the Church with comparative calm. There were no English
battlefields and no English martyrdoms. Only after Mary Queen
of Scots, fleeing her own country, had come to England and
formed a rallying point for her co-religionists in the North did this
enviable state of affairs change. Far from London, where the Nevilles
and the Percies carried on feuds and border warfare unhindered,
and where the mass was celebrated in defiance of all the laws and
punishments, rebellion broke out.

The Livery Companies received a precept for soldiers fully armed
with calivers, flasks, touch-boxes, morions, swords, daggers, and so
on. In addition they were ordered to provide their troops with a
jerkin apiece and a pair of 'galley slops' made of broadcloth. The
revolt was soon suppressed and, as many of the rebels paid with
their lives, even the far-distant North began to realize that Elizabeth's writ was stronger than that of the local lords. She was firmly
established and men were content that it should be so. They had
supped full of the horrors of tyranny and disorder: for this reason
the Pope's bull of excommunication absolving them all from their
oaths of allegiance was a resounding tactical failure: the plottings
that ensued were foredoomed amongst those who, satisfied with
the régime, wanted no interference from Rome.

Thus the plan of Roberto Ridolfi, supported by the Duke of

Norfolk, to remove Elizabeth and put Mary in her place, with the aid of the Duke of Alva and Philip of Spain, was heavily handicapped right from the start. In October 1571 the Companies were called to their respective Halls and received from the Lord Mayor the news 'of the horrible and heinous conspiracy pretended, against the Queen's Majesty and the whole realm and namely the City of London, by the Scottish queen, the Duke of Alva, and the Pope with other their adherents.'

Norfolk and his chief associates had been arrested. The members of the Companies were admonished that 'if in case any of them shall hereafter see and hear by any word or deed, writing or cyphering, countenance or suchlike' anybody who favoured the conspiracy, or who was an accomplice to it, or who disapproved of the imprisonment of the Duke of Norfolk, they should 'incontinently apprehend the same, or cause them to be apprehended and brought before a Justice of the Peace to the end that they may have condign punishment for their offence to the example of others.'

Liverymen were appointed, as usual, to guard the gates and posterns from six in the morning till five at night: they were to stop 'every idle and suspect person' coming in and out.

By January 1572 the crisis was over. Norfolk was executed. Elizabeth's triumph was complete. It was celebrated in a manner which by its lavish display, against a background of drab austerity, subtly stressed the power of the State over the individual: when the rulers were prepared to be gracious the ruled might enjoy – and pay for – the splendours of a Show.

At the end of March, with what was an unusual degree of advance warning, precepts were issued to the Companies for men – 'good, tall, cleanly and of the best picked persons' for a Show before the Queen on May Day. In the intervening weeks there was much parading and rehearsing. Some of those picked were rejected and others chosen; those who wore black morions were told to go away and get white ones; all the handguns were exchanged for calivers; every man was ordered to parade with a good sword and dagger. Training took place on various days: sometimes it was at Mile End, sometimes at St. George's Fields. At last, on the evening of 30 April they all collected together and set forth towards Greenwich to the Muster before the Queen, to the sort of generic triumphal Show that, to later generations, became symbolic of all that was typical, and enviable, in Elizabethan England.

While the Company were settling down to the management of their new estates, and administering the charitable trusts attached to them, the dispute with the Armourers flared up before dying down for another term of years. In 1567 it had been ordered by the Court of Aldermen that, until further consideration of the matter, the two Companies should share the duties of the Search. Now, in 1571, there was a full hearing of the dispute, the matter was deliberated and, at last, a 'determinate order' was made: from henceforth neither Company should intermeddle with the search of the other among their own fellowships but that at Bartholomew Fair, they should operate under a joint authority. For the moment an uneasy truce was established.

There was a wider issue occupying their thoughts, a feeling that some steps should be taken to reform the 'custom of London.' One of the aspects of this traditional usage of the City was that it 'enabled the citizens who had obtained the freedom in any Company (generally through inheritance) to practise the trade of any other and prevented any Company having complete control over the trade it represented.'[132]

Fourteen Companies, the Cutlers amongst them, petitioned the Court of Aldermen that there might be a return to the condition of ancient times when each Company had the sole exercise of its art or handicraft and things were 'truly, substantially and workmanly made.' By achieving this reform the aldermen would 'purchase everlasting renown and immortal fame here on earth with the fruition of the immortal God in the world to come.'

The attitude of the ruling classes was, on the whole, unfavourable to the movement – after all, it was argued, under the system citizens were protected against the 'foreigner' but, at the same time, they were able to transfer their capital from one trade to another. It was inevitable, in the event, that, although some concessions were made – particularly in the following century – there was no immediately noticeable result of the petition. Life continued according to the custom of London.

It continued, however, on a somewhat more austere scale. In the first place the City had been 'credibly informed that the Nobility and gentlemen about the Court are much offended at the great number of Bucks being consumed in the Halls of Companies within London at their feast dinners. . . .' And although it may now be difficult to imagine a situation in which Livery Companies would in the least care about any such jealous touchiness on the part of courtiers none the less many self-denying ordinances were made restricting the number of bucks to be consumed at any one feast.

But apart from this somewhat dog-in-the-manger interference with the activities of the Companies there were other reasons for austerity. In times of national efforts to achieve a buoyant economy, restrictions are, inevitably, placed on personal pleasures and at this time the need for such restrictions was greatly increased by a great dearth of provisions. In 1573, a precept from the Lord Mayor laid down that there should be no feasts, dinners or suppers in the City Companies for elections and the like. On quarter days they might have only a 'reasonable' meal, and they were to entertain no guests other than those indispensable to the business in hand. Dinners arising out of legacies, or on Lord Mayor's Day, were still permitted – but without guests at the table or venison upon it.

On 12 September the Lord Mayor issued a further precept for the loan of Wheat Money – a demand which made reference not only to 'the great and excessive price of wheat and other kinds of grain and meat necessary for men's sustenance' but also to the 'greedy and covetous minds of the people, owners and possessors of the said grain . . . and the intemperate weather that hath been of late. . . .'

With the money the Government proposed, if necessary, to import grain from the Continent. 'The wealthy and able' of the City Companies were to be taxed for the purpose.

Soon another precept reported that the Queen was most displeased with the amount of money raised: further loans were urgently demanded. As it transpired the money when it was, eventually, forthcoming, was not spent 'in Danske and other places beyond the sea' to the best advantage. For of the corn provided 'so much of it by reason of the so unreasonable harvest, contrary winds, foul weather and long lying on the way, became musty and not wholesome to be spent and a good quantity utterly lost and meet to no use as doth well appear by two hundred quarters and upward which doth yet remain in the Bridgehouse by reason whereof there is lost £2100 or thereabout.'

The Lord Mayor asked the Companies to decide how this loss might best be borne. And he added 'There is two thousand quarters and more of good wheat of the City's provision lately made in Sussex, part thereof already shipped and the rest ready to be shipped, over and above the two thousand and odd quarters of good sweet grain now remaining in the Bridgehouse of the last year's provision. . . .' Perhaps the Companies might like some of this grain to be delivered to them, for them to store themselves, in part repayment of the Wheat Money already owing to them for two years.

What the Cutlers replied to this optimistic suggestion is not known: at least one other Company returned the sort of reply not usually accorded to a precept.

In such times of scarcity and unemployment there was always a preoccupation with apprentices: if there were too many of them they competed unfairly with the fifty-shillings-a-year journeymen. They were now indentured for ten years – from the age of fourteen to twenty-four – and, as a token of disciplinary power over them, the government decreed precisely how they should be dressed. According to Stow they wore their 'hair close-cut, narrow falling-bands, coarse side-coats, close hose, cloth stockings . . . blue cloaks in the summer and blue gowns in the winter. But it was not lawful for any man, either servant or other, to wear their gowns lower than the calves of their legs, except they were above three-score years of age; but the length of their cloaks not being limited they made them down to their shoes. Their breeches and stockings were usually of white broad-cloth, viz., round slops, and their stockings sewed up close thereto, as if they were all but one piece. They also wore flat caps . . . as well apprentices as journeymen and others, both home and abroad; whom the pages of the court in derision called "flat-caps".'

The Companies were ordered at the end of 1572 to see that these regulations – the dress for the numerous girl-apprentices is not described – were strictly observed. It could be considered that the government might have had more essential things to think about but, in fact, the effectiveness of a rigorous control of such details as what a man may wear, or how short his hair must be, may be seen in the boiler-suited millions of Chairman Mao. (Like Cultural Revolutionaries, too, the apprentices proceeded to 'molest and evilly entreat' many of the 4600 aliens in the City – always a popular target in times of hardship. The wording of contemporary complaints that they did this 'indiscreetly and without order' and must immediately desist, may, perhaps, be significant.)

More obviously reasonable was the control of the number of apprentices and of their entry into the trade: in 1575 a precept from the Crown commanded that in future no one should take an apprentice whose father was not the son of an Englishman born within the Queen's Majesty's dominions. Nor were the sons of Englishmen who had been, or who still were, 'of the allegiance of any foreign prince or estate' permitted to become apprentices.

To the hardness of the times and of their normal lives was added the constant demands on purse or person: three thousand young men to be provided by the City as a permanent defence force; 'warlike' caliver men to be ready at an hour's notice to serve in Ireland; a loan for the Queen to be levied, expressly, out of the Companies' funds and not by a poll-tax; further loans for building a new harbour at Yarmouth . . . in all these and many more the Cutlers must have borne their share.

Sometimes there was a variation on the theme: instead of borrowing from the City the Crown would insist on a Government loan to the Londoners: in 1576 it was £110,000 for a year at a rate not to exceed seven per cent. Every Company must accept a proportion of the unwanted loan.

In 1578 the demands were larger still. The country, threatened with an invasion to liberate the imprisoned Queen of Scots, was put upon a warlike footing. The City must supply two thousand 'able and sufficient persons, being Journeymen, apprentices or others which are freemen of this City and inhabiting within the same, being of Agility and honest behaviour between the ages of nineteen and forty years which are fit to be trained for arquebus shot, every one of them having a Morion, a sword, a dagger and a caliver with furniture for the same and half a pound of powder, beside touch-powder.' Nominal rolls with addresses were to be drawn up; the names of those suitable to be Captains and lead the men were to be indicated. All were to be ready within a fortnight. The expenses of such an operation were alarming. Soldiers were, by the standards of the day, highly paid. Eight days' training in the arquebus – for which the Mayor provided an instruction manual – for one hundred men cost some £43; the maintenance of fifty-six soldiers for a month more than £250.[133] These were horrifying figures: the rich were to be charged with paying them and a note was to be made to the Crown of how much each had raised. There were many complaints and a considerable amount of dispute within the Companies about the unfairness of individual assessments. Rash remarks were made and legal actions followed.

Just how disputatious was the atmosphere in the Livery Companies of 1579 may be seen from the Lord Mayor's precept:

Forasmuch as men of Christian profession ought to seek by all means unity, peace, concord and brotherly love in that commonwealth where they are and, in as much as in them is, to suppress hatred, malice, and disorder which in these days aboundeth too much, to our great shame, the gospel God's word being manifested unto us. And to avoid such suits at law, for words which are but wind, to the great charges of many men and also great hindrance and loss of time to those that appear on Juries for the same.

In consideration of the premises these are to will and require you, with the advice of your assistants, to take some order for redress therein and so to call the whole body of your Company before you and will them that if any person being a freeman of any other fellowship do offend any of them in words, that they do first go to the wardens of that fellowship that he is free of and to them declare the offence to him done, who have order from the Lord Mayor to pacify or punish the offender according as they shall see and find the weight of the offence. Wherein I would have you do the like if any of your brethren do offend in words any person of any other fellowship. And, if you find any so obstinate that you cannot pacify the same, then send to me in writing the names and surnames of both the parties that I may call them before me and I will do what I can therein. And if I find such obstinacy that they will needs to the law, I may perhaps be Chancellor in that matter.[134]

Many men were shewing the litigious sides of their nature: some were engaged in attempts to alter the law for their own purposes. The great Richard Matthew was one of them. Somewhere about this time he had secured 'a Privilege from Her Majesty under her Great Seal for the making of Knives and Daggers with a new kind of Hafts. But this was complained to have been, and further would be, the Decay and Overthrow of the whole Company of Cutlers within the City, besides their Wives, Children, and Apprentices; and the Prices of Knives and Daggers excessively enhanced, prejudicial to the Queen's subjects.'[135]

There must have been some potentially awkward moments when he encountered at the Hall those who insisted that their occupations would be gone.

It is by no means clear what was in his mind when, as a warden of the Company, he appeared before the Court on 13 February 1579 asking to be allowed to make 'humble suit unto the lords and others of her Majesty's most honourable privy Council for a general reformation to be had and taken against the wearing of long swords, rapiers and daggers, with the like pikes in bucklers. . . .' Nor is it clear why the Court agreed that it should and might be lawful for him to do so. There had already been proclamations to this same effect in 1557 (as the result of public disorders) in 1562 and in 1566 (as a sumptuary law); the Cutlers' interest in reviving them is obscure. A year later, on 12 February 1580, the petition bore fruit: 'Item, her Majesty ordereth and also commandeth that no person shall wear any Sword, Rapier, or suchlike weapon, that shall pass the length of one yard and half a quarter of the blade, at the uttermost: nor any dagger beyond the length of xii inches in blade at the most; nor any Buckler with any point or pike above two inches in length. . . .' The penalty for disobedience was a fine and the forfeiture of the weapon. For a second offence the culprit was to be banished from the town where he lived.

This was supplemented by a precept from the Lord Mayor. The Livery Companies were to place watchers on the City gates, there to remain from seven in the morning until six at night, until further notice, 'for the Reformation of all such persons, both men and women, as they shall see pass by them which shall wear any manner of apparel, swords or daggers, bucklers with long pikes, great Ruffs or long cloaks, or carry their swords loose under their arms or the points upwards, contrary to her Majesty's late proclamation and the laws and statutes of the realm. . . .' Anybody who offended or who refused to reform was to be apprehended with the aid, if necessary, of the Constable.

Both the proclamation and the precept were widely disregarded. On 8 March Lord William Howard, brother of the Earl of Surrey, passed through Aldersgate, 'wearing ruffles very much out of order and one of his men a sword of forbidden length and carrying it with the point upwards.' 'Because of his quality,' those who watched the gate did no more than remind his Lordship about the ruffles 'and they directed his servant to carry his sword otherwise and also deliver it to be cut shorter; whereupon the servant offered to draw his weapon and strike the citizens; and his lordship reviled them with very odious names of culines, rascals and such like which might have bred disorder of the citizens had they not been discreet men. This being the third time his lordship had put the orders to contempt, to the peril of the citizens,' the Lord Mayor requested the Lord Treasurer 'to take such steps to redress the same that the citizens might not be discouraged in their duty.'

The Lord Mayor, on 27 April, also wrote to Francis Walsingham reporting that the Cutlers had complained of the losses they were sustaining due to the non-observance of the proclamation 'which not being enforced in other cities and town rendered their wares unsaleable.' He prayed that that law should be generally enforced.

The answer came next day from Lord Burghley. He had caused a search to be made among the cutlers in Westminster for swords and daggers exceeding the length limited by the proclamation. He had, indeed, found some 'disorders' there – there were blades in the shops which infringed the laws – but the cutlers had excused themselves alleging that the London cutlers themselves sold forbidden blades. He therefore politely requested the Mayor that search should be made and that the law should be generally enforced in the City.

It was about this time that the two thousand men, trained two years earlier to use the arquebus, were called-up. In some Companies, the masters of the Yeomanry were responsible for collecting them together, press-ganging anybody who resisted. A four-day 'refresher-course' was held at Mile End and it was impressed upon the troops that they were not to go about London loosing-off their weapons either 'to the peril of others or to the trouble of the City or unnecessary waste of powder. . . .'

On 9 July there was another precept – this time for 300 men – to be ready for the Queen's service in Ireland. At the end of September 500 more citizens were called-up. With their aid the troubles in Ireland were soon put down. The rebels had been organized from Spain and accompanied as they were by a papal legate, the incident served as a further warning to Englishmen of the sort of foreign mischief that was plotted against their Queen. It doomed still further the future of the Catholic cause.

But the times remained serious and the Government was determined to make it apparent.

Two years later there were new regulations: young men had been indulging in too much luxury and wearing clothes too splendid for their station in life. Apprentices were now forbidden to wear anything but the plain garments provided by their masters – no bright colours, no ruffles except at the neck, no gold or silver or silk trimmings to their doublets, no rings and no weapons other than knives. They, as well as servants, journeymen and children, were forbidden to go to plays, hunts, or 'interludes' either in the City or out of it – the growing Puritan element in the Government believed in Strength through Drabness, in depressing regulations that would bring home to people that life, with the growing threat of a war with Spain and actual troubles in Ireland, was real and earnest and must be lived under strict discipline. It was also a year of severe plague and when a scaffold collapsed at Paris Gardens, killing a number of citizens, this, too, was said to be God's judgement. The thin-lipped unsmiling portraits by Holbein tell us much about the atmosphere of Merrie England.

In addition to the other problems of living in that age the City Companies now faced that of a renewed and quite unreasonable extortion: the matter of 'Concealed Lands.'

These were properties which – so the Crown alleged – had been overlooked, deliberately or otherwise, at the time of the Reformation when, it will be remembered, a return had been demanded of all lands left in trust to the Companies for supposedly superstitious uses. The rents of these lands had been seized by the Crown and then sold back to their rightful owners. After four hundred years and with the complexity of many of the trusts involved it is probably now impossible to determine whether the Companies had, in fact, been guilty of any appreciable evasions. Least of all is it possible, in the absence of records in the Cutlers' Company, to know how they fared. But every Company about which any information remains seems to have been, guilty or not, the prey for many years to come of any man who could obtain a patent from the Crown to indulge in a little legalized blackmail. And since it is known that the Cutlers too, at the time of the Reformation, had owned properties to which religious trusts and duties were attached, it is a reasonable assumption that they, like the other Companies of the City, were now harassed by the problem and by those licensed to exploit it.

The difficulties were primarily those of interpretation: thus, in a bequest amounting to £15 a year a Company might well consider that only the £8 allocated to the costs of the obit and of the priest's stipend were returnable as superstitious: the Crown, on the other hand, argued that potations, gifts, grants of coal to the poor, and so on, should also have been included because the recipients were expected to pray for the souls of their benefactors.

It was, said Strype,[136] 'Sir Edward Stafford and others who had obtained patents from the Queen for finding out obits and chantry lands concealed. . . . Certain prying fellows, hoping thereby to make some gains to themselves, had made discoveries of them to these patentees . . . who examined narrowly into all these concealments and what was discovered became the patentees', the Queen having some small part. . . .'

In cases where there was some doubt about the legal interpretation of the matter it was obviously cheaper to settle with the patentee on the best terms obtainable.

But a more serious threat had to be faced in 1582 when the City Corporation and the Companies, individually and collectively, were called upon by Sir Christopher Hatton to defend themselves and their properties in the Exchequer Court. The better part of their argument was an appeal to reason: if the claims by the patentees succeeded in full the Companies would be ruined, the poor would lose their alms, and the Queen, being no longer able to call upon them for money, corn, arms and soldiers, would lose far more than ever she gained from the small sums payable to the Crown by the patentees. It was sound reasoning. In May, Hatton replied that he was willing that two judges, one of them appointed by the City, should hear all disputed cases. If the law so decided he would leave the Companies in peace; if the judges found in his favour he would, none the less, offer the Companies 'reasonable and favourable composition' – the definition of what was reasonable in each case he was prepared to submit to the judgement of the Lord Chancellor, the Lord Treasurer and Master Chancellor. He must insist, he said, on an answer by 'Friday next, the same to be brought by one or two and no more.' Their consultations together must be 'with as good secrecy and as little common bruits and rumours as may be.' If they rejected his terms he reserved the right to submit to any composition whatsoever.

The Companies accepted. With the judges of what was reasonable including such eminent names it was obvious that any degree of defence was going to prove expensive to the Companies.

In due course of time – two years or thereabouts – figures were agreed and the Companies paid their decreed sums.

But, of course, then as always, the blackmailer was not to be content with a single payment from his victims. In later years, the Companies were again to suffer the extortions of those private individuals into whose hands the Crown was always prepared to sell its loyal subjects.

The threat of public law suits against the Cutlers was accompanied by the reopening of their private battle against the Armourers. In 1584 it was reported that armourers had refused to let the officers of the Cutlers search their shops. In view of the previous rulings in the same long drawn-out dispute it appears, at this distance of time, that the Cutlers, by bringing a complaint before the City authorities, were indulging in vexatious litigation: after all, each Company had previously been ordered not to intermeddle with the other except on the occasion of their joint search at Bartholomew Fair. Indeed, on 6 August, a discussion was held at the Queen's Head between representatives of the two Companies to make arrangements for the search of the Fair that year.

Yet by the beginning of September the quarrel had clearly broken out again. On the first of the month the Master and the Court were to be found at the Hall looking among the records for 'certain grants for Searching between us and the Armourers.' When they had finished they all repaired to the Star Tavern to thrash out the matter over a potation. A fortnight later they again met at the Hall, drew up a supplication to the Lord Mayor, and their work done, repaired to the Swan in Dowgate. The next day the Master and wardens delivered their petition against the Armourers to the Lord Mayor, calling in as they did so for a drink at the Star. The Armourers were warned to attend a hearing in two days' time. (It may here be observed with the resumption of the Company's own records that, during the unminuted years, the social activities of the members outside the Hall had greatly increased: more business was now transacted, or celebrated, in taverns than on their own premises. It seems almost as if there must have been at this time some deficiency about the Hall premises that made the holding of functions, even of dinners, at various inns a more attractive proposition than meeting under their own roof.)

Organizing such a petition was always expensive both in time and money. The Mayor's officer went around the City summoning the armourers; another officer was sent for their Master. The Town Clerk perused the petition; so did the Recorder. On 22 September the Armourers put in their reply – some of the masters among the cutlers attended the Star Tavern after hearing it read to them. On 24 September the Common Crier 'carried in one Christopher to my Lord Mayor against the Armourers' – presumably as a key-witness in the proceedings. The case, conducted for the Cutlers' Company by their Counsel Mr Smith, dragged on. On 1 October the Master, wardens and clerk, waited at the Star Tavern for the Lord Mayor's Court to act but it was not until a fortnight later that the Master was called upon to attend the Court. On 16 October all the masters were summoned before the Lord Mayor and, at last, on 21 October, the Lord Mayor delivered to Mr Smith his ruling in the case. The Company records give no indication of the result but it has, however, been reasonably inferred[137] that, rather surprisingly, the matter was decided in the Cutlers' favour. After it was all over they presented a knife to an official 'to give warning whether any bill was preferred in the Parliament house against us by the armourers' – an indication that the Cutlers felt, perhaps, that their victory was based on very unsubstantial ground.

The Company had emerged in 1584 from the dark ages of its record-less state in tolerably good shape. The number of the Livery does not seem to have increased: only 39/- was raised in quarterage. There were forty-one apprentices, and eleven cutlers set up shop for themselves. Four cutlers came on to the Livery from the Yeomanry, the wardens of which collected 30/- in quarterage from the junior body – a figure that suggests a membership of about forty-five. The Court still kept a watchful eye upon the trade: they levied fines upon individual members: for setting a 'foreigner' to work without permission from the Master and wardens; for 'having a 'prentice a year before his other finished his year;' for 'having a 'prentice more than his number.' A stranger they fined for arresting one of the Company without a licence, and Mr Tedcastle had to pay 8d. 'for speaking indecent words in St. George's Fields.'

Their accounts, which ran each year from the Feast of the Annunciation, were now kept personally and in holograph by the Master and the Renter respectively. The Master's account that

year, when the expenses were more than £44, was some £16 in debit.
But the rent roll was a respectable £110 which clearly left considerable room for financial manoeuvre. Their properties occupied by
working members of the trade now included some sixteen melting-
houses, mostly in Shoreditch – sometimes they were rented with a
garden, sometimes with a tenement, often in pairs.

The Court were much concerned, too, as they had always been,
in the registration and control of trade marks. There had been, as
early as 1490, a Company mark and, it is fairly clear that in 1586 there
were occasions on which this was misused, for the Cutlers began a
Suit for 'Repressing the Mark of the Company and the repressing
of such persons which would work for themselves' not being
denizens. On 13 March the Master and wardens 'went abroad
themselves to survey the strangers for their marks and who were
denizens and who not.'

As a result, application was made to the Lord Mayor and aldermen for a general warrant to control the city marks. They were
advised to address their suit to the Lord Chancellor. They seem to
have had little difficulty in achieving their purpose – although, as
usual, it was a fairly costly process. There was boat hire to Westminster; the Lord Chancellor's porter to be paid at the Water
Stairs; a pair of 'rich knives' worth thirty shillings, damasked, and
originally made for the Queen, for the Lord Chancellor's Secretary
who prepared the warrant; a ten shilling knife-dagger for the Lord
Chief Baron; a similar knife to Mr Recorder together with a piece
of silver-gilt plate and a book – the *History of Abraham and the Death
of Christ*. Back in the City it was necessary to shew appreciation to
officials there – a knife with a scallop shell, damasked with gold, for
the town clerk; a fair pair of knives with a silk string for his wife;
and lots of knives of lesser worth all round to officers and their
men. Nor were such gifts the only expense – there were drinks at
the Three Tuns with the Mayor's officers and drinks at the Mermaid
with the Recorder and his man: whether it was post hoc or propter
hoc the Recorder issued a warrant to attach an alien named John
Garrett. Obviously it was all well worth while. The 'strangers' who
had recently, on receiving a summons from the Cutlers to bring
in their marks to the Hall, declared that 'they would not be re-

formed' now brought in bonds for their future good behaviour. There were drinks on that occasion, too. The Cutlers were highly sociable and the Renter's account for 1585–6 lists forty-four official visits to inns and taverns: when the precept for the Lottery was made; when the Survey of the Armourers was made; 'after we had been at the Hall about Gittins and his man'; after having 'talked to the Livery touching their Marks'; on View Day; 'at the "Grey-hound", the Master being there'; 'when Parker made suit for his lease'; 'when Wicker Bunt complained of his Mark'; 'when Widow Elkins had her pension granted'; 'the day that Jerome, the Beadle, was given 20/- to buy himself a cloak' – clearly these were worthy occasions for celebrations at the Mermaid, the Star, the Greyhound, the Swan, the Boar's Head, the Dagger, the Horn and others of the City drinking houses.

If anything in grim Elizabethan England justified the adjective 'Merry' it must have been the Cutlers' company about their day-to-day affairs.

Yet in the greater, outside world all was not well. The compulsive intriguing of the Queen of Scots, the Throgmorton and the Babington plots, all seemed to point towards an imminent onset of the Catholic 'Enterprise' against England. In April 1585 a Spanish invasion was anticipated and the City was ordered urgently to muster four thousand men, the largest Livery Companies being called upon for nearly 400 persons. Twenty-seven cutlers were called up and in addition the Company had to provide forty other soldiers who were 'pressed' at 1/- a head. The operation was launched enthusiastically on its way on 17 April with a dinner at the Mermaid, no doubt to celebrate the fact that they had collected that day towards the expenses £11. 15s. 0d. from sixty-one members of the Company and £5. 17s. 2d. from twenty-five aliens. They had another dinner two days later at the Dagger in Cheapside and, the day after that, a dinner at the King's Head. From these occasions there emerged some kind of a fighting force equipped with all the due panoply demanded – culivers, morions, banners, handguns and so on. There was a barrel of beer, too, for the soldiers. The Company had its own tent that was carried to the encampment at Blackheath and carried back again to the Hall when the week-long operation was concluded. Inevitably there were those who proved awkward – Carey Matcham had to be sent to the Compter; inevitably, too, there were those who were unfortunate – Gittins got hurt and Crookes was sick: each of them received 18d. in compensation.

In the event the troops were stood down after only seven days but the operation had proved a severe strain on the resources of the Companies. All had their own armouries and many employed a full-time armourer but such demands took a great deal of fulfilling. The cost for every man mustered was probably in the region of thirty shillings and, for this reason alone, there must have been great relief when the emergency came to an end. The relief was, of course, purely temporary. The immediate danger of a Spanish invasion might for the moment be ended but there were other military demands. The Earl of Leicester's expedition, reluctantly committed by Elizabeth to the Low Countries, proved a bottomless pit for men and money. The Cutlers were involved, from the very outset, when there came a precept for five men for service in Flanders. The accounts of their expenditure were kept in great detail and included such usual occasions as the Master's dinner at the Boar's Head, and, of course, drinks at the Swan the day the five men, with their calivers, their bows and arrows and bowstrings, were presented to the Lord Mayor. The men were paid board wages of 8d. per man per day, as well as money for drinks in the field; it is clear that before they were finally sent overseas they hung around the City for a fortnight, having breakfast at the Company's further expense.

Wasteful though the Netherlands campaign was, Elizabeth's intervention there had the effect of preventing a Spanish victory. This, from Philip's point of view, was bad enough but he suffered a further and constant source of irritation in the repeated 'unofficial' raids, by men such as Hawkins and Drake, upon Spanish shipping and Spanish trade routes. As long as Mary still lived, the defeat of Elizabeth would have meant the accession of the Queen of Scots to the English throne and the establishment of France in a paramount position over both England and Scotland. But in February 1587 Mary was at long last executed. Now, if he conquered England, the throne would fall to Philip: he made immediate preparations for mounting a great invasion by sea – the 'invincible Armada.' Drake's celebrated exploit against Cadiz delayed the sailing of the great fleet but by April an attack was so imminent that the citizens were kept hard at work arming themselves against it. There came a precept to the City for men and ships.

Of the demands upon the Cutlers' Company there appears to be much that is unrecorded for they must surely have contributed more than the comparatively trivial items which began, on 3 April, with two corselets with pikes, swords, and daggers, and one musket with headpiece, rest, sword and dagger.

A fortnight later the Captains in charge of the operations complained that there was a shortage of muskets which could not be supplied in the wards on the scale demanded by the assessments made upon them. The Cutlers must supply another musket (with a good and sufficient rest, flask and touch box) before 21 April to any Captain authorized to receive it. After use, it was promised, the musket would be handed back to be kept in the Company's armoury. On 11 May this demand was repeated with, four days later and almost as an afterthought, a precept for a man to serve with the musket.

Then Mr. Wilbraham, the Common Sergeant, gave a morale-raising address to representatives of the Livery Companies at Guildhall. He reported how the Queen had sent for the Lord Mayor, with some of the aldermen, to shew her gratitude for the City's great efforts. It was not, in fact, at all usual for the City Companies to get any display of official gratitude for their patriotic efforts and for this reason alone Elizabeth's words must have been of great propaganda value. As reported by Mr. Wilbraham, the Queen told the Lord Mayor:

We greatly thank you in the name of all Our faithful and good subjects of Our City of London for your and their diligent forwardness and willing expedition, together with their liberal contribution towards Our necessary affairs so lovingly done unto Us, in setting forth and so well furnishing their sixteen ships and four pinnaces and other great charges so willingly and diligently expedited. And I pray you, my Lord Mayor, tell them I thank them all for it and desire them to pray for me and I will pray for them and that I would be sorry mine enemies should have the same subjects, for I think no Prince in Christendom hath the like, or can have better, for whom I am greatly bound to God. And I assure you the same shall be employed for the weal and honour of my country.

The Lord Mayor, who had been kneeling for a long time, had to be helped to his feet and his reply – if accurately reported – seems to indicate that he had been overcome not only by stiffness but by the greatness of the occasion.

Oh, most precious Prince and Jewel inestimable, [he began] whose hairs of her head her subjects are, I heartily pray unto God that if she hath any loose hairs that will not stick to her that she may cast them into the fire and burn them. For as long as Samson had his hairs fast to his head he was able to overcome one thousand men but when it was taken away his strength failed him.

She is our Princess and we her subjects; she is our mother and we her children. We read that as Amphonus and Astrophus carried their aged father out through the flame of the fire put into a City by an enemy, even the very flame yielded from them as though it had favoured their piety and pitied their extremity. We read the same of Anchises done by his son Aeneas when Troy was afire. I am with you greatly to thank God and I heartily rejoice that I, the least of a thousand, am in place to speak these glad reports unto you and that you are so happy to hear the same – being from so excellent a Queen, the heavenly dew of God's blessing: Who long bless, keep and preserve for the mother of His children and give Her Highness the victory over all His and Her enemies. Amen.[138]

There were, after this, a few further demands upon the City for meeting the threatened invasion. There was not much more that the City could provide. The armouries were empty, the funds exhausted. On 20 July – the day after the Armada was sighted off the Lizard – the Cutlers were called upon to provide a caliver, flask, touchbox, headpiece, sword and dagger; ten days later, when the danger – had they but known it – was over, they were ordered to provide a coat, costing 13s. 4d., for the man who carried the caliver.

In fact, the news of the victory was long arriving. The driving out of the Spanish fleet by fireships from their anchorage off Calais; the way in which they were outgunned and outmanoeuvred in the battle that ensued; the escape of the survivors in a squall – all this was fairly quickly known. But that the invasion would now never take place was still to be learned. The Spanish fleet had simply disappeared. It was thought to be, perhaps, refitting and regrouping somewhere in the Baltic. In Spain the news was at first of a great victory for the Armada: it was not until later that it was discovered by both nations that the demoralized fleet, so far from seeking to refit and renew the attack, had fled northwards, hoping for a homeward passage around Scotland and Western Ireland. On the way a storm completed the wreckage of Spanish hopes – barely half the ships of the invincible Armada succeeded in limping back to their home ports.

It was on 20 August that the Lord Mayor, his prayers dramatically answered, and the citizens went to St. Paul's to thank God 'for our delivery from the Spaniards and driving them out of the narrow seas.'

The real celebrations, however, took place in November on the anniversary of Elizabeth's accession. The Cutlers were warned to be ready with the whole of the Livery in their best apparel to attend on 18 November and wait for Her Majesty on her way to St. Paul's to hear a sermon there. They were told that their stand must be strong and well-railed and covered with a fair blue cloth; their standards and streamers must be set up; they must be attended by whifflers in coats of velvet, wearing gold chains and carrying white staves. The event was postponed for six days but, at last, on 24 November, the Queen came from Somerset House to the City.

The Cutlers' stand 'was on the right hand going up Fleet Street, next the Conduit save one, and we stood in this sort – on the right hand was above us the Pewterers and Clothworkers and beneath us the Waxchandlers. And on the left hand the Leathersellers and Vintners. . . .'

The Show that they watched was characteristic of such occasions. First came the Queen's gentlemen at large, her officers of the Household, knights, Sergeants of the law, the aldermen and knights of London in their scarlet gowns, the Judges, the Lords and Earls, the Lord Chancellor and the Lord Treasurer. Then came 'the Mayor of London carrying her scepter and the Marquis her sword before her. And her Majesty in a fair and seemly throne carried by the force of Two horses where in a Chair she did sit, her ladies of honour following a horseback after her. And thus she passed through Fleet Street where the Companies a both sides railed in. And in their best liveries with their streamers and standards did welcome her into the City. And so passing forwards she went to Pauls and there heard a learned sermon. And dined at the Lord Bishop's of London. And in like sort with torchlight returned back again. . . .'

The first of the occasions on which England owed her survival entirely to the Navy was over, the celebrations ended. But the war by land, notably in the Netherlands, went on. And with it, inevitably, there was much work for cutlers to do.

8

A Question of Quality

1587–1603

IT was only natural that the testing time of war should bring into prominence the question of the quality of the weapons used. Puritans among the Elizabethans had long been scornful of the highly decorated arms that were fashionable. As one of them wrote in 1585,

... they have their rapiers, swords and daggers gilt twice or thrice over their hilts with good angel gold, or else argented over with silver both within and without; and if it be true, as I hear say it is, there be some hilts made all of pure silver itself, and covered with gold.

Othersome at the least are damasked, varnished and engraved marvellous goodly; and lest anything should be wanting to set forth their pride, their scabbards and sheaths are of velvet, or the like; for leather, though it is more profitable and as seemly, yet it will not carry such a port or countenance as the other.[139]

It was one thing to be able to turn out expensive works of art to satisfy the personal pride of the owner: it was something quite different to produce a sufficient number of serviceable 'warlike' weapons. It was natural that in such dangerous times the question of the quality of swords and the control of their manufacture should become a public issue. The year after the Armada there was some considerable but badly documented activity by the Cutlers' Company on the subject of blades.

Many of these were imported and, apart from the dangers inherent in relying in time of war on imported weapons, there were doubts about the quality of the foreign blades.

The Cutlers began to petition both the City and the Crown for special privileges to be granted for blade-making. They spent 12d. 'for drawing a petition to the Lord Mayor and Court of Aldermen for our Company for blades making.' A similar sum was spent on a like petition to the Queen. Two aldermen went to Cutlers' Hall and, calling the Company before them, heard their opinions about the petition. There are indications that the Cutlers were anxious about the outcome – there was a special trip to Greenwich, to deliver their letter to Counsel, which had an urgent ring about it; and, no doubt to strengthen their hand, they arranged an inquest to test the quality of imported blades. The jury's reward and the dinner they were given cost the Company 32s. 3d. There was the usual handing out of knives for favours received or anticipated: 'to the Clerk of the Council to prefer our Suit, a rapier and dagger, black varnished, with velvet scabbard' as well as 'a velvet girdle fringed and stringed'; to the doorkeeper of the Council a knife with ivory haft and silver rivets; to the Lord Chamberlain, a knife with his arms; to the Lord Chamberlain's wife, a pair of knives with black hafts, gold damasked, stringed and in a case of gold. It was all money well spent. The Queen's letters patent and commission for the Company to make blades was duly received. And the Lord Mayor issued a precept which clinched the matter. 'Disserviceable sword blades,' he noted, had been made 'of sleight stuff brought into this Realm and uttered and vented into divers counties unto such as in these doubtful times have been enjoined to furnish themselves with Armour and Weapons whereby her Majesty's subjects are not only deceived but a great abuse is committed in that kind of provision which should serve to the defense of the Realm being altogether unserviceable.' To redress 'this Lewd Abuse' he ordered that the wardens and other experts in the Company should be called together 'with such discreet persons as they may care to chose' to carry out a search of all warehouses and shops 'where deceivable blades are to be found.' Such blades were to be defaced and a bond taken from the offenders not to import or sell any such material in the future.

It was all part of the power struggle.

There had been consultations with their old enemies the

Armourers. Now, in October 1589, an order gave the Cutlers the right of search of swords and other weapons on condition that the wardens of the Armourers were associated with them.[140] There is a faint implication that the Cutlers thereby enjoyed a certain priority but six months later the two Companies were put on an equal footing in a search for 'naughty and deceitful sword blades' on sale in the City: two of each craft were associated in the search with the representatives of certain other Companies.[141]

A subsequent search by the Cutlers, both of their own and other Companies, resulted in a haul of 335 blades confiscated on the spot and a further 648 blades left in their owners' hands to be brought in to Cutlers' Hall to be defaced at a later date – a date on which there was a celebratory potation at the Mermaid. The Cutlers compiled, at the same time, a list of the merchants whom they believed to be importing the offending blades.

There was a move, too, against those who sold their wares other than on established premises: three warrants were obtained from the Recorder to apprehend Hawkers and at least one alleged offender was brought in by the Mayor's Officer. This was the opening shot in a new campaign to rid the City of something that they considered an intolerable nuisance; the next move came, on 14 June 1592, in the form of a Petition for the Repression of Hawkers and the Abuse of Trading.

This document 'in lamentable manner sheweth . . . the poor estate of the said Company arising . . . by the multitude of strangers using their Art and occupation.' It was well-known, said the Cutlers, that there were twenty such denizens – aliens who had been naturalized – in and about the City. But there were also another fifty-seven non-denizens of whom seventeen were actually householders. All these strangers worked in secret places not known to the petitioners. Nor was this all: as well as the strangers there were 'English foreigns who (were) by way of hawking in the streets and highways with deceivable wares appertaining to this Society. And (there were) merchants . . . being retailers in the said occupation with like deceivable wares. . . .'

As a result, the poor householders were so impoverished that many of them were obliged to abandon their trade and become day-labourers, porters or watercarriers. The Company, the petition stated, had spent a considerable amount of time and money in trying to take the offenders by surprise but they had failed: for they did not only hawk in the City but for miles around. The Company had vainly tried to suppress the aliens but had been thwarted by their friends. Knowing the weakness of the petitioners they were able to overcome and hinder by cunning sleights in the vending of their deceivable wares by retailing within the City as any other the Citizens do, thus undoing the poor Freemen. It may be thought that some inconsistency is to be remarked in this argument but the Company was in little mood for rationalizing an outrageous situation: the aliens refused to take the oath, they refused to submit to the Court, they refused to pay quarterage. Yet the poor petitioners were 'charged from time to time with Scot, Lot, Subsidies, Taxes, and other charges which the foreigners escape.'

The petition was laid before the Lord Mayor.

There had, indeed, recently been a number of charges upon the Company. In January 1590 the Cutlers had received a precept to supply 480 pounds of good and serviceable gunpowder, 'to be carefully and circumspectly kept in such convenient place as may be without danger and peril to this City.'

That same year it was demanded that they should supply 18 quarters of wheat and 9 quarters of rye: there was an additional complication – 'all the said rye to be provided from foreign parts.'

There was good reason for this stipulation. Grain bought in the English countryside to store in London granaries for the benefit of the evergrowing capital merely meant that in times of scarcity other towns were deprived.

This increase in the size of London had long been a problem: it caused difficulty of government; it caused a dearth of victuals, a multiplication of beggars and a corresponding inability to relieve them; it caused an increase of artisans, more than could live together, while other cities were impoverished of inhabitants; it caused lack of air and lack of space in which to shoot or walk about; it caused plague – in 1592; the sickness was so 'dangerously disposed in sundry places of this City' that no dinners were to be held on Lord Mayor's Day and the money thereby saved was to be given to those of the poor who were already, or were soon to be, infected.' London was clearly breaking down. But, to avoid further strains upon the resources of the countryside, its future needs of grain must be met from abroad even although this must inevitably prove more expensive to the City Companies who were assessed to provide it.

All this the scheming aliens were enviously seen to avoid.

They avoided too the precept in June 1591 for the provision of six ships and a pinnace, all ready for war, with men and victuals and all the furnishings necessary for active service for which the total cost was then estimated to be 'at least' £7400. By September the cost had escalated to £8000 'or thereabouts' and the first assessment, of which the Cutlers' share was £27, had raised only slightly more than £6750. A new precept was given – which the aliens also avoided – for the extra money that was needed: the Cutlers were compelled to find a further £4. 19s. 0d. There was a considerable incentive for the Companies to comply with the precept for it was ordered that if anyone failed to pay, or if any of the previous assessment remained unpaid, then the wardens of the defaulting Company would be committed to prison, there to remain until every last penny had been paid.

There was a further precept for wheat that Autumn, and in November 1592 the Cutlers were forced to supply another 480 pounds of Gunpowder, together with a proportionate supply of match. To ensure that they did so, a certificate, in writing, shewing how much they had actually supplied, was demanded of them.

There had been other taxes, too: there had been two 'fifteens' – a kind of payment of Rates – for the Queen. All these expenses came at a time of the slump that had followed the opening of war with Spain. Many traditional export markets were now closed; many trade routes were, to a greater or lesser extent, cut off; the dangers of sea transit added greatly to the cost of goods; the difficulties of export – where it was not actually impossible – led to a scramble for the home markets. There was certainly no room in the Cutlers'

K

world for unofficial and illegal traders such as the hawkers, the aliens who paid neither Lot nor Scot.

But still their petition to the Lord Mayor lay unrewarded.

It was time again to take up the fight.

In October 1592, four months after their abortive appeal to the Lord Mayor, they decided to address themselves to the Queen.

Their petition to the City had been a plea ad misericordiam: the Mayor and aldermen had remained unmoved. To Elizabeth, then, they would appeal – after stressing their own miseries – on grounds of a disinterested patriotism, demonstrating clearly wherein lay the public good.

The document they produced, with its unintended note of farcical black humour, is absolutely characteristic of its age

lamentably complaining and shewing unto your good Lordships' how the Company of Cutlers of London who, getting their honest living by their good labour, have always provided good wares and true workmanship in their faculty for the use and service of her Majesty's liege subjects, are now utterly decayed by want of a speedy redress and like to be utterly undone by certain idle, dissolute and vagrant persons who, keeping neither house nor open shops where due search may be made ... wander from place to place on her Majesty's highways and there, as hawkers and forestallers, utter and sell deceitful wares and weapons to all sorts of passers-by so that the soldier in war and the traveller in peace, and all kind of people that buy of them, when they are occasioned to make trial of that fraudulent stuff are utterly deceived and find their money cast away – their swords and rapiers bending and standing more like lead than any well-tempered metal, and themselves left either to death, maims, or mercy of their enemies.

'Again, the long permission of those vagrants unpunished hath so multiplied their numbers that they swarm in most places, and increase in all their pernicious sect, having more shifts than one to help themselves: for, if their highways market fails them, then fall they to mischief, rob or murder her Highness' subjects, spying out places of opportunity by their daily prowling to and fro, and having weapons ready to furnish themselves and other stout rogues of their consort whose former misdemeanours bar them from buying swords in any City or good town – for which offence some of the said Hawkers have been apprehended, convicted and executed.

'By this enormity, Right Honourables ...' and here the Cutlers were gathering strength for their real point '... your said petitioners to the number of four hundred persons with their wives and children here in London, besides far greater numbers elsewhere, are extremely impoverished, loiterers maintained, labourers decayed, vagabonds succeed [sic], good commonwealth's men that pay all impositions to her Majesty subverted, true men oppressed, thieves and rogues strengthened, many abused, and all sorts deceived. . . .'

It was an impressive catalogue. To put matters right the Cutlers pleaded that warrants might be issued to various justices to arrest the offenders, seize their wares, and punish them condignly. Because the Hawkers 'have no certain place of abode, neither are of ability to pay' it would be necessary to have special Warrants for the attachment of their bodies or wares. If their Lordships were to do so they would be performing, so the Cutlers urged, a very charitable deed by which they would bind their poor petitioners, with their posterity, 'daily to pray for their prosperous estate &c.'

They had struck exactly the right note. Within a matter of days rather than weeks the Council had agreed: they sent out letters in just these terms to the appropriate Justices.

A fortnight later, on 10 November, the Justices, in their turn, acted, ordering all Constables, headboroughs and other her Majesty's officers to go out and 'look at the Highways and if they find any hawkers of swords and daggers to arrest them at once and bring them to [a] house near London Stone.'

Three days later seventeen such officers were summoned to the Hall: thirteen of them appeared and were issued with Justices' warrants. They rode off in all directions – one group went 'Hertford way', another 'towards Knightsbridge'. Others went to Highgate, Stratforde atte Bow, and Brixton Hundred in Surrey.

How many hawkers were in fact taken in this search is not recorded but it is known that difficulties arose: some of the offenders sought the protection of other Companies[142] and those old enemies the Armourers supported a certain stranger named Tilman Childe in a law-suit that continued for many months. And one of the posse was actually arrested for apprehending a hawker – the Cutlers gave him six shillings in recompence.

Seventy years later hawkers were still a problem.

The Cutlers' Company had taken a high moral stand in their petition to the Crown; they had drawn a dramatic picture of the unwary customer of the hawkers finding himself at an embarrassing disadvantage the moment he first tried to defend himself with his deceivable weapon; they had claimed that they themselves had 'always provided perfect good wares and true workmanship.' But not everyone was prepared to endorse this latter statement. Sometimes the Cutlers' own morality was called into question.

And you, cutler, you are patron to ruffians and swashbucklers, and will sell them a blade that may be thrust into a bushel; but if a poor man that cannot (assay the) skill of it, you sell him a Sword or a rapier new overglazed and swear the blade came either from Turkey or Toledo.[143]

Clearly in every Company there were to be found those who were either dishonest or incompetent, or both, but the very close searches that took place – searches in which, by 1597, the Cutlers seem finally to have been confirmed in a position of superiority over the Armourers[144] – tended to reduce this to a minimum. The Cutlers were, in any case, faced with a competition that was potentially more serious than that of the hawkers and that must have been an incentive to produce good work in the City – this was the great rivalry that Sheffield and Birmingham shewed to London. As early as 1586 Sheffield knives were being exported from Liverpool and Chester to London's foreign markets.

'The deplorable feature of this competition was the systematic manner in which London marks were counterfeited by the country makers – a breach of commercial honesty which bore fruit in later years when London got the credit for much fine Sheffield cutlery. Nor was the blame confined to one party, for the London cutlers themselves were accused of stamping Spanish and other marks on their goods. The provincial cutlers, however, seem to have been constant offenders – seizures of Sheffield knives and Birmingham knives, swords, and daggers being frequently recorded, and the complaints of the London cutlers were loud and continuous.'[145]

In spite of their complaints about the imminence of ruin from the hawkers and from Sheffield and Birmingham and in spite of the general trade depression there are indications that the cutlery trade was – as might, in time of war, be expected – modestly flourishing.

In 1593 there were fifty-five apprentices and fifteen members set up in business for themselves which suggests a certain individual prosperity. Corporately, too, the financial situation was reasonably healthy: there was an income of more than £200 with a credit balance of £89 on the Master's account and the rent roll was now a very respectable £145. 10s. 6d.

They received, too, a dividend on the money that they had invested in a free-booting expedition against the Spaniards – the prize was valued at £12,000 of which the Cutlers received some £45. The Crown gave: the Crown took away. They received at the same time a precept addressed to those 'as have adventured by sea with Sir Walter Raleigh and are thereby interested in gains of the Carrick goods.' In it they were ordered 'all excuses set aside' to call all the freemen together and 'by all the best means' persuade them to give one-third of all clear gains towards the building of a hospital being planned by the City – a pest house for victims of the plague.

Once again London was greatly infested. Company meetings were reduced to a minimum – there were only twenty-one Court Days in 1593 compared with thirty-six the previous year – and there was to be no feasting. As on previous occasions, the money thus saved was to be devoted to those in infected houses unable to sustain themselves. The Master and wardens were summoned to Guildhall: they were told to bring with them a certificate stating how much they usually spent on such occasions. The Cutlers said that they usually spent 'six pounds or thereabouts whereof the House pay three pounds and the Wardens pay the rest.'

The times of pestilence meant also a diminution in the number of official visits to taverns – there were only fifteen that year, including the day when 'old Mr. Tedcastle was buried', and they were all lumped together under the heading 'Charges in Diet Laid out by the Master.' The general air of gloom that hung over the City must have been greatly increased by the precept – evidently anticipating some general unrest – which was headed simply 'That servants and apprentices go not abroad.' The householders in the

City, its liberties and suburbs and in the Boro' of Southwark were to be summoned to the Hall and instructed that 'they from time to time look so carefully to their apprentices, journeymen and servants, especially upon Sundays and holydays, that they keep them within their dwelling-houses unless they repair to church in their masters' company to hear divine service, and also at none other times none of them to be suffered to wander idly in the streets or abroad in any part of the City, and also to lock and keep from them all manner of Armour and weapons, which every householder hath in any of their said houses. . . .'

If they failed to do so and if any tumult arose they would be held individually responsible for their servants, journeymen and apprentices. There is no record of the length of time during which this precept was in force, or for how long these wretched creatures were kept confined to the tiny shops and their cramped quarters. It is another example of how far removed from reality is the imagined spirit of the great days of Elizabeth the First.

It was a time, too, of increasing taxation. The winter of 1593-4 saw demands for corn money, for no less than three Fifteens for her Majesty, and a whole subsidy of £5. 6s. 8d. due for the Hall. They were followed by a direct precept for nearly £14 for Ship Money for her Majesty's 'important service'. It was not, all things considered, the most favourable moment for Lord Burghley to intercede, at the instigation of the French ambassador, on behalf of four of the hated strangers – 'four poor Frenchmen who were being hindered and grieved by the Master and Wardens of the Cutlers.' His Lordship asked that the Master and wardens be called, together with the Frenchmen, before the Lord Mayor, and if the Cutlers could not be persuaded to help the strangers ('being, as he has heard, of the French church and therefore to be favoured') then, Burghley suggested, he himself should hear in private the Frenchmen's grievances.

The Cutlers reacted strongly. They submitted a petition to restrain strangers (who, they did not fail to point out, paid no taxes) from exercising the trade without submitting to the Company according to the laws of the Realm. Others, they added, had already been sued in the Courts and had been ordered to obey the

laws of the country in which they had chosen to settle – for this
reason they did not think that, in fact, even if they wished to do so,
they had the power to go against the Court's decision just to make
a special case of the four poor Frenchmen concerned.

Unrest among the workers and the apprentices was now such
that the Lord Mayor appears to have considered putting the City
under martial law. The Crown, in order to keep people duly in
their places, desired that the Statute of 1569, about the wearing of
caps, should in all points be put into operation. Those whom it
concerned must be called together and admonished to see that they
and their employees conformed. But the Cutlers' Company does
not seem to have been afflicted with the same amount of internal
indiscipline as was to be found in some of the other Companies.
There were comparatively few fines for misbehaviour – Oliver
Plunkett was fined for giving uncomely words to Warden Siddon
and a few members of the Court were mulcted for coming late to
meetings – but on the whole the business of the Company continued quietly enough. Their gradually growing list of properties
occupied much of their energies. In 1593 John Davies charged his
estate at Bowes Farm, Edmonton, with thirty shillings a year for
ever to the Cutlers 'for the use of the poor men of the said Company.' There were annuities to be paid out of Buck's Lands – including one to the Armourers – and Craythorne's Lands. Other entail-
ments included prison relief at the Marshalsea, Kings Bench,
Newgate, and Gate House; there was an exhibition to be paid at
both Oxford and Cambridge; there was a long drawn-out law-suit
concerning a wall in Houndsditch which proved immensely
expensive – there were three counsel at the trial, the defendant was
arrested, four witnesses had to be paid, the jury alone cost ten
shillings, and somewhat mysteriously 'to the old woman's
daughter that brought us to Arrowsmith and to the old woman'
twopence was given. After the dispute was ended the arms of the
Company were taken to Houndsditch and set up on the boundary
of the property – later there was an extra charge for adding the
'Ollifan'.

With these sort of expenses it is not surprising that the annual
credit balance on their rent roll of nearly £149 was apt to be only

about twenty pounds. From the Master's account there was an endless succession of taxes or forced loans to be paid: in 1596 it was money for ships, pinnaces, and men 'to annoy the King of Spain'; for equipping first 'the Soldiers which should have gone to Calais' and then those who, in fact, went to Boulogne. Some of the Company must have been among those forcibly pressed for service. The following year there were soldiers for Picardy; the year after that it was a contribution towards the cost of suppressing the rebels in Ireland and providing men, horses and equipment for the war there.

Every year there came a demand or demands for grain. 1596 was the third successive year of bad harvests, poverty and starvation. People were dying in the streets of the City that year. The supply of grain became an overriding preoccupation. In October ten thousand quarters of wheat over and above any amounts previously demanded had been ordered from overseas 'upon the City's adventure', and three thousand quarters of rye had been bought in Amsterdam and were 'daily expected'. It was to cost thirty-five shillings a quarter and the Cutlers were ordered to take up fourteen quarters at a cost of £24. 10s. Then in December a demand reached them for a further £19. 10s. payable, however, in three instalments; next March another £13 was demanded because the merchants who had brought grain from Dansk were still unpaid. Because 'of the present dearth and scarcity' the Companies were ordered to 'forbear to feast during this summer season to prevent great consumption of victuals' but that October it was announced that there was still a dearth of grain in the Kingdom: ten thousand quarters were to be bought overseas, imported, ground into meal and sold in bushels, or lesser measures, for the relief of the poor. Towards this amount the Cutlers were assessed to provide forty-five quarters and, to help them, they were to join with the Grocers' Company to make their provision together: it was the senior Company that had to provide the initial capital. The first half of the grain was to be ground by 31 December, the second half by May Day, and the whole operation cost the Company more than £80: although various individual members contributer, the Cutlers lost some £14 on the transaction.

In addition to all these levies there were the usual Fifteens and subsidies and the water rate was increased to 26s. 8d. Yet with all these outgoings the Cutlers still had money to spend on the counting house at the Hall. From the amount of work which went on – tiling, carpentry, painting, glazing and matting – it appears as if the counting house was, in fact, being created rather than restored. Fifteen ells of painted cloth were used, too, and the arms of the Queen and of the Company were regilded. The carpenter also made 'a defence for the Hall Door against pissing'.

As the century drew towards its close all was not well with the City. The country was in the grip of a depression exceeding anything in the previous fifty years. Bad harvests had forced up the price of wheat from twenty shillings to nearly sixty shillings a quarter. Industry was stagnating and trade was, because of the war, at a standstill.[146] Poverty-stricken countrymen had drifted into the major cities in general and into London in particular – a London which, as we have seen, was already breaking down. The City authorities had been compelled to take action to provide the social relief that had once been the concern of the monastic establishments. It was the Councils of various cities who had first transferred their charitable assessments from a voluntary to a compulsory basis, who had provided cheap food and fuel in times of dearth. Now the problem had become too big for local government and the system evolved by the municipalities was taken over by the State in two Acts which established Poor Laws at a national level.[147] The first of these, in 1597, seems to have passed unnoticed over the Cutlers' heads – their preoccupations were still with troops for Ireland and the home Counties, with their £90 share of the forced loan of £20,000 from the City, and with their own pensioners of whom there were now sixteen. But the second Poor Law Act, in 1601, was brought to their notice by a precept which admirably summarized the situation:

Whereas the Lord Mayor and his Brethren the Aldermen duly considering of the great number of Idle, Lewd and wicked persons flocking and resorting hither from all parts of the realm, who do live here and maintain themselves chiefly by robbing and stealing, by cozening and abusing of men's children, servants and apprentices and by all other wicked, unlawful and ungodly means to the great offence of Almighty God, the damage and hasard of the state, and the evil example of other idly disposed persons. And to the end that this kind of idle and dissolute persons may not be suffered here to live Idle but that so many of them as from time to time may be apprehended and [caught] shall within this City, Liberties and Suburbs thereof be sent to Bridewell. And there employed and set to work and labour. . . .

To the first Elizabethans the greatest sin against the Holy Ghost was idleness. 'Sturdy beggars' were hated and, therefore, feared. Weals upon their backs and the holes bored in their ears were evidence of that even though the high noon of Tudor cruelty was past. They must be set to work. And although their treatment may seem unsympathetic to the second Elizabethans, with their lesser insistence on the virtues of industriousness, the fact that anybody (for whatever reason) cared about unemployment set an example to other countries in the contemporary world and provided for those genuinely seeking work a measure of security previously unknown.

It was, of course, an expensive operation. For an experimental period of a year £500 was to be raised from the City by assessments based on the proportionate contributions set by the Companies for buying grain.

It was not only the poor who were feared by the State. The sight of anybody behaving in a manner above his divinely allotted station in life was almost equally displeasing to the Crown.

The opening year of the seventeenth century had been marked down, in advance, as another year of scarcity, because of the wet weather 'and of other occasions best known to her Majesty.' It was certainly no year in which to indulge in vulgar display. In May the Queen summoned the aldermen to Greenwich. She was, she said, grievously offended with them for their carelessness 'in suffering such excess and disorder in apparel as is daily worn within this City by the Aldermen's wives and their daughters, by Lawyers and Citizens wives and their daughters.' She gave a special command to the Mayor to see that there was an immediate reformation: he himself would have to answer for it to the Queen if the 'intolerable pride' and the 'daily disorder' continued. The Companies, Elizabeth ordered, were to be summoned to their Halls, informed of Her Majesty's 'gracious pleasure and Commandment', and ordered that 'as they regard their duties to Almighty God and obedience to her Majesty, they cause a present reformation of the excess of apparel of their wives and daughters and not to suffer the like disorder ... but that they may go decently and modestly apparelled, fit for their degree and calling. ....'

It was different, of course, for men – especially for men called upon to support the pageantry of State. When the ambassador from the Emperor of Moscovia arrived in London in September he was 'to be received with all honour.' The Cutlers' contribution to the welcoming posse of horsemen was three 'of the gravest, tall, and comely personages, well horsed and apparelled in velvet coats and chains of gold.' They were to parade at Tower Hill and accompany the Ambassador to his lodgings. And, in November, they received an equally demanding precept 'To attend the Queen's Matie from Chelsea to Westminster.' This time there were to be four horsemen to ride from Cheapside to Chelsea, from Chelsea to the Palace, and then back again to the Lord Mayor's house. The Companies were ordered to make sure that all their representatives were fitted out in such a manner that 'no man for insufficiency in any respect be turned back again to the disgrace and discredit of his Company as a man unfitly furnished and appointed for so Honourable a service.' There was no question there of anybody being accoutred above his station.

From the other end of Company rolls, four men were to be 'pressed' for the Queen's service in Ireland – the selection was to be made from those most easily spared, certainly those without wives or children.

But there were not to be many more autocratic demands from the old Queen. She was seventy years old and had reigned for forty-five years. The Tudor dynasty was passing into history. It was not a dynasty upon which the sixteenth-century Cutlers could then look back with nostalgia. But the Stuarts were waiting in the wings and, in the first half of the seventeenth century, there must have been many who looked back with a real regret for the old times which, harsh though they were, may well have seemed, when they later compared their corporate lot, to have been halcyon days.

9

Adventuring with James I

1603–1611

THE Cutlers, though they did not know it, were at the beginning
of what was, perhaps, the most eventful century of their whole
existence. All they saw, at that moment, was that the beginning of
a new reign was, inevitably, a time of great expense. There were all
the festivities to be paid for, the presents to the King, the costs of a
new charter and so on.

Elaborate preparations were being made to greet the new
monarch. On 1 April 1603, a week after the accession of James I, a
precept was received for four citizens 'of good sort', on horseback,
with velvet coats or, as a possible concession to fashion, velvet
jerkins with sleeves of the same material, and with chains of gold
were to be made ready for employment at very short notice. And
because, the precept continued, in the past there had been many
insufficiencies – either in the men or in their dress – the Company
was immediately to see to it that everything was properly prepared.
This injunction applied equally to the rails and stands for the
livery and the furnishing of the barge. Everything was to be ready
not only for speedy use but it was to be kept in readiness always
and for any occasion. Eight days later it was announced that a
show would be prepared to greet the King on his arrival from
Scotland. The City was to spend £2500, of which the Cutlers' share,
to be paid to Mr. Cornelius Fish, amounted to £11. 10s. The whole
Company was then summoned to the Hall – the wardens of the
Yeomanry went round the City, warning them to appear – and
'were severally demanded what they would in their liberality

give towards the new making of our banners & other charges which the Company is now to be at. . . .'

There were, at the time, thirty-nine Liverymen including the Court, sixty-nine Yeomanry and twelve aliens and 'foreigners' and between them they raised the respectable total of more than £54. Red taffeta was bought for the King's Banner and, for the other banners and streamers, the Company laid-in blue taffeta, red taffeta sarcenet, black fustian and silk fringing. All was ready when on 7 May the King at last came to the City. The Cutlers celebrated the new reign with potations at the Swan and The Cross Keys but, in fact, the festivities were greatly curtailed and the general rejoicings marred by the worst epidemic of plague since the reign of Edward III. More than thirty thousand citizens – fifteen per cent of London's population – died in a single year and it was not until the following March that the coronation took place. The Cutlers duly received a precept for the beautifying of streets and lanes. The King and Queen with their nobles and great personages were about to proceed 'in pompous and magnificent state from the Tower of London through the City.' The Company were ordered 'all excuses and delays set aside' to prepare for the occasion. The standings were to be lengthened so that every man had three feet of standing space for his greater comfort and for the better look of the thing. Their banners and streamers were to be 'featly set up' for the garnishing and beautifying of the rails.

And so James I came to his long-desired heritage. For his immediate needs a forced loan of £15,000 was demanded of the City: it was to be repaid before March 1606. All thirty-nine of the Livery and seventeen of the Yeomanry contributed the £67. 10s. which was the Cutlers' share.

About this time it becomes noticeable that the fraternal spirit within the Company was exhibiting signs of stress. The number of disputes between members increases. There are instances of indiscipline and insolence towards the Court. The degree of insult is sometimes hidden by damage to the manuscript but the general tendency is clear. One member accused another of bringing 'base company to his shop and cozening him of a sword worth twenty pounds': adding insult to this injury, he had called the complainant an [illegible] and his wife 'tallow-faced'; William Davis, one of the Yeomanry who had already been fined for refusing to be a Whiffler was further charged with uttering words against the Court saying that he was wronged; Davie Rogers, one of the Livery, was committed to Ward because he wilfully refused to pay the twenty shillings with which he had been cessed for the payment towards the coming of the King into the City; Richard Benney, another Liveryman facing a similar charge, 'after some words of discontent and unwillingness' agreed at last to pay within a fortnight. By this time Davie Rogers was again in trouble: he was charged with 'unkind dealings' to the Company in reviling the servants and refusing to obey orders. 'And required, according to my Lord Mayor's commandment, whether he would confess his offence and submit himself to this house . . . he first denied that he had given any offence and that he was wronged by the Master and wardens and would seek and take his remedy by law against them. And that they had wronged him and not he them.' John Stubbs was fined for beating and abusing his man, Richard Hales, before the Court; Richard Hales was, in his turn, fined for trouble-making and, in carrying tales, behaving 'like an Ambodexter.' Then William Watkins called the Court 'rascal knaves and bald knaves and bald [illegibles]'. He was committed before the Lord Mayor, as were two other members who on several occasions had disobeyed orders to appear before the Court. Much of it was small beer: the members quarrelled frequently among themselves about such neighbourly matters as to whose responsibility it was to sweep the gutter in the street outside their properties; a husband and wife brought before the Court the dispute they were having with their servant. But it was all symptomatic of an unrest which came to its head in a curious incident in 1606.

A new reign meant a new Charter: very often it was no more than an 'Inspeximus' or confirmatory charter but on this occasion it had been suggested to the Company that their working charter of 1416 was not only out of date but contained clauses that might prove to be defective. To strengthen their position, both as property owners and as a corporate body, it was therefore in February 'agreed that a suit shall be brought and presented by the

Master and Wardens to the King for the obtaining of the new Grant for our Corporation with some addition to be therein for the further purchasing of lands. And the confirming of other things for the good of the Company but before anything be put in execution it is agreed that the Court shall be called and the Assistance warned to know what they and others of the Company will [desire] about this suit.'

At the next meeting of the Court it was determined that the Master and wardens should take counsel's opinion about the best way of acquiring the new Charter, and in March the Court authorized its purchase, with ordinances devised by learned Counsel. 'And the house by agreement is to pay and bear fifty pounds and no more' – any extra cost was to be collected from among the members.

'By colour whereof some private members of the said Company, especially one Oliver Plunket, taking upon them the following of this business, procured a new Charter, soliciting the same in the name of the whole Company. And in the said new Charter had excluded all the same Company other than such as are working cutlers to bear office as to be Master or wardens of the said Company, a matter contrary to the orders, rights, and usages of all the Companies in London. And procured without the direction and liking of the then Master and Wardens of the said Company. But secretly by some working cutlers of the said Company who would not suffer the Master and Wardens and principal men of the said Company to be acquainted with the contents of the said new Charter until the same was thus obtained under the Great Seal.'

The new Charter was, in fact, brought before the Court on 16 May. With consternation the majority of the members heard read to them the clause empowering the Company to elect yearly as Master 'one of the freemen of the said Mistery of Cutlers who at time of such election shall be a cutler and use the Mistery of a cutler.' With added alarm they heard the same formula applied to the election of the wardens. At once somebody demanded 'how many of the Court gave allowance or liking thereto? And it appeareth that these persons ensuing utterly dislike . . . the said Patent in the words in which it now passeth.' There followed a list of the names of those who dissented. Mr. Hawes spoke for all the other rebels when he expressed his dislike of 'the division of the Company which it is expected will grow by this Patent.'

In fact it appeared that there were only two members of the Court who approved the new Charter – Mr. Oliver Plunkett, a past Master, and Christopher Hatfield, the Senior Warden – and 'none of the rest knew of the contents of the Charter until it was brought in.'

It was an extraordinary incident and it seems almost incredible that those working cutlers who had planned this naively bare-faced attempt to seize power in the Company could ever have supposed that it would succeed. If they were relying on their fellow members of the Court not paying attention to their business or if they thought that no one would dare to speak out against a document obtained under the Great Seal of England at such great expense, they were much mistaken. The non-working cutlers instantly appealed to the City authorities and on 20 May a Com-mittee of Aldermen was appointed to consider and report upon 'the dispute in the Company of Cutlers touching the new letters patent obtained from the King.'[148]

On 12 June a Court of Aldermen examined both parties in the dispute. They decided that 'the matter in question being of great consequence to the City . . . may be very dangerous in example to all other the companies in London' and they ordered, therefore, that all the Cutlers, working or otherwise, should operate under the terms of the old Charter until the Court of Aldermen could bring the matter to the notice of the King or the Privy Council.

In the meantime the annual election of the officers of the Cutlers was approaching. It was clear that disputes might arise since the Company were now utterly divided 'some claiming by the former patent and some by the later which may cause trouble and dissen-tion amongst them if the same be not timely prevented.' The Lord Mayor, therefore, would nominate two aldermen to attend the Cutlers' election personally to 'see that no trouble or disorder grow, which this Court mistrusteth.'[149]

Under their supervision it seems that the election took place peaceably enough. The new charter might be unacceptable where elections were concerned but it had, none the less, its uses. At the next Court 'were summoned most part of the foreign working cutlers, in and about the City and suburbs of London when . . . was published and read the Corporation anew granted by the King's Majesty and certain rules concerning them. And they were generally charged every man to observe the form of the Patent which they promised.' In particular they promised 'to reform their marks and to strike a proper mark by the allowance of this house, whereon is, on a part thereof, to be struck the dagger being the Arms of the City.'

Meanwhile, behind the scenes, the activity to replace the Grant by a new Charter continued. That same June three knights on the Court of Aldermen together with the Recorder went to Sir Edward Coke, then Attorney-General, 'for reformation of certain grievances complained of by divers of the Company of Cutlers touching matters contained in a new Charter lately procured by some of the said Company, not only prejudicial to the general government of this City but hurtful to the said Company'[150] Nothing seems to have come of this deputation. But in October, when Coke had become Lord Chief Justice of the Common Pleas, the Lord Mayor wrote to him in that capacity 'complaining that this new Charter was contrary to the usage and custom of this ancient City and requesting him to examine and report upon the differences between the Old and the New Charter.'[151]

Five aldermen were summoned to attend the two Chief Justices at Serjeant's Inn and although no records of this meeting have survived later events suggest that the verdict was given in favour of the non-working cutlers. For the Court resolved to apply for a new patent. It should be the same as the one recently, and mistakenly, granted except for the rules for the election of the Company's officers; they should be as they had always been.

Victory, for the moment, was to the traditionalists. But the constitutional crisis within the Company was not so easily to be settled.

In the meantime, in the divided Company, life went on.

The weather was, as always, unseasonable. There was a very small yield of grain and prices were rising. The Cutlers had first to certify how much grain they held ready to put upon the market and then to supply, 'with expedition', twenty-five quarters more. In July the streets were beautified for the coming of King James and the King of Denmark and their respective trains through the City from the Tower. The Company were to have everything prepared by 30 July with an azure blue cloth upon their stand – a stand they certified to be 107 feet long – and 'with banners and streamers in the most beautiful manner as may be.' There were to be at least six Whifflers for every twenty liverymen, with staves in their hands and standing over against the Company rails for the better and quieter ordering of the streets.

The pageants alone cost one thousand pounds, towards which the Cutlers' assessment was £4. 10s.

The Account dinner, too, was held at the Hall in the old manner, that July: in spite of the recent financial crisis in the City there was a handsome balance on the Master's Account and, with eighty-five apprentices and fifteen new shops opening and twelve admissions to the Livery, the Company was, at any rate financially, in good shape. They had paid the Clerk £11 that had been outstanding since 1600 for a basin and ewer that they had bought from him for £21. They had paid the fifteens and subsidies that were continually demanded; they had paid for the expenses of obtaining their ordinances; which had not been involved in the dispute about the charter; they had taken action against a Frenchman who had brought prohibited cutlery into the realm; they had contributed to the building of Aldgate and Moorgate; they had taken a benevolence of £6 'according to the ancient manner' to the Lord Mayor; they had mended the Yeomanry Hall and they had paid an officer 'to carry Matcham to the Counter' after dinner at the Robin. And still they had a credit balance on the year of £134.

The Court voted a sum not exceeding £10 towards an Act of Parliament to strengthen and confirm their so-called 'Concealed Lands' which had once again been called into question by those newly-licensed by the Crown to engage in extortions.

They confidently faced, too, the costs of obtaining a revised charter: surplus funds were still available from the sums collected for the Grant that they had rejected and a further amount was still to be collected from those who had defaulted on that occasion. Four members – Oliver Plunkett among them – promised 40s. each towards the expenses; any further monies that might be required were 'to be borne by the body of the Company or the house.'

In January 1607 they gave notice to the Lord Mayor of their intention to purchase a new charter 'which shall be to the liking of us all.'

The revised Grant received in April from James I, since it was for so long the working charter of the Cutlers, is worth considering. The scope of the trade had been defined as including all persons 'making or working for sale . . . any manner of swords, daggers, rapiers, hangers, wood-knives, penknives, razors or surgeons' instruments, or small knives, skeynes, hilts, pommels, battleaxes, halberts or any other weapons or blades or other things belonging to the mystery.' Now, to summarize, the grant was made, on the petition of the Company, 'for its better rule and government, and for the prevention of divers abuses practised in cutlery to the loss and damage of His Majesty's subjects. It conferred on the executive the power of making ordinances for the government of the craft, and of search and correction over the trade in London, and within three miles' radius, and the right to call on the civic authorities and all others for assistance in carrying out the law; it approved of the Constitution of the Company as composed of a Master, an Upper Warden, an Under Warden and twenty Assistants, of whom all were to be elected out of the Commonalty – the Master and Wardens annually on Trinity Eve and the Assistants for life.'[152]

Very importantly, the value of lands that the Company could hold in Mortmain was raised from £20 to 100 marks, or more than £66.

Obtaining the charter had been an expensive business. £10 had been paid for the signification of the Royal Pleasure and the same amount for the actual Royal Signature; £6. 13s. 4d. went to the Attorney General and the same amount was charged for engrossing the document; £8. 9s. went to the Great Seal; £5 for the Privy Seal; £4 for the Privy Signet – all this was in addition to seemingly endless fees and gratuities to lesser palms. Altogether some £80 was spent and for all their prosperity there was great difficulty in raising so much money. There were many defaulters, and the non-working members of the Company proved particularly recalcitrant: Mr. Beckwith, called upon to pay the 20s. at which he had been assessed, answered that 'when this new patent is used in the choice of the Master and Wardens according to the ancient use of the house, like to their first patent, he will pay.' There were at least four others, including a member of the Court, who were of the same mind: it was decreed that they were not to be summoned to Company functions until they complied. It seems that their discontent arose not so much from their assessment as from the slowness with which the promoters of the new grant brought it into operation – it was, as we shall see, two years before the matter came to a head.

The Court, however, armed with their reconfirmed powers shewed great activity in their executive functions. Some aliens and no less than fifty-three foreigners were called to the Hall where the charter and the rules of the house were read to them. Some of them brought in their trade marks to be registered. The Court admonished William Floyd, free of the Goldsmiths, to leave off striking his mark because he did not do his own forging. He surrendered his stamp and promised in future to buy from those of the Company who were allowed to have marks. They brought a suit against certain cutlers 'for not being denizens and for working in our mistery not being prenticed according to the custom of the City of London.' Their authority in these matters was clearly respected: 'John Commyne, Stranger of the town of Soling[en], under the obedience of the duke of Oleava [*sic*] brought in letters patent under the great seal of England ... whereby it doth appear he is made a denizen of the said realm of England.' They registered his trade mark and they fined Charles Finch for counterfeiting or stamping his wares with the mark of the half-moon instead of his own proper mark, the spectacles.

Increasingly their time was occupied with the problems of trade marks: in a most unbrotherly manner members were continually counterfeiting the marks of better-known or superior craftsmen. The half-moon, in particular, was a mark that was constantly being counterfeited. The offenders were sometimes sent to prison; almost always their 'deceivable blades' were confiscated and often broken. In July 1608, for example, a large number of knives were delivered to the Court – a pair of spotted knives with ivory hafts, a knife with a box haft taken in Ironmonger Lane, more than five dozen knives and sheaths taken at Bartholomew Fair, counterfeited blades, some of them with the half-moon and other marks: on this occasion many of them were returned to the owners on the payment of varying sums of money.

Two years later, on counsel's advice, the Court decided to 'prefer a Bill into The Star Chamber against such obstinate persons as do strike marks or otherwise wilfully offend in contempt of the King's Charter lately granted to this house.' The Court also 'deliberately heard' a quarrel between William Oldrenshaw and Richard Warren which began with the latter reproving the former at Stourbridge Fair 'for selling wares appertaining to this mistery in deceitful manner' and which ended with Oldrenshaw behaving 'contemptuously and unbrotherly' towards Warren, 'plucking him by the beard and challenging him to the field.'

Later, the positions were reversed with Oldrenshaw abusing Warren and Warren assaulting Oldrenshaw. The Court fined them and ordered them to be friends again.

More seriously 'John Swan was for divers abuses done to his Mistress and for drunkenness and for beating his Mistress, by the testimony of the Neighbours under a petition, adjudged to be whipped and was whipped with half a dozen stripes.'

But, above all, the Court busied themselves with putting into order the affairs of the Yeomanry – 'from henceforth there shall be no more assistants of the Yeomanry than Twelve, besides the two Wardens, but those that are in place already to continue until, either by death or otherwise, they be removed.' The Court's approval must be sought for anyone becoming a Yeomanry Assistant.

Their wardens must render accounts, each year, to the Livery wardens and must summon their members, through the agency of the Beadle, to appear on quarter days: they were authorized to fine any who disobeyed the summons. The Assistants of the Yeomanry, too, were to be fined unless they came to the Hall 'in decent manner' in their gowns. The inferior situation of the junior body was, however, stressed: 'on the quarter days the Wardens of the Yeomanry shall appoint eight persons who shall serve and bring in supper, who shall be attendant for the use of the Wardens of the Livery to serve at the tables and after supper is ended the same eight persons shall have their diet in competent manner provided for them and they shall then sit down with such officers as have not supped.' All these rules and ordinances, together with the Charter and the Act of Parliament in Confirmation of the Cutlers' Lands – all the authorities under which they operated – were written out in a parchment book for which a leather case was specially constructed for its better preservation.

But for all their external shew of strength the internal constitutional struggle between the working and the non-working cutlers, the divisive dispute which had been instigated by the Charter, still continued.

In June 1609 Christopher Hatfield – who, it will be remembered, was one of the two assistants who had plotted to obtain the first rejected charter – was elected Master and, almost immediately, 'divers of the Principal men of the Company of Cutlers which were not working Cutlers by trade' petitioned the Lord Mayor against the working cutlers.

The Committee of Aldermen gave the ruling that Hatfield was to continue in office for a year – instead of the then normal two years – and he was to be succeeded by Reynold Greene, one of the complainants. Three members of the Court, who had been dismissed during the course of the dispute, were to be reinstated and were to pay the assessments which they had refused. Their money was to be used for the expenses of the amended charter only and was not to be applied towards the costs of the grant obtained by Oliver Plunkett and Christopher Hatfield.

This ruling did not satisfy the working cutlers and their activities remained such that on 26 May 1610 the Lord Mayor found himself compelled to issue a precept to the Company 'to proceed to an orderly election of the Master and Wardens.' He recalled to their notice the ruling of his predecessor that an orderly election should be held 'without distinction or exception of men of other trades or occupations.' He pointed out that by virtue of his office he was 'Master of all the several Companies of the City and cares for the good of all the Companies.' He noted, with regret, the recent differences among the cutlers, differences in which the Master and the two wardens were on one side and Mr. Thomas Green, a Past-Master, Mr. Blathwaite and Mr. Beckwith upon the other. It was a highly undesirable situation: in order to prepare the business of the election and to do everything possible to ensure a quiet occasion the Lord Mayor decreed that the three rebels should submit 'decently' to the Court and be reinstated into their positions as Assistants. To avoid all dispute, the very form of their submission was dictated to them: 'In whatsoever I have offended this Court I am heartily sorry for it and desire to be received into your good opinions and I will be a good and dutiful Brother to this house.' As for the 20s. that each of them had been ordered to pay towards the charges of the very charter that had excluded them, 'to prevent disorder and Circumlocution of speech which otherwise may then rise about the same' the Mayor ordered that they should pay only such arrears of search and quarterage money as might have arisen during their period of disbarment. And, finally, Mr. Reynold Greene was to be elected Master for the year ensuing.

In due time the three rebels made their submission. Unfortunately for the hopes of peace within the Company, and contrary to the Mayor's command, when a fortnight later the democratic election took place, Mr. Christopher Hatfield was again elected.

The non-working cutlers launched yet another appeal. They complained to the Lord Mayor of 'the undue and disorderly election of the Master and Wardens of their Company out of the younger and meaner sort, being working cutlers, and passing over and refusing to chose merchants and others of their Company

itlers' Hall, a drawing by Hanslip Fletcher, 1938 (photo: Eileen Tweedy)

The Carrington Salt, presented by Robert Carrington, Warden, in 1658. The body is encrusted with pearls and garnets. The ears, tail and trappings of the elephant, the rim of the stand, the castle and the cup are silver gilt (Photo: Eileen Tweedy)

The Beadle's staff head, in the form of the Company's crest. Silver; said to be sixteenth-century, it is not hall-marked and no record of its origin exists in the Company's archives

The Belle Sauvage inn, *circa* 1840 (Photo: Eileen Tweedy)

being more ancient and against whom no just exceptions could be made. . . .'

The Lord Mayor ordered that the election be held again and that the orderly and normal procedures were to be observed: if they were not, he said, he would himself come to the Hall in his role of Master of all the Companies and see that the decencies were observed.

On 19 July a proclamation was read to the whole Livery: Mr. Reynold Greene had been elected Master and from henceforth every person or persons of the same Company of what art or profession soever he or they be, shall be nominated, elected and chosen unto office or place in the said Company according to his Ancienty, unless there be just cause to be shewed against such person or persons to the contrary.

Victory was for the traditionalists and the non-working cutlers: in fact, the Company was no more than keeping in line with most of the other Livery Companies where for many years a great dilution of trades had taken place.

Though the atmosphere within the Cutlers' Company can hardly have been a happy one and there must have been many highly embarrassing Court Meetings, the constitutional struggle was for the moment ended.

The members could more whole-heartedly direct their attentions towards the potentially more profitable subject – both morally and financially – of the new overseas Adventures.

The first of these was revealed in March 1609 by a precept in which the Companies were to be called together in their respective Halls and their Masters and wardens were to tell them all about the Virginia Plantation (which, founded by Sir Walter Raleigh, was now being reorganized) and to do everything within their power to persuade their members to adventure money in the project: the amount that they raised was to be certified to the Lord Mayor, in writing.

There had already been an attempt to raise sufficient money among the merchants of the City to launch the revised project but this had proved unsuccessful. The appeal to the Livery Companies was at first no more effective. In July, therefore, the promoters of the scheme issued a prospectus.

Whereas the Lords of His Majesty's Council, Commissioners for the Subsidy, desirous to ease the City and suburbs of a swarm of unnecessary inmates, as a continual cause of dearth and famine and the very original occasion of all the plagues almost that happen in this Kingdom, have advised your Lordship, and your brethren in an ease of state, to make some voluntary contribution for their remove into this plantation of Virginia which we understand you all seemed to like as an action pleasing to God and happy for this Commonwealth. We the Council and Company of this honourable Plantation, willing to yield to your Lordship, and them all, good satisfaction . . .

had tried to work out how much would be the cost of transporting a private person or a private family. They did not wish, they said, to *exact* any money; they wished, only

that you may see as in a true glass the true charge which we wholly commend to your grave Wisdoms, both for the sum and the manner of Levy.

They had to point out, however, that they could not accept any sum of money less than £12. 10s. – administratively a lesser sum would be much too much trouble and would cause difficulties when it came to working out the dividends that were bound to accrue.

Any arguments that those inmates ordered to emigrate might have were discounted in advance: if they said they had nowhere to go and asked how they were to maintain themselves upon the journey, and what might be their prospects, they were to have held out to them a glowing picture.

They shall have meat and drink and clothing with a house, orchard and garden for the meanest family and a possession of land to them and their posterity, one hundred acres [?] for every person that has a trade or a body able to endure day labour, as much for his wife, as much for his child that are of years to do service to the Colony with further particular reward according to their particular merit and industry.

And if your Lordships and your brethren shall be pleased to put in any private adventures for yourselves in particular you shall be sure to receive, according to the proportion of the Adventure, equal parts with us Adventurers from the beginning. . . .

Because they were appealing to aldermen of so great a City the promoters were content that there should be no difference in status between them and those who had borne the heat and burden of the day: anyone who adventured £40 or more would be immediately made a councillor on exactly the same footing as 'us who have spent double, and trouble as much as is required, abiding the hazard of three several discoveries with much care and diligence and many days attendance. . . .'

Aldermen's deputies could become partners and assistant-councillors for only £25.

Read with a twentieth-century eye, there seems something decidedly untrustworthy about this appeal and the peroration with which the document ends does little to improve matters

And thus, as an action concerning God and the advancement of religion, the present ease, future honour and safety of the Kingdom, the strength of our Navy, the visible hope of a great and rich trade, with many secret blessings not yet discovered, we wholly commend the cause to the wisdom and zeal of yourselves and your brethren, and you and it and us all to the holy protection of the Almighty.

The Cutlers, in their wisdom, seem not to have been greatly impressed. The early results of the expeditions were disastrously bad – the quality of the settlers, of all classes, was appalling and the motley crew were quickly decimated by disease, shipwreck and Red Indians. It was soon clear that there was little profit to be expected from that quarter. There were occasional lotteries to raise funds for the Colony and, on one occasion, 100 wretched vagrant children were shipped out there. In 1612 the Cutlers' Company, under repeated pressure, adventured ten pounds: by this time, in any case, they were deeply involved in the second of the two adventures – that of the Plantation of Ulster.

It had long been an article of faith in English political thinking that the best solution to the eternal Irish problem would be to settle that difficult country with Protestant Englishmen. The confiscation of the estates belonging to the Earls of Tyrconnel and Tyrone provided an opportunity to secure the land necessary for the operation and, in the same manner as in the case of Virginia, suitable citizens were invited to become emigrants or, at any rate, to invest in Irish property. On 1 July 1609 came a precept 'for the Plantation of Ireland.' It was accompanied by a printed book on the subject and to London was granted the first opportunity 'of so worthy an action which like is to prove pleasing to Almighty God, Honorable to this City and profitable to the Undertakers. . . .'

The most substantial men of the Company were to be called together and from their number four men of judgement and experience were to be chosen to join with similar representatives from other Companies. They were to act as a joint-committee to confer with the King's Council of the Realm of Ireland about the project. It seems that the Cutlers, in common with the other Livery Companies, wanted no part in the scheme for, three weeks after the precept, there came a complaint that 'by reason of some mistaking, the committee . . . made answer in writing before any conference had with his Majesty's said Council of Ireland which was ill-accepted by the Lords of His Majesty's Privy Council as hath been publicly delivered at a full assembly. . . .'

Now that the Companies had heard the explanations about the likely profitability of the adventure all their members were to be called together – their yeomanry as well – and all their names taken so that their intentions might be known, and recorded, in a matter of such great consequence.

(It may be noted that this was a favourite and effective device often employed by those such as the Council who were responsible for raising large quantities of voluntary subscriptions: anyone refusing to volunteer was summoned before the Council and asked to state publicly the reasons for his refusal.)

On 26 July the members of the Cutlers' Company assembled at the Hall and the details of the scheme were read out to them. The Court reported soberly to the organizers 'But none will be Undertakers in your Plantation but divers willingly will be Adventurers. And many will contribute in small sums so that they may be advertized how their contributions shall be disposed of or what profit may produce for the same and to whom. Some being contributors of 10s. and some of 5s. which does not amount to above £40.'

Such a derisory response led the promoters to indulge in a publicity display. A conducted tour of the Irish Lands was arranged for selected persons of influence in the City. They were received with every kind of blandishment and shewn all the roads and properties that would create the best impression. It was a successful promotional scheme, the visitors reported favourably both on the properties they had seen and on the likely profitability of the venture: the City decided to raise £15,000.

This, the Privy Council decided, was insufficient – they must raise at least £20,000. In January 'the year of our Lord God according to the computation of the Church of England one thousand sixteen hundred and ten' – a strange variation in style – a precept for this sum was issued: the assessments were to be based upon the payments of corn money and the money was to be raised in each Company by a poll tax. In exchange the City was promised the interest in 400,000 acres of land. The Cutlers' share of this forced investment amounted to £90. A quarter of this sum was to be raised immediately and paid before the Feast of our Blessed Mary the Virgin next ensuing on 10 February.

On 8 March it was pointed out to the Cutlers that they had made default, either in part or in whole: they must not only pay immediately but they must take notice that the second instalment was due before the Annunciation of Blessed Mary. Any member of the Company who refused or failed to pay was to be committed to one of the City Compters and the Mayor was to be instantly informed of the fact.

By the beginning of August the Company's corn assessment had been raised to 40 quarters and, therefore, the third instalment of their Irish Land money was proportionately increased from £22 10s. to £30. There were still arrears owing on the first two instalments. Their position was beginning to become untenable and worse was to happen. On 21 January 1611 it became clear that the money they had already spent was likely to be irrecoverable. They were asked if they would accept still further lands in Ulster 'in lieu of moneys by you already disbursed or hereafter to be disbursed . . . and so to build and plant the same at your own costs and charges.' All such work had to be carried out to specifications laid down in the Book of Plantation. Or would they refer the letting and management of their lands to the Governor and Assistants of the Irish Society? To this the Cutlers replied that they would accept the lands but would not themselves plant them: they would leave their management to the Society.

At the end of February the final thirty-pound instalment of their proportion was due. The same threats attended its demand and, as usual, arrears were sought.

There was an additional complication. The Cutlers were warned that before 13 March 'you must signify your consent in writing . . . that you will accept of your proportionate share of the County lands and manage the same at your own Charges as eighteen Companies have already agreed to do.' They were still, however, permitted to entrust the management to the Irish Society who would build on the land and let or dispose of the properties.

By July a serious situation had been reached. The Society reported that the twenty thousand pounds raised with such difficulty had all been spent. Another ten thousand pounds was needed, of which the Cutlers' share was sixty pounds: they were to call their members together and ask them whether they would accept this new assessment: if they refused they would lose everything they had already paid. The first instalment of £30 must be collected at once. The Cutlers agreed. There was really very little else they could reasonably do. A year later, in 1612, they still owed £30 when the next instalment fell due. They paid off one sum but by October the other was still owing: on the thirteenth of the month the Master and wardens were told that they must pay within seven days or face imprisonment and such other punishment 'as the quality of the Contempt shall deserve.' Those individuals who had not paid were warned that they would be considered to have ceased to participate and their previous payments would all be lost. Ten per cent interest was charged on all arrears: in May 1613 by the time everything had been paid off another £10,000 was demanded from the City. Somehow – by taking the money still owing out of the 'Treasury' or Communal chest on at least one occasion – the money was raised and in December of that year a reckoning took place. Forty thousand pounds in all had been raised by the City. Those Irish estates as were divisible were divided into twelve equal parts: one part was allocated to each of the Twelve Great Companies who had subscribed £3333. 6s. 8d. and any major Company that had not subscribed such a sum was joined to a number of minor Companies whose subscriptions would bring the amount to the requisite figure. Thus the Salters who had only raised £1954 were joined in Division 10 with the Dyers, who had raised £580, with the Saddlers contributing £390, with the Cutlers, whose total now amounted to £225 and, finally, with the tiny Company of Woolmen who had collected £20.

Although the conveyance of the proportions was made by the Irish Society to the Chief Companies and their Associates it was the major company in each division who, in fact, had the sole right of management, without any voice on the part of the Associates. Such properties as woods, ferries and fisheries which were deemed insusceptible of division were retained by the Irish Society who received the rents and profits and accounted for them to the twelve chief companies.

Thus was established the Protestant settlement of Londonderry and Coleraine. By 1615 the first of what were to become quite reasonable dividends were being paid to the Companies. Three hundred and fifty years later when, fortunately, the Companies no longer had any connection with the Province, the Plantation of Ulster paid dividends of a very different kind.

A Company Divided

1611-1625

THE Irish lands were, henceforth, to provide a continual source of work for the Court but, during the years since the first precept in 1609, they had been faced with other problems and other expenses.

As has been stated, their precept for grain had been increased and, with it, had come a demand for a contribution towards building new granaries at Bridewell. In January 1612 they were ordered to provide 60 quarters of foreign wheat and in March – since the Livery Companies' record of compliance with such orders shewed an inclination towards delay – they were further commanded to state in writing how much grain they had already bought and where they stored it. The Cutlers answered that they had 30 quarters of wheat which was stored in the Clothworkers' granary at the Bridgehouse. The rest they would provide as soon as possible: they would, in fact, have done so already if they had anywhere to store it. Since they had contributed to the new granaries at Bridewell might they not be allocated some space there?

In July that year the stocks of grain began to be called upon: every Wednesday two quarters of wheat-meal were to be taken by the Cutlers to the meal market in Leaden Hall. 'And there sold to poor people by the half peck, peck, half bushel, and not more than a bushel each.'

In fact, although the grain precepts presented a continual call upon their finances, it was quite common for the money to be eventually recovered in full. Only if there had been damage to the stored grain or if – an unlikely eventuality at this period – there had been a fall in the price did they lose more than the time and effort involved. As with grain so it was with coals – in 1611 the Company's assessment was for forty sacks of great coals: these, too, were eventually disposed of without appreciable loss.

This principal of financing the supply of necessities to avoid price fluctuations and, perhaps, profiteering, was capable of extension. In August 1611 Mr John Porter, one of the Court, 'brought in a paper tending in effect to the public good of this mistery. That there may be consideration had by this Company for the making a stock for the buying of wares, as well [those] which shall be brought into this kingdom, as for the taking and buying of wares which shall be made by the workmen of this Company and afterwards to be vented by the Company. And this Company and board have thought upon it. And . . . referred it to a Committee.'

No more is heard of this scheme. It seems likely that the merchants of the Company were not over-enthusiastic at the idea.

It will be seen that the administrative business of the Company was now considerable: it cannot have been made any easier by the division caused by the dispute between the working and non-working cutlers. This continued against the background of a general spirit of unrest in the City. In April 1611 the Company were called together to hear an Act of Common Council

for reforming of the abuse growing by reason of the excess and strange fashion of apparel used by many apprentices and by the inordinate pride of maid servants and women servants in their excess of apparel and folly in variety of new fashions and to admonish them to have a due and special care to see speedy reformation had in everyone of their servants So as they may avoid the same penalties in the said Act contained.

Authority has always been worried by the revolutionary attitude of the young as expressed in their clothing or hair styles but, at this particular stage of the Cutlers' history, authority, in the form of the Court of the Company, was itself not setting a very good example in the divisiveness and in the further upsurge of strife that, as we shall see, was very shortly to arise once more. In the meantime, on the surface, all appeared unruffled and the social life of the Company, connected as it was with the daily administration of

M

affairs, continued. Although the Account Dinner of 1611 – nine messes of meat and eight dishes to a mess – was held at the Hall – most of the occasions of feasting were held at taverns. It seems probable that, in spite of the kitchens in the Cutlers' Hall, it was then easier and the results more satisfactory to eat on the premises of a professional caterer. And a list of such functions held during the Company year 1611–1612 is not without interest in giving a fairly comprehensive picture of the Cutlers' Court activities:

16 July	Paul's Head	Dinner at the eating of the venison given by Mr Johnson
18 July	Swan	Supper after Court
23 July	Mermaid	Dinner on View Day
31 July	(Hall)	Account Dinner
5 Aug.	Paul's Head	Dinner for Gowries Day
6 Aug.	Swan	Dinner for Search Day
5 Sept.	Swan	Court Supper
26 Sept.	Swan	Dinner the day the poor were paid
4 Oct.	Mitre	Dinner by Mr Hawes, Mr Plunkett, Mr Johnson, the Renter, and others in visiting Mr Hatfield in his heaviness
9 Oct.	Paul's Head	Supper when the Master and Wardens conferred about a gown for Mr Ashott
15 Oct.	Paul's Head	Eating of Mr Johnson's venison
29 Oct.	(Hall)	Dinner on Mayor's Oath Day
5 Nov.	Paul's Head	Gunpowder Day
21 Nov.	Swan	Dinner for Search Day
26 Nov.	Swan	Supper the Day the Assistants were sworn
6 Dec.	Mitre	Dinner. Coal distribution day
20 Jan.	Swan	Court Day supper
10 Feb.	Three Cranes	Court Day supper
3 March	Three Cranes	Supper for Search Day
18 March	Mitre	Dinner. Coal Day
24 March	Mitre	King's Day dinner
– April	Mitre	Dinner at sealing of Mr Clarke's lease
6 May	Mitre	Dinner for Search Day
6 June	(Hall)	Buns and wine at Election of Master
	Mitre	Dinner after Election
16 June	Mitre	Court Day Supper
20 June	Mitre	The paying of the Poor
24 June	Mitre	Midsummer Dinner.

However, in October that year, the Cutlers were told that they were 'to be spared this year the Guildhall Feast' to which they usually sent an allotted number of representatives at the Company's expense.

The Prince had decided 'to grace the Guildhall with his presence and that of the Count Palatine Elector and other great Estate of foreign nations and divers of the Peers and Nobility of the Realm.'

The number involved meant – especially as it was desired that the Prince and his Company should sit in view of all the guests – that there would not be room for even the usual number of representatives from the Twelve Great Companies. The Master and warden were, therefore, instructed to call the Company together and 'persuade them not to take it in ill part but for this one time to be pacified. . . .'

Pacified they seem to have been and pacified they also eventually were after an incident involving the yeomanry, an incident which must, at first sight, have seemed as though it was the opening shot in some revolutionary demonstration. For when the Master and wardens of the Livery came, in January 1612, to the Hall to read out the Trade Marks book the wardens – there were four of them that year – and assistants of the yeomanry 'were at the Tavern . . . and were not in place to sit down and take their place when the others of the Company did sit down. . . . But the Master and his Wardens were fain to send for them at the Tavern, which offence was generally, by the Master and Wardens and Assistants and Livery, taken in evil part. And thereupon, in the open Hall, before all the Company, they were rebuked. And fined. As aforesaid.' They were, in fact, fined, variously, 12d. and 6d. each but so far from exhibiting an attitude of revolt they were overcome with apologies and even produced two excuses where one would have been sufficient. ' . . . They acknowledged the offence And by protestation and apology by them made that their going was only in Love to give to their late Warden Catle a pint of wine, who was to go to Ratcliff and could not, by reason of the lateness of the evening, tarry. And also that their only Ancient, John A Lee was not well [so] they went to comfort him.'

The Master and wardens, to whom the fines properly belonged, were pleased to be gracious. ' . . . after every man had paid and laid down his fine upon their submission aforesaid and promised not to give [again] any such evil [they] delivered to every man his fine again.'

There, with a display of rather self-conscious magnanimity, the matter ended. But the constitutional split in the Company was once again to become embarrassingly apparent.

The first hint of the troubles to come arose in November 1611 when three members of the Company were summoned to the Hall and accused of abusing one of the wardens, Miles Banks. As it happened, the evidence was conflicting and it proved impossible to decide which one of the three had actually been abusive: the Court were compelled to fall back on the device of dismissing the case but warning the accused that if they got into trouble again the present offence would be remembered and taken into consideration. Then, early in the new year, Banks complained in open Court and 'laid down many wild words which Mr Oliver Plunket should call him.' The Court wished only, after the previous disagreements, 'to set them at peace and unity' and left it to the wisdom of the Master, Reynold Greene, to achieve this end.

At the same time it was hoped that the Master would also settle the quarrel that Banks, by making offensive observations, had picked with Christopher Hatfield. For the moment reason seems to have prevailed: Miles Banks undertook a second year of office as younger Warden and presented the Company with the piece of plate – in this case a silver-gilt tankard – customary on such occasions.

That the quarrel was still that of the working cutlers against the members in other trades is indicated by a restatement in the Minutes 'No person or persons to be debarred from being Master and Wardens of this House' so long as they were free of the Company and lived in the City or its purlieus. Nor, in accordance with the Charter, did he have to be a working-cutler.

Once again an uneasy truce prevailed for a time at the meetings of the Court. A palpable non-working cutler, William Segar,

Garter King of Arms, was 'elected and chosen a brother of this Company to be warned of all our solemn meetings.'

At these meetings the normal work of the Company had still to go on uninfluenced, so far as was possible, by the partisans of either side. Much of the business of the Court was taken up with the affairs of apprentices, of whom there were now as many as eighty-seven. Apart from enrolling them, turning them over to new masters, disciplining them, protecting their interests and seeing that they obeyed the various sumptuary and disciplinary laws, there were other problems. One master, contrary to the orders of the Company, sold his apprentice to another; a master was fined for enticing an apprentice; a third master locked his apprentice out and the Court sent the Beadle to take the boy to the master's house with the order that, if he were not received into service, the Lord Mayor's officer was to be summoned. There was all the usual business of controlling the established traders: for a fee of 10d. marks were registered; any one who wished to sell his Mark to another was licensed to do so upon the payment of various fees – 2s. 6d. to the Company, one shilling to each of the wardens, the Master and the Clerk, and 6d. to the Beadle; a chapman from Coventry was summoned to the Hall for selling at Bartholomew Fair counterfeit knives struck with the London mark of the dagger and, even though he pleaded ignorance and promised never to buy or sell any more of the same sort, they confiscated his knives. Their searches were sometimes made more difficult by the attitude of those searched: even one of their own wardens of the Yeomanry shewed 'unreverent behaviour' towards the Master and his wardens. He was fined 20s. (which he refused to pay), dismissed from his office and proscribed from being an Assistant of the junior body 'until he be better reformed.'

The usual feastings that perhaps compensated, to some degree, for any unpleasantness that might arise, were greatly restricted. In May 1614 it was noted that 'all kinds of victuals are somewhat scant'. The prices, moreover, were excessive partly because of the usual unseasonable weather and partly (so it was somewhat mysteriously alleged) because 'the Commonest of people' were in the habit of repairing to Parliament to find out the prices – both of which factors it was considered were likely to make the rates rise rather than fall. 'And whereas the accustomed times for the Companies of the City to make their feasts doth now approach, which will also be an occasion to enhance the price of victuals. . . .' the Cutlers were ordered to be 'very sparing in the provision of diet and provide only what shall be needful and necessary and not to exceed in the same.'

In June, therefore, the Court decided to make neither feasts nor dinners. But they nonetheless declared, in October, that if the Lord Mayor was going to have his usual dinner at Guildhall then they, too, would have their own customary feast 'unless there is a commandment to the contrary, with eight messes and eight dishes to a mess – viz. Capons in white broth, Butter and Cullets, Long and Greenfish, salted salmon, eel pies and mince pies, Capons roasted, Custards and either smelts, warden pies or larks.'

Whether they dined on this occasion or not, they would give the usual £6 to the Lord Mayor 'to gratify him.'

Among their other business there was, too, the continued pressure of levies of money for Ireland. The Salters might be organizing the management of the joint estates but there was still much money to be raised. Everything about the project had cost more than had been estimated: in January 1616, another £7500 was needed from the City. £5000 must be raised speedily, by the end of the month; the remainder was to be paid by the beginning of May.

The Cutlers' contribution was fixed at £45 which, rather than submit to all the trouble of trying to raise the sum from individual cutlers, they took out of the Treasury of the Company. Later that year they were to be asked for another £30 but in the meantime they had received the first of their dividends on the Irish Plantation. It came from the fishing rights and the amount accruing to the group headed by the Salters was £80. The Cutlers had, by this time, paid out nearly £300. Now they got back £4. 17s. 2½d. It was a beginning. And there was clearly more to come, for the Salters, on behalf of themselves and their associates, granted a sixty-year Lease of the properties at the rate of £160 a year.

The emigration policy of the Crown was beginning to show results.

The emigrants of one nation are, unfortunately, the immigrants of another. And London was finding itself faced with an immigration problem. In July 1615 the Lord Mayor requested the Livery Companies to make a note of all the grievances they had against strangers born and other foreigners and submit them to the City authorities for consideration how redress might be made.

The Cutlers were quick to reply:

The number of them are many and without the liberties and suburbs are grown to hundreds who not only sell their wares in deceivable manner in the King's Highness' Court, highways, streets, inns, gentlemen's houses and chambers, and suchlike places But also to Ironmongers, Brokers and other such persons that do intrude into the same their occupation To the undoing of the said Company. . . .

Furthermore, aliens imported ready-made cutlery 'and the same to Personages of great worth do put to sale.' The Cutlers' Company had, they said, long endeavoured to put an end to this state of affairs by Acts of Parliament. But some of the offenders 'being countenanced by great Personages have prevailed . . . and the said Company discouraged.'

The problem of dealing with the immigrants was, however, complicated by the fact that many of them had 'grown aged and got large families and cannot be suppressed without great calumniation to the Company and a great charge on the parishes they live in.'

The Company suggested that all aliens coming to the City should be viewed from time to time and if it were found that they were intending to settle, an attempt should be made, there and then, to remove them. This would not cost the parish very much and 'the redress will of itself, as we think, follow.'

The problem was, however, one that proved to be remarkably enduring.

Such day-to-day difficulties were, as always, interspersed with the lighter relief of public pomp and ceremony. In October 1616 a precept was received for the reception of Prince Charles coming from Richmond to Westminster to be made Prince of Wales. There were thirty-six barges involved with all the usual accoutrements including the Companies' Banners and streamers and – a new touch – 'Trumpets or other Loud Music.'

The flotilla was to form up in two lines, in order of Company precedence, near the Three Cranes by eight o'clock in the morning. Room was to be left between the two ranks for the Mayor's Barge to row through to take up its position at the head of the station. Then all were to proceed up-stream. When the Lord Mayor met the Prince, all the barges were to stop, turn round and return in reverse order until they reached Westminster where they were to stop and allow the Mayor and the Prince and his nobles to sail through the two lines of barges. When the great personages were safely disembarked everyone could go home. It seemed likely to be a long day: every Company was to carry in its barge twelve torches 'to light my Lord Mayor home if need shall be.'

There was a certain note of unease in the precept. There had been an earlier occasion in 1610 when Henry, the previous Prince of Wales who had died two years later, had been received on the river Thames by the City. Evidently things had been less than perfectly organized on that occasion: the Lord Mayor wanted no repetition of the sort of débâcle that, reading between the lines, can be clearly seen to have occurred. He issued a second, similar, precept in which the instructions were set out in more simple terms. The number of barges taking part had risen to fifty. The Mayor wished, he said, to avoid 'the confusion and errors committed in former times.' Instead of everyone dispersing independently after the show was ended, the flotilla was to proceed downstream from Westminster in orderly manner, line up between the Three Cranes and Bridewell, and let the Mayor sail through to disembark first. During all the proceedings the Companies were exhorted to keep their barges at a distance of forty feet behind one another with eighty feet between the two ranks. They were to try and keep in line, both to make the passage easier and 'the view more comely and pleasant. . . . Likewise that every barge row slowlier, lest disorder happen.'

There was another Royal occasion the following year when the

King was to be accompanied from the causeway at Knightsbridge to the Court at St. James and to his Palace at Westminster 'with no less show than was put on for [her] late Majesty.'

In addition to the Master and wardens there were to be four of the most grave, tall and comely personages of the Company, all to be well horsed and apparelled in velvet coats and chains of gold. Every man was to be attended by a footman carrying two staff torches and all were to be ready by one o'clock in the afternoon. (It may here be remarked that chains of gold were no indication of the wealth or status of corporations or individuals: they were customarily hired for the occasion.)

The Cutlers, nonetheless, seem to have been at the time in a reasonable degree of affluence. They were able to lend out money every year to suitable members of the Company: in 1617 eight loans, of which the largest was £10, were made to a total outlay of sixty-three pounds. There was even a very welcome allowance to the Master and wardens 'towards our ladies gowns, viz to every one of us 20s. a year.' Their properties were well managed and they were able to command a premium of £350 for a thirty-three year lease, at £20 a year, for the Belle Sauvage.

There was, however, still a degree of uncertainty – pretended or otherwise – about their title to those lands previously devoted to the so-called superstitious uses. The Cutlers had no doubt thought, in 1607, when they had paid for an Act of Parliament to 'strengthen and confirm' their properties, that they would be at last free from the blackmailing patentees of Concealed Lands. Once again they had been wrong: in 1618 the whole weary and expensive business was to be done again. A precept containing a number of notes and questions about their lands was received. Among other properties called into question was Woolsack Alley in the Hounds-ditch estate. The Cutlers were not alone in their trouble. In May the Lord Mayor announced that he and the Court of Aldermen, on behalf of the whole City, had petitioned the King to confirm and secure all the land holdings there. The Master and wardens were authorized to go to the Recorder, take counsel's opinion and to agree to any fine or compounding that might prove necessary. The Master and wardens accordingly went twice to see Sir Thomas

Wolverton, the King's Attorney; they consulted the Recorder of London; they took counsel's opinion and conferred also with Mr. Jones, the Common Sergeant of London. At the end of the discussions they told the two latter to 'compound and use their discretion' to settle the affair. It proved an expensive settlement. When, in May 1619, the King confirmed the Land holdings of all the City Companies, the cost to the Cutlers for their share was £110. Nor, whatever might be professed, was this, necessarily, the end of the affair. It was not, in fact, until 1623 – by which time other Companies had been again attacked – that an Act was passed which made their lands secure.

However, for the while, they were reassured and enjoyed their rents, and the occasions on which they inspected their estates, in peace and quiet.

Their relationship with their tenants seems generally to have been good – the principal tenant of the Catherine Wheel Estate at Egham, Gilbert Clarke, citizen and grocer, went so far as to present the Company with a very fine loving-cup.

It was unfortunate that their own relationships, one with the other, were less satisfactory.

It had long been the custom that each of the offices of Master, Senior Warden and Junior Warden was held for two years with a gap of at least one year before being promoted from the lower positions. There had never been any option of paying a fine to avoid service. Then, sometime in the first part of the seventeenth century, it was enacted that the ancient and increasingly invidious duties could be avoided on the payment of twenty nobles – £6. 13s. 4d. And in 1617 the Upper Warden actually refused service and elected to be fined. It was an unwelcome break with tradition – 'this Court finding many inconveniences to arise hereby.' Not the least of the inconveniences was, no doubt, that recently the 'younger sort of the Livery' had 'made Combination together to bring in Innovation': they supposed that anybody who had been elected Master or Warden could demand to be excused. They objected in any case to having to serve two years.

The Court made a desperate attempt to maintain the ancient traditions of voluntary service.

For the future good of the Company it is ordered and decreed that from henceforth no manner of persons so elected . . . Master, Upper Warden or Under Warden shall continue less time in their service places than two years according to the old and Ancient orders of this Company Unless there be especial cause found to the contrary by Judgement of this Court. And that none shall escape the said service by way of fine but by like Judgement. . . .

There was, then, to be no automatic opting out: only the Court could give permission. As for the amount of fine to be paid, if permission were given, that would not be fixed: it would depend in each case upon the circumstances in which office was refused. It was not a very happy, or indeed a practicable, ruling: to insist on some unwilling member actually taking up office was not likely to improve the efficiency of that office. Eventually, of course, the rule had quietly to be dropped and soon – certainly by 1627 – those who actually chose to serve as officers were doing so for one year only. In the meantime the troubles in the Court continued. William Langton, one of the working cutlers, who as a Liveryman had been greatly involved in 'the disorderly practices' attending the elections during the early days of the constitutional struggle, proved to be just as troublesome now that he had come upon the Court. For, after George Harberd had paid his fine of twenty nobles to escape the duties of Under Warden, Langton approached Henry Addams, one of his fellow-assistants, and asked him how much of the fine he had received, implying that he believed that there had been an illicit share-out of the money. Such action was clearly indictable for 'indecency' because the Master was reasonably felt to be impugned by such a slanderous suggestion. When charged with this offence Langton was quite unable to deny the accusation but he made such a 'simple' sort of reply that the Court was at first unable to come to any decision. The matter was adjourned and, before the Court could meet again, Langton added to his offence by some remarks that he made about the case to a member named Stubbs who was not even on the Court. He was asked what more he could find to say by way of excuse for his offence? He not only made no reply but failed to attend the meeting. In his absence the Court declared that his remarks to Stubbs were 'not well taken by this Company.' Nor – and this was perhaps the root of the problem – was his 'combination with those of the younger sort' at all popular with his colleagues. They decided that until he made a sufficient apology he was 'from henceforth not to be summoned to any meeting at this house.' His behaviour, as a member of the Court, was reprehensible enough. But worse was to follow. The deep-seated malaise in the Company was fully revealed when, at the elections of 1617, Miles Banks became Master. At the first meeting of his year of office it is to be remarked that although there were fourteen assistants present – a marginal increase on the usual number attending – the majority of them were not those who had regularly served the previous Master. The Beadle, so he said, had given everyone due and proper notice of the meeting. But those who had not turned up had all made different excuses for their inability to attend. Those who were present sat

and continued till about Eleven of the Clock and, none of the masters appearing, the Master, master Miles Banks, did lay open the cause of his warning the Court which, in effect, was: First, he found himself aggrieved that the masters would not accompany him, according to former custom, on the day of his election to his house where he had in kind manner provided for them a Banquet. Next, that having solemnly bidden them and their wives to dinner at his Oath Dinner, against which time he had made provision according as other men had done, they, the said masters, after they had given to the Master and his Wardens their Oaths, pretended other business. And the Master and his Wardens for their part expecting the dinner of the said masters and their wives none of them did come. But went and dined elsewhere: which unkind dealing . . . the Master and his Wardens aggrieving at it, did summon this Court to know the cause why the said masters should be offended. And that if he and his Wardens (James Tackley and Nicholas Skinner) had given any cause of offence they might reconcile themselves . . . for that they would have no rancour or malice grow in the Company.

Upon which allegations of the said Master and Wardens of their griefs aforesaid this Court did think it good that there be a time taken by the Master and his Wardens, at their pleasure, to warn anew the said masters to know the true cause of their absenting. And that in the meantime the Court will take no order till they hear what the said masters can say in their defence.

The trouble was undoubtedly based in the continuing deep-seated constitutional dispute between the working and non-working cutlers. Miles Banks, so the past-Masters and other 'Ancients' complained to the Court of Aldermen, had allied himself with the 'younger sort' who were, for the most part, actively engaged in the cutlery trade and had persuaded them to elect him Renter as well as Master, setting aside John Porter the member who was due that year for the rentership.

The aldermen at once ordered Banks to give up the post of Renter. He refused, and six weeks later was sent to Newgate. His Master's account for that year actually includes the sum of £21. 18s. 2d. spent 'in the controversy about my commitment to Newgate.' That this sort of behaviour caused him to be disliked seems probable yet a reconciliation did in fact take place.

At the Court of 19 August 1617

the former order concerning unkindness to the Master and Wardens being read . . . (those) as were charged to offend therein having severally answered for themselves and conformed themselves to this Court it appears now . . . there was cause of offence given to the Master and Wardens . . . but the Court, in regard they wish no rent to be in the Company, but that due reverence may be given and continued to the elders of this house, do Order that, if it pleases the Ancient masters and others to acknowledge their errors, then they do . . . order that all former injuries shall be forgot and forgiven and no more repetitions to be had in that business. . . .

Forgiven the matter may have been: Miles Banks, in fact, continued for his two full years as Master. But forgotten it can never have been and the Cutlers' Company must have continued, during all the years that the rivalry between the working cutlers and the non-working cutlers was a matter of practical consequence, to form an uneasy and unhappy brotherhood.

Miles Banks and his Court were thus, at any rate nominally, reconciled and William Langton, too, came before the assistants and apologized humbly 'for the former speeches he had been charged with. . . . Upon which words he was dismissed. And the court think good, upon summons the next Court to be given, he shall be received in his former place.'

They were less forgiving to the Beadle, James Whetstone, against whom 'divers demeanours were objected . . . for which abuses most part of this Court gave consent [that] he shall, for a time, be removed. . . .'

It was perhaps fortunate that during this time of division there occurred a number of problems involving the trade, and therefore the welfare, of the whole Company which tended to hold the two warring factions together.

In 1619, for example, the goldbeaters of London received a charter of Incorporation. The immediate result was a petition to Parliament made jointly by the Cutlers, the Painter Stainers – many of whom were themselves goldbeaters – and the Bookbinders. Their general ground for complaint was that gold and silver leaf (foliat) had long been imported from abroad. Now some thirty persons skilled in the art had combined together for their private advantage and, with the assistance of Dr Eglesham, one of His Majesty's physicians, and Sir Henry Bretton, 'had obtained the grant of a charter for the sole making of gold and silver leaf and a proclamation prohibiting the import of those articles from abroad.'[153]

They noted, for what it was worth, that Dr Eglesham had been awarded a salary of £200 and Sir Henry was receiving £50 a year for his part in the affair.

The Cutlers and the other petitioners complained that they were now forced to buy the foliat from the new Corporation. Six Goldbeater wardens controlled the sale of the material from Goldbeaters' Hall: great oaths had been taken that it should be sold nowhere else, at no lower prices and by nobody other than they. The Cutlers, as a result, now had to pay 15s. for gold leaf which had previously cost them 12s. For silver leaf that had cost them 20s., they must now pay 30s. Worse still was alleged: the leaf was now 'thinner and deceitfuller.' It faded quickly, too – a great disgrace to all who used it.

The Goldbeaters seemed to be quite ruthless – certainly as ruthless as the Cutlers themselves had been – against those who sought to break the monopoly. The petitioners alleged that a craftsman named Spencer who had tried to work in secret places was chased from one hide-out to another: eventually, his tools were confiscated, he was imprisoned and a £400 action brought against him. And when the petitioners, in their charity, tried to help him financially and secure his release from prison, the Gold-beaters, through their Clerk, Norton, exhibited a forty-six-page complaint to the Attorney General in Star Chamber, accusing the petitioners (and their wives) of 'molestation'. It had cost them £20 to defend themselves.

The Cutlers, at least, must have been well aware from their own past experiences that a simple plea ad misericordiam was apt to be ineffective if not accompanied by some patriotic appeal tending towards the public good. In this case they chose to take their stand on the matter of economics. The Goldbeaters used bullion valued at between £3000 and £4000 every year: this could otherwise be used for making coins and if imports of foliat were once again allowed there would be more bullion available and, therefore, more coinage to help trade and traders.

The petitioners anticipated one of the Goldbeaters' replies: the latter would allege that the foliat formerly imported from the Low Countries was 'base gold and made deceitfully' whereas it was just as good as the Goldbeaters' product, and cheaper too.

They exposed the scandalous fact that when they had com-plained to the Goldbeaters about the price and the thinness of the leaf the alleged reply had been that they 'had better be content for if they did find fault therewith they would pay more for the same' – a threat in the best traditions of monopolists everywhere.

To this destructive petition the Goldbeaters made a most reason-able reply: ever since 1486 the import of gold and silver leaf had, they said, in fact been forbidden. The deceitful imported foreign product was used only by the Painters and the Bookbinders: the Cutlers had always used the Goldbeaters' foliat but if it turned out that they had also been using imported material then they had been doing so contrary to the law. Goldbeating, they continued, had for centuries been an English trade and it should be controlled under charter in the same way that other trades were controlled. In answer to the specific charges brought against them, they admitted that they had given gratuities to get their charter but the money for them had come out of their corporate funds and they were no more than any other Company had done; the bullion they used was foreign bullion worth no more than £2500 and their charter expressly provided that no one might exercise the craft until he had signed a £500 bond not to use any English bullion or coinage to make the leaf; there had, certainly, been a rise in prices but this had merely kept pace with the general rise in the cost of living; they denied utterly that they had threatened to raise prices still further if complaints were made; they sold the foliat at their Hall because that was where it was brought to be viewed – an obvious convenience which was operated without the wardens making any personal profit; it was quite untrue that the leaf had become thinner since Incorporation; certainly, they agreed they had persecuted Spencer – he had been the prime mover in obtaining their Charter and had then refused to pay any of the dues for which he had given his bond. Finally they admitted to creating a monopoly: the same, they said, could be argued against all the other Livery Companies. They ended with the powerful counter-allegation that the Cutlers and their allies had made the petition for unworthy reasons: before the Goldbeaters' Charter his Majesty's subjects had no idea of the price of gold and silver leaf because the manufacturers were few and their whereabouts not generally known. The Cutlers and the others had, therefore, been able to buy the foliat and charge two or three times the price for what they used in their own manufacturing processes. Now they were afraid that the nobility and gentry would know the price, would buy the gold and silver leaf themselves and give it to the petitioners to be worked – thus cutting down their inordinate profits.

On 12 July 1620 the matter came before the Privy Council at Whitehall. They, because of the allegation that the ban on imports was 'a great cause of interruption and stand of trade in some of the most staple merchandizes of the kingdom, think fit and order that Mr Secretary Calvert, Mr Chancellor of the Exchequer, the Master of the Rolls, Sir Edward Coke, knight, and the Master of the Wards, or any three of them . . .' should consult eminent lawyers and call before them representatives of the Goldbeaters and the Cutlers to discuss the matter.

This, no doubt, they did but the result of their deliberations is not recorded: according to one authority,[154] the Goldbeaters' patent of incorporation was overthrown. Certainly they seem to have bothered the Cutlers no more.

Of far greater importance was the problem that confronted them at the same time: the quality of the steel available to the manufacturing trade. Gold and silver leaf was a pleasant and profitable adjunct to their business. It was of artistic rather than strictly necessary worth. But steel was the *sine qua non* – without it there would be no cutlery and no cutlers – and there were growing complaints about the standard of steel, particularly of the steel made in England.

On 20 November 1617 the artisans of the Company petitioned the Court

tending in effect for the reformation of bad steel and for no Imbarment of foreign steel but that they may be at their pleasures to buy for their good what they may. And that the Master and Wardens would be pleased, for the general good of this mistery, to join in suit with them to the Lords of the Council for reformation. . . .

The Court agreed that the Master and wardens should, at the expense of the artisans, join in such a petition 'whereby no Imbarment may be made or had of [foreign] steel': it was to be drawn up in the name of the Company as a whole.

The trouble arose, as usual, from a monopoly.

This had been granted to Sir Basil Brooke and the trouble that led to the artisans' petition came to a head early in 1619 in a spate of complaints.

First of all, on 25 February, there was the certificate of certain cutlers, blacksmiths and locksmiths protesting that steel made by Sir Basil Brooke, under a patent granted to two manufacturers, Elliot and Meysey, was worthless: they requested permission to use foreign steel, as they had previously done, until the case which was pending in the Court of Exchequer had been settled.[155]

Then, the same month, the old patentees made a statement about the badness of the steel: they offered to pay £5000 to the King for renewed permission to make steel and promised, at the same time, not to interfere with foreign imports.

N

This was followed by two certificates – one from the men of twelve trades who denounced the badness of Sir Basil's steel, and the other from a number of working smiths, gunmakers, and cutlers in favour of the steel made by one Matthew du Rocher: they appended a list of names of aggrieved users of the inferior steel.

Clearly Sir Basil Brooke was beginning to come under a considerable and well co-ordinated pressure. On 27 June, and again two days later, the Master and wardens went down to Greenwich to see the Privy Council about the matter. And in the first days of July new and powerful allies entered the field – the Deputies of the States General of the United Provinces.

The United Provinces of the Netherlands – so called to distinguish them from the Spanish Netherlands – had long been under attack by Spain but, since 1609, there had been a truce. The Protestant region of Belgium remained under the influence of the English and the French and maintained representatives in London. These deputies now complained to James I that free trade had been interrupted, quite contrary to the treaties between the two countries, 'especially in the commodity of steel by occasion of a Patent granted to Sir Basil Brooke, Knight, for the making of steel within the kingdom and prohibiting the importation of foreign steel. . . .'

The Privy Council 'forasmuch as there had been many complaints likewise made against that patent by such artificers as work in steel' arranged to hear the matter on 2 July when 'the artificers of all trades using steel being present, and specially the cutlers, did complain that the steel made by Sir Basil Brooke is insufficient and unserviceable, and shewed many proofs and instances to make good their allegations. And though some few stood for the patent, yet they did not insist upon the goodness of the steel made for the present, but said they hoped it would still be made better and better, and withall confessed that they wrought Flanders steel in the mixture of steel made by Sir Basil Brooke.'

A long debate ensued: at the end of it the Privy Council ordered that the Attorney-General 'should take a speedy and real course, by way of *quo warranto*, for the voiding of the foresaid patent, and proceed in the prosecution thereof in the Court of Exchequer according to the course of law.'

By the end of November Sir Basil was required to surrender his patent to the Council. He asked that, since he was now acting in the interests of free trade, he might be released from his covenants and from such payments as were due to the Crown. He also asked that he might 'have a new grant for the sole making of steel (without bar of importation) according to the inventions within the use and practice of the former patentees.'

The Council agreed. But, as will be seen, the whole highly-important question of good-quality steel was by no means ended.

In the meantime the business of the Court continued as usual. Most of it was the routine business of regulating trade and trade marks, of administering their estates and of sharing to some lesser extent in the problems of the Irish lands. But one of the search days in 1618 was evidently attended by a certain degree of drama: a warrant was subsequently issued for the arrest of William Cope, a knife-maker, 'for that he abused the Master and his Wardens in their Search, offering to have struck the Master with a Bar of Iron and wounding the Beadle, his Hand and Arm, who by command-ment of the Master and Wardens took into his [care] certain counterfeit blades which were struck by the said William Cope.'

And there was also one of those disputes between master and apprentice which is typical of all such Court business of the period. This time it involved William Banks, the son of the unpopular and controversial Master. '. . . the apprentice did pretend many wrongs offered unto him by his master besides want of diet. And it appeareth that his master, for some fault by the apprentice com-mitted, did give him correction in some sort tolerable and in some other sort that the Court alloweth not well of (if the apprentice doth say true). But it appeareth that the master and apprentice have taken such unkindness, one against the other, that the Court can hardly reconcile them together.'

The master wished to be rid of his apprentice; the apprentice did not wish to stay with his master. The Court, unfortunately, could find no legal reason for cancelling the indentures. So they told the master to take the apprentice into his service 'and to hold him and well use him . . . and not to give him any unreasonable correction.' If he disobeyed and if he did not give the boy enough meat and drink and other things necessary for an apprentice, then the lad would be taken from him – a clear incentive, it might be considered, for the master to disobey the Court. However, for the moment, a reconciliation of a sort took place: the master promised to be good and kind and the apprentice promised to be dutiful and serviceable.

The Court faced, too, the normal demands for the usual commodities – wheat and coal. They received also a precept to report how much gunpowder and match the Company held in store. Their reply was simple and to the point: 'They are altogether unprovided.'

Other Companies were, no doubt, in like state.

In July 1619 the King ordered the City to replenish its stocks: 53,636 pounds of gunpowder were to be bought, together with an appropriate amount of match. The Cutlers' share of this rather large amount of explosive was 322 pounds of powder at 6d. a pound and two bundles of match: they were responsible for taking delivery and for storing it in a safe place – away from fire, it was particularly stressed.

They were still faced with the problem of competition from outsiders trading illicitly in cutlery. In November 1619 the Court of Aldermen considered a complaint by the Cutlers' Company against the 'Country larrymen, cutlers and nailers and their factors, that keep private warehouses within this City and sell by retail to foreigners the cutlers' wares. Contrary to the Charters of this City.'

It was not a problem that the Aldermen found easy to solve. In the following January they suggested that the Masters and wardens of both the Cutlers and the Ironmongers, with any others they thought fit, should meet together and seek a remedy for their own grievances – and for those of any other Company similarly afflicted: they were to 'set down and appoint a place Certain within this City where the Country Larrymen, Cutlers and Nailmen shall sell their wares.' Hardly had they made the ruling than they were faced by another demand from the Cutlers against certain citizens 'for the suppressing of an abuse offered as well in swearing and taking to them foreigns professing the art of Cutlery as also in that, contrary to the King's Majesty's grant to this Company, they give to the same persons, being knife-makers, marks which in right, as this Company do suppose, belong to the granting of this house.'

Before this had been settled a new controversy broke out between the apprentice William Banks and his master James Wright. The boy complained not only of a 'want of meat and other victuals and of instruction in his trade' but that his master had taken away from him patterns which he was keeping to help him in learning his craft. It might be thought that James Wright had seized the opening offered him by the Court on the previous occasion. But it was found that the apprentice, in fact, had no grounds for complaint about meat and drink

for that, if he would, he might have had sufficient for those days he pretended want, but he would not take it when he might have had provision. And for the patterns that were taken from the said apprentice, they were his fellow-apprentice's. And the said master protesteth he did not take the same patterns from him on any purpose to hinder him from the practise of his well-working but is ready and willing, by all the means he may, to further him in good workmanship. And would be ready, upon any request made by the said apprentice, to deliver unto him for his instruction the same patterns, or better, with instruction and information from time to time as he might require. . . .

The Court accepted these protestations and the apprentice again promised to be dutiful: reconciliation was made for a further six months' service.

Into this workaday life there still broke in, from time to time, some Royal occasions.

There was a feeling amongst those responsible for organizing such affairs that the City Companies were somewhat failing in their obligations: there was, for example, a great disorder in 'not coming to the solempnities in their gowns faced with fur accordingly as in ancient time.' A Court of every Company was to be held to work out a decent order of furred gowns, not only in the winter season – from Michaelmas to Easter – but, specially, for those times when there were 'many noble and worthy spectators, as well foreigners as also Native born.' Gowns were to be worn decently in order of precedence; they were not to contain a mixture of furs but were to be fashioned wholly with the pelts appropriate to rank – Budge or Foyne powts or Marteners ('which the chief Companies do wear') or Martens powts.

They were to be properly dressed when, in March 1620, the King came one Sunday to St. Paul's to hear a sermon and the usual call-out of the Company was ordered: there were to be ten whifflers in coats of velvet and chains of gold and the stands were to be strong and well-nailed. The Livery were ordered to repair to their seats and forms in the preaching-place at St. Paul's Cross and to stay there until the service was ended. To make sure that everything went smoothly the rails and so on were to be sent down to Fleet Street the preceding Friday night.

The Court Minutes contain the marginal note:

Sent to Fleet Street for rails, being 18 trestles, 18 rails, 17 boards, 2 turned posts. And there came back but ten trestles, the rest were broken and lost, 17 rails and 16 boards broke, with the two turned posts as they were delivered. And note: strangers stood in the rails, not known from where they came, being of no benefit to this house or to the officers of the house.

Royal occasions were followed by Royal demands. In December the same year the King asked the City for a 'reasonable sum of money' as a contribution

towards recovering the Palatinate already invaded by the enemy, being the Ancient inheritance of His Majesty's son-in-law which is to descend to his Majesty's posterity and a matter of that importance which every good subject is sensible of and how much it doth and may concern His Majesty himself, his Children and Posterity and welfare of his Kingdom and the state of Religion there. . . .

The City gave £5000 of which £30 was the Cutlers' share:

the Livery and divers of the Yeomanry were warned to know what, out of their benevolence, they would give to the King of Bohemia and his Queen, to relieve them in this their distress. And the Livery were contented to give every man 10s a man and the Yeomanry 5s a man.

Since there were thirty-two liverymen and seventy-nine yeomanry and the Company had been asked for only £30 there turned out to be an actual profit made upon the precept which was not at all a usual state of affairs.

And all the while that these matters were engaging their attention the question of the quality of steel was steadily becoming more urgent.

On 8 August 1620 'certain Frenchmen brought in a proof of certain steel made by them in England and desired that the Court would, in their favour, as they found the goodness make certificate thereof.' The Company had only the Frenchmen's word that the stuff was made in England; neither, as yet, had they tested its goodness. The Court, therefore, asked for time to think the matter over: the Frenchmen left some of the steel to be tested.

Towards the end of September, the Privy Council took up the enquiry. They recalled that they had often discussed the matter of making steel in England and had, in fact, withdrawn Sir Basil Brooke's patent. Now, they reported that 'Robert Fludd, doctor of physick, hath, at his great charge, drawn over from foreign parts certain persons, and amongst others one John Rochier, a Frenchman, skilful and expert in making of steel, and being a humble suitor for a patent to set them on work in that mistery for the good of the public, did this day offer to the Board a certificate, under the hands of many cutlers, blacksmiths, locksmiths, and other artificers working in steel, that the steel made by the said Rochier is very serviceable, good and sufficient, and Doctor Fludd further undertaking to make as good steel as any [that] is made in foreign parts, and to vent the same at easier and cheaper rates than the outlandish steel. . . .'

There was a further great selling point: England had suffered a vast energy crisis. The supplies of home-grown timber had come almost to an end; the forests of the Weald had been consumed. There was little wood either for housebuilding or for heating or for industry. Now Doctor Fludd promised that his French steelworkers would 'waste no wood but only make it of pit-coal; that they desire no bar of importation more than what the goodness and cheapness of their stuff shall occasion, and that his Majesty shall have a third part of the profit arising thereby. . . .'

The Privy Council had considered the offer and both they and his Majesty, 'finding it very requisite to have the making of good and serviceable steel within the kingdom, did well approve of the offers made by Doctor Fludd herein and think fit that the letters patents be granted unto him and the said John Rochier upon security to to be first given as well for the making of good and serviceable steel as for ensuring the third part of the profit to his Majesty.'

Two months later the Council, writing to the Solicitor-General, asked him to draw up a warrant: they added the details that the patent should be granted for a period of twenty-one years 'with these prohibitions, that no person be suffered to work after the manner and invention of the patentees, and that none but the patentee and his assignees shall export the steel by them made, lest the realm be thereby disfurnished. . . .' They should be granted a licence to import any oils or other materials necessary for the making or working of steel as long as they paid the appropriate custom duty.

The decision was not without its political repercussions. If they were to make good steel in England they could make good swords there, too, and there would be no need for imports. But orders for weapons had already been tentatively placed overseas and were ready for delivery. The situation was a delicate one. The Privy Council wrote on 15 May 1621 to Sir Dudley Carlton, his Majesty's Ambassador to the United Provinces:

We perceive by your letter . . . that the proportion of arms which by former letters from this Board you were directed to provide and buy in those parts for his Majesty's use is now in a readiness, and that nevertheless you have in your discretion forborne to make any absolute bargain for the same, but are at liberty to take them or leave them, as you shall receive further orders from his Majesty. Wherein, as we do much commend your care and discreet proceeding, so forasmuch as upon further conference with the officers of the Ordinance [and] the Armourers and Cutlers here, it is found that the whole proportion for the arming of 12,000 men may be provided in the kingdom within the time required, and that at more easy rates, and of better condition, than those to be bought there, his Majesty, as well in respect thereof as also for gaining manufacture and affording employment to his own subjects, is pleased to be furnished with the whole complement here at home, and doth therefore require your Lordship to relinquish the bargain you now have in hand for the arms there. . . .

The King wished that there should be no misunderstanding of his motives in making this order.

And lest that upon this occasion there may be any opinion conceived that his Majesty doth any way slack or fall from his former just resolution for recovery of the Palatinate, we pray your Lordship to acquaint his Majesty's son-in-law with the true cause of his forebearing to be furnished with the foresaid arms from thence, which is only his Majesty's gracious care for the relief and employment of his own subjects, in supplying his occasions, especially upon such advantageous conditions, . . . and no alteration at all of his purpose for the defence and recovery of the Palatinate in case the course by treaty, now in prosecution, (whereof his Majesty ever hath and still doth conceive good hopes) shall not succeed.

This much you may likewise make known to such others as your Lordship may think fit and particularly to Mr. Trumball, his Majesty's agent with the Archdukes, to the end he may understand the true scope and intent of his Majesty's directions and be able to give satisfaction touching his princely purpose herein upon any occasion of discourse that may happen thereupon.

With the new and improved English steel there might be the ability to make English weapons at home on advantageous terms. But the business was complicated by the system of monopolies. This time it was the King's Secretary, Mr. Thomas Murrey, who was granted the patent for the manufacture of all sorts of sword and rapier blades. He was anxious to appoint licencees and on 13 July he wrote in a somewhat unsecretarial style to Mr. South, a member of the Court of the Cutlers.

I have been willing to make the first offer of the Patent of the sword blades to your Company. I have had no answer from the Company. My desire is only to know whether they would accept my offer in the whole or in part and upon what conditions. Therefore I desire you to require a final resolution of the Company. And that one or two or three come hither the next Sunday . . . [when] I may confer and conclude, or otherwise that I must take some other course. And that your Company hereafter may not complain that I have neglected them. . . . And let me have your answer the next Sunday here in Court.

Representatives of the Company – the Master, John Porter, together with Mr. Thomas Cheshire and Mr. South – 'took occasion to go and see the engine whereby this Manufacture should come to pass.' They reported back to the Court. They found 'according to our best knowledge the platform very fitly placed' but little else, 'the house and wall requiring some large expenses for the finishing thereof.' They were doubtful, too, about the carrying out and continuance of the work 'being to be performed by strangers coming from the parts beyond the seas.' Then, there was, so they were 'given to understand, one Captain Powell which hath a part therein. And offereth it to sale to sundry persons . . .': this was certain to cause confusion. The Court, faced with this less than enthusiastic report, decided 'that neither the house itself nor any particular persons of the Company will have any dealings therein before such time as the Mill and all things concerning the same shall be finished. And, withall, the sufficiency of the work and workmen to be seen.' After that they would consider any reasonable proposition for their involvement in the project. And they wrote to Mr. Murrey, explaining their decision and asking him 'to cause to be set down certain articles of agreement in writing at your worship's pleasure as you shall think meet, unto which, upon perusing in some reasonable time, we will likewise give an answer thereto.' They thanked his worship for his 'kind love in offering the same', however the affair might turn out, and committed him to God's merciful protection.

There are no records of Thomas Murrey ever having submitted any such proposals and it is possible that the project of the mill which needed so much capital to complete was never achieved. For, as we shall see, the work of supplying the necessary blades was undertaken by individual cutlers, apparently working in their homes rather than in a central manufactory.

While this correspondence was taking place there were, in the background, the reverberations of three previous affairs. First of all the controversial figure of Miles Banks again took the stage in yet another constitutional dispute. Mr. John Porter was the Master in 1621, for the second of his two years in office. He was due to be succeeded, in order of precedence, by James Tackley who had been

Senior Warden during Banks's Mastership. Tackley refused to take office, insisting upon being fined, and at once the quarrel flared between the Master, Wardens and Ancients upon the one side and the rest of the Court and the Livery on the other. The traditionalists, it will be remembered, stoutly maintained that every man should serve in office if elected, without the option of buying himself out; the 'younger and meaner sort' considered that the duties of office were both invidious and excessively onerous and, as such, to be avoided by those who did not wish to undertake them. Both sides in the dispute appealed to the Court of Aldermen and on 26 June the matter was referred to the Recorder.[156]

On 11 July the Court of Aldermen learned 'that Mr. Miles Banks and others of the Company of Cutlers did yesterday in very rude manner and, contrary to the use and custom, without the consent of the Master and Wardens, take upon them the nomination and choice of one George Harbert to be Master of the Company. And notwithstanding that Mr. Recorder hath not yet delivered unto this Court his opinion in the cause in difference. . . .'

The aldermen summoned Miles Banks to Guildhall that very same afternoon to give a bond for his appearance at a meeting of their Court next day; the new Master was not to be sworn until the aldermen had met. On 12 July they ordered all proceedings to be stopped until a further meeting, four days later, when both sides were to be heard. On 16 July the aldermen ordered that John Porter be nominated for a third term of office and that, in future, the elections were to be held in the manner laid down by the Charter – by Master, Wardens, Court and Livery.

Then there were echoes of the action the Cutlers had taken to suppress the Charter granted to the Goldbeaters. In March 1622, the Court decided that the Master and wardens 'shall, either by suit of law or otherwise by Complaint to the Lord Mayor and Court of Aldermen, do what they can or may to recover and receive of the Painter Stainers such money as formerly they promised to the Company for suppressing the Goldbeaters.'

Moreover, two persons – Beedon and Martin – were to be paid £10 for their part in the 'overthrowing' of the patent. There were those in the Painter Stainers Company who opposed any payment to their allies in the fight: it became necessary for the Court of that Company in December to order that anyone questioning or opposing payments to the Cutlers of certain sums laid out by them in the struggle against the Goldbeaters should be fined 40s.

It seemed, too, that the whole problem of gold leaf was still not entirely resolved for in 1623 the Court of the Cutlers learned that there was a patent 'which is thought to be procured by certain persons from his Majesty for Gold and Silver foliat and for gold lace which is also thought will be prejudicial to this Company.'

A committee was formed 'to learn and understand the substance and true tenor of the Patents'; if it appeared that they were harmful all possible steps were to be taken to get them suppressed. In fact, in 1624, the Cutlers brought an action in the High Court and submitted a petition to Parliament against a patent granted to Sir Thomas Villiers for silver and gold wire.[157]

Thirdly there were repercussions of the Court of Aldermen's order of January 1620 that some place in the City should be selected where country larrymen, cutlers and nailers must sell their wares.

Leadenhall had been chosen as the public market where all such traders must sell their goods instead of at 'inns, chambers, and other by-places'. A suitable number of shops were built of freestone 'with all conveniences for the purpose' at the cost of the City, and two days a week were set aside as market days.

As an added incentive cheaper rents were demanded for the shops than the foreigners had to pay in their 'lurking-corners'.

In spite of an act of Common Council made in 1622 that all nails, knives, or other wares made by foreigners of iron, or steel, or iron and steel, and cutlery should be taken only to Leadenhall and nowhere else there to be shewn, searched, housed and sold, the law was still not being universally obeyed. In 1623 a petition by the Ironmongers and Cutlers to the Lord Mayor made it clear that although the Loriners and Nailmen were at last conforming, the foreign cutlers had refused to do so 'and had taken shops in the Friars Minories, a privileged place, where they uttered their false wares at their pleasure.'[158] The Lord Mayor petitioned the Privy Council to ensure that all were made to toe the line, but a year later the same complaints were being voiced about the seemingly intractable foreigns.

The Company were, in fact, occupied with matters of trade and manufacture to a greater extent than in any other period of their existence.

It has been shewn that many aliens had been brought over to work in the cutlery trade: in April 1622 the Privy Council asked for returns to be made of all strangers living in England. The Cutlers produced two lists, the first of which named twenty-seven French and Dutch aliens in the cutlery trade in or near London and Westminster. These were ordered to appear before the Alien Commissioners to be examined.

It has been suggested[159] that the 'Dutch' were probably Flemings speaking a Teutonic dialect and that the 'French', too, might have come from the Netherlands where Walloons from the metal-working districts spoke French.

But, naturally, it was the native-born cutlers, the members of the Company, whose affairs took up so great a part of the technical business at Court meetings.

There was the continual and most unfraternal habit of infringing one another's trade marks: it should not have been necessary for the Court to note that 'divers persons of this Company strike counterfeit marks. And do commit sundry and several abuses in contempt of the rules and ordinances' against which, action must be taken as soon as possible. The bunch of grapes seems to have taken the place of the half-moon as a desirable Mark to be counterfeited, sometimes it was merely a matter of transferring it without consent from one maker to another; at other times it was simply and blatantly infringed.

Such abuses must instantly be stopped. Furthermore, the Court ordered that only artisan craftsmen should be allowed to have marks: 'no man from henceforth shall have any proper mark unless he be a forger and be able of himself to forge and temper his stuff as a workman should do.'

The acute problem of trade marks was further exacerbated by the behaviour of the cutlers of Birmingham and Sheffield, who persisted in their habit of striking the mark of the dagger, 'the public and general' mark of the Cutlers' Company, on their own wares. Nor did the foundation in 1624 of the Cutlers' Company of Sheffield – later to be known as the Cutlers of Hallamshire – do anything to bring about a higher morality: for many years to come – since there was then no legal protection of marks – they continued to give the dagger mark to their own members.

So bad did the situation become that in April some of the London knife-makers petitioned the Court to frame a Bill for Parliament not only against this infringement of the London mark but 'concerning certain abuses committed by the makers of knives one against the other.' They intended, they said, to bring an action against offenders but wished, first, to obtain the consent of the Court. Their request was approved and the Court contributed £20 towards the costs of the action. As it happened the Bill failed to be presented at that session of Parliament and the money was returned to the Clerk.

Then, too, the Privy Council were still interesting themselves in the breaches of the law that wares made by provincial cutlers were to be sold only at Leadenhall market two days a week: they asked the Cutlers about the question of 'lurking-places'. They still existed and the proscribed hawkers still existed, too. Sixteen Birmingham knives were taken from one George Smythe of Ripon as he went hawking with them in the streets; a female vagrant hawker also lost five plain white-handled knives – all were brought into Court to be defaced and disposed of. Sometimes such confiscated property was broken, sometimes – as in the case of eighteen ivory-handled knives, judged to be counterfeit and deceivable – they were sold for the benefit of the poor.

It will be seen that there was much business for the Court in general and for its officers in particular: apart from all the work involved, the nature of the tasks faced by the Master and wardens in dealing both with offenders and with those who felt themselves aggrieved is sufficient to explain the reluctance of some of the Assistants to accept the higher ranks. In March 1624, there was all the extra work arising out of a controversy amongst the Livery wardens and the yeomanry whose wardens and assistants brought in certain orders which they had drawn up for their own government. They wanted the rules to be ratified under the Seal of the Company – a suggestion that the Court probably regarded as presumptuous – and a Committee was set up to consider the whole affair.

Later that year the Court handed back the rules, which they had revised, expressing the hope that the Yeomanry would accept the revisions. Consideration of the matter was deferred and, before the Yeomanry left the meeting the Court enquired blandly about their accounts: they had been delayed without any reason being given. . . . And with all the business of trade and man-management there continued, too, their other preoccupations such as the business of property-management and of raising the money demanded by the usual precepts. The Company, it may be noted, had become, in common with other Companies, even less prompt than they had previously been in the payment of Corn Money. In January 1622, for instance, the Lord Mayor had voiced his suspicions that the Livery Companies had not bought the full quota of grain demanded the previous July: they were ordered to do so immediately. In August they were ordered to put wheat meal on the market every Friday; in November a precept noted that they had failed to do so and ordered them to comply. In February 1623, perhaps because of their laxity, the Companies were told that the City had bought the wheat: they were ordered to take cash in hand and collect their allocation. The same month came the order for supplying the market with meal; four months later a further precept indicated that they had again failed to do so.

The voluntary system of organization certainly imposed a heavy strain on those who served it while having, at the same time, to make their own living. And for the working cutlers of the Company there was more trade at hand. For, as the reign of James I neared its end, the demand for a supply of swords which the King had refused to buy from the United Provinces in the interests both of the economy and the domestic industries had at last to be met.

On 20 April 1624 the size of the order that might be expected became known. There was a meeting that day of the Court and some of the Livery when those present set their hands to an agreement by which they should supply monthly, when required by his Majesty, no less than 5000 swords with hangers and girdles.

In spite of the new inventions and patents for making steel the cutlery trade was still using foreign blades. In order to fulfil the King's order for swords a new procedure was instigated: the Company bought blades – usually they were French or Flemish – from wholesalers in London and Birmingham and sold them to their members at fixed prices, on eight months' credit. The blades were then made into swords and delivered to the Tower; accounts were settled and the Company repaid.

When the first order for a monthly supply to the Crown was received that April the Court decided to take money out of the Company treasury to finance the scheme. The assistants, two years earlier, had interested themselves in the state of the Company funds and it had been agreed that a small account book should be kept in one of the boxes. It would thus not be necessary to be forever counting the cash in hand – they would be able to know at a glance how much there was, or should be, in the account. They could now see, therefore, that they could afford £110 for the project: they bought, as a beginning, forty-eight dozen blades which cost them £92. 16s. 2d.

The scheme worked well. The blades were brought into the Hall from time to time and were sold there to the members.

In December 1624 'for the general good' £49 held by the Clerk and £53 owed to the Company by various members for various reasons was to be laid out on blades for 'intended service now to be expected'. The Hall became filled with blades which members could buy for 40s. a dozen. The Court Minutes contain page after page of receipts for blades handed out and, later, for the cash due for them. In June 1625 another £50 was taken out of the treasury to pay the merchant, Lewis van Hoobrooke, for a supply of blades. In September no less than seventy-one dozen blades, in chests, were placed in the Counting House. Mr. John Porter had left them in the Hall in his lifetime – he and Mr. Cheshire had bought them for the use of the Company.

Not all the blades were put to good use: in April that year the Beadle was given, for his pains, seventeen swords rejected as unserviceable 'when the Earl of Southampton and other honourable personages were employed beyond the seas.'

But, generally speaking, everything in the trade was well: there was, at any rate for sword-cutlery, an assured market and financial backing from a flourishing Company. And it was at this juncture that James I died. The reign that followed was to prove one of tyranny and extortion that tested the financial resources of the City to the full.

II

Aspects of Autocracy

1625–1640

THE accession of Charles I was marked for the Cutlers by the usual Royal progress, compulsorily attended by the Livery Companies in their stands behind their rails, through the City. But, as was so often the case, the festivities in particular and the social life in general was somewhat marred by an exceptionally bad outbreak of the plague that to a greater or lesser degree was almost perpetually present in London. It was only to be expected. The streets, as the King was to note, were 'very noisome and troublesome for passing in consequence of breaches of the pavements and excessive quantities of filth.' In 1625 no less than 35,000 people died in the City and there was a considerable falling off in the number of public gatherings that were permitted.

In particular it was noted that there was 'a Vain Custom of late taken up, of meeting of Countrymen of several shires and counties of this realm at Halls and Taverns within this City which meetings occasion much expense of money . . . many times by men that can hardly pay the same for provisions. . . .'

It was ordered, therefore, that 'particularly in this great time of Plague' the Companies were not to let their Halls for such provincial reunions.

The rich fled from the City. The streets, along which the plague carts rumbled towards the communal graves, were filled with beggars. Charles I, too, was in a state of penury. To the war with Spain, arising from the defence of the Palatinate which he had, to some extent, inherited from his father, was added in 1627 a war with France. He had inherited, too, his father's favourite, the Duke of Buckingham, a man greatly hated by the nation. Parliament had shewn considerable mistrust of Charles and during the first two years of his reign proved highly reluctant to grant any money to a King so clearly under the Duke's influence. When Buckingham was impeached, the King sent his accusers to the Tower and in the Court of Star Chamber the favourite was then acquitted. Parliament refused to be intimidated; they denied the King his supplies and were dissolved; Charles, desperate for money, was forced to fall back upon a forced loan. The City was assessed at £120,000 which was to be secured upon Crown lands – half of it was to be paid within the week and the Cutlers found themselves compelled to raise £360 immediately. A meeting was held and those present asked the Master and wardens in what manner other Companies of their standing provided the sums demanded of them. They all agreed that 'if they cannot in good manner avoid it' the money was to be raised but 'it shall not be levied by the poll but out of the stock and means of the Company unto which the Master, Thomas Tuck, with his Warden, Robert South, proposed a question that, if there wanted a stock, or money, what would they then have done? And the answer was made: The Plate either to be sold or impawned.' Eventually it was found that they could raise £290 without difficulty; the remainder was made up by the Clerk and the Master and wardens out of money which they were holding for the use of the Company in general.

But when, in June, there came a precept for a further £120 for the use of the King, there was no more cash available and the plate had eventually to be pawned to provide the ready money to pay into the Chamber of London. Yet the Cutlers shewed no immediate haste. The precepts from the City became ever more urgent: the demand for £120 was payable on sight, yet they had failed to do so. The King's needs were both pressing and extraordinary. Still the Cutlers failed to pay. The City authorities' requests became more strident – they themselves were being pressed: the Cutlers really *must* pay.

They were being hard-pressed financially but there were still signs of hope. The Irish Lands investment was one of them. The King, it was true, setting himself firmly on the course that was to lead him to disaster, was turning to the English Plantation as an additional source of revenue. Double rents were demanded on some of the lands that had been bought from Royal patentees or monopolists; the tenants found themselves allegedly due for services of tenure that were both tedious and costly; if they failed to pay their lands were distrained upon. Yet in spite of the new extortions there were many tenants coming forward for the lands administered by the Salters – in all, some forty-eight leases were granted, to both English settlers and to Irish natives, and the Cutlers' first share of these rents amounted to eighteen guineas. Between their properties and their preoccupation with the business of blade-making the Court became busier than ever. With more manufactures being carried out there were, inevitably, more disputes about marks and trade offences; there were more insults bandied and, consequently, more offenders to be tried by the Court.

In order to get through all the business it was necessary for the Assistants to attend punctually. Absentees and those who arrived late were to be fined – an order that immediately raised the attendance figure from fourteen to twenty-one.

One of those present – William Langton – was soon in trouble and appeared before the Court 'for certain speeches of scandal given': he had called the Master, William Davis, 'a base fellow and careth not what is spent of the house'; Mr. Hutchinson was 'a base slave for he hath gotten much [profit] since he came to his place'; Mr. Tuck was 'a Cocksome Bawd' and there were hints that he had taken part in an orgy at the 'Babylon' that was the Belle Sauvage; Thomas Cheshire 'in Idle manner' took upon himself to interfere with the business affairs of William Langton and his son 'so that they were beggars'. There were many other complaints in the same vein – far too many and far too serious to be overlooked: Langton was dismissed from both Court and Livery and although, two months later, he 'made means to be reconciled to the Company' they, considering also the earlier offences which, as we have seen, he committed in 1617 'will in no wise agree to accept him amongst them but he shall stand disabled. . . .'

Then there were complaints to be dealt with from the freemen Blademakers in the Company against Peter Carter for taking apprentices to the 'hindrance' of the freemen. The Court ruled that Carter should have no more apprentices from them and that 'for the better encouraging of the said freemen from henceforth they shall have as many apprentices as they will without any fine brought to this house' – an almost incredibly elastic ruling that makes it appear that the Blademakers were in a position to exert considerable industrial pressure.

There were more complaints about the activities of hawkers, this time from the Knifemakers, who asked that they might have the services of one Gregory Edwards to restrain them. The Court agreed. The Knife-cutlers, themselves, were complained about for their 'many abuses . . . in selling of unlawful knives with the mark of the Dagger and inlaid with tin instead of silver.' A Committee, appointed by the Court to stamp out such offences, seems to have acted, at any rate initially, with some firmness: almost immediately they seized from Joseph Elsmore two gross and eight knives with black hafts, one gross ten dozen and nine knives with white silver-chased hafts and some sheaths. All the knives were Brummagem ware, stamped with the dagger, and although the sheaths and his fine of 20s. were returned to him on his promise to be of future good behaviour, the knives were all forfeited.

At the same time fifty-four dozen and five knives were confiscated from Adrian Hendrik, a merchant-stranger.

Trade marks became subject to new and stricter safeguards: any member applying for a mark to be enrolled was compelled to forge a blade and strike it with his mark in the presence of two members of the Court. Arnold Cornelius and Thomas Cament, two knife-forgers, were forbidden to utter or sell any unmarked blades; this order was perhaps aimed at hindering Richard Briginshaw who, it now appeared, had for many years past been buying unmarked blades and, before selling them, engraving them with the best marks belonging to the brethren of the Company. Briginshaw was already in a state of some dispute with the Company – he had rather unwisely brought an action against the Master and wardens in the King's Bench: now, he was ordered by the Lord Mayor to apologize for the contempt he had committed in having them arrested. The Court were clearly determined to be seen to behave strongly and uphold their internal ordinances. When, however, it was a question of obeying the orders of the Crown they were, perhaps, because of the great expenses to which they were being put, increasingly non-compliant.

The precept for grain was the chief matter on which they shewed their intransigence. As usual the orders were received but, now, unusually, they began, in spite of repeated demands, altogether to ignore them. The demands became more urgent and still the Cutlers took no action. In January 1629, when they were asked how much wheat they had in store, they replied, without explanation or apology, that they had none. In 1630 their lack of co-operation became more marked and more noticed by the authorities. It was another year of great sickness in London and in May the Lord Mayor issued a precept 'for as much as the visitation of the Plague is much feared to increase within this City . . . it is not now a time of feasting but of fasting and prayer to Almighty God to avert his Judgement from us. . . .' There were, therefore, to be no public dinners or feastery, and no meetings for burials, marriages and the like. The savings effected by this self-denial were to be spent on the poor. While he was on the subject of feasting the Mayor observed that the Company had failed to certify how much wheat they had laid in – a fact that 'maketh me conceive you are wholly improvided.' It was true. In October the wheat was still unbought and the Mayor reported that the King himself was grievously mispleased. The Company had been very 'remiss and negligent' in that they also failed to put wheat-meal on sale at Queen Hithe as they had been told to do for the benefit of the poor.

The Company had been told that they must devote any savings from their enforced economy in feasting to the poor: in view of the way they had utterly disregarded the provision of grain it was likely that they had failed to make over their savings to the poor: the Lord Mayor ordered them to bring half of all such money to Guildhall.

By December the Mayor was obviously irritated. He ordered the Cutlers to send a double portion of wheat, every Monday, to the market; he ordered them, too, to pay in the savings immediately to Guildhall. By the end of the year they had still taken no action: the Privy Council sent an order supporting the Lord Mayor. The Cutlers' Company and others, their Lordships noted, had not been obedient. On the contrary, they had been remiss. They *must*, without fail, provide the corn which in a time of such scarcity was more than ever important. The Council added a warning and a reminder – the grain must always be bought from places remote from the City: the Companies were not to rely on supplies from bakers and chandlers. The whole point of the operation was to increase the amount of grain actually available in the City.

The Cutlers bought it neither from within or without the City; they simply took no notice of any orders received on that particular subject. In February 1631 the Mayor wrote to the Company, recalling his former precepts

but we have been by you too much neglected which hath been the cause that I have been, and daily am, pressed by the King and Lords and have been taxed of remissness in not seeing the same effected, whereby it merely ariseth by the neglect of you, and other the Wardens of Companies of this City, who should have been more careful to execute the commands of the magistrate in these things.

The King, the Lord Mayor continued, had ordered that some of the ports should be opened for bringing corn from all parts of the kingdom to the City. A great quantity of corn was expected to arrive so that those Companies who lacked would be able to buy.

By May the corn had arrived and was to be had – so a precept declared – at very reasonable rates. In addition to buying their proper share of the grain the Cutlers were urged to put as much wheat meal as possible – more, in fact, than their basic requirement – upon the market.

In June it was remarked that merchants trading with the East had imported great quantities of rye which was as good or, even, better than the corn usually available in London. But they were unable to dispose of it – in fact, in order to be rid of it, they were prepared to sell it at 6s. 6d. a bushel which was 13d. below the market price. The Privy Council, wishing to 'relieve the merchants and encourage them' and thereby ensure future supplies for the City, asked the Lord Mayor to press the Companies to buy from the merchants: the Cutlers were, as a result, ordered to buy half their allocation of sixty quarters from the merchants.

By July the price had fallen to 4s. 9d. a bushel and still the Cutlers did not buy. The precept of June was, word for word, repeated and the Privy Council wrote to say that the price was very reasonable. The Companies really must take up their share: already the merchants were asking permission to export the rest of it to foreign markets.

In September the wardens of twelve companies – the Cutlers, Cooks, Dyers, Haberdashers, Innholders, Ironmongers, Leathersellers, Saddlers, Salters, Scriveners, Skinners and Tallowchandlers – were summoned to Hampton Court and there, no doubt, castigated by the Privy Council. They were to make a provision of corn and they would be overseen by two Aldermen. The display of threats was equally ineffective. By April 1632, it was noted, the Cutlers had still failed to provide any of the corn demanded. By their inaction they had hazarded his Majesty's displeasure. They had hazarded, too, the same sort of crisis as had struck the City, through lack of corn, the previous year. They were reminded that they must not cheat, as some other Companies had already done, by encouraging bakers and chandlers to store corn in the Company granaries. The provision was to be immediately 'made and laid up *bona fide* without fraud or colour as they will answer at their perils.'

This led the Court to report gloomily in October that they had actually bought sixty quarters of wheat but could only sell forty-two quarters – the rest had been damaged by high tides and had gone musty in the Granary.

In any case the perils of disobedience were evidently small. Eighteen months later it was noted, with a faint air of hopelessness, that 'the Companies are not stored and provided with grain for the service of this City.'

At a time of great autocracy, when a literal belief in the Divine Right of Kings to rule, subject only to God the Father and Christ his Son, was genuinely held and when disrespect for authority was, therefore, a mortal rather than a venial sin, this recalcitrance on the part of the Cutlers and some others of the Livery Companies and the failure to react to it on the part of the City, the Council, and the King – all of whom had compromised their positions by issuing stern orders and injunctions – is strange indeed. Not thus, it may be felt, would things have been in the great days of Elizabeth: the inside of the Compter would soon have brought the wardens to a right and proper frame of mind.

Inevitably, as the demands and threats and final notices are issued and sink without trace disregarded and unremarked in the unresponsive Companies, there comes the feeling that the City was, to use a twentieth-century cliché, rapidly becoming ungovernable. It is tempting to see in such intransigence the slow underground working of the popular will that was finally to erupt in the death of the King.

In their own house, however, the Court of the Cutlers demanded strict obedience. In 1631 some members who had 'offered contempt to the Yeomanry' and subsequently to the Master and wardens by not appearing before them to answer to the complaints, although repeatedly warned to do so, were jailed. They wrote to the Master letters of ignominious submission: they desired him to do the best he could for them with the Lord Mayor to secure their release. 'We are sorry and grieved' they protested 'and we remain beholding and thankful unto you as long as we live, thus hoping you will do what lieth in your power.'

Others who had been trafficking with hawkers or brokers submitted humbly and promised never to do such a thing again. An apprentice who was denied admission to the Freedom because he refused to take the Oath of Supremacy was forced to submit and, to make quite sure that there was no misunderstanding, the oath was entered in the Minutes:

You shall swear that in heart you do acknowledge our Sovreign Lord Charles, by the Grace of God, King of England, Scotland, France and Ireland, defender of the Faith &c, to be the Chief and Supreme head over the Church within his dominions and territories, next and immediately under God and Christ his Son.

At the same time as they briskly wielded their powers it seemed that they became suddenly doubtful of just how far they might legally go. In 1632, the Master, wardens and some of the Court, together with Constable Benjamin Eley entered and searched the shop of a broker or seller of old garments, in Long Lane. They alleged that 'he usurpeth on the Trade or Mistery of the Cutlers', for they found, trimmed and all ready to be sold, a number of new swords, scabbards, blades without hilts and the odd new hilt without a blade, ready to be trimmed. They also seized and brought to the Hall, for inspection, a new sword, ready to be trimmed and sold, which was riveted together with a small nail.

But then – perhaps as the result of the broker's protests – they decided to take counsel's opinion on what, exactly, their rights might be.

They were advised, firstly, that anybody could buy and sell anything he wished provided he did not infringe any Statute or ordinance of the place he lived in: the old-clothes man was, therefore, perfectly entitled to buy and sell ready-made swords. But, if he bought parts of swords and assembled them, then he must be regarded as exercising the art of cutlery and be liable to a fine of 40s. a month. Secondly, counsel restated the old rule that no alien who had not been naturalized was allowed to carry on a handicraft within the realm: by doing so he risked losing all his goods to the Crown and even a naturalized foreigner could only work as a craftsman if he had completed the normal seven years' apprenticeship in the relevant Gild.

Finally, counsel considered that the Cutlers' charter did not permit them to search for or seize goods in any but cutlers' houses 'and not in the hands of the buyer and seller only of swords and other things. . . .'

The case against the broker was, no doubt, hastily dropped. But it proved useful as a simple restatement of law as it then stood.

The making of swords and rapiers was now the chief preoccupation of the Company. In 1631 a commission had been granted by the Crown to the Armourers and Gunmakers, to the Bandolier men and the Pikemakers for the making of armours, guns, bandoliers and pikes for all the trained bands of England and Wales. There had been no mention of the making of swords or rapiers or any of the other weapons which had always been made by the Cutlers. Robert South 'the King's Cutler' and a member of the

Company, with two or three others, suggested that the Cutlers, 'to prevent a mischief for times to come', should declare their interest in fulfilling part of the commission 'lest the Armourers should trench upon our profession'. They asked that if they could come to an agreement with Mr. Kirke, one of those who had obtained a monopoly for making swords and rapier blades, the Company might either take over the whole production of such blades as Mr. South and his associates might be licensed to manufacture, or they might take up a third share in the enterprise 'upon gain or loss' or, if they wanted to take a less active role, simply to lend them, upon security, £100, free of interest. The Court decided, eventually, on the latter course and Robert South and William Cave, acting in the name of the Cutlers' Company, entered a petition to the appropriate Committees requesting that they should be included in the Commission. Their action was successful: it was thought 'very fit' that they should be so joined.[160] For the moment the prospects for trade seemed to be promising.

They needed a substantial trade for the demands upon their purses were heavy. In addition to the supply of Corn money which, whether they paid it or not, was a constant threat, there were any number of other claims: in 1632, for instance, there were no less than four 'fifteens' levied on the Company. And there was a very pressing appeal for the restoration of St. Paul's Cathedral. As the Bishop of London wrote:

A great dishonour it is, not only to this City but to the whole State to see that ancient and goodly pile of buildings so decayed as it is; but it will be a far greater, if care should not be taken to prevent the fall of it into ruins. And it would be no less disgrace to religion happily established in this Kingdom if it should have so little power over the minds of men as not to prevail with them to keep these eminent places of God's service in due decent repair which their forefathers have built in times (by their own confession) not so full of the knowledge of God's truth as the present age is. . . .

The Company, whose members, at the end of the sixteenth century had defaced the south side of the cathedral by building shops along it,[162] agreed to subscribe £5 for five successive years.

As was often the case when money had to be raised the Company were apt to make a large number of admissions to the Livery to collect the entrance fees. No doubt, due to the mortality in the severe outbreaks of plague, there were a number of vacancies available: one year twenty-two members were admitted and in 1632 the sixteen new members of the Livery 'did make their dinner at the Cutlers' Hall, the Master and Wardens did lend them their plate and other things useful for the said dinner which was performed in good order. They invited the whole assistance with the wives of those who have borne office with their own wives; the diet was six messes of meat – roasted geese, capons, minced pies, rabbits and tarts. Who were bountiful to the officers of the house, viz., to the Clerk for carving 3s. 4d. and to the other officers their fees.' With the prospects of the trade which was to come to the Company the new Liverymen no doubt felt that it was all well worth while.

There were, at the same time as they prepared to set to work on their share of the great scheme for arming the trained bands, the usual petty distractions. These were 'Brokers and Hawkers and Birmingham men' indulging in their usual 'sinister dealings and deceits' – new attempts were to be made to suppress them.

There was a continual undercurrent of unrest among and concerning the Yeomanry – it had to be kept within reasonable bounds.

There was William Wall, a promising apprentice who had served his time, who asked, through his father, to be translated to the Fishmongers – the Court 'would not give way to the loosing of a person so promising as [he] may hereafter prove . . .' and prepared to enter a caveat in the Chamber of London.

There was Nicholas Skinner, an old member of the Court who had failed for many years to attend any Company meetings of any kind: he suddenly put in an appearance, demanding to take his place next to the ancient masters – there was no room for him and he was sent away. Again and again he turned up at meetings until eventually the Court ingeniously disposed of him by demanding a vast backlog of fines and dues and quarterage which he refused to pay and was, consequently, struck off both Court and Livery.

There was the trouble in which the City found itself after failing to arrest the murderer of the astrologer William Lamb – the Cutlers' share of the communal fine eventually worked out at no more than 2s. 6d. a head but the principle caused trouble and discontent.

There were too the usual distracting squabbles between the brethren. Liverymen gave 'hard words' to the Master or insulted members of the Court: they had to be dealt with. The Court fined two of the Livery, Stephen Scarborough and Jasper Churchill, 20s. each because on 27 March 1634, the anniversary of the coronation, at the Three Tuns in Paul's Churchyard, in the presence of the Master, wardens, and the greater part of the Livery they 'did unreverently and rudely behave themselves both in speech and action, viz., the said Stephen, after many angry speeches past, daring the said Jasper to throw a bowl of burned wine at him . . . the said Jasper . . . did fling in the face and on the apparel of the said Stephen *two* bowls of wine the one after the other not respecting the time nor place where they were in.'

But the chief obstacle in the way of their rearmament programme was the opposition that came from a Liveryman, Benjamin Stone, who owned a blade factory at Hounslow.

This Middlesex town was then a centre of sword-making. In 1629 Henry Hoppie and Peter English had been brought over from the Continent by the King and Sir William Heyden and had set up factories there. And Benjamin Stone, although he lived in the City, had set up his works on Hounslow Heath to avoid what were, centuries later, to be referred to as 'the restrictive practices of the Cutlers' Company.'[161]

In December 1634 there was a visit by the 'ancient masters' as well as Robert South, the Master, to Benjamin Stone's mills, probably in connection with the programme for sword-making, but it turned out badly. Stone 'in the hearing of divers strangers' uttered 'disdainful words and reproachful speeches' for which he was summoned before the Court, but refusing to submit, he was eventually sent to the Counter. And although, at the command of the Lord Mayor he eventually apologized to the Company and paid his fine, he was intent on securing the contract for blades for himself.

His first action in July 1636 was to petition the King to buy 2000 blades 'which were then in readiness and to cause the Lord Treasurer to advance present money for the same, thereby to encourage the said manufacture which never heretofore was brought to such perfection.'

The King referred the matter to the Attorney and Solicitor General. They investigated and reported that the petitioner certainly seemed to have 2000 blades in store (another 2000 would be ready by Michaelmas) and to have gone to great expense in making all sorts of blades for the Services. They noted, further, that 'by reason of the petitioner's great expenses in the said manufacture, and his being indebted to persons in the City of London, he dares not walk about in respect they threaten to arrest him. Beseeches he may have present money upon delivery of the 2000 blades and a letter of protection for one year.'

It was noted that blades had previously been made in foreign parts and, if the Crown did not buy those from Hounslow, Benjamin Stone 'having no vent for his blades is like to be undone.'

Later that year, Stone again petitioned the Council. At a cost of £6000 he had perfected the art of blade making so that he now made 'as good as any that are in the Christian world.' He alleged that great complaints had been made by the Lord Deputy of Ireland and others of the unserviceableness of the swords delivered to the Office of Ordnance by the Cutlers; in fact, he said, his Majesty had ordered that he, Benjamin Stone, should be made a member of the Ordnance Board and he guaranteed to supply 500 blades a week. In spite of this, the Cutlers had now been given orders for 4000 blades 'which for the most part are old, decayed, swords' although he himself had a great number on his hands, all ready to be delivered to his Majesty. If, said Stone, the Cutlers were allowed to cross him in this manner it would be 'to the great disserve of his Majesty and overthrow the science of blade-making now brought to full perfection in this kingdom.'[163]

The Council, if Stone is to be believed, were clearly impressed. They ordered the Lieutenant of the Tower and the Lieutenant of Ordnance to take another look at the goods delivered to the Armoury. An appointment was made for the Cutlers to attend the survey. But according to Stone, already calling himself 'his

Majesty's blademaker' it was never kept. He prayed, therefore, that special warrants be issued by the Privy Council to resurvey the swords in the compulsory presence of the Cutlers and that the swords that he had on his hands be received into the Ordnance Office.

The Cutlers did not sit back idly under this attack. They counter-petitioned in 1637 with weighty technical arguments. They backed these arguments by a counter-attack against Benjamin Stone: 'the swords which he petitioneth to be received into the store and pretends to be blades of his own making are all bromedgham blades and foreign blades and for the bromedgham blades they are in no way fit for his Majesty's store.'[164]

The following year Stone returned to the attack. He had, he claimed, now spent £8000, the whole of his estate, on the manu-facture of swords: he was ready to deliver to the Government one thousand blades a month. In the tail of his petition there was a sting: he prayed that he might have 'the power of hindering the stamping of Spanish and other marks upon blades made by workmen of the Cutlers' Company.'

The decision of the State was that 'the petitioner is to make as many swords as he can and they shall all be taken off if they be serviceable and good.' How many fell into this category may not now be determined. It is possible that there were but few for one historian of the steel trade refers to the 'Hounslow fiasco'.[165]

In all this dispute – and coming from a Liveryman of the Com-pany it must have been regarded as verging upon the sacrilegious – it is hard to evaluate the truth of charge and counter-charge. Members of the Company, we know, were liable to err: they had long been accused of counterfeiting Toledo marks. Moreover, in 1635, it had been agreed that everyone would do all he could 'to suppress and utterly abandon the working and trimming up of swords, rapiers and skeins, with brass and copper hilts and pummels which are cast in moulds or any such deceitful way.'

On the other hand, in attempting to evaluate the evidence given against the Company, we are entitled to consider the character of the witness.

STONE, Benjamin:

1618 Fined for 'striking other men's marks and other abuses'; committed to prison by Lord Mayor for the additional offense of Contempt in not having appeared before the Court although warned several times to do so.

1620 May. 'summoned and warned that from henceforth he do desist from buying knives which are not made within the City of London. And yet are glazed and otherwise wrought and framed to be knives made in the City whereby there is much counterfeit . . . [and] secret deceit . . . so that the common people . . . cannot discover where they are made, many of the knives having the bunch of grapes. . . .'

October. Fined for going to Stourbridge Fair unsearched; admitted three or four similar offences; claimed not to know of the Order, having failed to attend at Quarter Day to hear the rules read.

1621 Fined 'for disorderly behaviour and uncivil speeches to certain masters and other Assistants . . . at the Tower of London upon delivery of certain swords to his Majesty'; refused to pay fine; committed to the Counter.

1622 Ordered by Court to pay a widow for thirty swords which he had sold and for which he had not paid her.

1624 Fined for not enrolling his apprentice although frequently ordered to do so; committed to the Lord Mayor for contemptuously refusing to pay this fine.

1629 Fined 'for speaking disgraceful words' against the Master and Wardens before the Lord Mayor; refused to pay fine; to be 'forborn to be warned to the Hall as a Brother until he shall submit. . . .'

1630 Demanded use of Bunch of Grapes mark, already enrolled by another; hearing promised if he paid his fine; 'in contempt refused and left the Court.'

1633 Fined for coming to the Hall, improperly dressed, 'in a falling band.'

1635 Fined for insults to members of Court during a visit to Hounslow.

These offences, although by no means unusual among members of the Company, do not, taken as a whole, entirely create the picture that Stone wished to present of himself as a serious supplier of blades to the Crown as 'Cutler for the Office of the Ordnance' as he liked to be known.

And, after this eruption into the limelight of the national records, Benjamin Stone makes but one more public appearance, in 1641, when the Court appointed some of the freemen of the Company to bring a suit against him 'for divers abuses and misdemeanours by him committed as well against the persons of the Master and Wardens as also against the whole Body of the Manufacture of this Company. . . .' But then came the Civil War and there were other weightier concerns for the Court.

In the meantime the irreversible acts, the inexorable progress of the King towards Civil War and death, were being enacted.

Since he had dissolved Parliament in 1629 the King had been ruling without any constitutional source of supply. Yet money had to be raised for running the country, for paying for the war, for the King's own expenses. His principal source of revenue came from customs duties, which, under protest, the merchants paid. Ship money – a direct tax on real property to pay for the Navy – would not, on the whole, have been regarded as unreasonable if it had been levied by Parliament. In fact, when it was first demanded, in 1634, from the City there were no general objections from elsewhere in the realm: it was only when, in 1635, Ship money was demanded from the country as a whole that non-payment was declared a matter of principle.[166]

Much worse, and indeed indefensible, was the action of the Crown over the Irish Estates. There had long been accusations that the Companies had failed to carry out their obligations under the grants of land made to them. There was a certain degree of truth in these allegations and there were great efforts to bring the properties up to the standards laid down in the Book of Plantation. It was not until 1635, for example, that the consortium headed by the Salters' Company at last faced the necessity for building a new church in Londonderry. But a lack of conformity to the agreements made in respect of the Irish Lands was not the reason given by the Crown for its action in bringing a suit in Star Chamber against the City.

It had been decided, said the Attorney General, that the letters patent of 1613 for the Plantation of Ulster had been 'unduly and surreptitiously obtained to the prejudice and deceit of his Majesty.' They must therefore surrender the estates to the King.

P

Apart from the obvious injustice of the demand, the administrative problems to be envisaged were enormous. The lands were not a matter of simple ownership; they were held in trust for all members who had subscribed. Many of the original subscribers had died and their executors were now involved with the lands: the difficulties were incalculable.

The Companies, after asking for time to consider what action to take, decided that they must accept the best terms that they could get from the King. He at first demanded £120,000 for the return of the properties to their owners but the outcry was such that eventually Charles magnanimously accepted £12,500 'in consideration of his Majesty's several grants to this City and pardon to the several companies for misgovernment.'

The money he gave to his Queen, a foreigner and a Catholic. It was an action that the City neither forgave nor forgot: it was to have a serious effect upon their attitude towards the King in the vital struggle that lay ahead.

By 1636 when the collectors of Ship Money actually arrived at Cutlers' Hall, demanding £15, the Company were in debt. The Master avoided the necessity of having to pay out the money, there and then, to the collectors by telling them that he had instructions to pay the money direct to the Lord Mayor. But it was only a temporary respite. In any case there was insufficient cash in hand. The Court turned to the plate cupboard and determined that as much should be taken out of it as could be pawned for £60: Robert South agreed to lend them the money on this security and they were thus spared the indignity of having to resort to some outside broker.

But there were further extortions to follow. The King demanded in 1638 £12,000 from the City for 'passing the Books and Patent under the great Seal of England.' The Cutlers' share of this was £80 and was additional to the amount they had already paid the King, on his accession, for the confirmation of their own Charter.

How, the Court wondered, was such a sum to be paid? Should they pawn or sell some more Plate? Or should they borrow upon a Bond? It was a matter of some urgency. Eventually they decided to take sixteen new members upon the Livery – fortunately there were a number of vacancies – and charge them £5 each for the privilege.

But they were angry with the City over the demand. They disputed the basis upon which their assessment was made; they disagreed with the manner in which their £80 demand had been calculated upon the Corn Rate and they said so. But, for once, the City authorities, who had suffered so much and so long from the intransigence of the Company in their response to precepts, suddenly hit back. The Master and wardens were committed to gaol, there to remain until the money was paid.[168]

The sixteen new Liverymen were enrolled in December and paid the entrance fee demanded of them. But the following May, seven of those so elected petitioned the Lord Mayor against the Master and wardens. They claimed that such a charge for coming upon the Livery was excessive and unconstitutional. Counsel 'learned on either side' heard the arguments and eventually the Court of Aldermen ruled that the newly-chosen Liverymen should enjoy the places to which they had been elected but that the Master and wardens should remit 30s. of the £5 fine – a considerable set-back to the Court's efforts to balance the Company accounts.

It is possible, therefore, that there was less than general enthusiasm when the King and Queen, with the Queen Mother of France and divers of the nobility and great personages passed through the City. There were the usual orders to attend the ceremony: all the Livery 'except such as be of the Trained Band' were to attend and they were to spread themselves out, 'to enlarge themselves in their number and distance that the Companies may fill that side of the street in the whole passage from Aldgate to Temple Bar if it may be.'

If the reception was mixed, it was because the richer Londoners, upon whom the burden of taxation fell, had less cause to rejoice than had the masses who, under the autocracy, had enjoyed a surprising degree of poor-law relief and employment.[167]

But the Cutlers' Company, in its corporate capacity, had little reason to cheer the passing Monarch who was, himself, in ever-increasing financial trouble.

This time funds were needed for a war with Scotland 'whither, as to a weak and distempered part of the Body, all the rheums and fluxes of factions and seditious humours made their way.'[169] Charles had in 1637 attempted to enforce a new Prayer Book upon the Scots. They had risen against him to a man. A truce was agreed, in 1639, at Berwick but Charles refused to agree to the Covenanters' terms, and he demanded now, to carry on the struggle, a loan from the City of £100,000. The City authorities, their recent treatment over the Irish Lands still rankling, refused. But war against the Scots, even under an unpopular leader, was always a popular cause: the City voted the King a free gift of £10,000. To vote such a sum was one thing, to collect it another. Eventually the total sum was achieved only by appointing sixteen Sheriffs who were unwilling to take office and who could be fined for their refusal.

But it became clear, even to Charles, that to wage war against the Scots he needed a more assured source of income. He was forced to take the advice of the Earl of Strafford and recall Parliament. The years of autocracy came suddenly and unexpectedly to an end.

For Charles it was too late. Those who were recalled to Parliament, were, after eleven years, in no hurry to grant supplies to the King. Not even the fact that the Irish Parliament had voted Charles £180,000, not even the popularity of a war against Scotland, could change their minds: their grievances must be met before they would grant a penny to the King.

The scene was set for the ultimate conflict.

12

Civil War

1640–1648

IN that springtime of 1640 there was everywhere in London a great discontent. A double watch was mounted in the City, where papers inciting to rebellion were found to have been posted up, and householders were warned to keep their apprentices and servants at home until further notice. The trained bands, which had taken the place of the old standing watch, were called out. The resolve of the Commons, led by John Pym, to prefer grievances to supply had led to the dissolution of the Short Parliament after only three weeks.

In the absence of Parliament it was to the City that Charles had to turn for money. He demanded a loan: the City authorities refused it. The King threatened them and, although he did not follow the Earl of Strafford's advice to hang a number of the aldermen, he imprisoned four of them and said that he would depose the Lord Mayor.

The City stood firm. The lists of wealthy citizens which the King demanded were refused to him. There were riots until Charles, momentarily alarmed, released the aldermen.

Two petitions – one from the City and one from the Lords – were then sent to the King: they demanded the recall of Parliament to deal with their outstanding grievances: taxes, both import and export; Ship Money – in spite of the naval protection it should have provided, merchant-ships and goods were still being taken by Turkish and other pirates; imprisonment for the non-payment of Ship Money; monopolies, patents and warrants in restraint of trade; innovations in religion – when in church, should one, or should one not, bow to the altar?; the great concourse in London of Papists, all busily plotting; the irregularity of Parliament; and, oddly enough in the circumstances, the danger to his Majesty's sacred person in time of war.[170]

The next move must clearly come from the King.

In the meantime, it was business as usual in the Cutlers' Company. Wherever their sympathies with Crown or Parliament may have lain, their trade was to supply King and country with arms.

On 23 January 1640, the Court decided 'for the benefit of the whole body and for the service of his Majesty there shall be bought ... such blades as can be gotten and for the money for the payment of them the Master and Wardens shall give security for One Hundred pounds of the Seal of this House.'

In fact, a week later, the Company borrowed £312 for which they sealed a bond for £600: as a result the Court were able to order that

There is to be provided for his Majesty's service within one month to the number of 3000 swords, ready trimmed, to be brought to the Cutlers' Hall by several workmen of this Company . . . every workman is to bring in those swords that he maketh, not trimmed with Irish hilts nor black blades, and every blade to be above nine handful long. . . .

Various freemen of the Company contracted to make varying numbers of swords: their names and particulars were entered in a record that the Master kept.

In February there was a meeting at the Hall at which the Master and wardens delivered sword and rapier blades to divers workmen 'to be trimmed up for the service of his Majesty . . .': the number of blades and the amounts of money owing by the workmen were written in a book entitled *A Book of Debts for Blades Delivered*.

The swords would soon be needed, it seemed, against the hated Scots who, in July, were reported to be massing upon the Border. The King again demanded a loan from the City: he promised that if £200,000 was raised without more ado, he would refrain from putting into circulation the debased coinage that he intended to use. Although the Court of Aldermen were, with difficulty, persuaded, not all the Livery Companies co-operated. Among those who did so were, it seems, the Cutlers whose contribution amounted to £360: they were told that if they were not satisfied about the security that the King was offering for the loan, the Lord Mayor could explain it all to their satisfaction.

This was by no means the only contribution to be demanded. In August and September they were forced to buy four barrels of gunpowder (to be stored safely in a 'remote room') and four barrels of bullets for the service of the City and to certify how many complete sets of arms they held ready in their armoury.

For his immediate needs Charles both debased the coinage and seized the Spanish bullion that was held in the Tower. In August, as his army marched northwards, the Scots crossed the border. The two forces met at Newcastle where the Royal army at its first encounter with the enemy very quickly broke off the engagement and fled. The Scots occupied the town and the northern counties. In October the King, at Ripon, was forced to sue for peace, and to agree not only to leave the enemy in control of Northumberland and Durham but to pay the Scottish armies until a new Parliament met.

It was therefore imperative that the King should recall Parliament: it was equally imperative that even before it met he should raise the money needed for 'preventing the imminent Calamities and settlement of the present distempers and distractions' in both Kingdoms. The Lords decided that the English army, such as it was, must not be disbanded before that of the Scots. There must be 'a goodly supply of £200,000 to be levied for their continuance and orderly dismission.'

Charles had already asked the Lord Mayor how such a sum might be raised as a loan: now the lords, too, wrote persuasively to the City. His Majesty was graciously resolved to hold a Parliament at Westminster on 3 November so that the people might be informed and 'their just grievances' relieved. They were trying to conclude a treaty with the Scots but if the terms proved dishonourable the enemy would have to be fought. The counties occupied by the Scots were in a condition they described as 'miserable' and the future safety of Yorkshire and the parts adjacent to it now depended upon the continuance of a standing army. The disbanding of this army, when peace came, if come it did, would have to take place in an orderly and phased manner 'lest in their Return his Majesty's subjects should undergo any of those inconveniences that soldiers sent away dissatisfied are too apt to put upon them'.

Their Lordships declared that they were persuaded that the City of whose unanimous loyalty and affection they were aware could well afford such a sum: they themselves would supply security for the loan.

On 3 October the Lord Mayor conveyed the message to the City, adding his recommendation of the scheme. £50,000 was to be raised by the twelfth of the month. The Cutlers' share was £500. The spell in prison that the Master and wardens had suffered the last time a precept was ignored had evidently had its effect. The money was paid and paid punctually.

On 3 November Parliament, in no very good humour, met. They started to arrest a number of peers for high treason; Judge Berkeley, too, was arrested on the same charge 'which struck a great terror in the rest of his Brethren then sitting, and on all of his Profession'. They removed from office Members who were monopolists and sniffed out Papists the tolerance of whom, as was well known, 'led to the swarming of lascivious and idle books and pamphlets, play-books, and ballads as, namely, Ovid's *Art of Love, The Parliament of Women,* Barnes's *Poems* and Parker's *Ballads.*' They also voted £300,000 for the relief of 'our Brethren of Scotland'.

Matters were rapidly coming to a head. Strafford, the arch enemy of the City who, in urging that it be plundered, fined and ransomed, had said that things would 'never be well until some of the Aldermen were hanged up', was impeached on the somewhat obscure charge of having broken the unspecified 'fundamental laws'. Charles, in the face of threats from Parliament and the London mob, broke every promise he had made to his minister and signed Strafford's death warrant. In May there were further tumults in the City. A thousand sailors and others marched against the Tower carrying a ship's flag. The trained bands opened fire and killed two of them. And to the trained bands, too, was entrusted the protection of the Queen Mother. Parliament voted £400,000 to be raised by poll tax for the great and pressing affairs of the Kingdom.

In June there were plans for disbanding the English and Scottish armies: in addition to the money already owed to the soldiers there was to be a demobilization grant amounting to one month's pay. £610,000 was still needed and an Act of Parliament was passed in order to raise the money by poll tax. The scale of taxation was fixed according to rank: in the upper levels dukes paid £100, while, lower down, in the Cutlers' Company the Master and wardens were assessed at £5 a head, the Livery at half that sum and the freemen at 10s. each.

At the end of July the Company were called together and given notice of the tax – returns were to be made of the names of those who had paid, and the amounts, and lists were to be submitted with the names and addresses of those who had refused or neglected to pay.

On 6 August there came a stiff note from the Commissioners complaining that there had been great neglect in raising the money. Defaulters would be forced to pay double. If the Master and wardens 'conceive that any of your Company have any money to lend' they must entreat them to provide what they could spare.

In November there was an urgent demand for a loan from the City of £50,000 for an expedition to Ireland. It proved difficult to raise the money although the rebellion was spreading rapidly. There was, it seemed, a great deal of readiness in the City to meet the demand but there was already so much money outstanding that, for lack of liquidity, trade was difficult and the lending of money for the good of the nation even more so. The City with its properties in Ireland was well aware of the situation there: it was suggested that the persons of some of the Papist lords and Quality in England might be secured for the Loan.

As soon as the armies had been disbanded the King hurried to Scotland in an attempt to rally a Royalist party there. He had miscalculated: it was, in fact, in England that a party was beginning to form to defend the King and the Church,[171] already hotly assailed by the Puritans. Charles returned to London. The City made the usual preparations to meet him. The Cutlers selected suitable members 'to ride on great horses with chains of gold, with velvet Jackets and other decent Habits, with each a lackey in violet kersey suits trimmed with white and red ribbons, each lackey to have a white truncheon in their hand for the forenoon service and a torch for the afternoon service. Also, one other in like habit to ride before them bearing a pendant of the Company's Arms.' Two of the Livery were to serve at the Guildhall in gowns of foynes, the rest were to line the rails 'for the Credit of the Company'.

It was the last Royal occasion that the Company were to attend for many a long and dangerous day.

On 4 January 1642 Charles made the fatal mistake that precipitated the Civil War.

There were, at the time, a spate of the wildest rumours. The Commons, and the City of London mob, believed that the Papists were preparing a rising in England, as they had already done in Ireland, to destroy the Protestant religion. Men marched through the City crying 'No Popery! No Bishops! No popish Lords!' The Commons impeached twelve Bishops and prepared, so the King thought, to impeach the Queen. Charles had already lost almost everything by giving way before Parliament – prerogative courts had been abolished, taxation without the consent of Parliament had been declared illegal, an act for the regular summoning of Parliament had been passed, a treaty with the Covenanters had been signed. Now Charles decided to strike back with an impeachment of his own against five selected members of Parliament. But when his officers entered the Commons the members were no longer there: they had taken refuge in the City which, even though the King appeared in person at Guildhall, refused to surrender[172] them. Civil War could not now be long delayed.

In later years it was often taught that the chief reason for the war was the King's disrespect for the Constitution and for the Liberties of Parliament. Such abstractions do not make very powerful rallying points for the man in the street: the Londoners knew well enough the reasons for the conflict, emotive causes to which any red-blooded Englishman would rally and for which he was prepared to fight and die in defending himself. The Catholics were everywhere. Even the officers who had violated the sanctity of the House of Commons were Papists! Papists were committing 'unheard-of rapes' in Ireland – it could happen in London, too. 'A Humble Petition of Gentlewomen, Tradesmen's Wives and many others of the Female Sex', Londoners all, protested:

To see our Husbands and Children murdered and mangled and cut in pieces before our eyes; to see our Children dashed against the Stones and the Mother's Milk mingled with the Infant's Blood running down the streets; to see our Houses on flaming Fire above our Heads: Oh, how dreadful that would be![172]

There were, of course, those in the City who were by no means uncritically enthusiastic about Parliament. When it was sought to raise a militia to protect the King against Papists, one George Benyon spoke for the rest when he refused to subscribe so much as a groat and expressed the opinion that rule by Parliament would mean four hundred tyrants in the place of one. But, on the whole, the City which had been so long a victim of Royal extortion was very willingly prepared to support the King's enemies.

In March Charles withdrew to York and, in his absence, the Parliamentarians summoned a Common Hall at Guildhall to demand from the City a one-year loan of £100,000 at eight per cent for the relief of Ireland 'secured and repaid upon the public faith of the Parliament'.

It had been known for some time that the Irish Lands were in trouble. In March, the Lord Mayor, Sir Richard Gurney, had revealed the miserable distress of the people of Londonderry and the Cutlers had agreed to pay forty marks for their relief. Then in May the Mayor reported, further, that the Protestants were in a state of miserable calamity and distress 'through the inhumane and bloody cruelty of the rebels there who spare not the Protestants wheresoever they come, taking away their lives in a most diabolical and barbarous manner utterly extirpating whole families and towns'. Dublin and Londonderry were both besieged and likely to be lost.

There were difficulties in coming to their relief, for Parliament was chary of raising an army which the King might then use against it. And among the City Companies there was a great amount of indignation at the use of their Common Hall for the governmental raising of money. The richer Companies were especially outraged because the 'greatest number of Liverymen being of the inferior Companies and men of very mean and poor estates were careless of what they granted in regards they were neither willing or able to bear any considerable part of the said charge or burden. . . .'[173]

The Cutlers' share was £1000: to obtain such a sum they borrowed from three men – not members of the Company – on bonds guaranteeing double the amount. They already owed £500 on the bond which they had taken out to contribute towards the disbanding of the armies. This had to be renewed.

It meant a crippling burden of debt but the money for the relief of Ireland was paid at the beginning of July: it was certainly a loan and as such was due to be repaid. But any interest that the loan earned was already ear-marked for the interest on the money they had been forced to borrow and the times were so uncertain that the eventual recovery of their money seemed highly speculative.

In August 1642 the King set up his standard at Nottingham and the first important battle between Essex – who led the Parliamentarians – and Prince Rupert – who led the Royalists – was fought at Edgehill. Both sides were fairly evenly matched: neither gained an appreciable advantage[174] (though the City seemed to regard Edgehill as a defeat[175]); the Royalists occupied Oxford and Essex withdrew to London. It was, in fact, from London that the best part of his army came: the only competent body of militia in the kingdom was that belonging to the City. Rupert, on the other hand, commanded, from among the gentry and their country retainers, the only available body of horse – and it was the cavalry that were the decisive factor in seventeenth-century warfare.

In September 1642 the King marched towards London. At once the citizens, men, women and children, rallied to the Parliamentary cause, digging fortifications and carrying earth. On 12 November the Royal forces captured Brentford. Shops in the City were shut to release employers and employees for defence; apprentices were encouraged to enlist; promises were made that all who took up arms should have their jobs back when the fighting was over.

Twenty-four thousand men were in this way raised and rushed to Turnham Green: faced by such a display of determination, the King, without joining battle, retired with his army to his winter quarters at Oxford.

The extraordinary zeal displayed by the City for the Parliamentary cause has been attributed to Isaac Pennington, who, after the Royalist Richard Gurney had been removed, became Lord Mayor for two years.[176]

In any case 'the Parliament now had the City of London so much at their devotion' that the citizens presented, by a deputation led by a Mr. Shute, a petition and proposals of considerable length to the Commons. The King's strength, they said, lay in horse, yet Parliament had no such body: they would provide a force of cavalry. They would 'man out every Man his Man and make their own Captains and Officers and live and die with the House of Commons and in Defence thereof'.

This, they felt, entitled them to criticize.

The Sabbath Day was everywhere profaned: Edgehill had been fought on the Sunday and it had proved the day of their ruin. Yet the *Book for Tolerating Sports on the Sabbath Day* had still not been burnt by the public hangman.

No expiation had been made for the Marian martyrs.

The Officers of the Army (always excepting the Lord-General Essex) were not as diligent as they ought to be, nor all of them to be trusted.

Something should be done about the prisoners who were present in the City 'in great numbers and of Dangerous Condition'.

In spite of these criticisms, however, they assured the Commons that 'You have our Persons, Purses and Estates, all at your Command: You may do with us at your Pleasure.

'We come in the name of the Godly and Active Part of the City.' This last sentence revealed that there were others in the City who did not share their sentiments: they were henceforth to be known as the Malignant Party – a conveniently categorical division of the citizens into the opposing forces of Good and Evil.

The Commons expressed themselves gratified. They put first things first and ordered that the Book should be publicly burnt by the hangman: then they gratefully accepted the offer of horse and foot. They called-in the citizens to inform them of both these decisions. The Londoners had, in the meantime, had further thoughts and Mr. Shute expressed them:

'The Coming of the Lord-General's Army into the City of London and staying there so long as they did is another Thing that troubles them; which they forgot to express before. Another Thing is that some present and more severe Course might be taken with Malignants; and amongst them the Malignant Ministers. And then the Citizens withdrew.'

They had, in fact, engaged to raise 1000 light horse and 3000 dragoons for the service of Parliament. They were to be commanded by the Lord General alone and to be accountable to none but him acting under the orders of both Houses. Their immediate commander in the field was to be Sergeant-Major-General Skippon, with Colonel Hurrey as second in command.

The General was, obviously a bluff military-man, unused – as he might himself have said, clearing his throat – to making speeches.

He addressed the newly-recruited force of Londoners, bluntly:

Come my Boys, my brave Boys, let us pray heartily and fight heartily. I will run the same Fortunes and Hazards with you. Remember the Cause is for God and for the Defence of yourselves, your Wives, and your Children. Come my honest brave Boys, pray heartily and fight heartily and God will help us.

Their fighting was not yet, however, to begin. The King had not pursued his victory at Brentford: there was, even, talk of a treaty. It was talk that alarmed Mr. Shute. At the head of several citizens he arrived on 21 November at the House of Commons: they were all, he said, 'grieved to think that there might be an Accomodation'. If any such thing occurred the Malignant Party must pay its share of the costs. Later he again presented himself with his followers at Westminster. This time they submitted ideas for raising money for continuing the war. There was, for instance, the plate in the Livery Halls; there were subscriptions from the wards that had not yet been collected; weekly subscriptions could be raised among the Companies; money could be saved by reducing the number of unnecessary officers, by doing away with Musters, by making foreign merchants contribute, by having 'indifferent honest men' to collect the subscriptions. In December he again appeared before the House of Commons. He complained that the Godly party were being accused of not wanting peace: the Malignants, who accused them, wanted a treaty only to give the Royalists time to regather their strength and collect more Gunpowder.

But, understandably, the Commons were beginning to tire of Mr. Shute: he found himself, to his discomfiture, rebuked for using un-Parliamentary expressions. The Parliamentarians did not, however, receive kindly a petition from those whom Shute would have dubbed 'malignant' – those who protested that Civil War was a terrible thing and they were all being ruined by it. These petitioners were also denounced by the Lord Mayor, the aldermen and the Common Council: no petition that was not attested by the Town Clerk, they said, genuinely came from the City.

Nonetheless, the peacemakers continued with their unpopular cause.

In January 1643 the King at Oxford received a petition from some of those in the City. It contained great protestations of loyalty – which Charles appeared to doubt – and begged him to return to Parliament and restore peace to the country. The King asked that a Common Hall be summoned at which both the Petition and his reply could be read. At this the Commons became highly suspicious: if the reply was the same as that which had already been issued in book form, then it was full of matters scandalous to Parliament and likely to cause a mutiny. They decided to send to the Common Hall representatives prepared to speak out in denunciation of the King's answer: in the meantime a Precept was sent by the Committee of Lords and Commons for the Safety of the Kingdom to all the Companies.

Whereas there are divers letters pretended to be sent by his Majesty to the Masters and Wardens of the several Halls in the City of London with two little books therein enclosed th'one entituled 'The Humble petition of the Mayor, Aldermen and Commons of the City of London to his Majesty' and th'other entituled 'His Majesty's Letter and Declaration to the Sheriffs and City of London' dated the 17th of January which evidently tendeth to sedition and setting the whole City in Combustion. . . .' The precept was 'therefore strictly to command the Master and Wardens of every Hall in the City to whom the said letters and books enclosed shall be directed to forbear to publish or open any of them until both the houses of Parliament shall give further order therein. And the Masters and Wardens . . . are required to bring the said Letters with the Messengers thereof to the Committee which they will take (as) an argument of their good affection to the Parliament.

The Cutlers had received their letter from the hands of Henry Davis, one of the King's messengers who lived in Westminster, but there is no indication that they went so far as to take him before the Committee.

They received another precept that the Beadle was to summon the Livery together on 13 January before eight o'clock in the morning. All were then to proceed in an orderly manner, in their Livery gowns, to be at Guildhall before 9 a.m. where they were to hear read out the petition and its reply.

The petition was duly read but, when it came to the King's reply, the messenger, Captain Heron, tried to escape reading it: he had been told, only, he protested, to deliver it into the hands of the Lord Mayor; moreover, in so great an assembly he would be unable to make himself heard. However, at last, he was persuaded. The gist of the message was that the King had always wanted to live in the City but the lawlessness there had driven him away. They had collected money for armies to fight him and had done everything to act against him. How was it possible to trust them when Pennington the Mayor was imprisoning the supporters of the Crown and cherishing Brownists, Anabaptists and other Schismatics? Was that respectful towards the Protestant Church? The King warned them that, if they did not reform, they would be punished when eventually he returned to the City.

Captain Heron, who had indeed made himself heard only with the greatest difficulty, was asked to repeat his performance in the Clock House. He did so and some Malignants 'an inconsiderable Company near the Door, made some Offers towards an Acclamation; but finding no expected Echo to answer their Shout they wound up in a little Modesty and a great deal of Silence.'

This was the opportunity for the Parliament observers to speak out. The Earl of Manchester, amid thunderous applause, described the King's reply as a great slander to the City – but they could rely on Parliament to protect them. Mr. Pym also addressed the meeting. It was quite untrue, he said, that the King had been forced to leave Whitehall because of tumults. In fact, the day after he had come violently into Parliament, Charles had come to the City without any guard, had attended Common Council, had dined with the Sheriffs and had returned home without any expressions of anything but Fidelity from the citizens. . . .'

He dealt with all the King's objections, demolishing each in turn. Finally he reiterated the promise that Parliament would protect the Londoners, a statement greeted with enormous applause and repeated cries of 'We will live and die with them!' The Malignants, so it was claimed, were confounded and ashamed to see their powerlessness and thus the City was united instead of divided.[177]

This disappointing reaction to the Royal reply caused Charles to write to the sheriffs, on 17 January, asking that Masters and wardens should call their Companies together, with 'the Freemen and Apprentices (whose Hopes and Interests are so much blasted in these general Distractions). . .' and read his answer to them. Charles added that Pennington had never been legally elected Mayor – Mr. Cordwell had secured more votes – and had never even been sworn-in. He declared Pennington to be no longer Mayor: he ordered his arrest. But the King's writ no longer ran in the City. The Sheriffs informed Parliament and Parliament ordered the Companies to disregard the request: they were not to summon their members together as Charles had demanded.

Nonetheless there were still attempts to patch up some kind of a peace with the King. The Citizens were, in fact, beginning to tire of doing good to Parliament, of pouring vast sums of money into the purse of a cause whose forces were really not gaining any comparable success. The flame of their enthusiasm began to flicker. They began to complain. The City in relation to the country as a whole was, they claimed, being over-assessed. More of the money collected should be devoted to the defence of London and the expense should fall not only on the Godly but on the Malignants as well. The citizens had already been asked for £60,000 – now

Q

the enormous sum of £10,000 a week was demanded. As far as the
lump sum was concerned the City would not pay it until ordinance
for its eventual repayment had been passed. Parliament conceded
the point: repayment would be made with eight per cent interest
and the principal sum would be paid from the weekly collections.
The money was desperately needed. If what the King alleged was
true the sum collected to suppress the rebellion in Ireland had
been spent, so it was said, on the Parliamentary army. More arms
were urgently required: the Companies were ordered to hand over
everything in their armouries to the Auxiliary Forces. The weapons
would, eventually, be returned or replaced. Great amounts of
pay were still owing to the troops. There was a grave danger that
they would disband if money were not forthcoming. The City
authorities were ordered to sequester the estates in the City of
those who supported the King.

They were ordered, also, to consider the risks of fire in the City
in time of war: as a result the Cutlers received a demand for 'a
sufficient number of Buckets, Ladders, Hooks, Pickaxes and other
instruments fit to be used on a sudden occasion. . . .'

With all these demands for money or for goods it was obvious
that the Cutlers must soon find themselves in great financial
trouble. In May the Court decided to raise £200 by selling some of
their Plate – the money was to be apportioned, in particular, to
the £10 which was their share of the weekly assessment, to the
interest money that they were paying on the money they had
already borrowed and, more generally, to the 'many other urgent
and pressing occasions the Company is put into at this time'.

A committee of both Houses sat at Haberdashers' Hall to collect
the money raised by corporations and individuals. Anyone who
would freely lend any money was to be allowed interest of eight
per cent. Those who would neither lend, give, nor pay their weekly
assessments were to have their goods distrained: the Committee
were allowed 3d. in the pound for the expenses of the process and
informers who could tell where goods were secreted were allowed
five per cent of the value of the goods discovered.

In June the Cutlers were forced to make out two more bonds in
security for sums borrowed to repay some of their earlier debts

and, not surprisingly, they decided that no Account Dinner should be held that year 'in respect of the great sessments and divers other charges and impositions'. The Parliament at this point had the good fortune – or, perhaps, the good management – to uncover a plot. The Companies were summoned again to Guildhall and reminded of their own importance – they with the Parliament and the army comprised all that was vitally important in England. Yet there were plotters amongst them: Mr. Pym retailed the details of the affair at enormous length; he proclaimed a day of thanksgiving for their deliverance from the Plot and, with a magnanimity surprising in the circumstances of a real conspiracy, added that any plotter who was stricken by remorse might own up and be forgiven.

Everybody was to swear in the most solemn manner: 'I, A.B., ... declare vow and covenant ... not to lay down Arms as long as the Papists are fighting Parliament' – another clear indication of what the man in the street considered to be the real cause of the War.

But the City was becoming increasingly discontented. It would have been one thing to dispense vast amounts of money and goods and be rewarded with victory: it was quite another to find the Army in a miserable condition, largely unpaid, demoralized and gradually losing so much ground that the Royalists occupied two-thirds of the country. The Londoners needed no reminder of what would happen to the loans and themselves if the Parliamentary cause were to be defeated.

They were faced with the depressing truth when the Lord Mayor called both for a day of public fasting for the defeats of the Parliament in the North and West and a capital tax in a weekly levy.

In August, the Court of Common Council being 'very sensible of the great and imminent danger this City is in by the near approach of the King's forces and of the great and pressing necessity for money . . .' demanded a loan of £50,000 for six months at eight per cent: the Cutlers were assessed at £500.

The Court considered this new demand. Martial enthusiasm was wearing thin: they decided to pay £250 and no more. Yet another bond was sealed to raise the money and plunge them still deeper into debt.

It is not surprising that rumours of another proposition for peace began to be heard. The idea caused great alarm among the Godly: Pennington summoned the Common Council and a petition against peace was presented to Parliament. This time there was a counter-petition: women, in particular, were becoming vocal in their demands for an end to the fighting and it was alleged that some of the rabble, dressed as women, joined in the shouts of 'Peace! Peace!'

The Malignants were, however, in a minority. The Godly made further warlike demands: in September 1643 there came an urgent precept from Sir William Waller for five thousand men to be 'pressed' from various counties. 'In which the very Watermen on the Thames were included; alleging "That in time of Common Danger and Necessity the Interest of private Persons ought to give Way to the Public".'

The more men were enlisted, the more money was needed to pay them. In October the Cutlers were summoned before the authorities to know why they would not pay more than the £250 towards the recent loan. Their reply is not recorded but it may be noted that the Court decided to sell more of their Plate.

In November the patience of the City, under its financial and material burdens, crumbled dangerously. The Committee of the Militia of London went so far as to present to Parliament 'A Remonstrance of the City of London of their great Wants and Necessities'.

Through their spokesman, Alderman Gibbs, they declared that their wants could be, basically, divided into two. Firstly there was a great lack of money: the City had advanced great sums at various times both for this country and for Ireland. They had contributed to every kind of tax and levy and subsidy and they had received no benefit. Secondly, they had made many large disbursements on arms, ammunition and victuals. They had spent great sums of money on various armed units particularly to raise forces under Sir William Waller 'when he was broken all to pieces'.

The City troops in the field were without pay: two regiments of horse and three of foot had been on active service for a month. There were three more regiments with Waller. £10,000 was needed for the troops with Essex and perhaps another £5000 for those with Waller. The City, the Remonstrance protested, simply had no longer that amount of money. 'Our rich Men are gone because the City is the Place of Taxes and Burdens; Trade is decayed and our Shops shut up in great Measure; our Poor do much increase; we desire you for future Taxes, that we may bear but their Proportion, and be not over-burdened. . . .'

The accusation that the Godly were warmongers who did not desire peace was deeply resented: 'these are bitter Aspertions out of black Mouths and bitter Pens'. All they, in fact, desired was the glory of God and the safety of religion – and a grant of money to continue in business. This reversal of the accustomed roles, which found the City asking Parliament for cash, struck an unexpected and unwelcome note. The Commons declared that they must have time to think: in the meantime, the City might rest assured that they were grateful for all that had been done and they would do all that they could to help.

The Malignants were still a power to be reckoned with. In January 1644, with Sir Basil Brooke as their leader, they plotted to make a separate peace treaty between the King and the City. Safeguarding the Protestant religion was to be the *sine qua non* of the agreement – another indication of what the common man conceived that he was fighting for – and, hardly less important, all loans that the City had made were to be repaid. The Liberties of Parliament were not mentioned.

In all this activity Parliament saw quite clearly the hands of the Papists in general and the Jesuits in particular, attempting to subvert the City. The Godly, for their part, expressed themselves so happy that the plot was discovered that they asked the Lord General Essex and representatives of both Houses to dine at Merchant Taylors' Hall – an invitation that was gratefully accepted for, said the Parliament men, they recognized what a support the City had always been and this gesture they recognized as another example of affection.

The cause of the Parliamentarians had reached its nadir. Then, at the beginning of 1644, they joined forces with the hated Scots and a Committee of Both Kingdoms was set up to direct the war. This step proved, in the long run, to be conclusive. From henceforth the King was on the defensive and the tally of Roundhead victories began to mount.

The fortunes of war still fluctuated: though Cromwell and his 'Ironsides' gained a brilliant victory at Marston Moor and York surrendered to the Parliament forces yet there were Royalist victories in the West and in Scotland under Montrose.

In March, that year, everyone in London and Westminster gave up one meal a week and the money thus saved was devoted to the Army. Essex was demanding more men. He was, he said, certain that the City, who, as he pointed out in a fulsome manner, had always been so resourceful and willing in that sort of affair, could provide them. He chose 9 April – a thanksgiving day for the victory of Waller's troops at Winchester. The Companies were called together and addressed by a number of eminent speakers: they were thanked for their past efforts on behalf of what was actually described, to keep the main objective firmly in the public view, as the 'Defence of Religion and Public Liberty'; they were greeted with a rousing slogan by which they were encouraged to join their 'Persons, Purses, and Prayers'. To all this display of over-enthusiastic exhortation the Recorder replied sombrely only that they would do what they could. With this the notables on the platform had to be content and, in fact, in October that year, the City sent out five regiments of foot to oppose the King as he approached Dorchester from the West. In the meantime the Commons had voted support for a Scots army in Ireland and a Committee was sitting at Goldsmiths' Hall to devise means of raising the money. They decided that the City should raise an extra £300 a week for necessities in Ireland.

The citizens – or, at any rate, a large part of them – were still demanding Peace: it seemed that there was a disagreement between the Lords and the Commons on the subject and the City desired that the quarrel should cease.

That London was suffering an appalling draining away of the money that was its life's blood is obvious: yet, somehow or other, each time the screw was turned, a little more blood, figuratively speaking, emerged. Literally speaking, too – at Tallow Chandlers' Hall Collectors were stationed to receive subscriptions for the wounded soldiers. Increasingly the City shewed a desire for the end of hostilities. Yet an attempt to make a treaty at Uxbridge failed and the Civil War continued. The remains of the five Parliamentary armies that had been in the field against the Royalists were now re-formed into one 'New Model Army', under Fairfax. By a self-denying Ordinance the old commanders retired and 'simple soldiers' took their place. Whether the army was new or old, money had still to be raised. The assessment on London and Middlesex combined was more than £8000 and for the maintenance of the Scots army alone the City had to contribute nearly £2200 each month.

In addition to such sums taxes had been placed on a wide range of goods. Further sums were raised by Tunnage and Poundage.

In March both Houses of Parliament passed a resolution to borrow more money from the City. They had already decided to raise £50,000 a month from the whole country. An immediate £80,000 was needed to put Fairfax's army in the field and they would pledge the credit to be raised from the nation-wide monthly collection to the City to raise this urgent sum.

Once again the City used the demand as an opportunity for airing criticisms of how the war was being waged: more action must be taken; Fairfax's army must be brought up to strength; soldiers like Cromwell, who had been excepted from the self-denying ordinance, should be allowed to get on with the fighting in their own way – they should not have to await orders from Parliamentary Committees before every campaign.

The results of all this reorganization and soul-searching were soon to be seen: the year 1645 was one of sweeping Parliamentary gains. But victories were no less expensive than defeat: £30,000 was wanted for the Scots army approaching Newark but the response to an assessment was disappointingly sluggish. The Collectors at Goldsmiths' Hall reported that the money was simply not being brought in to them. Parliament decided that 'some Gentlemen' should be sent into the City to borrow the money. Where the politicians had failed the gentlemen no doubt succeeded: the Godly were rewarded and the war, in spite of peace negotiations, went on.

In May 1646 the King gave himself up to the Scots and the first part of the Civil War was ended.

Where, in all this, had the Cutlers stood? There is no reason to doubt that, as a body, they were on the side of the Godly. As a body, too, they had been mulcted continuously and painfully. Under assessments based on the scale of Corn Money their contribution was one per cent of everything demanded from the City. It was no small amount and it can be remarked only that it was, somehow, always eventually forthcoming. In 1644, for instance, they admitted twenty-seven members to the Livery and their admission fines provided a welcome amount. But on the whole it was money that could be raised only by becoming ever deeper in debt: at least four bonds for various amounts were sealed in 1643; two more were taken out in 1644; and the following year they sealed six bonds totalling £2000. Their tenants, too, were finding life difficult; at Egham the occupier had been compelled to carry out repairs totalling some £200 and was demanding an extension of his lease to compensate him for all that he had spent.

Against the terrifying background of the Civil War the Court had continued to govern the Company but the amount of business had greatly fallen away. While on a national scale the nicely differentiated forces of good and evil were slogging it out, on the more modest battlefield of the City the Cutlers were engaged in their own small but vitally important battles. It was ironmongers who were now causing trouble – they, and other tradesmen, profiting, no doubt by what must have been an exceptional demand for weapons, were making up swords and selling them 'at under rates to the spoil and ruin of the Company of Cutlers'.

The Company petitioned Parliament that such abuses should be rectified, and they determined that there must be a general tightening of controls: they would prosecute any ironmonger who used the trade of cutlery.

There was a tightening, too, of the controls over their own internal affairs. In future, they decided, the Master and wardens must give securities to the Court for the proper execution of their offices; there must be an attempt made to settle their accounts – to Richard Evans was given the invidious task of attempting to recover some of the money due to the Company from the Government and elsewhere. In the event, some money was, against all expectations, recovered and, ten days after Charles had surrendered to the Scots, the Cutlers received back, from the Cashier-General at the Excise Office, no less than £180. But in view of the general situation of both Company and country it is hardly surprising that the Master-elect, in 1645, chose to be fined £6. 13s. 4d. rather than take up office.

The Brewers, as well as the ironmongers, provided a cause for conflict. They claimed that one of the Cutlers' Livery was a brewer and should, therefore, be a member of their Company. And if either the Cutlers or the man himself should refuse a translation they 'would take him from us perforce'.

In view of the general state of unrest in the country it is, perhaps, surprising that among the Cutlers, unlike many of the other Companies, there was, in spite of their recent great constitutional schism, comparatively little internal unrest. It is true that when John Treadwell and other hilt-forgers of the Company went on a Search 'for French hilts and such-like prohibited wares [and] came into the shop of John Fell, cutler, to search for such-like goods the said John Fell did not only refuse to let them search but abused them in deeds and gave them and all the Company very bad and ill-beseeming language'.

And in the Chamber of London Jeremy Peasely 'scandalized the Company' by 'falsely saying and complaining to Mr. Harrison, the Chamberlain, that the Company kept a false Charter and ruled or governed by it'.

But, eventually and quite easily, these matters were resolved and there was, within the Company, a gratifying state of calm.

It was very different in the City as a whole. The War had been fought, as all were well aware, in defence of the Protestant religion. Yet now that the fighting was over, although the Papists had gone underground and had, indeed, been banished from the City, Brownists and Anabaptists and all sorts of Schisms proliferated under the name of Independants. They held private meetings on the Lord's Day – there were no less than eleven in one Parish – at which there were even women preachers and new strange blasphemies. In May the City made a remonstrance and petition on the subject to Parliament. They demanded first that there should be no Private Congregations and that Sectarians should be prosecuted. They hoped at the same time that taxes would be reduced and loans repaid: the Committee at Haberdashers' Hall was one of their greatest grievances – its activities discouraged people from coming to the City and destroyed trade – and they asked that it be dissolved. They complained, too, that the City was constantly subjected to invective, scurrilous pamphlets, and attempts to make trouble with Parliament.

This petition, although the Lords approved it, caused great offence to the Commons to whom it appeared that the City were trying to dictate to them: it was obviously the work of the Presbyterian party and General Ludlow considered it insolent. By a strange act of punctiliousness a copy of the document was sent to the King, away up in Newcastle and a prisoner of the Scots; he made a gracious reply to it as if he were still effectively ruling.

In July, the City went further. They sent a petition to Parliament containing 'very many remarkable Expressions of Respect from this Body Corporate to his Majesty'; they expressed their loyalty, a hope for the settlement of true religion and peace and the union of England and Scotland, and they hoped, too, that the King – to whom they requested that the petition be forwarded – would return to the City.

Once more the Commons were outraged. They could not approve of the City acting independently: the City was all one with the rest of the Kingdom in any propositions that might be sent to the King.

It is again worthy of note, in determining the true reasons for the Civil War, that the first eleven articles of the proposed treaty with Charles were all concerned with religion.

In September 1646 there came a demand for £200,000 to be raised from the City. The aldermen suggested that people should lend an amount equal to what they were already owed and that the whole sum should then be secured on the sale of the Bishops' lands which were in process of being confiscated. To this the Commons agreed and nominated as additional security the lands of the Royalist delinquents.

In fact, the subscriptions came in so quickly that the whole amount was collected by the end of November. And the Cutlers sealed still more bonds and fell still further into debt.

In the meantime, on 21 September, the Scots had sold Charles for £400,000 to Parliament – the City's subscription was used as a first instalment – and had agreed to withdraw from England. The Royalist cause seemed to be finally doomed. And, indeed, everything might have been speedily settled had not the victors fallen out amongst themselves. Once again it was religion that was the cause of dissension. In 1643, when the help of the Scots was urgently needed, a 'Solemn League and Covenant' had been made by which the Churches of England and Scotland were to be brought to the nearest possible degree of religious uniformity. This had been highly distasteful to the East Anglian Independents in the Army who, under Cromwell, were the forerunners of the modern Congregationalists.

Now, at the end of 1646, there was a great divide fixed between the victorious and sectarian New Model Army and the predominantly Presbyterian House of Commons: to religious differences were added the no less pressing differences on the subject of finance.

There was a great demand that the size of the Army be reduced. On 19 December the City petitioned Parliament for 'Disbanding the Army and for Removing Preaching Soldiers &c'. Many of the military, it seemed, had not taken the Covenant with the result that the pulpits of the City were incongruously and quite unacceptibly usurped by soldiers preaching Errors.

The City had further complaints to make. In March 1647 they protested against Fairfax's army being quartered near the City – they were using provisions needed for the Londoners. The Army, it was said, should be disbanded and the soldiers sent to Ireland. But before demobilization, the Army had to be paid and extra money found for those posted to Ireland. Parliament applied to the City for another Loan of £200,000, the Cutlers' share of which would have been £200. Coming as it did so soon after the last demand the Citizens shewed no great enthusiasm but the matter was becoming one of some urgency: the military seemed to be getting somewhat above themselves and were actually beginning to petition their paymasters in Parliament.

The Commons were, by June, becoming nervous about the army which, they thought, was approaching London for reasons which could only be sinister. Civilians, too, were coming in a disorderly way to Westminster: the City trained bands were called upon to protect Parliament against the tumults that were daily feared.

The Londoners also were becoming nervous: they besought the Commons to pay the army – or give the soldiers some kind of satisfaction; to keep the King safe so that access might be had to him by both English and Scots Members and to allow the City its old power of raising horse and troops to search out, especially, Papists.

Next the Army, over the signatures of Cromwell, Fairfax and others, protested to the City: they were not, they assured the Londoners, seeking their wealth. The troops wanted only their rights: they had been called up for certain war aims that, now that the fighting was over, had not been achieved; they had been badly treated financially: they sought the help of the City in securing what was due to them.

The City was not reassured. Parliament was requested to order the Army not to come within twenty-five miles of London: at the same time, a letter was sent to Fairfax at Royston protesting that the City was not in any way opposed to the Army achieving their just desires but by coming to the City and by creating scarcity, they would cause riots which could only make matters more difficult for everyone concerned.

The reply from Fairfax came, alarmingly, from St. Albans. This was not only within the twenty-five miles postulated by the City but well within the forty-mile limit which Parliament had, in fact, ordered. The letter had in addition a slightly sinister ring: it appeared, said Fairfax, that the Londoners were raising troops to fight against the Army; that people were trying to start a new War.

The City, thoroughly alarmed, appealed to the Lords: the Lords informed Fairfax that no troops other than trained bands were being raised in the City – all other recruitment had been countermanded. Fairfax wrote again to the City. He accepted their Good Will and he noted what they said about disbanding the forces that had been unofficially raised but . . . recruiting was still going on and other things as well, all prejudicial to the Army. The General's note displayed quite a new tone. He demanded rather than requested; he talked of impeaching some of the leading Citizens; he asked for a better understanding and mentioned casually that some influential Londoners now resided permanently at his headquarters – though whether this was intended as a threat or an inducement is not quite clear.

The City authorities were now approaching a state of panic: they sent an inordinately long petitition to Parliament demanding the speedy payment of everything that was owing to the troops and a quick return to a normal state of life in the Kingdom.

This called for more money. Parliament demanded that £60,000 a month be raised – London's share was stated with great nicety as being £3907 19s. 2¾d. – and expressed great indignation that both the City and the Army – who were now demanding the impeachment of eleven Members – appeared to be dictating to them. Clearly the three victorious partners were completely at loggerheads and two of them in a state of fear against the third.

It was at this juncture that the apprentices, who had been remarkably controlled, joined in the fray. With the enthusiasm of the young they embraced a great list of causes in which they placed the preservation of the Protestant religion rather lower down the list of priorities than did their elders.

On 14 July a petition of 10,000 apprentices and young men demanded that the King be preserved, that the privileges of Parliament be respected, that the Government of the Church be secured, that the Malignants be tried, that the soldiers be paid, that the Army be disbanded and that foreigns be prevented from hindering the trade of the City. Ten days later they were joined in another great petition to the Lord Mayor in which 'Citizens, Commanders,

Officers, Soldiers of Trained Bands and Auxiliaries, Young Men and
Apprentices of London and Westminster, Sea Commanders,
Seamen, Watermen and divers others Commanders and Soldiers'
all protested that religion, His Majesty's person, Parliamentary
privileges and the liberties of the subject were endangered by the
existing state of affairs. They asked that all the City might engage
together to get the King to come in safety and honour to Parliament, without the Army coming near, and there to settle all
matters in difference. The petitioners then made a 'Solemn Engagement'. They had sworn a covenant for reformation and the defence
of religion, for the Honour and Happiness of the King, for the
Peace and Safety of the Three Kingdoms. All now seemed likely
to be destroyed, so they solemnly engaged themselves to en-
deavour to get the King safely and honourably to a meeting with
both Houses of Parliament.

Many officers and young men, so it was reported, were seen
going in to Skinners' Hall to sign this petition; many copies were
in circulation; many thousands of signatures could be speedily
expected.

The Commons were outraged. They ordered a Declaration to
be read and published by 'Beat of Drum and Sound of Trumpet'
in London and Westminster and, afterwards, throughout the
Realm. The petition was a great aspersion on both Parliament and
Army. It tended towards another war. Anyone who took any part
in organizing or signing the petition was guilty of high treason
and would forfeit both life and estates.

They wrote to the Common Council: clearly these wicked
fellows were intent on a war which would start there in the City's
bowels before spreading to the rest of the body of the Kingdom.
The council must look to what was happening at Skinners' Hall;
they must restore the command of the City Militia to those who
would suppress such excesses.

The Army took it equally badly. It provided them with clear
evidence that, as they had thought, there were ill-disposed people
in the City, raising troops, wanting war, disaffecting the others.
The approach of the Army towards the City had been to discourage
just such a situation and to preserve the freedom of Parliament

from such violent behaviour. Yet how mis-represented they had been and how justified they were now seen to be!

All unheeding of this joint disapproval great numbers of rioters assembled on 26 July in Westminster and 'the Apprentices and many other rude Boys and mean Fellows amongst them came into the House of Commons with their Hats on, kept the Door open, and called out as they stood: "Vote! Vote!"'

In a more orderly fashion the Lord Mayor and aldermen had also petitioned Parliament to restore the right of the City to choose its own officers for the militia. In another petition they demanded the right to make such petitions without being declared to be traitors. In support of these demands the apprentices and rabble climbed up to the windows of the House of Commons and threw down stones on the sitting Members. Others attacked the doors and were repulsed by Members with swords. The Speaker, trying to go into the lobby, was flung back into his chair by the 'insolent rabble', forty or fifty of whom had managed to get into the Chamber. At this point the Commons 'thought Convenient to give way to their Rage'. They asked the rioters what question they wanted to be put: the reply was 'That the King should be desired to come to London with safety and honour'. The Speaker negatived this but many Members cautiously shouted 'Aye'. The mob departed. And, to some extent, they got their way: the declaration that signatories to the petition were traitors and the ordinance for the militia were both rescinded. But their action gave Fairfax the pretext that he was seeking. He had always said that there was an unruly party in the City – now they had shewn themselves. In spite of a letter from Parliament assuring him that the City had no part in the apprentices' riot and that the coming of the Army into the City would cause tumults, Fairfax marched on London.

Many of the Parliamentarians then deserted to the Army, and in August without opposition from the City militia, mustered in St. James's Fields, Fairfax entered the City. The Lord Mayor and aldermen congratulated him, offered him a basin and ewer, all of gold and worth more than £1000, and invited him and his officers to a 'splendid Entertainment' at Guildhall. Both the gift and the invitation were contemptuously refused and the troops marched through London with laurels in their hats as conquerors.

In September a new militia was decreed and the Lord Mayor was impeached for high treason. The Recorder and several aldermen were also imprisoned, and the General threatened that he would billet 1000 troops in the City if the arrears of money due for the Army were not speedily collected.

The Cutlers were among those who still owed money to the Collectors. They could not pay. They still owed money on the Corn Precepts which they were still receiving in His Majesty's name. The Court, therefore, early in December, with admirable prudence, ordered that 'the Master and Wardens should take the plate and linen belonging to the Company out of the Hall and secure the same in Mr. Partridge's or Mr. Warnett's Custody in regard the Company was threatened to be plundered for two several sessments the Hall was sessed at and could not pay to Sir Thomas Fairfax.'

This daring attempt to secure their property from confiscation met with a disconcerting set-back. It is unfortunate that the relevant entries in the Minutes have been destroyed but sufficient fragments survive to shew that when the plotters arrived to collect the plate and linen, to take it to a safe place of hiding, Edmund King, one of the wardens, refused to deliver his key of the Treasury and said that he would not allow the goods to be taken out of the Hall – an unforeseen attitude in which he was supported by Thomas Freeman, another member of the Court.

It was all very disappointing and it made the Company extremely vulnerable to the sort of sanctions which the Army were imposing upon the City.

The situation was now not only extraordinary but one of considerable irony. Parliament had raised the Army and the Army had revolted against its creator. The City had been old friends and allies of Parliament but were now not only considered to be filled with 'sedition and averseness, questioning their integrity' but were occupied by the troops. Charles had escaped from the Army and had taken refuge at Carisbrooke where he made a new alliance with the Scots against Parliament who actually (and, as it happened, vainly) sent four Bills there to receive the Royal Assent for all the world as if he were still their King in fact as well as in law.

Political chaos was, therefore, absolute: early in 1648 the Civil War was renewed.

Royalist hopes of revenge must have been high. Their enemies were hopelessly split, there was a growing discontent among the citizens with the Long Parliament, and a new alliance with the Scots. But, in fact, the war soon went against them.[178] The King's campaigns were badly co-ordinated and the New Model Army was still intact. Equally important was the fact that at last Cromwell was convinced that it would be impossible to make any satisfactory treaty with Charles: the struggle must be fought, without compromise, to a finish.

There were those in the City who still supported the Royalists: in April there was a riot by apprentices demonstrating in favour of the King. They beat drums upon the river-side to get seamen and watermen to join them 'for God and King Charles' – they also looted houses, fired shots into the Lord Mayor's House and seized the drums from the trained bands.

In May a plot was alleged, in and about London, against Parliament: it was used as a pretext for sending all Malignants and Papists at least twenty miles from the City and it was about this time that the Parliamentarians decided that they should try and repair their relationship with their old ally. On 23 May some kind of agreement was reached. The City consented to adhere to Parliament and petitioned for the release of their officers; Parliament agreed to remove their Horse Troops from the Tower to Whitehall where they would be kept until the City certified that it could guard itself; they would not impeach the Recorder and they asked that the collection of arrears of payment to the Army be expedited. There was, in fact, in the reconciliation, a certain amount of give and take on both sides.

In the meantime a reconciliation had also taken place in the Court of the Cutlers. Edmund King, the warden who had been so tiresomely obstructive about hiding the Company's goods from

Fairfax, acknowledged his offence and his submission 'was accepted and lovingly passed by'. There was slightly more difficulty with Mr. Freeman who 'by some words he said was supposed to advise and abet Warden King not to deliver up his key'. He, at first, several times 'very peremptorily refused' to submit to their censure and was banned from all further meetings but within a month he, too, had fallen into line.

In June that year there was a petition from some of the citizens to the Lord Mayor demanding, among other things, a treaty with the King and in due course the matter was brought before Parliament. This time it was the Commons who were in favour of negotiating and the Lords who refused. The Presbyterian leaders did, in fact, carry on a series of talks with the King in the Isle of Wight but there were powerful forces working against a settlement. Cromwell, who had previously been in favour of some form of monarchy, was now against it; Ireton was demanding the setting up of a republic; even in the City those who were demanding a treaty with Charles were probably in a minority.

'Thousands of well-affected Persons' declared themselves, in a petition on 8 September, against any form of agreement with the King and demanded that Parliament declare itself the supreme authority of the nation. It was a very long petition and it received no reply. After only three days the petitioners tried again and descended on Westminster in large numbers in a determined effort to undermine any settlement. They declared that they had 40,000 signatures but added, sinisterly, that 5000 Horse would be more effective.

The Army, victorious in Essex, Wales and at the Battle of Preston, had, by this time, had enough. On 30 November Fairfax, from Windsor, announced his intention of marching upon London. There would be, he promised, no rapine, but he would occupy all empty houses and he must have an immediate £40,000 from the City on the security of the arrears they already owed him. Parliament was, as might well be expected, alarmed: the City was urged to buy Fairfax off as quickly as possible: the City, hardly less alarmed, promised to do so by the very next day. The Cutlers, faced with such urgent demands, decided that there was nothing for it but to sell all the plate: the linen and the damask which had not yet been made up were, however, to remain in the custody of Mr. Gabriel Partridge. The Commons informed Fairfax that the money would be raised and told him to call off the march. He took no notice and arrived in Whitehall, demanding the execution of the King. The Members of both Houses of Parliament were, however, in agreement: Charles' answers to their proposals were sufficient justification for seeking peace. The Army, not now to be deterred, acted. Under Colonel Pride, an armed band entered the Commons and arrested the greater part of the Members, sending them with typically bluff military humour to Hell – a victualling house of that name in Westminster – for the night which they spent in great discomfort. The remaining Members, or 'Rump', carried by a mere twenty-six votes against twenty an Act to try the King for a number of hitherto unheard-of crimes.

On 27 January 1649 Charles was sentenced to death. Many of the Commissioners who had conducted the trial refused to sign the warrant for his execution: it was, eventually, due almost entirely to the personal efforts of Cromwell that sufficient signatures were collected.

On 30 January the King, watched by a silent crowd, was executed. His death, contrived by a minority, was undoubtedly unconstitutional. Equally undoubtedly it grimly fulfilled the Biblical warning that they that live by the sword shall perish by the sword: a despot died by the hands of despots. To refer to his death as martyrdom was to devalue the deaths of all those, Protestant and Papist alike, who in previous reigns in England had suffered horribly for those faiths which had been basically responsible for the Civil War – faiths which in the years to come were to provide the pretext for many another holocaust.

13

Interregnum

1648–1660

THE effects of the new despotism were seen in the City even before the death of Charles.

In June 1648 the Cutlers had, in common with other Companies, received a precept reminding them of the Ancient Custom of coming to Guildhall to choose their Sheriffs, Chamberlains, Bridgemasters, Auditors of the City Accounts, and Aleconners. It was stressed that they must all foregather at the Hall and proceed to Guildhall in an orderly manner in their Livery gowns and hoods 'without which orderly coming it cannot be so well prevented but that others which have no interests in the said Elections may intrude themselves in borrowed gowns to the disturbance of the said Elections and to the prejudice of the franchises and liberties of the City and government'.

Now, in December 1648 the choice of their officers was greatly restricted. An ordinance commanded that no one in the following categories could hold office.

i. Delinquents or those who had assisted the King during either part of the Civil War

ii. Those who had aided the Scots army to come to England

iii. Those who had subscribed to the treasonable arrangement with the King in 1647

iv. Those who had aided and abetted in the Tumults.

It was a fairly comprehensive list but, even so, it did not go far enough for General Skippon, the military commander in London. There were, he said, many who were of a far more dangerous sort –

those who had at any time subscribed to any petition for treating with the King. Parliament agreed with him but the City did not: it was pointed out in a petition that if the net were so widely cast there would be no one left to take office. There would not even be any Scavengers or, for that matter, they added in nice juxtaposition, Collectors of Money for the Army – a proposition which the Lords thought reasonable but which the Commons refused to entertain.

By April Parliament had decided altogether to abolish the monarchy but when Abraham Reynoldson, the Lord Mayor, was ordered to proclaim the Act in the City he refused. He argued that, since he had taken an Oath to uphold the Monarchy, he was unable to preside over its abolition. Puritan consciences saw nothing incongruous in refusing the right of others to indulge in such Christian scruples. The Lord Mayor was fined £2000, committed to the Tower for a month, and finally, with four of his aldermen, displaced from office. A new Lord Mayor was elected and took his oath – to uphold the Commonwealth.

One tyranny had replaced another. Among the outward and visible signs of the change the Lord Mayor, on the appropriate official occasions, now had to offer his sword to the Speaker instead of to the King. Throughout the City and in the Livery Companies life began to return to a state that bore some resemblance to normality. After all that they had been through it was perhaps disconcerting that so little appeared to be altered. Old friends had disappeared, families had been divided, some fellow citizens had been killed. But, at the end of the day, there seemed to be very little that was different in the gradually reviving official business of the Company. There were enacted a rather depressing series of laws against anything that could be broadly classed as pleasurable. Christmas, Easter and Whitsun had already been abolished: they were superstitious. But, oddly enough under the circumstances, a Bill against the Vice of Painting, wearing Black Patches and the Immodest dresses of Women failed to reach the Statute Book.

Feasting was once again permitted, or, at any rate, came creeping back, encouraged by such occasions as the dinner in June in the City at which Fairfax was offered, for the second time, a basin and ewer in beaten gold which he, this time, accepted, and Cromwell was presented with a service of plate worth £300 and two hundred broad-pieces of gold.

With plate obviously in their minds the Cutlers considered their own situation: in spite of the fuss there had been over removing the valuables from the Hall and discreetly hiding them away, and in spite of the Court Order, noted elsewhere, that all should be sold, now their plate and their linen and their Common Seal were all produced by Mr. Partridge to whom they had been delivered 'for safer keeping' and were brought back to their old places in Cutlers' Hall.

In October 1649 the Court were summoned to discuss the plans for accompanying the Lord Mayor by land and water to Westminster as they had used to do. A barge decorated with red and white ribbons was hired for £2. 10s. to row fifty of the Livery: a dinner was held with five messes of meat and four dishes to a mess: two necks and two loins of mutton were provided for breakfast. It was all quite like old times. Like old times, too, was the precept that pointed out that the Cutlers were still unprovided with Corn of which, 'in this time of imminent danger' a far greater supply would be needed. And there was an all too familiar ring about the announcement that the assessment of £90,000 a month for the Army would be continued. There was a promise that next Lady Day the sum would be reduced to £60,000: in fact, it went up to £120,000.

With a likely resurgence of Company business – there had been little enough with which to occupy the Minutes during the war years – it was necessary to state one or two working rules for the Court: no Master or warden was to spend more than £5 about the Company's business without the consent of the Court; and in future a fine of 12d. was to be levied for the poor from any assistant coming to a meeting after 10 a.m. or being 'without his gown upon his back in the Parlour by that hour'.

In April 1650 the City was required formally to declare its loyalty to the Commonwealth but it is possible that not all the citizens were over-eager to subscribe to public expressions of their sentiments: in November there was still need for a precept to enforce compliance. The Committee of the militia demanded that an order in writing be left at the house of every Liveryman and officer of the Company telling them to appear at Guildhall 'to take and subscribe the engagement as is directed'. And the Master and wardens were to bring with them lists of the Livery.

The Commonwealth were, in fact, anxious to supervise the affairs of the City. All the Companies were ordered to make a certificate of 'the extent of their bounds and liberties' and their rights of search.

And, in May, the Committee of Corporations ordered the Company's Charter and any evidence supporting it to be submitted for inspection.

But, above all, 1650 was a year for trying to get back to the normal business of running a Livery Company and controlling its affairs.

In January some of the working cutlers appealed for assistance for redressing 'abuses' which they claimed were ruining the trade: the Court appointed a Committee of eight assistants to sit with an equal number of workers selected by the petitioners. The Committee were empowered to meet and adjourn when they thought fit with the sole stipulation that as long as they continued they must report their proceedings to the Court. Fifty pounds was voted for expenses.

In May, probably as a result of the Committee's deliberations, it was 'adjudged by this Court that all hilts, pommels and handles, or anything else belonging to a sword, rapier, dagger, scimitar, hanger and skein, cast in brass are unserviceable, deceitful and unlawful wares and destructive to the manufactury of this Corporation and Mistery of Cutlers'. All shopkeepers and workmen cutlers who were in possession of any such brass wares were to bring them into the Hall – under penalty of a fine of forty shillings – 'and their brass wares to be defaced and destroyed whereby the Common Wealth may not be deceived and abused'.

Then, the next month, the working cutlers asked – and the Court agreed – that anyone working as a cutler should enter into a legal covenant 'for the better suppression of the making, buying, selling, exchanging or bartering, filing, cutting, hatching, gilding, silvering, chasing, repairing and blacking of brass and copper hilts and other materials of brass and copper. . . .'

Such an extensive list of prohibitions demanded, to be effective, a reliable system of inspection and search.

This had not always in the past been the case. In fact, the late Master, Edmund King, was now fined for failing to carry out any Search during his year of office. The current Master and wardens were ordered to go round the members of the Company not only in Search but in seeking out those who had not signed the covenant and securing their signatures. The Committee appointed one Edward Spencer as Informer and offered him 20 nobles for the job: he refused and, in August, they chose Nicholas Webb as the workmen cutlers' 'Searcher for French wares, being prohibited, as well as Brass and Copper wares'. He was to keep a sharp look-out, too, for any kind of abuses in the trade and inform the Master and wardens. As to payment for these services he declared himself prepared, at any rate until Christmas, to rely upon the good-will of the Court.

The Company were as it happened not in any position to shew great liberality. They were suffering a burden of debt and a continuance of great taxation: in fact, when the freehold of the Catherine Wheel Estate at Egham became available that year they were unfortunately unable to raise the necessary funds to buy such a desirable property as they wished to do.

As always when short of funds the Court turned their attention to taking more members on to the Livery: there were sixteen this year and it was urged that they be selected with great care as able and honest men because one of the vacancies arose from a Livery-man having broken the law and having been made to stand in the pillory for which he was, of course, cast out for ever.

The re-organization of trade activity continued into 1651. There was a suggestion that silver hilts should also be suppressed but not all the Committee were prepared to subscribe to this step, and the idea seems to have been abandoned.

In May the Committee decided that every one who enrolled his trade mark must leave his punch, with which he stamped his work, to be kept at the Hall – a procedure which might be thought to have involved considerable inconvenience in the day-to-day working of the manufacturing trade.

There seems, however, to have been no objection made by the working cutlers, from whom trouble might have been expected at a time when throughout the Livery Companies there were great outbreaks of democratic aspirations amongst the Yeomanry.

In the Cutlers' Company the Court, no doubt looking nervously over their shoulders at the sort of trouble the Clothworkers, amongst others, were facing, reacted swiftly when, in May, the Yeomanry submitted a paper. The contents are not recorded, but may be presumed to have demanded additional powers for, after debate, the Court 'caused an ancient record

of ordinance made in Anno 1566, by which they [the Yeomanry] were then constituted after they had for their misgovernment been quite nulled and dissolved, to be read unto them. And after that, when they had replied what they had to say, the Court declared that they would not add anything to enlarge their ordinances and power given to them but that they might continue their meeting for as [long as] they would peaceably and lovingly demean and conform themselves according to the ancient ordinances and rules of government. . . .'

Meanwhile Prince Charles had fled to France, Cromwell had been victorious in Ireland, and the Royalist forces in England, represented by the Scots, were suffering defeat. There were a number of Thanksgiving Days for Victories over the King's Forces and there was a certain amount of discussion about the future state of the nation. Was it possible to rule the English without some element of monarchy? Were the liberties of the individual possible without something of monarchy in the constitution? Would not all the Laws be upset? Would it be desirable to have, say, the Duke of Gloucester as King?[179]

Undisturbed by such speculations, the joyless government of the Interregnum continued. There was reported to be an order that all cathedrals were to be pulled down and their materials sold[180] – but apart from general and widespread acts of official vandalism this does not seem to have been carried into execution. The law about the abolition of Christmas was, however, strictly observed. All shops in the City were to be kept open and there were to be no solemnities of any kind.

And a precept was issued that

having lately received information of several Maskings or Dancings that have been appointed and acted, or at least attempted, in some of the Halls or other public places belonging to the Companies of this City. These are straightly to charge and require you that there be no dancings, maskings, plays or any other unlawful meetings . . . as you tend the peace and good government of this City. . . .

The Government took yet another look at the powers of the City: in November 1652 it was thought 'agreeable and suitable' that all Charters should be held under the authority of the Common Wealth and an order was given to all corporations to bring them before a Parliamentary Committee. It so happened that the Cutlers were unable immediately to comply: some law suits were pending and their documents were before the courts. Even when the Charters became available there was some anxiety about handing them over to the Parliamentarians. The Court ordered that 'there should be a copy, verbatim, written of the Charter. And that, with the Charter itself, should by the Master and wardens be carried unto the said Committee and if the copy would not satisfy the Committee and they could safely without danger leave the Charter then they might leave it. . . .'

There was, perhaps, some good reason for their anxiety for the safety of their Charters. Once again there was trouble brewing between the Army and Parliament. Part of the Roundhead forces had been disbanded and soldiers had swollen the labour market: those who remained under arms were demanding a settlement of the arrears of pay still owing to them. The military in general were dissatisfied with the small unrepresentative Rump Parliament and there were divergences of opinion as to how the Commons might be reformed. For some time Cromwell acted as mediator but eventually he lost patience with the Members: in April 1653 he took troops into the House and, with the celebrated incident of removing the Mace, dissolved Parliament.[180]

Almost immediately the apprentices and young men of London and Westminster began to petition against this attack on the Liberties and rights: this time there was no respect for delicate political consciences and those who presented the petition were committed to a term of imprisonment, with hard labour, in Bridewell. And Oliver Cromwell, the small country gentleman with a military genius, became on 16 December 1653 Lord Protector of England.

The preparations to greet the new ruler were not less elaborate than had been usual on previous occasions. The Lord Protector was invited in April 1654 to dine at Grocers' Hall and to greet him in the City the Cutlers were ordered to erect and line their rails, to a length of 25 yards, in Cheapside. The Goldsmiths took priority that year, and all the other Companies took their place in order of precedence, extending westward from the Great Conduit. All the Livery were to be in their places by 10 a.m. 'in comely and decent apparel and in their best Livery gowns and hoods' and the Cutlers provided three messes of meat for them. There were hens and bacon, and roast beef, and capons, and tarts and mince pies.

They could hardly have done more if they had been greeting Royalty and, indeed, it was noted that Cromwell rode in state like any King. He was offered at Temple Bar, as a Monarch would have been offered, the City Sword and returned it graciously to the Mayor. He was welcomed by the Recorder with a fulsome speech and then he left his coach and rode on horse-back in triumph through the City with the Lord Mayor, bare-headed, carrying the Sword before him. At Grocers' Hall there was a 'magnificent Entertainment'; Cromwell knighted the Mayor and presented him with the sword from his own side. The bells pealed all the day long and the guns of the Tower boomed as he left the City. It was a truly regal reception – and there is little doubt that, in some quarters, it was resented. It is likely that, behind the defeat of Cromwell's party in a vote of the Commons in September that year, lay an uneasiness at his general king-like demeanour. Cromwell was alarmed by this display of intransigence and by the thought that he might be overthrown by the instrument of his own creating. He therefore warned the Lord Mayor to guard the City against disturbances and appeared before Parliament with reproachful and resentful speeches: members were not allowed back into the House until they had signed a declaration of Loyalty.

For his part Cromwell, reassuringly, turned down a proposal that he should, in fact, be elected King.

As far as the Cutlers' Company were concerned one ruler, be he

King or Commoner, was as bad as the last – and probably as bad as the next, too: the swingeing taxes had still to be found and the Corn precepts now had an authoritarian ring about them that discouraged evasion. Their own internal problems were perennial: brassware was still being made deceitfully and steps had to be taken to deal with such matters; the Irish Lands were again proving an administrative problem. But on this latter point at least there was sounded an unexpected note of good cheer. First of all Cromwell was pleased to restore the City to its former position in their estates and the Cutlers, having rejected an offer by two Dublin aldermen of eleven shillings in the pound for their properties, were in May 1655 told they could go to the Chamber of London and collect £625 – their proportion of the monies disbursed to the State as long ago as 1640.

In spite of this apparent return to normality there was suddenly a great falling-off in the business conducted by the Court of the Cutlers' Company. There were, for example, only five meetings in 1655 and, if anything of importance occurred, it was not recorded. It is just possible that the Court Committee was still functioning and carrying on the more technical business but, if this was so, no report seems to have been made to the assistants.

In March 1656, the Court were seized by one of their spasms of doubt about how far their powers extended under their Charters and ordinances.

They who had for so long ruled with a confident autocracy – committing to prison or sending before the Lord Mayor any of their members who might defy them – decided to take counsel's opinion about the way in which they should obtain any fines that they might impose.

That they received a reassuring reply is suggested by the way they now treated Thomas Grimshaw who requested to be translated to the Brewers who, he said, were persecuting him for not being a member and were putting him to charges. 'The Court pleased not only to grant him his desire but chose and swore him an Assistant of this Court and afterward chose him Renter for the year ensuing which he refusing to hold the Court fined him to pay £10. And to give a piece of Plate to the Company.'

It was an expensive translation and one that indicates that the Court still possessed considerable powers.

The Company's stock of plate was further increased in 1658 when Robert Carrington, who had been a warden – presented a salt-cellar in the shape of the Company's crest – the Elephant and Castle – which had been granted to them in 1622 and which possibly makes nonsense of the rather fanciful but widely accepted derivation of the well-known Tavern sign. This munificent and indeed unusual gift was described in an early inventory as 'an Elephant set with small Ragg pearls and some other coloured Stones and a little Silver cup screwed to the Castle, a small loose button of Silver, and a black leather case to keep it in'.

It certainly made a change from the normal gifts of plate given by the wardens who, until they had made such a presentation, were to receive from the Company neither 'groats nor gown-money'.

With a lack of incident in their affairs that matched the dullness of the Parliamentarian times the Cutlers carried on the routines of management: the granting of leases and other property matters occupied the chief part of the Court meetings.

The occasional alarms that affected the City were not reflected in their Minutes.

In March 1658 Cromwell informed the City and the officers of the Army that he had discovered a plot in favour of Charles II: Lord Ormonde had been about the City trying to raise supporters for an invasion that was planned. The authorities were told to settle the militia in the hands of reliable and trustworthy persons and 'to put the City in a Posture of Defence, that they might be in a Condition to suppress all Tumults and Insurrections. . . .'[182]

There was trouble, too, for Cromwell with the republicans who formed the Parliamentary opposition. Once again he was compelled to rely upon the support of the Army whose leaders were sworn to live and die with the Lord Protector. And once again, the urgent need for money made it likely that he would have to fall back upon Parliament. But before the matter could come to an embarrassing head Cromwell had died and was succeeded by his son Richard.

There were great ceremonies proclaiming him throughout the City; the Lord Mayor and aldermen went to Whitehall to pledge their allegiance and loyalty; there were 'repeated Shouts and Acclamations in the City' and volleys of shot from the soldiery.

The euphoria was short-lived. Richard, 'a mild and lazy country gentleman',[183] was not the man his father was. In April 1659 the Army under General Lambert removed the new Lord Protector and recalled the Long Parliament which Cromwell had dissolved in 1653.

There was now a great lack of money for the conduct of affairs – especially the considerable sums needed to pay off the Army, which had great arrears of debt owing to it. There was a project afoot to 'deal with certain Gentlemen in the City' and all the King's lands were ordered to be sold. Then, in October, Parliament proving obstinate, Lambert took a leaf from his late master's book, marched troops into the House of Commons and dissolved it.

The country was now once again perched on the brink of anarchy. The republican Council of State, dismissed by Lambert, appointed General George Monk as commander-in-chief and in, January 1660 he began to march with his Army from the North. He wrote to the City saying that his sole purpose was to restore the authority of Parliament and the freedom and rights of the citizens which were being infringed more despotically than had ever happened under the monarchy. The City welcomed these proposals and awaited his arrival: the Common Council declared that they would pay no more taxes until Parliament were filled with members who represented the people.

On 9 February General Monk took up his residence in the City.

He was greeted as a deliverer: bells were rung and bonfires were lit and wine and money pressed upon the troops. Young men bought rump steaks and symbolically burned them as a token of contempt for the Rump Parliament. The Common Council considered Monk's demand for an assessment.

It was unfortunate that, at that moment, an order came from the Council of State that the posts and chains protecting the City were to be removed, the gates taken off their hinges and the portcullises wedged open. The chains were at once taken away but Monk protested to his masters that he had not carried out the other orders because he feared that it would exasperate the Citizens who were on the point of passing the assessment that had been demanded. The Council were adamant and – to complete the matter – dissolved the Common Council of the City.

In due course Monk reported that he had obeyed the orders concerning the gates and portcullises but that he had done so with great regret, a regret that was shared by his soldiers because, in all its wars, nothing like this had happened to the City. Many sober people, the General added, were very grieved by all this. The soldiers carrying out the task were, it seems, 'angry but merry too' – as soldiers carrying out disagreeable orders sometimes may appear to be – 'but the General was dark and chewed his Tobacco'.[184]

Shortly after this, Monk, who commanded as well as the Army considerable popular support, declared himself in favour of calling a 'free Parliament'. This, as he perfectly well knew, would mean the restoration of the King because the Presbyterians who would now be able to regain their places had never been republicans and had always wished for a Monarchy provided it were upon the right terms. From now on the tide of Restoration was to flow fast and strong. Charles II by the 'Declaration of Breda' promised to grant 'liberty to tender consciences' and to leave to Parliament the punishment of those not covered by a general pardon. In May a mission from the new Royalist Parliament travelled to Holland to invite the King to return. Among his Majesty's many advance messages to his people was one which remarked how his spirits had been raised during the long troublesome revolutions by the Loyal manifestations from the City. . . . To this the City replied that their prayers had at long last been answered by the King's Restoration and they confessed that 'all those manifestations of their affections' which Charles had noted were only a very small part of the duty that they owed him. And the City decided to present £12,000 to his Majesty. The Cutlers' share was £120 and the precept that demanded it put the words into their mouths for them: the gift was 'a testimony of the sense that this Court and the whole City have of his gracious letter and declaration to them lately sent'. There were some – the Drapers in particular – who resented this way of putting it and who, while paying what was demanded, made a tart protest.[185] The Cutlers, however, seem to have seen no need to make such a demonstration: the whole thing provided so ludicrous an example of diplomatic verbiage that it was, no doubt, not worth bothering about. They raised the money on the Common Seal of the Company and paid it to the Chamber of London. On 5 May a day of thanksgiving was ordered: everyone was to go to St. Paul's for a Sermon and the Arms of the Commonwealth were to be taken down and replaced by the Royal Arms. On 8 May the King was proclaimed and by the middle of the month preparations were under way for his entry into London. The usual demands were made for eight tall, grave, comely, well turned-out cutlers, with footmen, to be ready when required. It was noted that the King's 'happy coming' was uncertain in date: it was thought that he did 'intend (God willing) very suddenly to pass through the City'. The eight persons provided were to be in velvet plush or satin, with swords, and their footmen, carrying truncheons, were to be 'apparelled in cassock or drawers of cloth or stuff, garnished with ribbons the colour of your Company as near you can'. All were to be prepared to 'randyvouse' at the Artillery ground at one hour's warning: in the event, they had two days' notice and on 29 May 1660 Charles II entered his capital amidst scenes of wild rejoicing and excessive drunkenness. The Liverymen of London were there upon the rails and in stands covered with blue cloth and decorated with streamers and the banners of King and Company, to see 600 of their number parade with their whifflers who, like their footmen, sported their colours – which in the Cutlers' case were red and white. The Company borrowed £100 at interest from a widow named Dorothy Mann to pay for the setting-up of the King's Arms in the Hall and for making the banners and decorations for the Show – to secure the sum of £103 it was necessary to seal a bond for £200.

And so the King came into his own again. The celebrations lasted all the summer.

14

Autocracy Renewed

1660–1688

THEY now had, once again, a 'constitutional Monarch' to whom the Members of Parliament swore an Oath of Allegiance and Supremacy. On 5 June 1660 the Company received a precept that informed them that the City authorities were going to take a similar oath: all those holding any kind of office must do the same. The Master and wardens must see that the precept was carried out both immediately and in the future, too.

The City announced the intention of borrowing £3000 for six months at six per cent towards the costs of entertaining the King and the two Dukes, his brothers, as well as Parliament and other great personages, at Guildhall in July. From the Cutlers they demanded £30: it was paid without delay. The feast was an important one. Those riding in the procession were to be ready by 6 a.m.; attendance on the rails was, as usual on such occasions, compulsory for the rest of the Livery: they were to be in their places – with no women or children – by nine o'clock in the morning and there they were to remain until the King and his train had passed by. They might then leave the stands in order to refresh themselves so long as they were back in position by 3 p.m. Because there would be so many provisions consumed, and so many cooks 'and other persons of like quality ministerial' involved in their preparation and service, there were to be no other solemn feasts at Halls that day.

But when the tables had been cleared the hard unpalatable facts of life remained. The King, like every ruler, needed money and

S

needed it urgently. Unlike every ruler, it was necessary for him to raise, through Parliament, extra money to pay the debts that he and his Court had incurred in exile.

In September his present needs were estimated at £70,000 and the money required for the Army was twice that amount. The Cutlers received a precept for implementing 'the Speedy Provision of Money for disbanding and paying of the forces of this Kingdom both by land and sea': in connection with this demand they were ordered to submit no less than seven nominal rolls of the various categories of the Company – Masters, past-Masters and those fined for Master provided the first, and widows, with the details of their husbands' rank in Society and their estimated incomes, the last. By the end of the year, when a two months' tax was levied upon them and the first fine enthusiasm for the 'happy return' was beginning to wane, mention was made of 'the backwardness of the City for lending Money.'

The Cutlers had, in any case, other things that they urgently needed to do with their funds. In August a chimney had collapsed at the Hall, breaking down, in its fall, joists and rafters in the Parlour. There were extensive repairs to be made: the Court decided to borrow £400 and start the work. While they were about it they considered the whole building: it was two hundred and fifty years old, or thereabouts; it was too small; it was inconvenient and it was in a state of decay. Soon the simple repairs to the parlour had become the more ambitious project of 'new building and re-designing of a Hall and Parlour and other accommodations for the use of this Company'. They would borrow £1000 at interest and a committee would 'treat and agree with able and experienced workmen for the well and substantial doing and finishing of the same'. The year was one of national renewal – to replace the complex of buildings was in accordance with the spirit of the times. The old pewter was exchanged for new pewter; a pair of brass andirons and green cloth carpets were ordered for Hall and parlour: two dripping pans were bought for the new kitchen, the building of which, according to the new designs, had displaced the widow Fanch from her room and led to the Company granting her £3 a year for life in compensation.

It was a considerable undertaking at a time when, already in debt, the Company were faced with all the inevitable expenses of a new reign. St. George's Day was appointed for the Coronation: the King would pass through the City to Westminster the previous day and the authorities announced an intention to demonstrate 'so far as can be uttered the unspeakable Joy, Love and Loyalty of this City, his Majesty's loyal Chamber, to his sacred Person and Government. . . .' Everything must be stately and sumptuous, which meant that £6000 had to be raised and, since time was short, raised quickly and certainly. There must be no possible reflection upon the City – nor upon any particular Company – for failing in their duty. The Cutlers' share of the expense was initially £60 but it was soon discovered that the total costs had been considerably under-estimated. Very shortly before the great day the workmen laid down their tools and would not continue until more money was forthcoming: another £3000 was immediately necessary if the City was not to be dishonoured. The Lord Mayor admitted that there had been complaints from some of the Companies that their proportions had been unfairly calculated: he promised to look into the matter after the Coronation. In the meantime the Cutlers must pay another £30 in addition to the £60 already demanded from them.

In January 1662 more money was needed, too, for the Hall: another £400 was borrowed only a week or two before a particularly suave precept was received in which it was 'conceived' that the Cutlers had failed to supply the Corn demanded of them the previous October. Now grain had become scarce and dear. Any failure on the part of the Cutlers to supply their quota could hardly fail to be an offence to his Majesty and prejudicial to the City. The Company were commanded to supply a certificate stating the amount of Corn held: if it proved that they had fallen short of their obligations they must fill their quota immediately.

The times had indeed changed: the Cutlers certified, with hardly any delay, 'we have taken care and shall be in readiness to serve our Corn in our turn and course according to the direction of your Lordship'.

Next they were faced with the £30 which was their share of a 'voluntary' present to be given to the King: they paid it without any recorded demur.

Work on the Hall, for which in October 1662 yet another £600 had to be raised, was perhaps proceeding more slowly than they had anticipated – the committee of four entrusted with overseeing the work was strengthened by the addition of a further six members. It was an age of committees: a second one was appointed to hear and to rectify, if practicable, the grievances of shopkeepers and workmen cutlers. It comprised three assistants, led by Sir Lawrence Bromfield, three shopkeepers of a surprisingly high social grade – one was an Esquire and another a Captain – and three workmen led by Thomas Birdwhistle.

The rules agreed by this Committee were engrossed after only one month and were submitted to all the members of the Company.

Yet a third Committee was set up for considering and redrafting the Rules and Orders of the Cutlers: it consisted of eight of the Court, eight shopkeepers and thirteen assorted workmen.

At no time during their history had there been so much consultation between the disparate ranks of the Company: it was, therefore, all the more disappointing that, at this precise moment, the Yeomanry organization was suddenly, on Trinity Eve, the election day, abolished. In their own words:

this Court taking into consideration the evil government and misbehaviour of the Yeomanry of this Company in that they have abused the rules and orders formerly prescribed unto them and lately they have presumed, without acquainting a Court of Assistants, to take upon their table twenty men over and above the number they had on their table before . . .

The Yeomanry were, the Court noted, limited to twelve assistants. Yet from each of the twenty extra men they had exacted a fine of 20s. for which they had not accounted to the Younger Warden of the Livery as they should have done. Neither had they for many years past submitted proper accounts of the quarterage they had collected. For these reasons the Court

finding them very faulty, useless and burdensome to the Company have thought it very requisite and necessary to lay them aside. And to take away the power formerly allowed them to keep Court as a table of Yeomanry. . . .

The Court stripped them of all their functions – they were no longer allowed to collect quarterage and 'those that were last Wardens' were ordered to surrender all the keys and records.

It was a sudden end, unanticipated in the Minutes, to centuries of tradition: that there seem to have been no repercussions indicates that the Yeomanry organization had, perhaps, indeed outlived its usefulness.

It was not that the Cutlers were any less concerned with the control of the trade. More than ever were they involved with search and the confiscation and destruction of 'deceivable wares'. The enrolment of trade marks – possibly as a result of the competition from Sheffield which was, however, nowhere referred to – became an almost obsessive feature of Court meetings. But the new rules and orders which had been drawn up in committee were quite quickly repealed: many of the shopkeepers and working cutlers had accepted them and had agreed, under seal, to observe their provisions but there were many others who had refused to do so 'which tended to the great prejudice and damage' of those who had signed.

The degree of non-compliance was such that the Court, for all its autocracy, felt that there was no alternative but to declare the new orders null and void and to continue to operate under the old regulations.

In the meantime the rebuilding of the Hall was nearing its conclusion. The costs of the four-year operation totalled £2733. 2s. 7d. and the Company's other extraordinary expenses were high. There was some delay in paying the various outstanding accounts. For it was in 1664 that the City undertook to supply £100,000 for his Majesty's 'present great affairs whereof the prosperous and happy estate of the City is especially concerned'. The Cutlers were told that it was 'fit and reasonable for the quality and reputation of your Company' that they should subscribe £1000.

The Court ordered that £600 should be borrowed upon a bond and paid over to the Chamberlain. If they thought that this smaller sum would, if paid quickly, be acceptable they were mistaken. The

Master, wardens and the whole Court were summoned to appear before the Lord Mayor before eight o'clock in the morning upon pain of being imprisoned for contempt, with the result that a very speedy order was made to borrow the £400 that was still outstanding.

Then, in March 1665, there were further demands: the multitudes of poor in the City, increased by the severity of the weather, the dearness of sea-coals and the smallness of the collections taken up in the wards, made great demands upon the Company's charity and the shortage of grain brought increasing pressure upon them to fulfil their corn precepts. The same month it was reported that 'an unhappy accident has happened to the *London*' – she had been blown up at the Nore – and that the City 'considering under what obligations of loyalty' they were to his Majesty had decided to build another frigate to replace her. The authorities had obtained the King's 'gracious permission (with favourable acceptance) to promote a free and liberal subscription for the building' of the vessel. The Companies were told to organize subscription lists and to do everything in their power to 'excite and persuade' their members to be generous. As an added incentive it was pointed out that the lists would be forwarded to the Lord Mayor (together with separate lists both of those who had refused and of those who had failed to reply) and that fair copies would be kept 'for present use and for the instruction of Posterity'.

In spite of this powerful appeal, only a small amount of money was raised – and that with the greatest difficulty and with great delay. For more than a year the business was constantly before the Court. In April 1665 the Lord Mayor was pointing out that the shipwright must be paid and that, therefore, any money already collected must be at once handed over; in May it was said that the work was actually held up for lack of funds; in March 1666 the money had still not been paid to the Chamber of London with the result that the ship, which was wanted for the summer expedition, had not been fitted out or finished as soon as had been promised to his Majesty 'to his great disservice and to the consequent dishonour of the City'. The Master and wardens were to approach persons of ability and excite them.

All was in vain. By May a total of only £4200 had been raised by the City and it was realized that there was now 'an utter unlikelihood' of the money being collected as intended. The outstanding £10,000 would be raised by precept and the Cutlers were ordered to provide £100 by the 24 May so that the ship – to be named *The Loyal London* – might be fitted out by the Summer.

It is right to point out that the City in general had been somewhat preoccupied, for in July 1665 the country had been struck down by yet another epidemic of the plague which, almost always present in the City, now occurred on such a scale as to fix it for ever in the minds of the English as 'The Great Plague'.

It did not impress itself at all in the Minutes of the Cutlers' Company. In the book of precepts was entered the usual order that there was to be no feasting and that one-third of all money saved was to be given to the poor who were afflicted by the shutting-up of their houses and by the cessation of trade. Parliament imposed various assessments for poor-relief and for the provision of Coals – the Cutlers' share is said to have been 75 chaldrons[186] – but the Company does not seem to have been otherwise greatly affected. Sixty-eight thousand inhabitants died in London alone but few, if any losses, occurred on the Court who only met on four occasions during the whole of the plague year.

There were, however, certain financial compensations: the Irish Lands were beginning, once again, to pay small but acceptable dividends and by June 1666 the final outstanding debts on the Hall were paid.

Three months later, in the first week of September, it was reduced to a blackened, smoking heap of rubble.

There was a new Clerk to the Company that year. Richard Evans, probably the first of a line of Clerks who were chosen from the Livery, resigned: in rather chilly terms he 'acquainted them that he would not continue Clerk to this Company any longer than the next Account Day. And therefore wished them to provide themselves a Clerk in the mean time.' He had been the Company's Officer for twenty-four years – during all but two of which he had been an assistant – and had served them well, having obtained for them a valuable property in Fleur-de-lys alley on Ludgate Hill. Like all the Clerks, he was only partially employed upon the Cutlers' business and his salary of £6 was in the nature of a retainer fee. He had become a figure of some importance in the City, having been elected alderman and fined for Sheriff – now, with something less than cordiality, he left their service. It was his successor, Thomas Bywater, who was faced with the chaotic conditions that followed the Fire.

Fanned by a strong wind and quickly out of control among the closely-packed warrens of lath and plaster, the Fire destroyed in six days 13,200 houses – four-fifths of the whole City.

The first meeting of the Court to take place after the holocaust was held on 18 September at the Bear at Bridgefoot. The Master, Jeremiah Greene, was ordered to provide a chest with four keys for the custody of the records and such treasure as had been rescued from the flames. Looters were hard at work: the Master was also to 'take care to have the Lead, Iron, Stone, and what other materials shall be found in and about the Hall, occasioned by the late Ruins, to be put into the Cellar . . .' and to be bricked in. The Clerk's salary, it was agreed, should be continued: he was given, in addition, 20s. for having rescued the writings, plate, and other things from the Fire and told to hand them over to the Master. The interests of the pensioners were not forgotten: Mr. Greene was allowed, at his discretion, to relieve them.

The next Court meeting did not take place for three months: it was then decided to sell not only the salvaged lead, iron and stone but also the Company plate. The Master, wardens and Sir Lawrence Bromfield were to decide whether any of it should be preserved. The problems of rents due to the Cutlers from properties which had been destroyed was also considered. In March 1667 the Court decided to demand the rents due from the grounds held by Samuel Boot – and by all other tenants, too. This policy seems to have been fairly general in the City: rents were to be collected as if the properties had not been destroyed and the Company paid, at any rate in part, for the rebuilding by extending, without charge, the term of years of the leases. The way in which this system worked in practice may be seen in the case of Mr. Walter Smith the lessee of property on Ludgate Hill. He asked, initially, that his lease, of which he already had thirty years to run, might be extended to sixty years and the rent be reduced by 40s. a year.

If the Court accepted this offer he would be pleased to rebuild the house that had been destroyed by 'the Sad and Lamentabell Fier'. To this proposition the Court replied that on Lady Day he must pay the £6 that he owed and continue the same rent: if he did so they would then consider the business 'and deal kindly with him'. It was a reply that did not satisfy Mr. Smith and he brought an action against the Company: eventually, after much consultation with counsel, it was agreed that his lease should be extended without premium to eighty years at an annual rent of £10. It was the same with the majority of tenants who wished to rebuild and continue to occupy their properties – though there were some, like Thomas Arnold, who were paid to surrender the remainder of their term of years.

For such payments money was urgently needed. Quite apart from everything else, the money due for the *Loyal London* had not yet been fully collected and the wardens on assuming office were ordered to make gifts of money instead of plate. The frigate was at last completed and fitted out – just in time to meet the Dutch raid upon the Medway where she was destroyed. A committee was formed solely for treating with the tenants about rebuilding or having their leases cancelled – eventually such was the pressure of business that the whole Court was drawn into the Committee. The meetings continued to be held in taverns – at the Bear, at the Pied Dog in Seething Lane, at the Peacock in Bishopsgate Street. Somehow trade continued and somehow the Company continued to control it. There was, for example, a search in December 1667 and more than thirty-one dozen knives bearing the mark of the dagger 'which properly belongs to the Company' were defaced and broken in the presence of the Court, the hafts being returned to their owners. As the Cutlers limped forward into 1668 they began to hold their more important meetings at Loriners' Hall although much of their work was still carried on in taverns. It was at the Pied Dog that the Court determined to write to the Birmingham and Sheffield Cutlers (it was the first time that they had officially mentioned the latter body) 'concerning the striking of the mark of the dagger upon their blades contrary to their Engagement' – an undertaking which had certainly been made by the Birmingham men only three years earlier.

It was at the Pied Dog, too, in October 1688, that the Court took a long hard look at the state of their finances.

In 1666 they had assigned to Sir Lawrence Bromfield the Bill of £600, lent to the King in 1664: it provided some kind of security for the money that the Company owed him. Now they considered the whole extent of the obligations, 'the great debts owing to several persons. Amounting in the whole to about £2,900 which by reason of the great Conflagration by Fire the 2nd of September 1666 having consumed a great part of their Estate, together with the Hall, had disabled them so that they found themselves not in a Capacity to satisfy their Creditors with their Interest and Principal.'

There was a long discussion from which two suggested solutions emerged. The first was that the debt should be paid in four equal instalments beginning at Michaelmas 1672 and continuing at three-yearly intervals until 1681 without in the meantime any interest being paid. The second proposal 'if the creditors do approve of it better' which also envisaged the non-payment of interest, was based on the Court's calculations of the annual income from their properties. After the deduction of annuities, quit rents, exhibitions and other obligations chargeable on the estates, there was an income of some £90 which, it was proposed, might be distributed to the creditors and allocated proportionately among them as they might think fit until the whole sum had been paid off: it was estimated that the final payment might thus be made somewhere around the year 1701. So much for the outstanding debts; there remained the expense of rebuilding the Hall on the old site: the Livery fines – to be fixed at £10 – would be allocated to this project 'and no part of the money to be put to any other use'. For a start, eleven Liverymen would be called and six of them would provide, as stewards, the Company dinner at Mr. Hall's house, the Woolsack in Ivy Lane, on Lord Mayor's Day – capons and white broth, roast beef, tongue and udder, fat geese, mince-pies and tarts 'with wine and other accommodation'.

The October Court was also held at Mr. Hall's house and it was agreed that the creditors should be summoned to the Pied Dog on 12 November to hear what the Company proposed. There appear to have been only two of them – Mr. Thomas Smith, a former Master, and Mr. Thomas Thorowgood – and they 'lovingly agreed to accept the plan of payment by four instalments'. The Court 'did return them thanks' and proceeded to make arrangements for workmen to clear the site of the Hall so that new foundations might be laid. If the creditors had any dark thoughts about the amount of money that would be spent upon the project while their own dues went unpaid – and earned them no interest – they did not record them.

Clearly a great weight was lifted from the Cutlers' minds. They were able to begin the new year of 1669 with an appearance of virtual normality.

Their first action was to appoint a committee of nine members to supervise the rebuilding of the Hall. The terms of reference were to examine tenders, accounts and so on and, at the same time, to expedite dealings with those tenants who had not yet made any arrangements with the Company about their leases. They carried out their scrutiny thoroughly: when they added up the figures they discovered that they had been overcharged £10 by the carpenter. After some considerable argument he agreed to correct it and to accept £400 'in full payment for all the work that was done and also he was to lay all the floors with extraordinary good boards which was concluded in the sum'.

To meet such expenses no less than twenty-nine new members were taken on to the Livery in 1669: five of them were described as Yeomen and they paid only £9 each.

Another committee was appointed 'to consider some expedient for the carrying on of the Affair of the Blades Trade'. It is clear that the Court now consisted for the most part of non-working cutlers for it was stressed that the committee would have 'better Experience by reason that they exercise the trade of Cutler and . . . the Court may have their advice in the procedure of that work'.

They were, no doubt, concerned with the trouble with the cutlers of Birmingham and Sheffield and other places who, as a petition to the Lord Mayor and aldermen complained, were striking the mark of the dagger which was the legal right of the Londoners whose work 'honestly and truly wrought and inspected and searched is thus known from the work of others'. And because the provincial blades, which were 'very ill and deceitfully wrought', had been sold both in England and in foreign parts there was a great 'disparagement of the trade both at home and abroad', to say nothing of the ruin that was brought to London cutlers. The knife-cutlers also suggested to the Court that the offenders at 'Brimiger', who had given bond to the Company for their good behaviour should be prosecuted. They asked that they might be allowed at their own expense to sue in the Company's name. Their request was granted at a Court in October 1669 and the cases were begun but, by the neglect of the knife-cutlers, were non-suited with the result that in 1670 the Company was faced with a bill of costs amounting to £3. The Court demanded an explanation and payment of the costs. But, when the knife-cutlers appeared, they not only refused to pay but behaved insolently to the Court: Daniel Treadwell, who was one of them, was fined 13s. 4d. for insulting the Master.

There was further trouble arising from the manufacture of brass hilts and the Court were forced to have the previous order against the manufacture of brass hilts reprinted and circulated. But their main preoccupation was concerned with the rebuilding of the Hall. A new gate was ordered; the plasterer was commissioned to make a ceiling of 'reasonable handsome fretwork'; a house of office and a drain to the common sewer were to be constructed; a good handsome batten door was to be made on to the leads from the garret; the buttery was to be floored and the boards stained; the plumber was ordered to make good the lead stolen from the cornice and lantern light so that the painter's work 'be not damnified'; work was to go on with the building next to the Hall. To meet the rapidly mounting expenses no less than thirty members were added to the Livery: there seems to have been a certain reluctance among some of those called: those who failed to appear or pay their fines were to be taken before the Lord Mayor and a warrant was to be sought from the Recorder to bring in those outside the jurisdiction of the City. Those owing rent or money borrowed on bonds were to be sued, and, on the other side of the account, a committee was appointed to deal, not without some difficulties, with the creditors. At last, in July 1670, there were preparations to consolidate all the workmen's bills into one account; the Hall was to be given as security, up to £500, for the wages and was mortgaged to Mr. Daniel Clarebutt. By September everything was sufficiently far advanced for the Company to envisage holding the Lord Mayor's Day dinner in the new Hall. And 'there being wanting several utensils for the Kitchen and tables and other necessary things for the Hall, and the water to be laid on for the use of the house' it was left to the Master 'to take care therein'. By Michaelmas they were installed in their new Hall – the fourth of their existence – and the first dinner they held in it included 'Westphalia Hams and Turkeys'. It was a memorable occasion, and only one note of prohibition was sounded: 'not any person whatsoever be allowed to take any Tobacco at any time in the Great Parlour'.

At about the same time that they were reinstated in their new home a poll tax was levied 'for the provision of monies to pay off the armies and navies'. Since the officers of the Livery Companies were assessed according to the class in which their organizations were ranked an interesting indication is provided of the official standing of the Cutlers' Company in the middle reign of Charles II.

They were of the same status as the Barber-Surgeons, Brown Bakers, Butchers, Carpenters, Coopers, Cordwainers, Innholders, Painter Stainers, Scriveners, Turners, Wax Chandlers and White Bakers and, therefore, the Master and Past-Masters paid £3 each, the wardens and past-wardens £2 and the Liverymen £1. There is a useful standard of comparison to be found in the fact that £3 was the tax demanded from an attorney-at-law and £2 the amount payable by all those with an income of £100 a year.[187]

Whatever its status, the Company had to live within its means. By June 1671 workmen's bills amounting to £675 were still unpaid: it was decided that contributions should be exacted from the members. Another twenty freemen were called on to the Livery but in September the debate was still continuing 'how to raise money for to pay and discharge the Workmen's bills for the building and finishing Cutlers' Hall and the adjoining building, the whole Building being about eighty foot in the front. . . .'

The Master's offer to advance the money upon interest was accepted. Other expenses were threatening: the neighbours were making overtures about a drain and since the kitchen of the Hall proved to be affected by a spring it was felt that perhaps a drain might be useful for the Company themselves as well as for the neighbourhood. The Hall itself had to be used to provide a source of income. The Court hired it out for weddings and funerals and for the meetings of other Livery Companies such as the Wheelwrights, Combmakers, Tobacco-pipe makers, Paviours, Feltmakers, Clockmakers and Pin-makers.

Then, in 1672, the Clerk asked for an increase in his salary: formerly it had been £20 a year but this had been reduced to £6 and the use of his house. He pointed out how well he had served the Company – he had saved the treasures in the fire and returned them to the Company at his own expense, he had redesigned the property at Belle Sauvage, he had attended many extra committee meetings, and so on. The Court decided, therefore, that the Hall buildings should be divided to make a dwelling for the Clerk. He should have the room on the left of the entrance with a cellar under it, a large room leading out of the Music Room, a room going out on to the leads, a large room over the Parlour and a little room at the top of the stairs. The Hall and the offices he could use for conducting burials and marriages from which he might take the fees. It was a not unreasonable arrangement and indicates the considerable extent of the property. By the time they had settled all these domestic arrangements they found themselves beset by a number of problems arising out of the searches which were increasing in their thoroughness. In March 1673 there was a particularly intensive search for the forbidden brass hilts and an officer provided by the Lord Mayor was at hand, in case any of the offenders should prove refractory, 'to have taken them into custody'. There were eighteen offenders and a few of them put up a show of resistance but were dealt with by fines rather than by imprisonment. Some of them had part of their penalties remitted and they were asked to remember the new poor-box which – shaped like an Elephant – had recently been presented to the Company. 'And all of them did give to the poor Lovingly'. There was trouble, too, among the members over the quality of the silver that was used in the manufacture of swords. Some of them complained 'of the great Abuse by the making of Hilts, Pommels, and other things of the Cutlerywares of Silver of base Alloy, so much lower than the Standard'. In October a bond was prepared 'to be subscribed by the cutlers whereby they obliged themselves not to make any work of Silver but it should be upright Sterling. Several subscribed to it but others refusing . . . it was laid aside'.

The following year it was seen just how deeply rooted was the offence: Mr. Birdwhistle, the immediate past-Master, was himself found to have sold two scimitars which, when assayed at Goldsmiths' Hall, were found to be 'worse than Sterling at six ounces in the pound which is in value about half a crown in the ounce'. In view of his position in the Company the matter was rightly regarded as being particularly scandalous and the Court took a vote to decide how much he should be fined – should it be 20 shillings, or 30 shillings or 40 shillings? The majority voted for the highest figure and, although he paid the fine, the matter created an unpleasant atmosphere in the Company.

On top of this the whole question of the manufacture of blades again came to the fore. In spite of all the long-forgotten activities of Benjamin Stone, and of the patentees with their ingenious mill, it appears that the condition of the trade was as it had been forty years earlier. The King, indeed, declared publicly that 'blades ought to be made in England', a clear indication that there was no longer any great activity at Hounslow and that the secret of the unexampled degree of perfection to which Stone had claimed to have brought the manufacturing art, had, if ever it existed, died with him.

Evidently, too, the project of bringing over craftsmen from Solingen had failed to improve the position: it is possible that they were like the Germans brought over and set to work at Greenwich who 'proved of so cunning and obstinate a disposition that they would never yet be brought to teach any Englishman the true mistery'.[188]

The Committee for the Regulation of Trade, set up by the Court of the Cutlers, recommended that a petition be presented to his Majesty not only for promoting the manufacture of sword blades but also for greater powers to redress the abuses and grievances in the cutlers' trade. This petition was organized in February 1674 but before it could be presented, Sir Thomas Cheetly, Master of the King's Great Ordnance of the Tower, summoned the Master and wardens to his house in Bloomsbury. They went there, together with some of the past-Masters, and they were told that his Majesty intended that a manufactory for sword blades should be set up in England. There was, Sir Thomas remarked, a great complaint about the bad quality of imported sword blades. And he added that it was possible that there might be created the Office of Proof-Master to inspect the wares.

The Master of the Cutlers answered that this was exactly what the Company themselves proposed in the petition they were at that very moment drafting: they had intended to call upon his Honour when their preparations were completed: now they would ask him to help them in their suit. He agreed to do so and promised that he would himself present their petition to the King.

The cutlers, well content with the encounter, returned to the Hall to which they summoned two sword-blade manufacturers, Peter English and Henry Hoppie, and asked them if they had any comments to make to the Court about the trade. They told them about the intended petition and told them, too, 'that the Company had them in their thoughts, that if they had success in their business, to make use of them. And intended them a very good encouragement in their Trade. And so at present they were dismissed.' Everyone was happy about the prospects for the future: a draft petition was submitted to Sir Thomas Cheetly for his advice. And there the matter remained. As so often happened, all the soaring hopes, the glittering visions of a revived trade gradually dissolved – a year later there was talk of sending a petition direct to his Majesty for their case to be heard since the application to Sir Thomas had proved fruitless. But nothing came of it; their case was laid aside and with it their aspirations. Only the millstone of their indebtedness remained.

In October 1673 the Court appointed yet another committee – to raise money with which they might pay what they already owed – especially to Mrs. Mann. There was nothing for it but to sell some of their properties at fifteen years' purchase and to raise a second mortgage on the Hall from Mr. Clarebutt. In this way they scraped together £815 which they paid out in December but they noted gloomily, at the same time, that by next June the second dividend promised to their creditors, Mr. Smith and Mr. Thorowgood, would fall due and that steps must be taken to meet these obligations when they arose.

The Court wished, too, to seek a new Charter but they were daunted by the expense. It was impossible to take any appreciable number of new members on to the Livery – perhaps they could persuade people to take up the Freedom at 20s. a head. In the event they managed to find twenty-two persons prepared to become Brothers as long as they did not have the subsequent expenses of bearing office thrust upon them. It was a miniscule contribution to their funds and was more than offset by the fact that since the Yeomanry had been disbanded nobody had collected their quarter-age. Among their other debts the Cutlers owed no less than £500, plus eight years' interest amounting to £240, to the Estate of Sir Lawrence Bromfield. The trustees had sufficient funds to lend even more money and they suggested that the Company should join with them and hand over all their properties to the Bromfield Estate to be managed until debt and interest be fully paid. It was an imaginative solution but it contained such implications of loss of sovereignty over their own possessions that the Court asked for

T

time to think it over. They appointed a committee to work out the best solution possible: the discussions with the trustees were difficult but by 1675 the committee had persuaded them to accept a mere £550 – part of which they raised by a third mortgage on the Hall.

They still owed the Estate £150 – 'an urgent occasion' – and four members of the Court were selected to raise the money on their personal bonds: the remaining members of the Court in their turn gave their securities to indemnify the four thus chosen. In this way the Bromfield trustees were at last, in 1676, paid off.

But, the following year, the four assistants who had raised the money were still out of pocket – the repayment by the remainder was long over-due. The Renter was ordered to find the money: tenants found themselves, almost for the first time, threatened with notices to quit, and £100 was raised. The Master supplied the remaining £50.

It was only natural that the Court should become more stringent in their policy of rent-collecting: tenants whose payments were in arrears were ruthlessly pursued. The Company's general state of insolvency led them, too, to revise the order under which the Clerk had been allowed to make what profit he might from carrying out his own business in Hall and Parlour: now he must share his profits with the Company.

The Hall was, in any case, becoming increasingly frequented. The Razor-makers were given the liberty of meeting there to consult about their aspect of the trade. So, too, were the Knife Cutlers. And, on Sundays, as we shall see, religious sects held their meetings on the premises.

In the cutlery trade, reliance was still placed upon the Court to see that rules and regulations were observed: the Knife Cutlers, for example, asked for help in prosecuting the perennial hawkers and the Knife Grinders sought protection against 'foreigns' who carried on their trade in the City – those, in particular, 'that do drive a Wheelbarrow about the streets to grind knives'. This was 'a noyance' that the Court agreed to suppress: and continued to do so until they decided that too much money, under the circumstances, was being spent upon the cause and discouraged any

further action. This penny-pinching situation affected the beautifying of the Hall. The Company had been offered an eight-piece
tapestry, as well as seventeen chairs and stools and a large couch –
'all of them Turkey work' – at a cost of £60. The special committee
to deal with the affair had offered £40 but this had been rejected
and the matter was put into abeyance.

With the death of the Clerk in 1677 the Company were able to
vary the terms of service slightly to their financial advantage. The
new Clerk, elected from the Court, was to have no salary but was to
enjoy such perquisites as the fees for binding, for making-free and
for drawing leases. He might have the house for his wife and family
but, in future, the profits from the Hall were to belong to the
Company. The benefits accruing to the Cutlers were evidently felt
to be sufficient to encourage the Master to buy the Tapestry and
the other items for the Hall at the price originally offered. And in
1678 the last great effort to settle – or at any rate to simplify – the
debts was made: £2000 was borrowed from Esquire George Arnold
on all the properties of the Company and all the other debts were
paid off. After everything was settled, there remained over
£32. 8s. 6d.

In the meantime, while this struggle for solvency was being waged,
the newly restored Parliamentary democracy was making its
presence felt. The Civil War had been waged for the supposed
cause of Religion: it was not to be expected that Faith would now
be allowed to escape the rigours of control.

In 1673 an Act of Parliament was passed 'for preventing the dangers
which may happen from Popish recusants'. It laid down numerous
categories of those who were to take the Oath of Supremacy – so
numerous indeed that the Judges came to the conclusion that all
who held offices of trust in the City must take the same oath:
they warned the Companies to take notice so 'that none be Surprised and suffer the penalties of the said Act for want of due and
timely Intimation. . . .'

But Papists were not the sole danger: there were other
schismatics. The Cutlers received a precept for the prevention of

Conventicles and the holding of private meetings and it was at once clear that non-conformists were in the habit of gathering together at the Hall, for in April 1676 the Court reported that they 'had dismissed the Meeting . . . upon a Religious account'.

Their compliance with the provisions of the act was, however, not long observed. In June 1678 an informer, named Stephens, reported to the Privy Council that there was 'in Cutlers' Hall in Cloak Lane a great Presbyterian meeting (I could not get his [the Minister's] name) frequented by the Earl of Wimbledon and Alderman Love and several other with their coaches. After their preaching was over, a private conference of the chiefest was held, near an hour, in the said place.'[189]

And the following year Mr. Coles' Congregation – an assembly mentioned on several occasions in the Minutes – were promised the use of the Parlour and Hall for £30 a year: they were told, however, that they would have to transfer the meeting to some day other than Wednesday and they would have to provide a cleaner – with all the necessary equipment – to tidy up after the meeting and before the next day.

Other, non-sectarian, bodies were also granted the use of the Hall: for £6 a year and ten shillings to the Clerk at Christmas the Combmakers held their Courts and Meetings there on the first Thursdays of the month. In September 1679 they wanted, additionally, the use of the Parlour on Quarter Days: they were told that, their rent would be raised to £10 'which proffer the Combmakers peremptorily and without further overture rejected, desiring the Liberty to take their Chest &c. which the Court accordingly granted'.

By letting the Hall, by strictly managing their estates and, especially, by a satisfactory flow of payments from their Irish lands, the Company gradually struggled back to a state of solvency. The first signs of recovery were seen when, in March 1679, they were able to grant the Clerk a yearly salary of £8. The following year they received an unexpected windfall when they learned that the Innholders intended to take on Edward Norman from the Cutlers' Livery and translate him to their Company. The Court summoned Norman before them. An election was instantly arranged. In alleged competition with the Clerk, Norman was chosen Renter; in further competition with the Clerk he was chosen Upper Warden; in competition with Mr. Evans – possibly the senior past-Master – he was elected Master. He then paid fines to escape all three offices and his transfer was granted. Both democracy and self-interest were satisfied. In such ways, gradually, the debts were paid: by 1681 they were able to buy back from Esquire Arnold for £154 the mortgage of the Belle Sauvage.

And as they began, once again, to flourish, a booklet was published which making, as it did, a critical survey of the Cutlers' trade repays consideration.[190]

William Badcock, the author of *A New Touchstone for Cutlers' Wares* bemoaned the fact that things were not as they had been in the days of the great Elizabeth: in those days the cutlers were concerned with all manner of iron or steel cutting instruments and their accessories 'and not as they are now intermingled' with gold and silver wares.

Which intermingling of several Trades, hath happened by divers persons unlawfully exercising some Trades jointly with their own proper Trades and bringing up Apprentices thereto. . . .

Although this was against the law, the apprentices, when they had served their time, could legally carry on the other trade. Now the cutlers were infringing the rights of the Goldsmiths – not always, it seems, honestly, for Badcock quoted from the Confirmation Charter of the Goldsmiths in 1604

. . . the cutlers in their workhouses cover tin with silver so subtilly, and with so much sleight, that the same cannot be discerned and severed from the tin; and by that means they sell the tin so covered for fine silver to the great damage of us and our people. . . .

Whatever might be the position of the Company the Cutlers' trade as a whole did not appear to William Badcock to be flourishing. In spite of all the protectionist laws enacted by rulers from Edward IV onwards there were still many abuses by which the industry was 'much decayed and like to be utterly lost'. He suggested that the existing laws be enforced and that new regulations be introduced to include Sword Blades which had been omitted from previous legislation.

All cutlers, in and around the City, should belong to the Company and the Master and wardens should have the right of search over the whole of England.

The chief cause, it was suggested, of the present sorry state of affairs was that the officers of the Company frequently were men with 'little or no skill to perform the duty of those places and unable to correct the abuses' and, since there were many cutlers who were not members of the Company, the offenders amongst them refused to comply with orders.

Bad workmanship destroyed good workmen: they were unable to compete against the low prices charged by the bad workmen except by themselves reducing the quality of their work. And the widespread counterfeiting of trade marks had had disastrous effects because it prevented 'the knowledge of good works and thereby discouraged the honest and curious Artists'.

It was very necessary, the author urged, to set up an English sword-blade manufacture: at the moment the English were still compelled to accept whatever was sent from abroad no matter how bad or how expensive it might be. In fact, because the country had no home sword-blade industry and no officers to check the quality, the imported foreign blades were often most defective.

In this, Badcock merely was taking up the agitation which had been sparked-off in 1674 when the King had announced the intention to institute a British sword-blade industry. But it is from this writer that we learn something of what happened to the previous attempts to establish the manufactory in the days of Benjamin Stone. At first it had seemed as if the enterprise would be a success but then 'the Merchants from beyond Sea brought in great quantity of untried blades at lower prices than ordinary which was partly the destruction of the work here. . . . '

There was no reason why England could not make as good blades as any other country but the manufacture, said Badcock, should be controlled by the Cutlers' Company: it would not then fall into the hands of Executors 'which otherwise it will be if it come into private hands, which was the destruction of this work at Hounslow'.

So, it seems, the collapse of all the proud schemes for a home industry for sword-blades had been due to imports and to private enterprise – two aspects of the economy that three hundred years later were still objects of blame for various ills.

Cutlery ought – the pamphleteer urged – to be encouraged in the same way as many less important trades were encouraged. 'Where,' he demanded rhetorically, 'be any of the Cutler's Trade that make any considerable proficiency in their Estates in comparison with other Tradesmen?'

It was certainly the argument of a partisan and the work ended with a splendid peroration:

The Sword is the principal weapon of War and the Sword in the King's hand is the emblem of his Authority (*Romans*. 13.3.) Although by other weapons more are killed, yet all are said to be slain by the Sword.

This Scriptural endorsement was clearly intended to inspire the highest endeavours among the Cutlers to whom Badcock finally addressed a stirring exhortation:

Now, to you of the Corporation and Mystery, I say rouse up your spirits and give a suitable active pursuit and attendance for attaining these things: you must expect to take pains before profit come: and if some rubs and difficulties happen, you may remember that many do attend the pursuit of the most valuable and profitable achievements: Remember the chief instrument of your Trade, the *Sword*; it is the Instrument of Victory and Conquest; then be your actions in these concerns of like merit: in being victorious conquerors of all difficulties that happen in your pursuit of all lawful and reasonable things that may in probability make your Mystery and Corporation increase in Riches and Honour.

The immediate effect of this propagandist literature seems to have been small, although there certainly now appear in the Minutes far greater details of searches – lists of members searched, how much they paid, what (if any) goods were confiscated. The areas of search were also more fully detailed: Westminster, Charing Cross, Strand, St. Martin's Lane, King Street, Drury Lane, Holborn and Chancery Lane indicate the sort of round carried out by searchers.

The Goldsmiths, too, may have been marginally inspired by Badcock when they refused to return some of the faulty goods submitted to them for assay by the Cutlers. But, generally speaking, life in the trade continued normally: the Court appeared unmoved by exhortation or abuse.

They were, however, concerned with new problems and new dangers arising from matters, on a national level, outside the specialized interests of cutlery: once again it was religion that caused the first disturbance in the daily ordering of their affairs.

The freedom of conscience promised at the Restoration had proved illusory: restrictions on acts of worship by those not subscribing to the Established Church varied in their severity but were nonetheless universal: 'sedition' was the charge made against those, Catholic or otherwise, who did not conform.

The Act to prevent and suppress seditious Conventicles led the Court to arrange a meeting in May 1682 with representatives of Mr. Coles' Congregation, for whose meetings the Hall had long been used, in order to secure indemnities in case the Company or Clerk were fined for anything illegal that the Congregation might do while they were upon the premises. In June a bond for £100 was obtained but there were those on the Court who considered that, in view of the dangers to the Company, to its Charter, goods, chattels and estates if the Act were infringed, this sum was too little. They ordered the Clerk to ask the Congregation not to meet at the Hall on the following day, Tuesday: if, none the less, they arrived, the door was to be shut in their faces and the meeting prevented. Mr. Coles with dogged non-conformist determination replied that he intended to preach as usual unless he had a direct order from the Company to desist. The Clerk told him that it was just such an order that was now delivered. Mr. Coles asked if he might then preach at the Hall on the next Sunday. He was asked to provide a bond for £500 against the commission of possible illegalities: the answer of the Congregation was to send a carrier to the Hall to collect their chairs and benches. Since the rent was paid in advance until Midsummer Day the Court could raise no objec-

tion and the connection with Mr. Coles' Congregation came to an
end.

There were, however, others to make up for the loss of rental:
Mr. Low the dancing master, for example, began to hold his classes
there and the Feltmakers, too, agreed to hire the Hall and parlour
for their various occasions. The Hall was, in fact, contributing
considerably towards balancing the budget of the Company. On
Sundays, it was true, 'boys and other rude persons' were apt to
deface the rails and banks of the garden and back-yard which led
to a certain amount of trouble and expense but 'a pair of good
strong and handsome hatches with iron spikes' soon put an end to
that and the Company prepared to face a new stability both
financial and operational.

But, at this moment, the Court were suddenly struck by one of
the attacks of unease about the extent of their powers which, as
we have seen, periodically overcame them.

It may have been for the reason that the Crown was once again
toying with the idea of acquiring control of the City. The advisers of
Charles II were arguing that the City had received its privileges
from the Crown: the Crown, equally, could remove them. There
were old scores to be paid against the Londoners who had proved
so great a stumbling block to the cause of Charles I. That the City
was still recalcitrant could be inferred by the way a jury of City
officers had acquitted Shaftesbury when he was charged with
treason. To gain control of the government of London an attempt
was made to 'rig' the elections of 1682 at Guildhall: when the
citizens protested swordsmen made a dramatic appearance among
the voters.

Whether or not this demonstration that external interference
with the destiny of the Company was still a very real possibility,
was responsible for the Court's sudden decision to seek reassurance
about the powers of the Company under the charters and
ordinances, they anxiously addressed a series of questions to their
counsel.

These, with the answers they received, were as follows:

1.   Q. What is the safest and best way for the Master and Wardens to carry out
     forfeitures under the Ordinances?

A. *Distraint or action for debt.*

2. Q. If any Member complains to the Master and Wardens that someone in the City, or within eight miles, is acting contrary to Law how far are the Master and Wardens legally obliged to take action?

A. *Not at all.*

3. Q. Are the Orders made by the Company in 1602 (if disobeyed) suable? And are the forfeitures recoverable? They not being approved by the Lord Chancellor.

A. *Yes. But the Company would not be advised to sue until each order is approved in particular.*

4. Q. In a Search can an Officer of the Peace break down a door?

A. *Probably not. The old Act talks of Searching Open shops and Warehouses.*

5. Q. Are the Master and Wardens bound to Search and seize foreigns' goods forbidden under the Laws?

A. *No. Except when they think needful.*

6. Q. Can an Assistant be discarded for revealing Secrets?

A. *Yes.*

7. Q. Are Brass Hilts absolutely prohibited and suable from a Founder or Brazier?

A. *No. The Acts talk only of the wrongness of gilding or silvering brass or iron handles – there is nothing that forbids brass or iron as such. And if there is no forfeiture by Statute then there cannot be any forfeiture by Charter or By-Laws.*

It will be observed that the general tone of these replies tended towards *laissez faire:* Masters or wardens who did not wish to go looking for trouble were by no means obliged to do so. The replies were, therefore, on the whole encouraging: the Court possessed powers but they were not obliged to use them.

But the Company's investigation had hardly been completed when their powers were called into far greater question by a writ of *Quo Warranto* from the Crown.

The unwelcome attention that Charles II had been paying towards the City, had been earlier manifested in the attempt to 'rig' the elections: it had not stopped there. Sheriffs who opposed the

Crown were arrested; aldermen were heavily fined. The Rye
House Plot of 1683 involved leading Whigs: because the dissident
citizens were mostly of the same faction, further attacks were made
upon the City. In June 1683 its Charter – together with the charters
of other cities – was declared forfeit.

It may here be noted that the King had no particular desire to
change the framework of local government: he had, however, the
keenest interest in obtaining municipal officers who were loyal to
himself and who would provide none of the opposition from which
his father had so fatally suffered. In London, therefore, he removed
the obstinate and independent aldermen and replaced them by
others nominated by Royal Commission. He nominated the Lord
Mayor, the Sheriffs and the Recorder to serve at his pleasure. But
the scheme was incomplete without a subservient electorate in
Common Hall: he must, next, secure control of the City Companies.

It was thus that, in April 1684, the Cutlers, in common with the
other Livery Companies, received, as a preliminary to removing
their privileges, the writ of *quo warranto* to demand by what right they
enjoyed them.

It so happens that at this juncture the Court Minutes become
singularly uninstructive: there are no records of any meeting being
held between February and May – by which latter month their
rights and privileges had been removed. We must, therefore, look
to other Companies to determine a course of events which was
doubtless common to all.[191]

The common form of reaction to the writ seems to have been a
grovelling but stylized form of grief at having incurred the Royal
displeasure and a humble submission to the Royal wisdom and
pleasure. To this the King replied that he

designed not to intermeddle or take away the rights, property or privileges of
the Company nor to destroy their ancient usages and franchises but only to
regulate the governing part so as his Majesty might, for the future, have in
himself a moving power of any officer therein for misgovernment.

A humiliating Instrument of Surrender was dictated:

We, considering how much it imports the Government of our Company to
have men of known Loyalty and proved Integrity to have offices of Magistracy

and places of Trust . . . do by these presents yield up, grant and surrender unto his most Gracious Majesty . . . all Powers, Franchises, Liberties and Authorities. . . .

Gone with all their other rights was the selection of their own officers or their own Court. All depended upon the King to restore them to their former position 'under such Reservations, Restrictions and Qualifications as his Majesty shall be pleased to appoint. . . .'

Obviously a petition to the Crown in the name of the Company was called for. But was it legal, the Court asked themselves, to take such action without reference to a Common Hall of the members. They put this new question to their Counsel: he replied it would be safer to call a meeting of the whole fellowship. On 13 June the Common Hall was held: the Master asked the Company if they would petition his Majesty to restore their former Liberties, Franchises and Immunities, by Charter, under such Limitations as his Majesty should 'in his princely wisdom think fit?'

A vote was taken and action by the Court agreed. On 29 June a deputation consisting of the Master, the wardens and five members went down to Windsor: their petition recited that their privileges, rights and immunities had been granted by the King's Royal Progenitors. They conceived themselves 'partly through Ignorance and partly through Poverty and Low Estate . . . to have been misled. Whereat to their great Grief they fear your Majesty hath taken Just Displeasure.'

They begged his Majesty in his princely compassion and charity to forgive their crimes and errors and restore their Charter. Then they waited.

They began to study their own constitution to determine how the new Charter should be worded. The old Charter – with such regulations as the Company should think fit – was to be cited in the new and in November the Clerk was ordered to have a copy made and sent to Counsel for his advice on 'the best, safest and cheapest way' for the Company to proceed. Economy was certainly called for: once again they found it necessary to mortgage the Belle Sauvage for £300 to repay an earlier mortgage on another property.

In January 1685 the Court decided that not more than £60 was to be spent on renewing the Charter. There were some who refused to sign the surrender of the old Charter but they were in a minority. The sorry business went ahead and at last on 20 March 1685 their incorporation was reinstated. But they were by no means restored to their former position: their ancient style and title was the same, and they still had the rights of perpetual succession, but now their officers had to be communicant Protestants approved by the Crown. Moreover, the Lord Mayor and aldermen – themselves either nominees of, or approved by, the King – had to control all admissions to the Livery. The fact that the King was now James II – for Charles had died in February and his Charter was posthumous – made no difference whatsoever. The new oaths were taken and in May the new Court of those acceptable to the Government took their seats. The Master, Thomas Pennington, and the Junior Warden, Daniel Wilson, had been proscribed. In their places were William Chiffinch and John Hawgood. Although the latter was a bona-fide member of the Company, the new Master had been brought in from outside and was not even made free of the Cutlers until later in the month. Nor did he attend more than one further meeting – his place being generally taken by a Deputy Master nominated to act for this Crown-appointed figurehead. The assistants included five Ancient Masters and eight cutlers who had had never held office. There were three vacancies.

It may be thought that the first meeting of the Court was not without its embarrassments and awkward moments and it seems that a certain element of mutual trust was indeed lacking: for it was decided that all members of the Court must pay £5 towards the considerable costs of the new Charter, and when it was further ordered that they should be repaid this sum from the first money coming to the Company it was thought necessary to add the words 'without any fraud or pretence whatsoever'.

The first meeting of the new Court was, of course, to take the two oaths laid down by law.

The first was of allegiance and supremacy, by which they declared their belief that it was unlawful to take up arms against the King and declared their abhorrence of traitorous attitudes.

The second abjured the 'Solemn League and Covenant' which 'was in itself an unlawful Oath and imposed upon the Subjects of this Realm, against the known Laws and Liberties of the Kingdom'.

The Court settled down to the uneasy task of making the new organization work. By the judgement of *Quo Warranto* and the seizing of the franchises and charters, the privilege of being a Livery Company was amongst those suspended. Now, in May, the Lord Mayor intimated that the King had decreed that thirty-one Companies – the Cutlers amongst them – were again to be granted Liveries so that the Liverymen, all of them hand-picked and loyal to the Crown, should be able to vote in Parliamentary elections. This granting of Livery was subject to the proviso that 'the number of your Livery men do not exceed the number appointed by his Majesty's Letters Patent lately granted. . . .' The Court were, therefore, to select 'the most discreet and sufficient members . . . being of approved and unquestionable loyalty.' Their names were to be submitted to the Lord Mayor for 'allowance and approbation pursuant to his Majesty's further directions. . . .'

The Cutlers submitted thirty-five names. All of them were approved, and elections were called for 15 May.

Some coats of arms were removed from the Hall windows and others put in their place. These manifestations of dictatorship – there must have existed a surprisingly efficient central system of information about the personal beliefs of a large number of citizens – did not pass without some counter-demonstrations. On 7 May it was announced in a precept that his Majesty felt 'high resentment of the Dishonour done to his Royal Person – apart from breaking the law and the dangers to peace – caused by seditious, treasonous, scandalous books, pamphlets, libels . . .' and so on.

The stationery trade, it was observed, had been used in printing, binding, stitching, and generally producing these items: those of other Companies who were stationers – there was one such Cutler – had clearly been disobeying the orders of the Stationers' Company. Arrangements must, therefore, be instantly put in hand to translate all stationers to their proper mother-company. Thus would the trade – and, incidentally, the seditious pamphlets – be controlled.

By June conditions had been sufficiently restored to normal for trade matters to make their reappearance in the Minutes.

There was a petition for the suppression of 'one Rowley and other Interlopers. Or at least that the Shopkeepers might be debarred from employing persons under such Circumstances.' London had been inundated with French cutlers seeking asylum after the Edict of Nantes and the Court agreed that they would take action against anyone employing foreigners or interlopers and many promises were made, both by the petitioners and others, not to work for that sort of person: only one rebellious member said stoutly that he would work for any customer he could get.

Then, in August, a woman member complained that the Blacksmiths had seized some of her goods and the Court agreed to take up her case. They agreed too with the Master of the Armourers that the two Companies should join together to suppress the irrepressible Hawkers. The Cutlers, however, had bigger plans for control of the Trade than the harrying of petty offenders.

At the beginning of 1686, the Deputy-Master and the wardens rode down to Windsor to Esquire Chiffinch – the nominal Master – in order to wait upon Lord Dartmouth, Master-General of the King's Ordnance, for his advice in procuring a Patent from James II for the testing, approval, and marking of all sword-blades manufactured anywhere in England.

All workmen should bring their blades to the Hall, or to some other appointed place, where they would be paid 'an indifferent and reasonable price'; all those wishing to buy blades should do so at the Hall; all imported blades, taken in searches, should be destroyed and not sold under licence.

This was really a considerable innovation and it appears that Lord Dartmouth reacted favourably to their proposal: at any rate, the Court sent another deputation to William Chiffinch 'for his advice in shewing gratitude to Lord Dartmouth'.

As with so many of their ambitious schemes apparently upon the point of fruition nothing more is heard of it. A Mr. Porter of Birmingham certainly announced that he was prepared to send up all blades that he made to the Hall, to lie in stock when approved and to be sold by the Company on his account, the money being sent to him from time to time. Articles of agreement were to be drawn up. But there is no further record of any action. The Letters Patent, it must be assumed, were never granted and, indeed, the Company within a very few days of their expressions of gratitude to the Master General of the King's Ordnance were opposing his proposals to manufacture Hollow Sword Blades with a Mill.

Although Dartmouth's monopoly does not seem to have been immediately granted the scheme eventually succeeded and the Hollow Sword Blade Company – to which the Cutlers became reconciled – flourished for many years.

Though they might not mark all the blades in England, the Cutlers now became increasingly active in control of the marks that came under their surveillance: Moses Carr's mark of the 'Sceptre and O' was so like William Dean's 'Sceptre and Half-moon' as to be unacceptably indistinguishable; at Chingford Mills, Mr. How was turning out knives with a great number of different marks when, according to the rules, he should have used but one.

The life of the Company was back to normal. It was laid down that the Court should, in future, meet every month. Their deliberations were directed towards the accustomed every-day matters of their organization: Mr. South, the dancing-master who now held his classes at the Hall, was in arrears with his rent and asked both for a lesser rent and time to pay it; new though the Hall was there were already dilapidations to be dealt with; a five-and-a-half per cent mortgage was raised upon the lands at Egham.

Then, quite suddenly, in October 1687, further action was taken under the writ of *Quo Warranto*: an Order in Council swept away twenty-one members of the Court and Livery. Many of those removed in the first purge were to be reinstated; a new Court was to be formed from those previously dismissed – with certain exceptions which confirmed that the Government's intelligence system was exceedingly finely tuned to individual opinions and practices. New Livery and Court lists were to be submitted. As might well be expected there were errors and omissions and anomalies. William Chiffinch, for example, was listed as a former assistant – though he had never attended meetings, never paid Quarterage and, as we have seen, was at no time a member of the Company until imposed upon them by the Crown; Major Spencer, who had acted as Deputy-Master, was given the status of Ancient Master although he had never fined for any office. Very naturally mistakes occurred: the Order removed the Master, John Hawgood, from the Livery – and, therefore, from the Court and from his office and Mr. Clapham was elected in his place. When the lists were submitted Mr. Hawgood was reinstated and became Master again. Confusion, for at least nine days, was absolute – and the spoiled state of the Court minutes of the period permits little clarification. By 24 October things seemed to have been straightened out, though at least one of those selected was now living in the country and unable to serve.

It is said that the Nonconformists – given legality by the Declaration of Indulgence as part of James II's plan for the re-establishment of the Catholic cause – now formed the majority of the Company,[192] and they addressed an over-fulsome letter of thanks to the King for his protection of their civil and religious liberty.

But they were not yet finished with the effects of *Quo Warranto*. In February 1688 there was a fresh rash of reinstatements in which both wardens were removed and the order establishing Major Spencer as an Ancient Master was rescinded: his arms were hastily removed from the window and two of those previously taken down were replaced. Another thirty-seven members were taken on to the Livery.

The despotic means by which the King sought to achieve the respectable ends of religious toleration were largely responsible for his downfall in 'the Glorious Revolution'. Many of those responsible for his ovethrow were those who, otherwise devoted to the Crown, went in deadly fear of popery. The City had behaved in a supine manner. London, once the maker and breaker of monarchs in the worst days of tyranny, had allowed itself to be intolerably interfered with; it had permitted the grossest intrusion into its personal affairs. Fortunately there were still those in the Kingdom who were prepared to act against dictatorship: they negotiated secretly with James's son-in-law, William of Orange. When the birth of a son to the King threatened by implication a

U

perpetually Catholic succession to the throne, matters came quickly to a head.

James, learning that the Dutch were preparing the invasion of England, tried frantically to back-pedal. Among other desperate expedients he tried to woo the City: in October 1688 he announced that he had been 'graciously pleased to restore to the City all its ancient franchises. . . .' Everything was to be restored to the state immediately before the writ of *Quo Warranto*; the Instrument of Surrender which, so it was alleged, had never been enrolled was, therefore, as if it had never existed; all those originally upon the Livery were to be reinstated. Confusion was thus worse confounded. In any case, the King had acted far too late. The Instrument of Surrender was handed back to the Lord Mayor a fortnight after William had landed at Torbay and a day after he had actually arrived in London. James II fled the country and, in as unsettled a condition as it is possible to imagine, the Cutlers' Company prepared to face the uncertainties of a new reign. They must surely have done so without any great degree of optimism. The Stuart tyranny was at last ended but their centuries of experience had taught them that a change of ruler was of itself no guarantee that their lot would be improved. The City had survived the extraordinary upheaval of the last two years through no merits of its own. It would have needed a peculiar lack of sensitivity to regard the prospects of a new monarch with anything more than a guarded pessimism.

15

A Company in Decay

1688–1729

IT has been said that the writ of *Quo Warranto* was 'the last public event of consequence in connection with the City Livery Companies'.[193] Efforts might be made by reformers altogether to abolish them but never again was there any attempt to control by statute the actions authorized by their Charters.

And, almost as if reflecting this as yet unappreciated state of ordinariness, the business of the Court, in common with the Courts of some other Companies, suddenly shewed a marked decline. In 1689 it was laid down that there should be no more than four Court Days a year, except in emergency. Nor does this seem to have arisen purely from the fact that there now appears to have been a kind of General Purposes Committee, engaged in carrying on the business of the Company in between the meetings of the Court. If they were busy they did not report the fact to the Court.

It was inevitable that the confusion and uncertainty of the last days of the Stuarts should have left their mark upon the Company's attitudes. Clearly there was a certain mistrust among the assistants. That Masters should be forbidden to spend more than 40s. at a Court Meeting if, as was again happening, it was held at a tavern, was a natural precaution. But it was less natural to emphasize the order quite so thoroughly: such expense accounts had to be countersigned by at least five Past-Masters; they were to include 'no expenses but such as shall be really upon the Company's business'; the order was to be read in Open Court so that no future Master could claim ignorance.

And when they came to the election day in 1690 a constitutional crisis, on a scale such as they had not known for a very long time, suddenly exploded. The day had started on a sour note with the rejection of Past-Master Wilson's account. This had been previously queried and his revised account was no better liked. It was remarked that he had not paid his fine for Renter and he was charged £10 in addition to the piece of plate – a silver tankard – that it was his privilege to present to the Company. The Court then proceeded to choose the new Master and wardens for election by the Common Hall. To their shocked amazement, with calculated impiety the Common Hall rejected the choice and demanded that Edward Bickerstaffe (who was not an official candidate) be put in nomination for Master 'Which the Master, Wardens and greater part of Assistants refused, alleging it was not yet his time . . . having served only Under-Warden and Renter and that by virtue of King James the Second's Charter . . . Whereupon the Common Hall was in great disorder and uproar.'

During the painful scene that followed one of the wardens and several of the Court made a tactical withdrawal: those that remained were able to contemplate 'some of the young Livery violently pressing the Master [so that they] caused the Master and Wardens and all the Assistants to be put in nomination for Master.'

Two names emerged: Mr. Bickerstaffe and Mr. Tunn. And at this juncture 'Warden Tunn, Captain Powell, and others of the Assistance returning, Ordering them to leave off and desist from further polling, the whole Company by consent went to dinner.'

There is something rather pleasing about this sudden cooling of the situation, this sudden break in the tension, at the thought of the election dinner waiting them on the table: after the meal the matter was fairly quickly settled. Some fourteen assistants withdrew to the Court Room and there declared void the poll that had already been begun 'having been surreptitiously obtained'. They then selected four candidates for Master of whom, by a show of hands, the Livery selected Mr. Tunn. The revolt was over. When Bickerstaffe brought, in consequence, a writ of *Mandamus* against the Company ordering them to elect him Master the Company decided to fight any such demand and a committee of defence was formed. Eventually the whole affair was amicably settled: both sides, paying their own costs, gave up any actions or disagreements they still had from the beginning of the world to date.

In the meantime, life and work at the Hall continued. In planning one of the dinners it was agreed that music might be had if Mr. South, the dancing master, would provide it against what he owed the Company in rent; four of the Stewards, showing the current revolutionary spirit, refused to pay more than £4 each towards the cost of the dinner and were haled before the Lord Mayor; £200 was borrowed from Mr. Folkingham to repay the long-suffering Esquire Arnold; 'some of Mr. Knowles' people' sought to take the Hall for a meeting of their Congregation; the Master of the Pipemakers wanted to rent the Hall for his Company meetings but only offered £5 plus 20s. a year to the Clerk for cleaning the Hall whereas the Cutlers were demanding £8; a subscription list for raising horse and dragoons for their Majesties' service met with a negligible response but in 1692 a collection under 'an Act for Granting an Aid to their Majesties of the Sum of Sixteen Hundred Fifty One Thousand Seven Hundred and Two Pounds towards the Carrying on a Vigorous War against France' was more successful.

Otherwise the Minutes during the last decade of the century were mostly concerned with the routine business of Presentments, Bindings and so on.

The state of the Company's finances was still far from robust: the problem was perennially that of borrowing from Peter to repay Paul: Mr. Folkingham's loan was still outstanding and the Renter paid him £60 interest of which £20 was borrowed from the Master; later it was agreed that the Cutlers 'for the further security of payment of £200 to Mr. Edward Folkingham which he formerly lent the Company upon security of the lands at Egham shall release and assign to him . . . the Equity of Redemption of the Hall and Clerk's house after [?repayment] of £300 to Esquire Arnold. . . .'

The following year, in 1695, Esquire Arnold died and his administrator demanded the money still outstanding: the Company borrowed £300 from Mr. Folkingham. It was fortunate that there were usually men of substance in the Company who were ready to come to the Cutlers' assistance and free them from the necessity

of having to borrow from outsiders. It was not easy to make economies. The Court, planning the Dinner, voted to go without wine
(beer only was served), women (except for the wives of officers)
and music. They took a more cautious approach to demands for
the hire of the Hall: in the past they had lost some good lettings
through being too greedy in their demands. When a Founder, a
Skinner and the Clerk of the Joiners offered £12 for the use of the
Hall on Thursday mornings and Sunday mornings and evenings
for the use of Mr. Beverly and his Congregation, the Court
demanded £20 but 'rather than fail' would accept £16 for one year
'if Mr. Thomas Beverly shall so long live'. They stipulated, however, that Mr. Beverly's People should not be allowed to fix any
canopy or sounding-board or any other thing to any part of the
Hall unless 'it be taken off and removed day by day so soon as
Mr. Beverly hath finished his Exercise'.

The Court still concerned themselves with the control of the
Trade: Searches were carried out but either they were less scrupulous or people were becoming more honest for the amount of
goods seized declined. Hawkers were still to be put-down so long
as this could be done without involving the Company in expense,
and a similar condition was attached to the granting of a petition,
in 1698, for the prosecution of strangers and foreigners exercising
the trade of handle-binding 'making sleight work and thereby
undermining and underselling'.

That their old opposition to the 'Company for making Hollow
Sword Blades in England' had ceased by 1699 was demonstrated by
an advertisement by that organization in the *London Gazette* which
announced 'That they shall put for Sale by the Candle, at Cutlers-
hall in Cloak Lane on Thursday the 20th Instant (July) at 11 in the
Forenoon what Sword-blades they have finished'.[195]

The outside world scarcely ever intruded. The fortunes of the
war with France fluctuated; across the Channel the exiled James II
in Calais waited and hoped. There were plots and rumours of plots.
In 1696 it was 'notoriously evident that there hath been a late
barbarous and execrable design of assassinating their Majesties
persons and invading these Kingdoms by domestic and foreign
enemies'.

Everyone was therefore required to sign an Association which denounced the 'Papists and other wicked and crafty persons' who wished to encourage an invasion from France and which agreed that they would all stand together in support of King William as their right and lawful ruler and 'should the worst occur' they would defend his succession.

The Association was signed by members of the Court and 223 Freemen who presumably constituted an almost complete nominal roll of the Cutlers. It was decided at the same time that as a means of paying the Company's debts, as many as possible should be called on to the Livery. Twenty-eight names were put forward but the general reaction of the nominees was disappointing. Only a dozen accepted on the spot, others appealed and were altogether excused, some were excused until another day and two altogether refused and were sent before the Lord Mayor. There was, in any case, a limitation to the numbers eligible – an Act of the Court of Aldermen in 1697 insisted that 'no person shall be allowed to take upon himself the clothing of any of the twelve Companies unless he have an estate of £1,000, of the inferior Companies unless he have an estate of £500.'

As the century came to an end there were 110 members of the Cutlers' Livery[194] to enjoy the dinner on election day. There was now a general acceptance of the way the Elections were conducted: the Livery had some sort of say in the matter – a choice was put to them and if they usually selected the Court's nominees that was all part of the order of things. They were able, without rancour, to sit down together to a meal consisting of a large sirloin of beef ('to stand on the sideboard'), three dozen chickens with bacon, and 'sparagos', lumber pies, neats tongues, roast udders, marrow puddings, and tarts and custards. The food was washed down with beer and a gross of tobacco pipes was provided. But in the interests of economy there was no wine.

They certainly began the new century with a great burden of debts although there are no precise details of their extent.

They had introduced, as one method of raising money, the sale of annuities: for £250 they made a yearly payment of £15. It is uncertain whether the scheme was actuarially sound but it provided some kind of immediate relief. On a smaller scale of finance the Court instituted a great drive for collecting Quarterage. Some of the members had obviously failed for many years to pay the small sum of 4d.: one of them who now had to provide no less than £1. 7s. 8d. was, by inference, no less than twenty-one years in arrears.

Then 'the Court taking into consideration the great charge and expence the Company lies under and being willing to raise money the easiest way for discharge thereof' raised the Quarterage from 4d. to 6d. It can hardly have been more than a gesture to underline the seriousness of their situation; the financial effect can have been no more than marginal. However, they now felt they could afford to have the Hall reglazed, the tapestries taken down and washed and mended, and to wainscott the Green Room in the Clerk's House with 'all dry and seasoned stuff'. As a token of recovery, wine – not exceeding £7. 10s. – was permitted at the Lord Mayor's Day dinner.

By this time the majority of the Company's business must have been conducted in Committee – no Court meetings were recorded between October 1700 and April 1701 – but if there were any records of their deliberations they have not survived. By the time King William III was dead and Queen Anne was on the throne the work at the Hall had been completed and the accounts strictly scrutinized. Many of them were cut down by a few shillings and Mr. Bellamy offered to lend £50 towards their settlement.

The refurbished Hall continued to provide a steady income: another Congregation – that of Mr. John Smith – was authorized to hold meetings at the same rate as was paid by 'Dr. Beverly's People'; another dancing master held his classes there. But there was no money to spare for extra projects. When, in 1702, it was decided to take counsel's opinion about their bye-laws and, perhaps, revise them, the cost could only be met by abolishing the feasts at the election and on Lord Mayor's Day.

The only hope for saving the festivities would be if the stewards could be persuaded to undertake the whole of the cost of the latter

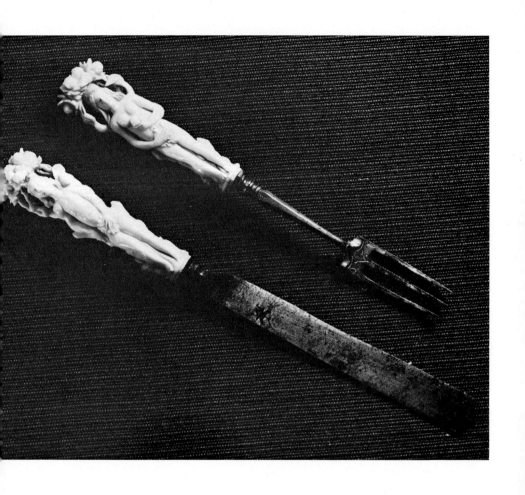

Folding knife, fork and spoon with stamped leather case. Copper gilt chased with hunting scenes. Prague or Karlsberg, first half of the eighteenth century

The terracotta frieze on the façade of Cutlers' Hall is by Creswick and is the only example of his work to be seen in London

The war-damaged Cutlers' Hall, 1940 (Photo: *The Times*)

dinner. The role of steward, because of the expense involved, had never been a popular one: now a demonstration of its unpopularity occurred. Two members of the Yeomanry, Andrew Ragdale and Samuel Strange, had refused some years previously to take up the Livery: now they appealed to the Court of Aldermen against the Cutlers' Company for attempting to force them to undertake the stewardship. They asserted that only members of the Livery were liable for this office but their plea was not accepted and the aldermen fined them £3 each for their refusal.[196] The matter was not, however, as we shall see, to end so simply.

In the meantime the Court discussed the bye-laws. Arising from their discussions there was promulgated a new standing order for themselves: 'for the better avoiding of disorder, noise, and confusion in all Courts of Assistants . . . every member of the said Court shall always keep silence at the commandment or desire of the Master. . . . '

Not more than one of them was to speak at a time 'so the opinion and judgement of every member may be heard and known without any interruption' and all, except the Master, were, when they spoke, to take their hats off.

On 12 February 1703 the various laws and ordinances were read out at a full meeting of the Court and five weeks later they were approved by the whole Company. And, in due course, they were confirmed by the Lord Chancellor, the Lord Treasurer Godolphin and two Chief Justices. Once again the Court could feel themselves, their authority full confirmed, masters in their own house. And, in October 1704, this feeling was put to the test: the Beadle was sent to collect from Andrew Ragdale and Samuel Strange the fines and fees for refusing to come upon the Livery.

They again refused to pay and appealed to the Lord Mayor. In January his Lordship ordered the Company to stop the prosecution: neither of the Yeomen possessed estates of £500 and therefore should be discharged from taking up the Livery. Faced with this challenge to their authority, the Court took counsel's opinion and were advised that the Lord Mayor and aldermen could not legally prevent them from taking action. They took the Charter out of the Company chest and prepared for battle. A year later the case was still dragging on and when the Court of Aldermen asked that it be referred to a special Committee, the Cutlers decided unanimously to continue to proceed at law. Counsel were retained but before the case could be heard both Ragdale and Strange had given in: they paid their £10 fines and the Company, with a fine gesture of generosity considering their financial condition, agreed to pay the considerable legal costs of both sides. It was an important victory for the Cutlers' Company, and especially noteworthy in face of the opposition from the Court of Aldermen.

Yet there were not now many occasions on which their authority seemed to be called for. The Court still enrolled marks but the incidence of such matters of trade control became increasingly rare: by the end of the reign it was only once in every three or four years that such a service was rendered. The time of the Court was occupied with trivia: Mr. Gere, the new dancing master in business at the Hall, demanded a grate with a shovel and tongs; his pupils demanded somewhere to change and were given 'the Liberty of the Clerk's dining room on Ball nights only'; the 'stale beer' provided at dinners gave way to the more generally acceptable Stout.

Perhaps it was fortunate that the assistants were not more busy: some of them were beginning to shew signs of infirmity. One was excused for deafness: another was too lame to come to the Hall. There was a moment of pageantry to enlighten the dullness of the times: Queen Anne came to the City and the Cutlers held both breakfast and dinner at the Hall. There was now plenty of wine provided, including a gallon of red wine that was sent down to the Company's stand to be drunk there to wash down the eighteen pounds of cake and the two dozen halfpenny rolls.

The Clerk died and when his successor was elected there was a break with recent practice – not only was he not a member of the Court but he was not even a freeman of the Company. The opportunity of changing the conditions of service was gratefully seized: in future he would have to pay £30 a year for his house.

The Cutlers needed every penny they could get. To add to their financial problems their profitable occupation of the Egham properties was coming to an end. When a precept was received in

1707 from the Lord Mayor to attend him upon May Day 'the Court taking into consideration the several debts they owe do think they can't attend his Lordship. . . .' The Clerk of the City works was therefore informed that some other Company could have their space and he was given a suitable gratuity 'for his Civility therein'.

Attempts were made to pay off some of the debts: one of those to whom they owed £200 refused to accept half that amount as an instalment and demanded the whole sum. The Master-elect was sent to the Salters' Company to try to collect some £168 long over-due to the Cutlers from the Irish estates.

The Hall was now rented to the Pinmakers as well as to the Clock-makers and there was a continual coming and going of assorted Liverymen, dancing pupils, congregationalists and so on, that could prove confusing. The long-established custom of conferring free-doms and binding apprentices on Lord Mayor's Day meant that the Hall was thronged and a great number of people came to the dinner who had no business or pretentions to be there: the custom was brought to an end and it was further ordered that no children or servants might be brought to the dinner.

No doubt the lack of security was responsible for pewter being stolen from the Hall: in future the Renter was to be accountable for all pewter, linen, knives and forks.

In addition to the members of the Court who were infirm – the Master now had gout – one of the assistants, Mr. James Abraham, was a prisoner in Ludgate 'and in a poor and low condition and in no likelihood of being further serviceable to the Company in that capacity'. His £5 Court fine was returned to him and a new assistant chosen in his place. For those still able to attend the meeting an Abstract of Titles and Leases, newly made in 1712, was read on Oath Day so that members might know something of the Company's business. The Minutes exude a general air of genteel decay and loss of purpose.

Many members of the Company were now refusing to pay the small sums of quarterage-money, pleading, very often groundlessly, poverty: in future all such claims were to be investigated by the Master and wardens and be subject to appropriate action.

The Master and the Renter both failed to put in their accounts and the Court deliberated how much they should be fined: eventually they decided upon 40s. which was the highest figure to be suggested.

Once again the Court were seized with uncertainties about their powers. The opinion of Sergeant Pengelly was sought on the subject of searching for faulty wares. The opinion of both the Attorney and Solicitor General and of Mr. Dod were canvassed in relation to the payment of fines for the alienation of leases. In both cases the answers were read to the Court; in neither case was any record made of what those answers were.

At this uninspiring moment in their affairs Queen Anne died and King George I was received in the usual way by the Livery who manned the stands after breakfasting on mutton at the Hall.

Despite the apparent slackness of the times the Clerk announced in January 1715 that he was becoming too busy to devote himself further to the Company's business. He asked that the attendance of Mr. Alexius Clayton should be held to fulfil his duty to the Cutlers. It is to be presumed that the desks for his clerks and the cabinets for his files recently set up in the lobby of the Hall must have been in connection with his own private practice. The Court agreed to this delegation of duty on condition that he held himself responsible for his deputy's actions.

Another great assault was mounted against the Company's debts. A member paid £1050 for an annuity of £100 and all but £50 was allocated to paying-off Mr. Folkingham. Mr. How, a past-Master, offered to take out an annuity for which he would pay £550 and offered also to lend the Company £200 at five per cent to take over Mr. Folkingham's security as security for his own annuity – a somewhat involved transaction to which the Court agreed.

An attempt was made to secure a reduction in the Land Tax and an increase in the amount of quarterage collected. There was to be a special effort to seek out those in arrears. Further lettings of the Hall were sought: the Paviours' Company were accepted as tenants at £4 a year.

Apart from their debts the Company were financially, at this period, just holding their ground. There was a balance of £42 on the Master's account; which did not leave much for emergencies; the Renter was shewing a miserable surplus of only £4 on the properties.

The transactions of the Court were becoming fewer and – either because the Hall was already occupied by tenants or because there was some economic advantage to be gained – their meetings were increasingly held at taverns.

This led to a decline in the standards of behaviour of the Beadles. There was a complaint that they were observed frequently to behave in a very indecent and rude manner and, on one occasion, not only was there an error in the Beadles' account – the same item was 'by mistake' entered twice – but the books got left behind in a tavern.

The Freemen complained too that the Beadles were extorting money from them by demanding 1s. for delivering printed copies of the Oath, although no such fee was authorized. For all these misdeeds warnings were issued.

As far as trade was concerned there were still apprentices to be bound: in June 1718 there were thirty-eight such enrolments.

But the control of the trade was rapidly waning.

In 1719 three members complained that 'several persons (not freemen of this Company) have set-up shops and follow the trade of Sword Cutlers in the City to the prejudice of the members of this Company'.

The Court, when asked for assistance in bringing a prosecution, gave orders that 'the Powers given for that purpose by the Charter and Bye-Laws be looked into against the next Court' and nothing more was heard of the matter.

Here, indeed, was a falling-away from greatness. Their rights and duties should, by now, have been well enough known: it was not thus that they would formerly have acted.

In January 1721 a mark was enrolled. But it was a solitary example. The problems of property management were now almost all their business. Any interest in governing the industry was almost extinct.

So the first quarter of the eighteenth century drifted uneventfully by in the 'squalid and pestiferous' City,[197] a City which, we may remind ourselves, was hardly less noisome than the one in which, 300 years earlier, the Cutlers had begun their history. London was a place of drunkenness and crime and violence and hard-living, a place of great contrasts between luxury and elegance and poverty and ugliness.

Between the very rich and the desperately poor stood the middle classes: the ordinary merchants and prosperous shopkeepers, many of them dissenters, who comprised the greater part of the 125 members of the Cutlers' Livery. The craftsmen and artisans of the Company – the journeymen and apprentices – were the bridge between the middle classes and the poor. It was the instability of their political opinions which varying, with boom or slump, with good harvest or bad, provided a perpetual source of disquiet to Government.[198]

Against this background the Court took stock of its Company. Their financial state as they were about to enter another 'dark age' (for which their records are either missing or so largely destroyed as to be valueless) was still extremely precarious. In 1725 they considered their debts to tradesmen and others – and to meet these they borrowed £300 from Mr. Shepherd. They also owed another lump sum of £500 – making, in all, £800 on which they were paying four per cent interest. In 1728 they were forced to borrow a further £400 to pay off their immediate small debts – £187 of this was raised on the Clerk's and £106 on the Master's expense accounts. On the income side of their ledgers the accounts were confusing. In 1726 it was reported after a View Day at Houndsditch that the estate there brought in £341 a year in rents but that there were vast numbers of repairs to be done. Yet in 1727 their entire rent roll shewed an income of only £211. 10s. out of which £183. 15s. 11d. was payable, leaving a rather insufficient sum for emergencies.

The state of the Company may therefore appear to have been unenviable: the City in which they lived was, by twentieth-century standards, a slum; their finances bordered upon insolvency; finally, serious constitutional trouble was stirring in the depths of the Livery. It came to a head on the day of the elections in 1728.

After the usual deliberations the Court had descended to the Hall and the Master, Richard Chapman, had announced that Thomas Cox had been duly elected Master for the year ensuing. This was, in fact, a break with tradition because, as we have seen, it was the practice for a nominal choice to be put to the Livery for their decision. And it arose from the fact that one of the two candidates had withdrawn leaving Mr. Cox alone on the field.

Immediately and disconcertingly the Livery rejected the announcement: they declared that another choice should have been made after the withdrawal of the second candidate and they demanded that a genuine choice be presented to them for their selection. The demand was refused with the result that the Livery formed what the Court referred to as a 'confederation' and clamoured for a poll to take place the following Thursday. For good measure they also demanded a poll for Upper Warden but that matter was eventually solved more amicably.

Pending the poll, the dissidents demanded a copy of the Charter and bye-laws 'in order to advise with Counsel about the last Election': the Court refused it. The representatives of the rebels then said that they would take legal action to compel a view of the papers: to this impious request the Court's somewhat sinister reaction was to order the Beadle to compile a list of all those taking part in the 'confederation'.

Meanwhile there was a state of uncertainty: under the circumstances Mr. Cox, the new Master, was unwilling to pay his fine for an office that might be overthrown and he was equally reluctant to do anything that might involve him in any expenses that might arise from a disputed election. However, the Court agreed to indemnify him against any financial loss and he duly took his place.

In July, some of the representatives of the dissatisfied Livery went so far as to swear an affidavit in the King's Bench in preparation for bringing a case against the ex-Master; others refused, as a gesture of protest, to pay their quarterage. There was a momentary lull during the Law vacations but it brought little general respite to the Court for Mr. Geary, the dancing-master currently holding his classes at the Hall, complained to them that Mr. Ragdale, their

Renter, 'had not only insulted him at his own door but arrested him for arrears of rent due to this Company.'

Mr. Ragdale replied that Mr. Geary 'had long trifled with him': he had many times gone to see Mr. Geary at the latter's request and in so doing had spent more on the Company's business than he had received in rent. He hoped that the Court would support him. The dancing-master was told 'to pay his rent better for the future'.

In October the Livery launched their action against Mr. Chapman, and the Court ordered the Clerk to defend it. They announced that, in view of the expenses involved, there could be no dinners for the Livery for three years.

The same month, the Company were all assembled at the Hall on Lord Mayor's Day, and, in their usual way, the assistants came down from the Court room to announce that the accounts had been audited and seemed to be in order: there was a debit of £8. 0s. 8d. on the Master's and a debit of £42. 11s. 7d. on the Renter's account. To this the embattled Livery replied that they wished to see a copy of Mr. Chapman's figures. The startled Court retired upstairs and debated the matter. They agreed that they would not let the Livery inspect the accounts. 'Whereupon several of them, with Mr. Woodcraft their Attorney, came into the Court Room and made a demand thereof. . . .'

The Master replied that the Court had already voted otherwise, and, therefore, there was nothing that he could do to comply with their request. In November the Court decided to take the advice of two or three Counsel about how the dispute with the Livery might be brought to an end: the Clerk had produced a case which was considered, paragraph by paragraph, and approved.

It was at this point that trouble arose with Mr. Chapman. He, when the case had first been threatened, had without any authority from the Court engaged Mr. East as an Attorney and now he and Mr. Hyde – the Warden joined with him in the case – demanded that East be directed to handle the case, a request that led the Clerk to deliver the ultimatum that if that were done he himself would have nothing more to do with the affair.

At once the Court was divided. The Master insisted that before any such decision could be made he must take counsel's opinion:

Mr. East was a stranger employed without the knowledge of the Court on a case that was likely to be very harmful to the Company. 'And thereupon the Master left the chair and the Court was adjourned until further notice.'

Christmas passed in an atmosphere of complete division in the Court and in the Company. In the new year there came an order from the King's Bench to produce the Charters, bye-laws, Orders in Court, Orders in the Minute Books together with Mr. Chapman's account and – presumably for purposes of comparison – the Master's account for the year 1714. The Court were clearly shaken by such an order: they appointed a committee of three to meet the Livery to see if some accommodation could be reached. Though they were not to make any treaty with the Livery without the consent of the whole Court the Committee were to tell them of 'the Disposition the Court is to preserve the tranquillity of this Company', and see whether they might not be able to agree together.

On 6 February the Committee brought in the Livery proposals to the Court Meeting. They found to their dismay that there was no quorum present to whom the suggestions could be put. The Master dispatched the Beadle to Mr. Bully, Mr. Tipping, Mr. Warden Hyde, Mr. Chapman, Mr. Alcroft and Mr. While to demand their immediate attendance.

In due course the Beadle returned with the information that 'Mr. Chapman went out of Town this morning, Mr. Hyde was busy and could not come, the like from Mr. Tipping, the like from Mr. While, Mr. Bully was not at home and that Mr. Alcroft was sick in bed.'

They all adjourned to the Feathers tavern and sent letters to Mr. Sheriff, Mr. Russell, and Mr. Spitzer, demanding their immediate attendance. It transpired that 'Mr. Sheriff had company and would attend the Master another time, Mr. Russell went to Chelsea this morning and Mr. Spitzer said he intended to have attended the Court but his horse had broke his Mill which prevented his attendance.'

Those of the Court who were present considered that all those who had made these excuses were perfectly well aware that the

x

meeting was being expressly held in an attempt to come to an agreement with the Livery and that, without their presence no arrangement could be made: the result was that the Company would be involved in further legal costs to say nothing of utterly wasting the time of the Committee who had bargained with the Livery. They were 'of the opinion that the said Members . . . have been guilty of a very great affront and indignity on the Master and members now present who desire the Master may acquaint the next Court thereof'.

At the next Court, however, no mention was made of the affair. Mr. Warden Hyde's motion that Mr. East, the attorney, be allowed to peruse the Charter and bye-laws was agreed without comment. In May a special meeting of the Court was held to receive the subpoena from the King's Bench which ordered them to produce their papers, and at last Captain Thompson and Captain How were able to submit their report about their dealings with the Livery.

In order to put an end to the suit against Mr. Chapman the Members were insisting on a number of points. First of all Mr. Chapman must be removed from the Court: then, if the Livery were summoned, they would confirm Mr. Cox as Master and the respective wardens in their offices. Next they considered the method of election: the practice of nominating a past-Master and one other of the Court as candidates meant that there was in fact no effective choice for the Livery. They demanded, therefore, that the three members next in succession should be nominated for election and that after one of them had been chosen the other two should be joined by a fourth nominee for the choosing of the Upper Warden. The same procedure should be adopted for the choosing of the Under Warden.

As for promotions to the Court the three senior Liverymen who had served as (or fined for) Renter should be put forward for selection.

The Livery demanded that all their 'just expenses' – about £12 – which had arisen over the case, should be paid together with their costs: the instant reaction of the Court was that this was 'unreasonable and not fit to be complied with'.

They did not record their opinions on the other demands.

Trinity Eve that year was on 31 May and when the Court entered the Hall they submitted to the Livery, as usual, two names for the election of Master – Mr. past-Master Hyde and Mr. Bully.

The resulting outcry should have been entirely predictable. The Livery demanded that the Charter and the bye-laws be read out to them. They insisted that under the Charter they had the right to choose whom they wanted from the commonalty and that no bye-law could alter so essential a part of the Charter – ever since the new ordinances had been made their choice had been restricted: a great injustice was being done to them. They asked that the Senior Master be put in nomination with the two senior assistants below the chair. If the Court refused their demands they would choose their own Master from the commonalty according to the Charter.

The Master, Mr. Cox, rather unexpectedly declared that he found the proposal perfectly acceptable and the Court retired to vote on the matter. In the Court room those who had found so many excuses for failing to provide a quorum rallied and were able to form a very narrow majority against the Livery. They all returned to the Hall to explain what had happened.

'Many debates arising' and the Livery insisting on having their own election the Master again declared that he was personally in favour of the Livery but that since he had been outvoted by the Court there was nothing he could do about it except to propose a seven-day adjournment. Everyone gratefully accepted this breathing space.

In the interval the Clerk prepared a State of the case between the Livery and the Court. Three counsel were consulted: Sergeant Sir John Cheshire, Common Sergeant Mr. Lingard and Mr. Reeve. Acting with – for lawyers – unusual promptness, all their answers were received within the week and their opinions expressed.

Q. *Had the Livery the right to proceed to their choice according to the Charter or were they bound by the Bye-Laws?*

A. Sir John Cheshire: If the Bye-laws were accepted by the Company duly summoned together then the right to choose for themselves had been delegated into the hands of two or three sufficient persons.

	And, to avoid confusion, the Bye-laws have always been regarded as valid.
Sgt. Lingard:	A Corporation by Charter can, by its Bye-laws, abridge the number of electors and the number of those from whom the choice may be made.
Mr. Reeve:	It is doubtful whether a Bye-law can be made repugnant to the Charter.

Q. *If they are bound by the Bye-laws ought the Court to submit two or three names below the Chair?*

| A. Sir John Cheshire: and Mr. Lingard agreed: | They ought to give a Choice. |
| Mr. Reeve: | If the Law is good they are not bound to give a Choice but it would be Convenient to do so. |

Q. *Has the Master the power to nominate someone put up by the Livery? How can he quit the Livery without upsetting the rights of the Court?*

A. Sir John Cheshire:	The Master ought not to. But he ought to put up two or three below the chair.
Mr. Lingard agreed:	The Court would be much at fault if they did not give the Livery an effective choice.
Mr. Reeve:	The Court ought to consider the wishes of the Livery.

The advice of three eminent lawyers had been taken and their opinions had been unusually straightforward and in agreement. It made no difference to the objectors on the Court: against eight liberal voices there were ten votes for not giving way to the Livery. At the postponed elections only the same two names were submitted to the Livery: the explanation given was that the names put forward on Trinity Eve could not now be altered. The Livery asked that the minutes of the Trinity Eve meeting be read; they asked that counsels' opinions be read. When both these demands had been satisfied they asked, not unreasonably, why the Court would not do as counsel had suggested?

The Master replied apologetically that the Court had voted that way and there was nothing that he could do about it. The long delayed vote was taken. Mr. Bully was elected, on a show of hands.

The Livery demanded a poll. Mr. Bully was again elected. Many of the members 'conceived themselves very much injured by the Court and their Partial and Arbitrary proceedings'. The spending of Company money on such unsatisfactory legal occasions they regarded as a 'fraud to which they would no longer submit'. They demanded to see the accounts of Mr. Chapman, the Master against whom the original suit had been brought. They were refused. In July the Court considered a motion to pay Mr. Chapman's costs in his case against the Livery – he had, after all, originally been indemnified. Against this point of view were the facts that he had spent a lot of money on his defence without the Court's authority with a Lawyer of his own choosing and had then, when the case was ready for trial before the Lord Chief Justice, given in. Moreover the Lord Chief Justice had warned them that they ought to take care about any orders they might make about costs.

The case dragged on, splitting the Court and poisoning relations amongst them, and estranging the Livery. The latter, the bit between their teeth, were, by February 1729, making definitive demands for restoring peace and quiet to the Company: their conditions for the selection of candidates must be met and, further, the Accounts must be audited by three of the Livery. No amount of argument would persuade them and the committee appointed to deal with them thought it necessary to accede to their demands. After all, the committee reported, putting as good a face upon their defeat as they could muster, the Charter entitled the Livery to choose one of their own number as Master so the 'concession', to offer them a choice of two or three of the Court, fell far short of that. Then, too, the choosing of a Senior Liveryman to be brought on to the Court had only recently ceased to be the rule and the new habit of passing over the Seniors and electing one of the Juniors had not only caused great offence but was making the Livery more stubborn in their attitudes. Their demand to audit the accounts arose from a natural anxiety at the great expenses the Company had been put to: the committee felt that since it was unlikely that there would be anything in the accounts that would not bear scrutiny such a concession would not be prejudicial.

The Court considered this argument. In May they informed the

Livery that they would concede all their demands except the one concerning the auditing of the accounts. 'And the Livery accordingly agreed to waive the same.' The principal action by the Livery was over. It had ended in what was virtually a complete victory for the liberals. There were still arguments to come about the payment of costs but at this point the yearly succession of Minute Books comes to a temporary end, plunging the story of the Cutlers into a second 'Dark Age' from which only occasional flashes of illumination are to be found. But, if the history of some other companies is considered, it seems not improbable that there was, in fact, little of interest to record.

16

A Century of Progress

1729–1838

THE Cutlers were now in a greatly reduced condition. In 1737 they were one of five Companies who pleaded poverty as an excuse for not attending Lord Mayor's Day. They were warned against any repetition of the offence and when, the next year, they were again accused of non-attendance they protested – as did also the Pewterers – that they were, in fact, 'Out but had no Stand'. They were unsympathetically ordered to provide themselves with a stand before the next occasion. But still by 1743 the Cutlers, and other Companies too, were again reported to the Clerk of the City's Works for 'neglect of the Solemnity on the last Lord Mayor's Day'.

In the meantime they were involved in extensive building works: the carpentry alone cost £455 in Belle Sauvage Yard, £350 was spent on the house there and £450 on two houses in Houndsditch.

There was some welcome addition to their income from the Irish Lands where the salmon fishery of the Irish Society had been let to the highest bidder at £16. 5s. per ton. There were, as always, problems arising from Ireland: in 1735 there was a 'Scheme to Reform the Irish' and contributions were sought, in what was almost a Swiftian turn of phrase, for the building of English Protestant schools

as the only effectual means to convert the children of Popish Parents from the Errors of the Church of Rome by instilling into their Infant Minds the principals of our Holy Religion, likewise curing them of their Native Sloth and Idleness by inuring them early to work and labour especially in Husbandry, Gardening, improving and spreading the Linen Manufacture over the Kingdom.

The Company were in no state to contribute largely to such an admirable project. Their numbers were diminishing as well as their fortunes: the Livery, 123 strong in 1722, had sunk to 92 in 1730 and was to fall still further to 62 by 1740 at which low ebb it long remained. Their control over the trade was rapidly draining away and sometimes the will to maintain even the vestiges seemed to be lacking.

In 1745, for example, the Clerk felt compelled to write to Mr. Collett, the Master, saying that Mr. Hatton, a Liveryman, had been attempting to have a boy apprenticed to him. The Clerk had told him that he must get the Master's consent and that, in all his years with the Company, the Clerk had never known that consent to be refused. When it was not convenient to hold a Court or Committee for a binding then the Master always acted on his own. Now the Liveryman had reported back to the Clerk that the Master had refused his consent.

'I would make one observation to you,' the Clerk told the Master sternly, 'that were we not to bind but at a Court or Committee, unless we were very regular in having them for that purpose, it would be a great inducement for the Freemen of the Company to get 'em bound to other persons and turn 'em over to themselves which Mr. Hatton has declared to me he will do if this boy is not immediately bound.'

In 1747 the state of the trade was the subject of scrutiny. It was written of cutlers that

their Business is making, forging, tempering, (in which Part some have been remarkably famous) and mounting all Sorts of Knives, Razors, Scissars, Surgeon's Instruments, and Sword Blades; but making the Hilts is a different Trade'.[199]

The work in this 'ingenious branch of the Smithery' was described as

'not hard-work; many cutlers also keep handsome shops and deal in divers other Things, as Buckles, Buttons, Canes, etc, though not very numerous. They take with an Apprentice £10 or £15, who must work from six to nine; of Journeymen there are but few and about £50 will make a Master of him; . . .'

The Company, this year, appealed to the Common Council about the great number of unqualified persons who were carrying on the trade of cutler in the City. For many years cutlers who were not Freemen of the Company had been inducing cutlers free of other Companies to bind apprentices and turn them over to them – thus avoiding the burdens and obligations of the Cutlers' Company which thereby lost its Quarterage and other dues and was unable to defray the cost of upholding the civic dignity by attending on public occasions. There were many Freemen who realized that, because of the controls of the Company, they were working at a disadvantage with cutlers who were not so restricted and therefore bound their sons and servants to that sort of tradesman. The Court of Common Council made a number of half-hearted attempts to deal with the problem, and, at the request of those members who were observing the rules, the Cutlers' Company themselves made new bye-laws to prevent such defections. But the situation had got so far out of their control that it was not easily righted.

The members of the Court of the Cutlers at this time were provided with an incentive scheme to ensure their punctual attendance at meetings. Other Companies had rules whereby only the first to arrive – the numbers varied – were paid an atten-dance allowance: the Cutlers went one better and laid down a graduated scale for those 'who first attended to do Business'. Nine of them received 3s. a head; the next two were paid 2s. 6d. each and the two after them 2s. The remainder, if any, received nothing and some unseemly scuffling in the doorway of the Court Room may well have been the result.

In their relations with the Livery the Court continued to shew an element of democracy that distinguished them from some of the major Companies: they still acquainted the Livery annually with the state of the Master's and the Renter's accounts. But, nonethe-less, the control of the trade and the state of the Company were all the time declining. By 1755 a new low level had been reached. The Livery now numbered only thirty-three, many of whom lived remote from the City or who were in poverty: the result was that there were great difficulties in filling the vacancies on the Court. The finances of the Company were in such a state that the pensions of £2 allowed to twenty paupers had long been discontinued and were revived only (but properly) by sacrificing the dinners. The sum of £300 borrowed ninety years earlier after the Great Fire had only just been repaid.

The City authorities had still failed to achieve any solution of the problem of cutlers who were not members of the Company because they preferred to work unhampered by the Cutlers' regulations, and so on 12 June the same year the Court petitioned that no working cutler be allowed to take up his freedom of the City unless he first became free of the Cutlers' Company.

Eighteen months later, on 15 December 1756, there was made an Act of Common Council for Regulating the Company of Cutlers of London: it decreed exactly what the Company had asked for and it remained in force until 1838 when it was declared obsolete.

But it seems clear that there was on the whole an uneventfulness in the Company during the first two-thirds of the century that reflected the outside world.

In 1745 the Young Pretender's invasion had caused a stir in the City. The Londoners had pledged their loyalty to George II and, as the Scots, victorious at Prestonpans and Falkirk, had marched southwards under Prince Charles-Edward, the City gates were guarded and the trained bands called up. A collection was made 'towards the relief of the Soldiers employed on His Majesty's service for suppressing the present Unnatural Rebellion'. But after the Pretender's retreat from Derby and his utter defeat at Culloden there was little enough intrusion from the outside world.

Gradually, with great slowness, the Company during these days of tranquillity began to recuperate. By 1763 they were in a financial position to make elaborate preparations for attending the show of their own Lord Mayor, William Bridgen, 'with all Decorations and Ornaments suitable'. A Barge was to be procured upon the best terms – it was, in fact, an old one belonging to the Ironmongers which the Cutlers agreed to have repaired at their own expense – and, in addition to cakes to be eaten in the Barge, there was wine too, to be drunk on the river to the amount of £7. 5s. 6d. and the music included a pair of kettle-drums and two trumpets. The proceedings on land were controlled by a Marshal and an Under Marshal and there were, too, a Captain and twelve swordbearers 'in a decent uniform'. The Company's armoury contained no

more than six broadswords – the rest had to be hired. And to crown
the splendours of the day – splendours all the more welcome for
the length of time they had been foregone – the Court 'obtained a
Grant for the Elephant lately presented to Her Majesty to precede
their Company in the procession. . . .'[200]

It is to be hoped that the 'stress of weather', subsequently mentioned in the Minutes, did not utterly spoil their recaptured
pleasures.

That their financial recovery was considerable can be seen immediately the records are resumed in detail in 1767. Although the
Renter's income and expenditure exactly balanced, the Master's
account shewed a credit of £404 of which the Company were able
to invest £400 in four per cent bank annuities. There was, in fact,
some difficulty in getting Mr. Thirkell to hand over the money: it
was demanded on a number of occasions and was only eventually
secured by the threat of legal action.

That the new prosperity was no mere flash in the pan was shewn
by the fact that the following year they were able to invest another
£200 in the annuities. It gradually becomes apparent that they had,
in fact, by now built up considerable reserves: the extent and the
expense of repairs to the Hall which began in 1769 were evidence of
that. The estimated cost was £640 and £200 were paid on account to
both the Carpenter and the Bricklayer and £400 of annuities sold.
As usual the expenses, once begun, were found to be greatly
underestimated and in 1770 no less than £1200 of stock was sold.

There was only one slightly disconcerting aspect of their affairs –
the strange behaviour of senior members of the company. Mr.
Thirkell, who had so long delayed paying his account, still owed the
Cutlers £12 (eventually it was altogether waived) and now he was
dismissed from his place on the Court for non-attendance 'and
other sufficient reasons'. Joseph Hatton, elected Master in June for
a second year running, had, by October, failed to attend any meetings of the Court: those who had stood surety for him were
summoned and told that the balance of his account for his first
year of office must be brought in before Lord Mayor's Day. All
Tenants were warned to pay no more rents to him but, instead, to
bring the money to the Hall where the Clerk was deputed to receive

the money for the rest of the year 'or until the Master shall appear'. In fact, it was not until April 1771 that Mr. Hatton paid over the full £371 balance of his account. In October that year the Audit Day dinner was held at the Hall 'with a Supper and Musick and other Requisites for a Ball for the Entertainment of the Ladies in a Decent and Suitable manner for the Occasion'. It set the seal upon the completion of the repairs to the Hall of which the final act was to have the street light removed to the Clerk's door from the Hall Gate where it was replaced by two handsome Bracket Lamps – which in future were to be lighted all the year round by Mr. Majorum at the usual rates. For all his extraordinary efforts during the repairs to the Hall the Beadle was given a gratuity of £15.

Once again, after this brief display of activity, the Cutlers settled down to a period of apparent inaction.

It was a period during which they built up the resources depleted by the repairs to the Hall. In 1774 they still had £500 invested in bank annuities and in 1775 they were able to double this sum. The greatest part of their income derived from their properties which on Survey Day were viewed by a party which included several of the Junior Livery, an admirable innovation for involving younger members in the affairs of the Company.

These properties were quite widely spread: in Cloak Lane and College Hill, in Watling Street, in Fleet Street and Fleet Lane, in Ludgate Hill and Aldersgate Street and Houndsditch. The regained prosperity meant that the Company could be more generous to their charities. The hard winters of 1771 and 1776 led to bonuses for their pensioners, and rises in the cost of living – particularly in the price of children's clothing – spurred them into giving £5 instead of their normal £2 to the Charity School in Vintry Ward.

They were able to indulge themselves a little with the gift of silver medals bearing the Company's arms to all the members of the Livery, new mahogany tables and a Turkey carpet for the Court Room and chairs for the Hall.

But in 1781 they faced troubles that arose from the system of collecting the rents that provided so much of their income.

After the Renter Warden's accounts had been audited and his security-bond returned to him it was decided to have a second look at Mr. John Copous' figures. To the general embarrassment it was only then discovered that the Beadle had received, in the Renter Warden's name, £62 which had not been accounted for. Mr. Copous explained that he had employed Playsted the Beadle to collect the rents for him: it subsequently transpired that Playsted had, in some instances, persuaded tenants to pay eighteen months' rent and had then handed over only the year's rent that Mr. Copous was expecting. It was all a mistake, the Beadle pleaded; that he was at fault he admitted but he denied, not very convincingly, any ill-intent. He had, since the discovery of the mistake, paid over all he owed.

The Court, with an admirably charitable restraint, did no more than suspend him from duty and, after only six months, he was reinstated.

All this was domestic small beer. In the forty recordless years all connection with the trade seems finally to have been lost. Apprentices, it is true, were still being bound but whether they were genuinely working apprentices in cutlery is perhaps doubtful. When, in 1783, there was a national outcry against the indifferent quality of British blades and leave was sought to import both sword-blades and swords from Germany the Company was not in any way involved. And when, three years later, a trial of quality took place it was a Birmingham cutler named Thomas Gill who was the chief contestant against the Germans: he won by a narrow margin but the other English manufacturers shewed by comparison a great lack of skill and the shameful fact was established that the doubt about the quality of British blades was justified.[201] But the Cutlers' Company had no part and, apparently, no interest in the affair.

They were more concerned with the fact that 'great numbers of Strangers are frequently introduced to dine with this Court to the great inconvenience of the Members'. Rules were drawn up for the invitation of guests and the Chaplain was altogether struck off the invitation list for his non-attendance at their affairs. The Court could when aroused be hard: they utterly rejected the pathetic letter from Samuel Toten who professed himself 'only to lament that Fortune has not favoured me with one single Sympathy or friendly feeling for any part of my Sufferings now 13 years since; or I should have hoped within that Period someone would have stood forth in my behalf, to have moved for my being restored to my former Honour at your Board. . . .'

What he had done, what he had suffered – imprisonment or bankruptcy, perhaps – were nowhere mentioned. His appeal to come back upon the Court was rejected.

By 1785 the credit balance of the two accounts was £115 and the Company had, in reserve, the very useful sum of £2800 in three-per-cents. The Court treated themselves to an annual outing, on Oath Day, usually to Richmond, but sometimes to Blackheath, Turnham Green, or Tottenham, 'and each Gentleman be permitted to bring his Lady'.

Those who attended were allowed one guinea for the coach fare.

Now that they no longer assumed responsibilities of trade-control life was much more simple. It was perhaps the constitutional dispute in the Cutlers' Company of Hallamshire – similar to their own great dispute with the Livery sixty years previously – that caused them to consult the bye-laws to see whether it was permissible for anyone to be elected to the Court without having first served (or been fined for) the office of Renter. The precedents were clearly against any such by-passing the normal channels of promotion and it was reiterated that those who had actually served the office, those with appropriately greater experience in the Company's business, should be preferred to those who had been fined. And the three senior Liverymen were put in nomination each year for Renter Warden.

The Court found it necessary, too, to consult Counsel about an offer they had received from the East India Company to buy part of a house in Cutler Street in order to pull it down to make a wider entrance to their warehouse there. Were they allowed, they wondered, to sell any of their Estates? Counsel considered that they were not: the properties were vested in the Corporation for life and since that life was capable of continuing for all eternity they could sell no part of their Estates. Accordingly they began to bargain for the sale of a ninety-nine-year lease at a rent of one shilling a year.

The outside world, where some rather ugly activities were taking place, hardly intruded into this domestic scene. There had been the war with the American colonies and there had been the French Revolution the aftermath of which had led to great fears of a popular uprising in Britain, fears which inspired the Government to acts of political oppression almost as tyrannical – with the suspension in 1794 of Habeas Corpus – as anything in the Cutlers' long history. Now there was war with France. Yet of all such events the only reflection in the still waters of the Company Minutes was, in 1798, a £200 'voluntary contribution to the Subscription, now open at the Bank, for the defence of the Country'.

Of much more note to the Court was the rebuilding that went on in 1796 when an extension was added to the Clerk's house and, on the other side of the Hall, two old houses were pulled down and one substantial building erected in their place. Because of the noise and dirt from the operation the Court had to dine at a tavern and the new Beadle was given £4 because the Company did not dine at the Hall – a clear indication of the substantial fees and perquisites which were his upon the greater occasions of the Cutlers. In spite of all these improvements – £1000 was taken out of the reserves – the Clerk managed to get the land tax assessment on the Company properties reduced by nearly two-thirds, from £175 to £60.

And, as the internally uneventful century faded unremarkably away the Company, untroubled by anything other than the management of their Estates and by the administration of their Trusts, were all the time consolidating a financial state that, now that they were freed from their crippling debts, was beginning to shew signs of considerable strength.

They had, in 1798, it is true, after all the rebuilding and repairs had taken place in Cloak Lane refused the suggestion by Mr. Gotobed, the Duke of Bedford's agent, that they should buy the annual 11s. quit-rent of two houses in Watling Street for £16. 10s. on the grounds that the sum was too much 'from the present great scarcity of money'. But this may well have been a polite excuse: the three per cent interest involved was to be had with less trouble by investing in the funds – into which in 1800 they were able to put another £1000.

They were beginning to achieve the sort of solid property-based prosperity that was to make them comparatively invulnerable to the trade cycles of expansion and recession which had so often endangered them in the days of their trade interests.

In 1801 the administration of the Trusts, normally an uneventful branch of their activities, was enlivened by a dispute over the Craythorne Exhibition at St. John's College, Oxford – an Exhibition for anyone bearing the name of Craythorne or, such a candidate being unavailable, one who was a freeman of the Cutlers' Company. Since neither condition had been fulfilled, the Company for ten years had, in spite of protests from the College, failed to pay the Exhibition. Now Dr. Free, on behalf of St. John's, again demanded the money. The Court replied that they had no objection to paying the sum involved if Dr. Free could shew that, according to the intentions of the donor, he was entitled to it.

To this letter the Doctor's attorney Mr. Trickey replied: the College was entitled to receive the money because it had already been paid for fourteen or fifteen years. He himself had been to Doctors' Commons to inspect the original will and since the sum involved was less than £10 was it really 'worthy of your Company's consequence to dispute it under all the circumstances? Your decisive answer will oblige.' The Court, no doubt outraged by this display of non-legal argument, decided as a matter of principle that no answer was necessary. And, indeed, it was not until a year later, when Mr. Trickey wrote again in somewhat the same vein, that they decided that the matter was so trivial – about £5 was involved – that they would pay the money to avoid further pestering by Dr. Free.

They now had £2000 in the funds but they were no longer in the habit of presenting the accounts to the Livery. This sop to Cerberus had been quietly discontinued in 1794, had been re-established during the two following years, and then finally abandoned. That it was not greatly missed by the Livery is suggested by the lack of any protest in an age when protest was becoming increasingly vocal, when Reform was in the air and when young men, in sympathy with the French Revolution, wore their hair short.

The war with France does not seem to have impinged upon the Cutlers in the same way that it affected other Companies. For them there were none of the frustrations put in the way of those Companies, who, when they tried to recruit men for the forces, found themselves obstructed by a City Council which was apparently more concerned with preserving its exclusive privileges than with furthering the war effort. But there were subscriptions throughout London and the country for various patriotic and philanthropic purposes and to these it may be supposed that the Company contributed, but there remain so few Minutes of any moment that it seems as if much of the everyday business was conducted by an autonomous Committee not much given to reporting to the Court. Pipes of port were bought and hogsheads of sherry and there was the practical gift of twelve dozen doylies printed with the Company Arms. The number of the Livery was, in 1808, limited to one hundred and although there were no longer the same opportunities for increasing their revenues by enrolling new members the Company were, nonetheless, able to put away another £600 into three per cent Consols.

In 1810 they decided to make another review of their Irish estates on which, over the last fifty years, their average annual dividend had been nearly £47. They applied to the Salters' Company to inspect the plans of the joint properties and were amazed to receive a rather tartly worded and high-handed reply: it was most unusual for the Salters ever to grant permission to inspect plans of their properties; why did the Cutlers make such a request? To this the Court answered that 'they cannot comprehend the nature of the Salters' Company assuming to call an estate theirs which this Company as well as others are joint proprietors with themselves'. They would, further, 'deem it derogatory to assign their motives in requesting the copy of a Plan for the necessary expense of taking which they have paid their proportion'. They therefore renewed their request – a request so reasonable that, as they said, they could hope for no further impediment – and they further resolved, without any break in the Minutes, 'that any member pocketing the fruit or any part of the dessert be fined one guinea to the poors box' – a fine example of a clerical *non sequitur*.

The Salters' subsequent reaction was perhaps typical of the head of a family who had been, rightly, corrected by a dependent relative: they expressed great indignation; they were amazed at the wording adopted by the Cutlers; in asserting a general principle of behaviour they had had absolutely no intention of claiming exclusive rights. They had considered, not being aware that the Cutlers had paid anything towards it, that the plan was their own – that was why they had demanded the reason for the requested inspection. They could not, they said, understand why the Cutlers should wish not to disclose their reasons; such an explanation would, surely, be a natural enough thing between co-proprietors. Still . . . let the Cutlers send along their surveyor and he could make a copy.

In this unnecessary dispute the Cutlers scored a clear-cut victory and no doubt the Master's handling of the matter influenced the final exordium which had become a feature of the end of each year of office. The vote of thanks to the Master, so far from being a formally standardized expression of esteem, differed subtly each year and it was possible to deduce degrees of success in ruling over the Company's affairs. In 1811 in addition to the able manner in which he had carried out his duties and the regulation of the finances it was 'his polite and friendly attention to members of the Court and his constant exertions to promote the harmony and conviviality of the Company' that attracted admiration. In other years it was 'unwearied zeal' or 'the handsome manner' in which he met the wishes of all the Court, 'his polite and gentlemanly behaviour' towards them and 'his polite attention to visitors'. At other times mention was made only, and bleakly, of his 'upright conduct' and thanks for 'uniform attention to the Interests of the Company' was about as minimal a display of appreciation as could be recorded.

It was a time when Parliament was preparing with a no less

critical eye, to appraise the activities of the Companies themselves
and one of the first manifestations was a Bill in 1812 to compel the
registration of Charitable Donations: in April the Cutlers sent a
representative to a protest meeting, at Merchant Taylors' Hall, of
the Masters and Clerks of the principal Companies. But resistance was, in this case, useless and the Act very quickly became law.

As the war with France came to an end – and with it the grant of
£25 'to be sent to Lloyds Coffee House for the relief of the Sufferers
in the late Battle of Waterloo' – the Company invested another
£500 in three per cent Consols and now had the very respectable
reserves of £4000 in the funds. The number of the Livery had been
raised to 120, although new members were warned that not more
than 100 could be invited to the feasts.

There was still a continuing amount of trouble at the dinners at
which both unofficial guests and the Court themselves were guilty
of irregularities. In 1818 it was necessary to make a rule that 'if any
Member of the Court dine in any part except the Court Table he
shall forfeit £1. 1s. to the Poors Box with the exception of those
Gentlemen deputed to preside at the lower tables'. And 'any
member of the Court introducing a stranger to dine at the Court
Table was to be similarly mulcted' with the exception of the
Master and wardens 'who shall have liberty to fill vacant chairs
with their friends, nor shall more than 24 dine at the Court Table'.

In spite of their prosperous state it was decided that the order to
pay the 'Vocals' on feast days should be rescinded: the Master was,
presumably, once again to send invitations to his 'Vocal Friends'
who would then be expected to sing for their supper. In fact, in
1819 the Master was allotted ten guineas 'to distribute at his discretion amongst the Gentlemen who entertained the Company with
their vocal powers during the last year'.

1819 also witnessed one of the last occasions in which the Cutlers'
Company interested themselves, however distantly, in the matters
concerning the trade, when they took notice of the Act to Regulate
the Cutlery Trade in England.

The Act recited the renown of British Cutlery formed and forged
of wrought steel – though it was noticeable that swords were not
among the items listed – and its importance to the export trade.

And it went on to point out that there was a practice of making cutlery from cast iron in a mould which, by a chemical process, could be made to look even to the expert eye like steel. Because of this, the Act gave to 'Hammer Manufacturers' – that is to say to those who did not resort to casting – the sole privilege of marking their goods with a hammer. From henceforth it would be illegal to mark or sell cast cutlery with the hammer mark; it would be illegal, too, to use any marks or words indicating that cutlery goods were of a higher quality than they in fact were. The same restrictions applied to using such words as 'London' or 'London Made', unless the goods had been made in the capital or within a radius of twenty miles.

It is said[202] that this was in part directed against those London cutlers who put their marks on goods from Birmingham and Sheffield and sold them at higher prices than goods from those towns normally realized. It was a practice that caused great resentment, especially in Sheffield. In the '*New Times*' in December 1823[203] a writer demanded, 'How long will the men of Hallamshire permit Cockney manufacturers, including renegades from hence, to traduce their wares and persuade the public that they are inferior to town-made articles? London would have little 'title to boast if all its obligations to Sheffield were acknowledged.'

As far as the Cutlers' Company themselves were concerned there was little they could do: their ordinances for the control of the trade had fallen into disuse and had become ineffective even though it was still usual for cutlery dealers and workers to take out their freedom in the Company and even as late as 1880 apprentices were occasionally bound and enrolled.

Since the London Cutlers' Company could not – or would not – act, the Hallamshire Cutlers were prompted to propose legislation to put an end to the abuses. But there were difficulties: the masters were far from unanimous and the London traders were hostile.[204] However, in 1825, the Sheffield trade introduced another Bill on the subject of the marking of cutlery. The Cutlers' Company opposed it vigorously and in May, when the news reached the Court that the Bill had been ordered a second reading, they passed a resolution 'that this second attempt of Sheffield to legislate for all-England in the manufacture of Cutlery is particularly hostile to London and its manufacturers'. Later they passed a further resolution 'that any future efforts of Sheffield to restrict the free trade of London be strongly opposed, the regulations being hurtful to themselves, as well as to all manufacturing cutlers, and to the commerce of the country'. The Bill was defeated. The Cutlers' Company, well satisfied with this final intervention in the management of their trade, settled comfortably back into their role of managing their properties.

They now had £6000 invested in the funds. Their Houndsditch estates alone produced a rental of some £900 a year but the buildings were in a very dilapidated condition and it was clear that, quite soon, extensive repairs would have to be undertaken. Many of their properties were encumbered with trusts and, since the Commissioners, under an Act of Parliament, were beginning to investigate charities the Cutlers decided in 1820 to see that their own house was in good order – particularly in respect of the trusts created under the wills of Thomas Buck and John Craythorne.

The result was disconcerting: 'the Court cannot but express their deep regret to find that under Buck's will the donation to the poor of Fleet Lane, to St. Thomas' Hospital and for the repairs of St. Sepulchre's Church had not been paid since 1727 owing to the funds at that time being insufficient for the purpose. And that from the length of time the estate remained insolvent it had escaped the recollection of the members of the Court. . . .'

The rents, at the time that the trust had disappeared from view, had been £6 whereas the outgoings had amounted to £27.

The Court decided to make immediate amends: they would write to everybody concerned, ask them what their arrears might be, and make full satisfaction.

Some of the beneficiaries were aware of the situation and were able to reply quite speedily: St. Thomas' Hospital said that the Company were 114 years in arrears last Christmas at 20s. per annum; the Churchwardens of St. Sepulchre's went further when they wrote that the Company owed them £2 a year for their poor and £1 a year for the Church itself over a period of 114 years, making in all £342 which 'should be paid with legal interest thereon'.

The Churchwardens of Wilberton in Cambridgeshire, on the other hand, replied that they had no knowledge of anything to do with the trust – no records, no memories, nobody living called Buck – and they would rely upon the Cutlers' records and be grateful for anything that they might receive. The Court decided that they were owed £2 a year for ninety-three years. Altogether the total arrears amounted to £642 which the Court decided should be paid, in spite of the demands from St. Sepulchre's, without interest.

But, on the whole, their accounts had been well kept. It was only now, with the increasing complexity of their financial business, that the strain of operating an accounting system unaltered from the Middle Ages was beginning to be felt.

To simplify the administration of the Company an Estate Committee was instituted but, in spite of this, the Court remained greatly concerned with property business. They were also concerned with a general reorganization of the corporate life in a world in which trade was no longer their preoccupation. The Beadle had died and had been succeeded by an assistant who resigned from the Court especially to take up his new Office. It became necessary to state what were the functions of one who had originally been the chief officer of the Company but who now had lost all but the most nominal powers over the Livery. The Court decided that the business of the Cutlers' Company must be the Beadle's first consideration but that was not to prevent him from engaging in any other occupation which did not interfere with his Company duties. He must be strictly accurate in his accounts; he must collect quarterage; and prevent waste; he must be attentive and obedient. He must attend Common Halls and see that none but members of the Livery came in; he must oversee dinners – supervising the waiters, keeping a list of their names, seeing that wine and liquors were put upon the tables and preventing 'as much as lies in his power their being taken away'. At tavern dinners he must be there in his gown and carrying his staff and must 'see that no imposition is practised by the waiters'.

There were new bye-laws for the Court to compile – between 1703 and 1830 various ordinances, some of them conflicting, had been enacted – and it became necessary to frame and compile an entirely new set of laws.

At the same time, the Court took other measures for internal administration: there had, for example, been no increases in the various fines since 1748 and it was clearly reasonable that there should be general rises in the amounts charged. And they decided that it was reasonable, too, to cease to invite to the dinners any of the Livery who were more than two years in arrears with their quarter-age money. That the behaviour at dinners were sometimes apt to be high-spirited was seen by the notice inserted in the summons sent to each Liveryman in 1826: 'The Court of Assistants of the Cutlers' Company have received an apology from the Gentleman who caused the unpleasant proceedings at the last Livery Dinner and they take the present opportunity of applauding the exemplary conduct of the Livery in general on that day'.

In 1828 the age-old system by which the dinner on Lord Mayor's Day was provided by stewards who were nominated from the Company either to pay the costs or be fined in lieu of doing so, was called into question: the Court of Common Pleas, in a case involving the Coopers' Company, decided that the rule was not a reasonable one and the ancient tradition was abolished. Another tradition that was a victim of the general spirit of Reform was Quarterage: in 1831, 'the permanent income of the Company being sufficient', it too was done away with. At the same time the poor box – the carved Elephant 'tronc' from which minor gifts of charity had for so long been disbursed – was also dispensed with.

Amidst the general symptoms of change the Royal occasions were not what they had been: when George IV died and King William and his Queen came to visit the City in 1830 there were no longer any stands for the Livery nor was attendance compulsory. A Company property in Fleet Street was used by the Court alone for viewing the processions: each member was allowed a ticket for himself and a female guest. So far from contributing to the decorations of the City the Cutlers could be persuaded to lend their banners for the occasion only if they were fully indemnified against damage.

This spirit of reform had not spread to the Salters' Company in their dealings with their associates over their joint properties in Ireland. In 1829, when the Cutlers applied for a copy of the original conveyance of lands by the Irish Society, they received a chilling reply that the document was purely in the name of the Salters without allusion to any other Company and that the request was, therefore, 'emphatically' refused.

The affair no doubt concerned the variations that Lord Londonderry was seeking to make in the terms of his lease: the Cutlers considered that they should have been consulted about the Irish Lands in 1754 and that they should again be consulted now. They even, in their indignation, took it upon themselves to write to his Lordship about the matter and thereby called down the whole weight of the Salters' anger upon their heads. They had been, the senior Company told them, informed of everything that had taken place in 1754 – their acceptance of the accounts which included legal expenses proved it – but, in fact, the sole management of their Irish lands lay, at law, with the Salters: the fact that the Cutlers had written independently to Lord Londonderry could very well injure everyone including themselves. The Salters added that they had never refused information to anyone who adopted a like liberal course – but they rejected all claims that were unfounded or uncalled for.

The state of ill-feeling between the two Companies continued for a little while longer. It was not until January 1834 that the Master reported to the Court, with a faint air of surprise, that he had been invited (in his official capacity) to dine with the Court of the Salters' Company 'and was entertained with great hospitality and kindness' – a new-found attitude that was happily to persist for the future.

In the meantime the now unwanted affairs of trade-control had once again come to the fore. In June 1832 'a letter from Mr. John Evans of Old Change explaining proceedings he had taken to prevent the imitation of his Mark by Charles Johnson of Sheffield was read. Ordered that the subject of the said letter be referred to such Members of the Court who are or who have been practical cutlers.'

The committee of assistants thus created were of the opinion that action against any piracy of London marks should be left to individuals to pursue but that, in the general interests of the trade, they should prevent country wares from being London marked and that advertisements, warning manufacturers of the state of the law, should be inserted twice in each of the Sheffield newspapers as well as once in the *Times Public Ledger* and the *British Traveller*.

That year, 1832, saw the long-awaited passage of the Reform Bill and although individual cutlers cannot have been greatly affected by such innovations as the extension to others, outside the Livery Companies, of the right to vote for the Burgesses representing London, there was, nonetheless, a critical feeling in the country that put them on the defensive, that made them feel uneasily that they were unjustly beleaguered.

It has been pointed out that much of the trouble and the calumny experienced by the City Companies during the years of reforming zeal arose from the ignorance and sometimes excusable misunderstanding that prevailed among the critics. The Charity Commissioners' reports had, generally speaking, shewn that the Companies were fulfilling their obligations correctly: there were certain charities that, due to primitive accounting systems, had suffered change but such money as was due to charity was being paid to charity. Unfortunately a great decline in the value of money had occurred since benefactors had bequeathed their trusts; lands which had secured the payment of fixed sums to charitable objects had greatly increased in rental value but the Companies continued to pay to the beneficiaries the same sums which were now comparatively worthless. The critics of the Companies alleged that the rest of the money was being spent by the Companies on vast self-indulgences and banqueting – in fact the greater part of it was being devoted to other charities and to the rising costs of administration.

The members of the Cutlers were, in fact, constantly on the alert for ways in which their charitable roles might be fulfilled and extended. It was to one of the committees that the idea that the Company should found some almshouses occurred: it was their own idea and it did not emanate from the Court; all the members of the committee offered personally to subscribe certain amounts, varying from £10 to £200 and totalling £440, should the scheme come to fruition.

In September 1833 the Court received a summons for representatives to appear before the Royal Commission which, under Sir Francis Palgrave, was investigating the whole vexed question of the City Companies. Although the enquiry was by no means so antagonistic as those later in the century the terms of reference included a number of critical points to be investigated: the Charters; the powers and duties and emoluments of the various officers and the circumstances of their election; the position of the Freemen and the costs of election to freedom or to office; the incomes, outgoings, financial objectives and accountancy; and so on.

The Cutlers prepared their answers with care. If the accounts were given in any detail the critics would have seen that the net of their charities was widely cast: among many other worthy causes £10 was given in February that year to the Sea Arctic expedition to discover Captain Ross – an expedition that was obviously successful for in December Captain Ross and his son were invited to dine at the Hall. But the critics would have no doubt felt that their strictures were justified in the accounts for feasting and junketting. For in 1834 it was once again a cutler, Alderman Henry Winchester, who was Lord Mayor and who had to be supported in a manner suitable to the dignity of his office and of the City.

That the Company could afford to do so was to be seen from the state of the Master's account which, for the first time for many years, was recorded in the Minutes. From an income of well over £4000 there was a credit balance of £720 from which the £267 costs of their contribution to the Show was readily payable. They had a barge with sixteen bargemen and two lads, a thirteen-piece band in 'regimentals', pensioners carrying shields, the Beadle in a bow and scarf that took four yards of material to make. All of them had to be provided with food and drink. There were coaches and chariots and costumes to be hired, police at the Hall and all the concomitants of a municipal show – bread, beef and beer; flags, silks, ribbons and gloves. In the land procession attending the Lord Mayor the Livery were there in their carriages, the Court in theirs. The wardens had a carriage of their own and the Master was splendid in a Chariot accompanied by his chaplain and by all the panoply of streamers and standards.

Nor did the expenses of the Lord Mayor's year of office end there for the Company. In the following summer it was learned that he was going to accompany the King to Greenwich in a procession by water. Several Companies had been invited to participate: the Court passed a resolution that the Cutlers, inexplicably omitted, might suggest to their Lord Mayor that they too be included in the number. The reply was enthusiastic. The Lord Mayor was delighted: the request was not only highly gratifying and flattering to himself but properly respectful of his Majesty. The Company had not been originally invited through 'motives of delicacy'.

In the event, only four of the six barges shewn on the plan of the procession[205] actually took part, the Cutlers, with their watermen's dresses lent by the Ironmongers, proudly in the van, their barge well-equipped with such assorted refreshments as sherry, Madeira, Bucellas, Lisbon, port and brandy.

The occasion was a success. In August the Lord Mayor 'expressed the great satisfaction which the arrangements for accompanying His Majesty and His Lordship to Greenwich had afforded to him personally, and added that he had every reason to believe, from the expression used by the King, that His Majesty had been equally gratified by the demonstration of Loyalty he had received on that occasion'.

The Lord Mayor presented them with two silver-gilt dishes and his portrait: the Court decided that his arms should be set up in one of the Court-room windows.

Yet when all these expenses had been accounted for, the Master's balance for 1835 stood at more than £1000.

In spite of this respectable financial state of their affairs 1836 saw some attempt at a modest retrenchment. The cost of the dinners, including dessert and tea, was reduced from 12s to 11s. per head – perhaps with some idea of appeasing those critical of their personal expenditure. Reforming ideas were now beginning to intrude in matters of the City government: the Municipal Enquiry Commissioners had suggested a new scheme for the election of the City Officers, a scheme that would have deprived the Liverymen of their long-established rights. The Cutlers considered the matter and decided to oppose it 'as a very improper and unnecessary disfranchisement of a highly important and independent body of Electors intimately connected with the welfare of the City of London'. They adopted a reasonable attitude: they would not, they declared, object to the admission of householders and occupiers of premises in the City partaking of their electoral privileges – under certain circumstances – but they felt bound to oppose their own disfranchisement. Many of the Livery Companies, they pointed out, owned estates which entitled them to be highly interested in the welfare of the City. They demanded that a Memorial be placed before the Lord Mayor and the aldermen and Commons of London praying them 'not to sanction any such measure of deprivation'.

Should this measure of reform, despite their opposition, be accepted by the City authorities, then the Livery of the Cutlers would send a deputation to their members of Parliament to oppose the measure when it came before the House.

The Cutlers were pleased with this defence of their rights and decided to send copies of the Court resolution to the Clerks of other Companies as well as to the Lord Mayor, aldermen and councillors; they would also advertise it in the *Times* and four other daily newspapers.

Some of the Companies to whom they confided their ideas shewed a gratifying response: both the Goldsmiths and the Merchant Taylors asked that any further such resolutions should be communicated to them. And the Painters wrote at great length to the effect that if the Common Council caused new laws to be promulgated they would feel it their duty to combine with other Companies to avert the evil – although they felt that the time was not yet ripe they would, if the Cutlers felt differently, be prepared to consider taking action; in the meantime they had not been behindhand in sending their own memorial to the City authorities.

Gradually the excitement died away and in May 1838,

the Clerk communicated to the Court that the Memorial presented to the Court of Common Council on the subject of Municipal Reform had been taken into consideration by the Common Council and in consequence thereof a Resolution had passed by which the Municipal rights of the Livery were preserved to them.

Whether or not it was strictly true that the Cutlers had been solely responsible for so signal a victory they had every right to be gratified by the effects of their action and their correctness in having taken it; for many years the Liverymen continued to elect their officers. The report of the Commission is, in one respect, particularly interesting in the way it demonstrated that, even at this late date, it was possible for nearly half the lesser Companies to claim a real connection, as far as membership was concerned, with their several trades. In more than a score of cases half or two-thirds of the Company followed the nominal trade and it was still usual for those who entered that trade to take up their freedom in the appropriate Company. 'The Cutlers' Company, for instance, reported that though the bye-law requiring all persons exercising the trade of cutler to be free of the Company had not been enforced for many years, it was nevertheless common for working cutlers and dealers in cutlery to resort to the Company for their freedom, and that fourteen of the Court were, or had been, cutlers.'[206]

But before this report was published William IV was dead and the young Queen had begun a reign which in retrospect provided for the nation – if not for absolutely all its subjects – a positively Golden Age.

17

Of Railways and Reform

1838–1901

It was pleasant to find, with the new reign, that the Company's relations with the Salters appeared to be on a now permanently genial footing. The senior Company sent the Cutlers a copy of a work that they had compiled about the Irish Lands which they hoped would prove of interest: they added that they would always be ready to communicate anything of interest – the Cutlers had only to ask. The Master was once again very hospitably entertained at Salters' Hall and the Court resolved 'that as long as the present amicable feeling shall exist between the two Companies the Master of the Salters be invited to dine with the Cutlers' Company on Audit Day in each year'. While they were on the subject of dining they agreed to the proposal that the Company should have three Summer dinners in the country and that up to four invitations might be made 'to persons of public note and importance as occasion may seem to require'.

They did not forget, amidst such indulgences, their moral obligations and the Court, in 1838, 'being desirous in their prosperity to add to the welfare and general comfort of their poorer Brethren and Sisters resolve to build Almshouses and for that purpose they vote the sum of £2000'.

Although their finances were now indeed soundly based, the Title Deeds of the properties which were the source of their prosperity and their Papers in general were in a shocking state of disarray and a committee attempted to restore them to some degree of order. With a somewhat defensive air the committee thought 'it right to observe that they have conducted their investigation upon as economical a principal as possible, dining in the first and last days only at a Tavern and on the other five days of their meeting partaking of refreshments at the Hall'.

While they were considering their records – and arranging to keep them sealed up in boxes with lists of the contents for easy reference – they considered certain aspects of their organization: the right of search, for example, now seemed to the Court to be in principle unfair and in practice unworkable. They repealed all the relevant ordinances.[207] Their licence in mortmain was only 100 marks – or £66. 13s. 4d. – a year so they applied for, and received, permission to increase it to £200: with the extra freedom for manoeuvre they bought in 1839 some land in Islington in Balls Pond Road upon which to build their almshouses.

They now had a Company stockbroker who accompanied them on their outings to Richmond and some £9000 invested in Consols so they were able to proceed without delay. The foundation stone was laid on 25 June in that year and by April the following year there were seven almshouses ready to receive those out of the twelve applicants who were successful. The rules for the almsfolk included a strict test of moral and religious character. Every inmate was to attend (unless too ill to do so) some place of divine worship upon the Lord's Day; each house was to be provided with a large print Bible which was to remain the property of the Company. The restrictions were daunting: no dogs; no walking on the grass; no walking on the gravel in pattens; no drunkenness; no habitual spirit-drinking; no lodgers; no swearing or obscene talking; no lying or slandering; no quarrelling or provoking others to quarrel; no nuisance of any kind – in short, none of the pleasures which are the breath-of-life to old people everywhere. In 1841 some more land was bought in Balls Pond Lane and, after some difficulty in securing an estimate – the competing contractors proved prone to mistakes in cost-estimating which caused some of them to withdraw – another five almshouses were built. Mr. W. H. Pepys gave £100 in trust for the yearly purchase of coals for the pensioners who were soon safely confined and a medical gentleman was found who for £12 a year, including medicines, would look after the physical side of their welfare. The Company then, rather surprisingly and apparently voluntarily, turned their attention to the now almost forgotten matter of the cutlery trade.

By 1842 the Sheffield manufacturers made almost all the cutlery in the United Kingdom 'including that sold by the London merchants who marked Sheffield products with their own names and street addresses, but omitting the word 'London'. On the other hand, Sheffield at no time became a 'serious competitor with either London or Birmingham in the production of swords or small arms'.[208]

The Court appointed a trade committee the members of which met in May 1842. They considered the bye-laws of the Company and the Act of Parliament to regulate the cutlery trade in England and 'with a view to reporting to the Court the means which appear best calculated to secure the Public and the London Cutlers from the impositions at present practised recommend that the following advertisement be inserted four times in the *Times*, *Herald* and *Chronicle*:

Caution to Manufacturers, Dealers and Purchasers of Cutlery

The Worshipful Company of Cutlers of London have reason to believe that Table Knives and other Articles of Cutlery of inferior temper and quality and manufactured at a great distance from London are constantly sold to the Public with false marks and as being the genuine Manufacture of Cutlers resident in London and its immediate vicinity, [They] desire for the protection of the Public and as a Caution to Manufacturers and Dealers in Cutlery, to make more generally known the Statute of the 59 Geo 3, cap 7 (1819) by which it is enacted that all persons who shall mark any Knives, Blades, and other Articles of Cutlery, Edge Tools and Hardware requiring a Cutting edge with the word or words *London* or *London Made* or any words having a similitude thereto, unless such Articles have been manufactured in the City of London or within twenty miles thereof, shall in every case forfeit all such Articles together with the sum of ten pounds for any quantity not exceeding one dozen of the Articles so marked, sold or exposed for sale, and for every quantity exceeding one dozen ten pounds for every dozen thereof: such sums to be levied and recovered with costs, as is in the Act provided.

The Cutlers Company further give notice to Persons who have purchased Cutlery marked as above, and which is supposed to be spurious, that upon application to the Company, at their Hall in Cloak Lane, Queen Street, they can inspect the aforementioned Act of Parliament and receive such further information as may be necessary to enforce the provisions thereof against Offenders.

The whole thing – except that there was no reference to the imminent danger of financial ruin in which the workmen, their wives and children must inevitably find themselves if such abuses were not hindered – was extremely reminiscent of the notices, proclamations, and petitions issued in the old days of the Company when the Court was indeed a Court of trade law. Now it roused speculation as to how it was to be enforced. The Court had, as we have seen, only recently repealed the ordinances that gave rights of search over the trade. What action did they then contemplate to make sure that the Act recently passed for the protection of 'one of the Staple Trades of this Country' was upheld? 'A memorial from several London Cutlers' was considered and the Court decided that, in order to assist in preventing any infractions of the Act, they would arrange with a solicitor, versed in criminal law, to prosecute any well-established breaches of the law that might occur.

There is no record that those at the Hall were greatly troubled by purchasers of doubtful wares flocking to Cloak Lane and demanding to see copies of the Act. But if, by these activities, the Court seem to hark backwards to the earlier days of their power they nonetheless were gradually introducing modern practices into the Company. For instance, a new Banking account with the Bank of England was to be opened each year by the new Master and wardens, with two members of the Court, so that bills and so on might be more expeditiously dealt with. They had £7500 in the Funds and decided that the dividends should in future be placed with the stock in order to add to the principal. This meant that they must keep their annual expenditure within the balances of the Master's and the Renter's account. A committee was appointed to take a hard look at the state of their finances.

They reported that over the last seven years the ordinary receipts had totalled £27,244 against ordinary outgoings of £23,819 – an average yearly credit balance of £489. But there had been extra-ordinary receipts and, inevitably, extraordinary expenditure too and if these were taken – as they must be – into consideration the Company was, on average, about £152 out of pocket every year. The situation was one that need cause no alarm – the extraordinary payments had included the purchase of stock, licences in mortmain, freehold land, almshouses and so on – all good investments acquired without any diminution of the Company's stocks. So the Cutler's financial situation was basically extremely strong. But – and it was here the finance committee looked stern – the decision to fund the dividends instead of spending them would mean that the annual income with which to meet their expenses be less by about £225. Then there was the new property tax amounting to £101 per annum; the committee hoped that it might be a merely temporary burden but it had to be taken into consideration. In fact, if they took the previous year's figures as their guide, there would be a debit balance, after they had paid the dividends into the capital fund, of some £60. Moreover, when the tenancies expired on the Houndsditch estates, there would be a diminution in their rent roll of, probably, some twenty-five per cent.

For these reasons the committee recommended an annual reduction in their expenditure of some £200. And they suggested ways in which such savings might be achieved. Clearly it was both undesirable and impolitic to reduce donations. It was from the tavern and dinner bills that the whole sum could easily be saved. Lately there had been great increases so that Court and Committee dinners were costing more per head than those of the Corporation: 'a restriction should take place in certain luxuries as for example the supply of expensive wine &c &c.' Except during the summer months there should be no ice and, indeed, 'a little sacrifice by the Court alone' would practically balance the books without abridgement of their usefulness or hospitality. Or the abolition of Vocalists could achieve the necessary economies – the Committee had, so they said, many other suggestions into which there was no need at that moment to look further.

They concluded with the excellent advice that the Company should buy lands near London and let them upon building leases so that when the term of years expired they would own properties whose rentals would compensate for the probable decay of their existing properties – a step that would 'preserve and maintain the present respectable position of the Cutlers' Company amongst the London Corporations'.

The report was accepted by the Court and a great economy drive was launched. One of the first victims was the Appeal on behalf of the Refuge Lavatory and Cabinets d'Aisance.

By 1849 the question of economies had become even more urgent. In February the Court voted, by a narrow majority, to make an immediate cut-back in the sums spent on tavern and other dinners – in February, April, September and December the Court would dine at a tavern chosen by the Master: there would be no guests, no vocalists, and no butler and the luncheon (it was the first time they had used that word) would be of a less expensive character. In August a committee was to be formed to reduce the Company's expenditure to £500 per annum. They proposed that the March Livery dinner and the August Venison dinner should be abolished; the expenses of the three remaining Livery dinners should be reduced to £60 a time; the amounts spent on vocalists should be limited and there should be no champagne except upon Ladies and Audit days. By these devices £300 a year could be saved and in view of the fact that part of the Belle Sauvage estate was soon to be disposed of the Committee thought that this would be a sufficient reduction. In fact, much of the economies must have been lost in all the expenses of a Cutlery Shrievalty with pomp and ceremony and 180 diners at the London Tavern. The occasion was undoubtedly pleasant yet the expense in their present condition was to be deplored. Yet it was only a decade since they had been talking about their prosperity and seeking worthy causes, such as the building of almshouses, upon which to spend their riches. How had such a decline occurred?

The answer lay in their properties. The Houndsditch estate was in a decrepit condition and many repairs had to be carried out before new leases could be granted. In 1850 the credit balance of the Renter's account was only £9. 7s. 7d., which was a negligible amount to offset the deficit of nearly £248 on the Master's account. There was still a reserve of £8000 in the Funds but, with true Victorian prudence, the Company regarded capital as sacred and to be preserved: the day was still far distant when the wise man lived, as far as was possible, in debt.

Houndsditch might be in a decayed condition which was the responsibility of the Cutlers to remedy, but the state of Cloak Lane in which stood their Hall was a matter for the City. In 1849 the Company sent a deputation to the Improvements Committee of the Court of Common Council. They were 'fortified' by a petition from almost everybody in the ward demanding that the lane should be widened 'whereby the ventilation of that portion of the City and the health of its Inhabitants will be improved and the Public convenience will be promoted by giving the increased facility and transit in so important a thoroughfare'.

It was thought that, perhaps, burial grounds might prove an obstacle but, after all, burial grounds in the City were soon going to be done away with. Their remarks, it was reported, were well received but the Minutes do not record any action – if houses were pulled down to afford the speedier passage of traffic it was not the Hall that was involved: that was to fall victim to a later phase in the conquering march of technology in the era that was now ushered in with the Great Exhibition at the 'Chrystal Palace'.

The Cutlers seem to have been less concerned than were some of the other Companies with the Exhibition: there are no records of visits paid to Hyde Park or of opinions expressed. There were ten London cutlers who exhibited in the appropriate section of the Show. 'Except for table-knives, however, the cutlers of London in 1851 were merely factors for Sheffield firms, though in some cases they still hafted Sheffield-made blades stamped with London names to order.'[209]

But the advance of science was not to be resisted and what the all-mighty and virtually sacred car was to a later age the newly prospering railways were to the Victorians. The first mention of the despoilers had come, in the previous year, with the bald statement that the London & North Western Railway Company intended to have a place for the Deposit of Goods in the City: they invited the Cutlers to negotiate with them. By 1851 there was more than one railway project threatening the City and the Court voted that the Company should put in a 'neutral' reply.

They were now rapidly approaching one of the periodical nadirs of their financial position. Their holding of Consols, reduced to £6500, brought them no more than some £92 in dividends. In 1852 the Court resolved that the Luncheon in future should consist of coffee, bread and butter, wine and biscuits. The Hall, to which gas was now being laid on, was found to be in need of urgent repairs, the estimated cost of which rapidly rose from £600 to 800 guineas, and orders were given to still further reduce the luncheons and discontinue the supply of newspapers for a year. The numbers of the Company were declining – the Livery now totalled only seventy-one – and a committee investigated the question of the fines and fees payable on admission to the Cutlers by redemption: they found them to be far in excess of those charged by other 'Livery Companies of equal respectability and position'.

The amounts demanded had been increased in 1830 and again in 1846. Over a period of six years before the latter increase six new members had paid a total of £420: after the fees had been raised not one new member had been enrolled. Those who had applied for details had never been heard of again, a clear indication that the prices were too high. Those taking up the Freedom by purchase, the committee noted, 'are generally persons in favourable circumstances and on that account less likely to become claimants on the funds of the Company; and that the respectability of the Company, as of Corporations generally, is promoted by the occasional admission of those other than the Sons and Apprentices of Freemen.'

Since, too, the Freedom of the City was no longer dependent upon being a Freeman of a Livery Company it was 'especially impolitic to maintain the present high rates. . . .'

The Court agreed to some reductions and modifications. Something was indeed needed to halt the swift slide to insolvency for 1854 proved a year in which there was a terrifying outflow of capital. The Hall was found to be in so serious a condition that the strong closet had to be removed to the basement to relieve the weight upon the walls. The £5500 reserves in the Funds – standing at only 94 – were reduced to no more than £1000. The State of the Company

Finances were actually set out in the Minutes – usually a sign of emergency – and it could be seen that the Renter's account balanced almost exactly and that the credit balance of £170 in the Master's account would be wiped out the following year because there would be no income from investments. There would, it was true, be other sources of income but they would be largely absorbed by such added expenses as the increased Income Tax. The cheerful prospect that, in only two years' time, some houses in Cloak Lane would revert to the Company was offset by the fact that the Houndsditch estate would very soon have to be rebuilt in its entirety.

The position was further aggravated by the fact that there was, that year, no income from the Irish Lands, although some £500 a year was soon to be expected. If this yearly sum were invested in Consols they would have both income and a sinking fund towards the eventually inevitable expenses at Houndsditch. All in all, and perhaps surprisingly, for, on the face of it, there was no great apparent strength in the figures, the report was regarded as a cheerful one. It was felt 'tolerably certain' that 'before many years are over the Cutlers' Company may have the satisfaction of seeing their former income entirely restored with three of their most important estates, namely those in Houndsditch, Belle Sauvage Yard and Watling Street substantially rebuilt and all the expenses connected with the restoration of the Hall defrayed out of the savings of past years'.

In the meantime the last £1000 of precious Consols were sold in 1855 and the Company borrowed from Mr. Stammers, an assistant, £500 at five per cent for furnishing the Hall at which the Court dined in August that year 'to test the new Apparatus'. In all the works there – the building and the decorating and the gasfitting and the heraldic painting, the engineering and the stoves – they had spent £6650. At such a time it must have seemed an astronomically large expenditure yet their faith in the future had been justified: the Renter's balance now shewed a small but sufficient credit of nearly £200 and the Company were well situated at the end of the year. When, in 1856, the Crimean War came to an end they were able to celebrate the peace: behind the transparencies in the Hall the gas-lamps flared and the façade was illuminated with decorations which included a handsome gas-lit star.

A 'Committee of Taste' decided where to hang the pictures in the refurbished Hall. Peace and prosperity were to go hand in hand. The casual charities with their sometimes evocative titles were resumed: five guineas went to 'the Broadstairs Boatmen who relieved the Passengers of the American Ship' and the same amount was allocated to the families of those that perished.

By 1858 the Clerk was able to demonstrate that the annual income of the Company would now produce a credit balance of about £1000: he was also able to demonstrate that although he had been with the Company for twenty-four years he was paid about half the amount given to Clerks in other Companies of the same standing. He thought, in fact, that he was the only Clerk who was not granted extra money after the Irish Estates had fallen in – an event which brought nearly three thousand pounds to the Cutlers. The Court decided that instead of paying the Clerk an annual retainer of £150, separately from any payment made for his professional services to the Company, they would now give him £250 a year for everything inclusive – an indication that the amount of their professional business was perhaps small.

While they were considering the sudden swing in their fortunes they decided that in future the Renter should be elected from the Court – they, in fact, chose the Master for the office – on the grounds that 'several of the recent Renters have experienced great difficulty from their inability to communicate with the Court upon the subjects connected with the office'.

By 1859 they were able to repay Mr. Stammers and the increased rentals from the Bucks and Craythorne properties enabled them not only to increase the amount of the exhibitions attached to the estates but to endow an additional scholarship at Cambridge.

Even the poor of the Company seemed to be less needy: the almshouses were half-empty and there seemed no likelihood that any of the pensioners living in their own homes would want to enter them. The Committee therefore suggested that the empty rooms be let on low rents to very respectable people who would

neither alter the character of the place or annoy the surviving
pensioners.

By 1860 it was permissible, once again, to note in the Minutes 'the
present improved position of the Company'. The annual income
from various sources was £3300 and there would be an extra £170 a
year in rents from the restored Belle Sauvage; the Irish lands were
paying regularly and well; the Master had some £600 in hand and
during eight months of Mr. T. Boot's mastership a saving of £800
had been achieved. A special supplementary offering of £100 a year
was to be distributed among various charities.

A banker was appointed and all monies were to be paid – as a
sop to modern thinking – into the bank.

But there was a limit to the extent to which modernity might go
– the choice in the election of the Company officers was now
entirely nominal: the alternative candidates for the three main
offices were now the three senior past-Masters and although, of
course, it was theoretically possible that by some perversity the
grey-beards might be chosen, in practice it was otherwise. Nobody
objected. The system worked well for the old fires of dissent were
damped down. Dissent to the advance of the railways, however,
had succeeded to the neutrality which they had expressed in 1851
and the Company decided to oppose the proposed line of the
London Chatham & Dover Railway across Ludgate Hill. But by
1863 the whole weight of the onslaught by the railways against
London was upon them.

At first it seemed that the invaders might be repulsed, for the
Ludgate Station Railway entirely abandoned the project of seizing
any of the Belle Sauvage estate. But in December 1863 it became clear
that the property would be affected by the London Chatham &
Dover Railway plans. In addition, the London Low Level Railway
proposals would affect Cloak Lane, and the London Main Trunk
Underground Railway, the Metropolitan Railway and the East
London Railway all affected parts of the Houndsditch estate. In
each case the Company registered their protest. But the 'blight' on
the threatened properties continued: when the Elders of the

Synagogue in Houndsditch appeared before the Committee with a list of necessary repairs they were told that, since the East London Railway was likely to need the premises, nothing could be done. And alterations to the Washing Room at the Hall were postponed until it could be seen whether the property would be needed for the Metropolitan Railway schemes.

In 1865 they were in the thick of negotiations. Some of the houses in White Street, Houndsditch, were sold to the Metropolitan Railway. Some Fleet Lane property was sold to the London Chatham & Dover line. With part of the money from these sales they bought a house next to the ones they already owned in Aldersgate Street and invested the rest in the 'New £3 per Cents and East Indian Railway Stock'.

There now seem to have been no legal scruples or objections to the sale of their properties. Their objections to the Bill in Parliament for the carrying out of the Metropolitan Railway plans in which they were particularly involved were made, it would seem, more to ensure the suitable compensation for compulsory purchase than from any hope that the scheme could be averted. They were demanding £8000 for the properties to be seized from them. There were all sorts of problems, such as those concerned with rights of access, to be settled too. Eventually the promoters of the line paid £6238 for the properties in Houndsditch and the Cutlers were allowed, by Act of Parliament, to expend this amount in the purchase of other real estate.[210]

With all this activity the Cutlers' finances were rapidly increasing. By 1871 their reserves had risen again to £8000. The price of land was increasing, too. What, three years earlier, had been worth thirty shillings a foot was now worth more than three pounds: the Court decided to advance £7000 for the purchase of more land. They were now largely engaged in 'development' plans – the purchasing of leases and the putting up of new buildings – with all that that implied. Not all their dealings with the Railway Companies proved successful: on the London Chatham and Dover line, Holborn Viaduct Station was causing damage to the Cutlers' Belle Sauvage property. It appeared that the Railway entrepreneurs were exceeding their parliamentary powers – an accusation that they hotly denied and, when litigation was begun to claim the modest sum of £500, the railway company held out until such time that it seemed to the Cutlers that their chances of success against the giant combination were too slim to make the hazarding of further money in legal expenses justifiable.

By this time the Irish Lands were providing a diversion. The Salters, as managers of the consortium which included the Cutlers, were much in favour of selling the estates and suggested that a sum should be set aside, from any monies they received, to pay in perpetuity the charities already dependent upon the Irish lands. In 1874 at a meeting of those Livery Companies who were partners in the holding it was agreed that the properties should be sold on thirty years' purchase. As it turned out the estates were not very quickly disposed of and, indeed, in 1875 there were complaints from the minor Companies that so little progress had been made. So that when, in 1876, the Salters suggested that the consortium might buy the Saddlers share of the Irish Plantation, the Cutlers were less than wholeheartedly enthusiastic and gave their consent only in order to facilitate the general sale of the properties, a sale which they insisted should quickly take place.

In fact, an offer of £375,000 – the equivalent of about twenty-three years' purchase – was received and the Cutlers proposed urgently that this figure be accepted: since there was some difficulty in finding suitable purchasers they were of the opinion that it was better to accept a lesser sum from a single buyer rather than to seek to sell the estates piecemeal for a greater sum over a period the length of which might be considerable.

But, in spite of the irruption of the Irish business, it was, as far as the Cutlers were concerned, the Railway Age: even the majority of their reserves were now in East India Railway Stock.

It was also, as they were almost immediately to find out, a new age of municipal reform.

In 1876 the first shots were fired across the bows of the City in the shape of a motion in Parliament by Mr. W. James for a return of certain information from the Livery Companies.

Because they proved unwilling to supply it he put forward another motion, the following year, 'that in the opinion of this House it is the duty of Her Majesty's Government to make full investigation into the present condition and revenues of the 89 Companies mentioned in the second report of the Municipal Commissioners of 1837'.

For the moment nothing happened – unless it be cynically suggested that the sudden drive which the Companies now made to direct their surplus funds towards technical education was the result of this sinister motion. The subject was one that was already in the air. In 1873 the Society of Arts had put foward the first appeals for help in establishing technological examinations; then the Annual International Exhibition announced a conference for City Companies, presided over by the Prince of Wales, to discuss the subject; in 1875 the Plasterers' Company announced their plans for promoting technical education and they were followed by the Turners and the Coachmakers. The smaller Companies were followed by the greater – when the Goldsmiths advocated that the City Companies should interest themselves in the matter the writing was upon the wall and henceforth technical education was to be a subject which for at least the next hundred years was perpetually upon the agenda, and in 1877 the City and Guilds of London Institute was born. That the critical voices raised by radical members of Parliament and the highly defamatory and inaccurate articles in the popular press had their effect, particularly upon the waverers among the Companies, can hardly be doubted. But there were those who, either by a skilful interpretation of the *zeitgeist* or by the operation of their own tendencies to progressiveness, acted as free-agents in the matter, anticipating the needs of society in a very creditable manner. The Cutlers, so far as official participation was concerned, were not among the leaders of the movement. Nor were they among those who might possibly be charged with clambering on to the band-wagon as it went lumbering by. They simply refused to take part in any common enterprise. They were of the opinion in 1878 that 'it will not be desirable for the Cutlers' Company to take part or to assist in the promotion of the various schemes propounded . . . as being calculated somewhat to interfere with perfect freedom of action on the part of the Company and as tending to the promotion of a vast general scheme of Education rather than one specially suitable for Cutlers in the various branches of the trade'.

It was not that they did not recognize the importance of the whole subject – they simply wished to be free to indulge in individual action for the good of their trade, and for the improvement of its manufactures and for the good of their Company in persuading more Cutlers to become Freemen. The Cutlers felt that they should 'recognize the privileges inherent in their Charters and act in such a way as to invoke a feeling of mutual interest between the Company and the Trade: they would, therefore, promote a Cutlery Exhibition and Competition 'followed by a series of Technical Lectures, delivered by eminent professional experts at the Hall. . . .'[211]

On 1 May 1879 the Exhibition was opened by the Earl of Carnarvon. The Master Cutler of Sheffield was present as well as the Mayor of Sheffield and several Masters of other Companies. 'Three classes of goods were admitted: General Cutlery, Surgical Cutlery and Sword Cutlery; and the points to which exhibitors were recommended to pay special attention were: general excellence of material, temper and workmanship, novelty of style, practical and general utility'.[212]

There were no less than ninety-six competitors and the jurors were 'the most distinguished men of the day in the various departments': they awarded one gold medal, twelve silver and ten bronze medals and thirty-eight certificates of merit. The whole enterprise was a great success. In addition to the exhibits by the competitors there was a valuable loan-collection of antique arms and cutlery and a display of various items used in the trade – polishing wheels, steel bars and files, elephant tusks and ivory or horn handles in various stages of preparation. Moreover 'a large number of high-class paintings kindly lent by Mr. Henry Graves . . . added greatly to the appearance of the Rooms'.

On two evenings a week the exhibition was open until nine o'clock in the evening 'to give a better opportunity for the artisan class to attend' and in the fortnight during which the exhibition remained open more than 14,500 visitors attended the show and thanks to 'the unwearied attendance every day ... of a number of the Exhibitors who were never tired of explaining the various articles, the interest was unflagging from beginning to end. . . .' It was 'very gratifying to observe that although so large a number of persons have visited the Exhibition not a single article has been misappropriated nor has any case of misbehaviour occurred'.

It was also highly gratifying that the Duke and Duchess of Edinburgh and Prince Leopold were among the visitors. It was the first time in their long history that Royalty had ever visited their Hall and it was suggested that a commemorative plaque be put up to celebrate the occasion.

When the Exhibition was ended Mr. Cheesewright, a chronicler of the Company and one who was perpetually offering them his advice on various technical matters, felt that the Court 'would be naturally desirous that the best results should follow from such an undoubted success': he put forward a number of suggestions which, if they were adopted, would 'have the effect of materially assisting in creating an extended interest in the cause of Technical Education and further developing not only the usefulness of the Company in its influence over those belonging to the Cutlery trade but will gradually restore to the Company those duties in relation to that trade which were undoubtedly contemplated in the grant of its Charters. They will also have the salutary effect of assisting to counteract those adverse criticisms now so plenteously made as to the application of the funds of the City Companies. . . .'

This last was an important and significant point but, as we shall see, it did not in any way protect the Company from the rising tide of ignorant criticism.

Mr. Cheesewright's suggestions included an apprenticeship scheme for orphan boys with, 'as an inducement to their future good conduct', their probable admission to the Freedom and Livery of the Company; a reduction of fees for admission to the Company by Servitude; the enforcement of the laws about trade marks and further exhibitions of the same sort.

The Court were markedly less enthusiastic than Mr. Cheesewright: they wanted time to consider the apprenticeship scheme;

they did not recommend lesser admission fees for practical cutlers; they considered that, as they did not have the power to grant trade marks – so they considered – it would be out of place to interfere in the question of infringement; finally another Exhibition was a fine idea but . . . the timing of it was a difficulty.

However, the apprenticeship scheme was finally launched – 'bounties were payable to the masters during the term of three years and on its expiration to the apprentice, both in the shape of money and the freedom of the Company, when the report was favourable'.[213]

'It was,' wrote Hazlitt, 'a praiseworthy effort, but out of touch with the new spirit of commerce and the altered relationships between servants and employers.'[214]

In spite of this drawback it continued for many years, and, although no more exhibitions were planned, arrangements were made for a series of 'suitable' lectures at Cutlers' Hall by such experts as Sir Henry Bessemer, Professor A. K. Huntington and Henry Seebohm, Esq., 'the well-known Steel Manufacturer of Sheffield'. It was 'gratifying to the Company to recognise from the large attendance of masters, artisans and apprentices, and the attention paid by them during the reading of the papers, the great interest felt by them in the various technical matters connected with their trade brought under their notice by the talented and scientific gentlemen to whom allusion has been made. . . .' A copy of the script of the lecture was presented to those who attended.

As an introduction to the problem of technical education the Cutlers shewed at any rate a practical, if modest, interest.

The Company now had an annual income of some £6000 and their charitable commitments were increasing with their wealth. In 1880 they amounted to more than £900. It could 'truly be said' – and Cheesewright said it – 'that while they feasted all the great they never forgot the poor or small' – a quotation in which the underlining added a sardonic Ingoldsbeian note that was presumably unintended. The poor and small included many whose names sounded a resonant Victorian fanfare: Mrs. Ranyard's Bible

Mission; The Reformatory and Refuge Union; the Royal Female Philanthropic Society; the Ogle Mews Ragged School; St. Mary Magdalene's Convalescent Home; The Army Scripture Readers' Society and many, many others. Yet when Mr. Mundella, MP, applied for a donation to the Sheffield Distress Fund the Clerk was ordered to convey to him 'the views of the Court as to the Distress being caused by the prevailing strikes and intimating that the application could accordingly not be entertained. . . .'

And donations were refused to the Training Home for Young Servants and the Association for German Governesses.

The almshouses were now much decayed and not productive of much benefit to pensioners: it was decided that no money should be spent on them for the land could more profitably be used for building purposes.

Their credit balance at the bank was now nearly £2000 – a figure it was not again to reach for many years. They were able, by selling East Indian Railway Stock, to spend well over £6000 on the purchase of four more houses in Houndsditch but unfortunately their wealth and their faulty accounting system attracted unwelcome and indeed criminal attention.

At the beginning of 1878 a clerk named Allen asked to be allowed to leave the Clerk's office immediately in order to take up, upon the following Monday, other employment in Newcastle. He was told that his resignation was accepted but that the notice was too short and that he must wait at least another week. But next Monday he had gone – a circumstance which caused the Company to look a little harder than usual at their account books. They discovered to their alarm that there were three sources of peculation. The first was in the Midland Railway rent accounts: here, Allen had opened letters, forged cheques, forged the Clerk's signature on receipts, and suppressed any letters written to urge a prompt payment. Secondly, arrears of rent, when paid, had been misappropriated: the system of fraud was here made easy by the fact that the accounts were kept by the busy Mr. Cheesewright, an old employee in the Clerk's office and so knowledgeable of the Company's affairs that the Clerk never checked the figures. And old Mr. Cheesewright was no match for Allen with his series of fictitious rent rolls which were splendid copies of the real items. Thirdly, there had been the simple straightforward stealing of cheques – both those payable to 'Bearer' and to 'Order' – made out to pay the Cutlers' accounts. It seemed incredible to the Court that a clerk with no banking account could obtain cash upon the crossed cheques of a City Company made out to tradesmen. But obtain the cash he had, and the Company were £2266. 18s. 4d. out of pocket. Under the system by which Clerks to the Company still carried on their private business, Allen was an employee of the Clerk and not of the Company. It could therefore be argued that the Clerk – Mr. W. C. Beaumont, the second of what was to be a long succession of family officers of the Company – was responsible for the misdeeds of his servant. Mr. Beaumont was prepared for this financial blow: 'it would be mere affectation in me to pretend that it is an unimportant one to me. It is not.' But he and his father were agreed that much more important than the large sums of money involved was the question of whether he, as Clerk, had carried out his duties properly. If the Court should decide that he had not done so and must make good the considerable losses, he would do so. 'But, Gentlemen, I know well that such a conclusion will not be arrived at without the full consideration which I have ventured to suggest.'

It was not. The Court decided that the loss should be borne equally between the Company and the Clerk 'for whom they feel sympathy and respect'.

They suggested that, perhaps, in future, to avoid the actual theft of cheques and misappropriation of letters, that the Clerk should himself post all letters containing cheques. Mr. Beaumont was outraged: 'I am addressing gentlemen intimately familiar with the ordinary course of business; and I venture to ask, with confidence, whether any person in the position of principal in a firm posts with his own hands his own letters.' Properly abashed by this monumental rebuke the Court withdrew the impious suggestion.

As it happened, there were no further such unpleasant occasions. A far more unpleasant affair was now threatening – the City Livery Companies Commission to investigate every aspect of the Companies with a view to appropriating their properties to public purposes.

We have seen that in 1876 and 1877 demands had been initiated for a Parliamentary enquiry. In the years that followed Mr. James Firth, the demagogic Member for Chelsea and others – Mr. James Beale ('Nemesis' of the *Weekly Dispatch* and 'Father Jean' of the *Echo*); Mr. Gilbert (who wrote in the *Contemporary Review,* the *Fortnightly* and the *Nineteenth Century*); Mr. Phillips a magistrate whose pen-name was 'Censor'; and many others – carried out a public campaign of vilification against the Livery Companies. They demonstrated all the defects of popular journalism with none of its virtues: they displayed extreme antagonism with complete inaccuracy and employed one of the simplest of the calculated devices of such writing – that of describing ordinary activities in derogatory words. Thus no member of a City Company ever simply 'ate' – he 'guttled'; at Livery Dinners the habitual drinking was described only as 'guzzling'. By the time Mr. Gladstone came to office in 1880 the ground had been carefully prepared for the inevitable Royal Commission. The Companies were invited, politely enough, to supply information about their affairs and, after a certain degree of consultation together, they agreed to do so.

The Cutlers – in common with other Companies – submitted with their replies, a formal protest.

The accusations made against the Companies were many and varied and the charges cited here were typical of the whole:

The show of charity covers a maladministration of trusts and a reckless disregard of charitable intentions such as find no parallel. The fact is that in many cases these votes of money to charitable purposes are nothing more nor less than conscience money.

The conduct of the Companies has been such, in their Trusts, as if they had been private individuals, would have subjected them to have been treated as criminals.

The vast sums they hold, and which were designed for charitable purposes, are being wantonly wasted in weekly feasts and orgies of unbounded wastefulness.

C2

Large salaries and monies in shape of attendance fees on Courts and Committees are rewards paid to members of the Courts and that, in further addition to these, monies on the occasion of such feasts are slipped under the plates of the dining members.

Relatives of members of the Courts are educated in the Companies Schools and there accommodated with Exhibitions in the Universities free of expenses.

Members of the Companies are granted leases of Company properties at most advantageous terms and are thus enabled to make enormous profits from sub-letting.

City dinners are not a very elevating sight and nothing could be more disgusting than the condition of the Companies' Halls after these weekly orgies.

If the Royal Commission had not been nicely constituted with a view to giving vent at its conclusion to Radical prejudice, its members might well have been puzzled by the scarcity – in view of the considerable list of wrongs – of witnesses prepared to substantiate the charges. After some hesitation the Companies sent representatives to give evidence for the defence: the collective conscience of the City was, indeed, clear and the Charity Commissioners, who had no axes to grind, gave evidence of the faultless way in which the Companies administered their trusts. One by one the charges – many of them in fact ridiculous – were demolished. It is interesting to note that it was the Cutlers' Company who were alleged to deal so delicately with their members in the way they presented the douceurs beneath the dinner plates. Unfortunately the witness for the prosecution could not remember whom it was in the Company that had given him this information and, indeed, it is interesting to speculate just how such a fantasy had been created, upon what basis – since there was no grain of truth in it – the lie had been founded. The members of the Court, it was true, were handed their attendance fees – derisory sums if they were supposed to compensate busy City men for the loss of time about the Company business – modestly sealed up in envelopes and it is by no means unlikely that these envelopes were laid beside their places rather than being thrust into their fists.

As the false charges were swept away, a very different picture emerged from that painted by the detractors. The total corporate or non-trust income of the Companies, money which was theirs by law to spend in any manner they wished, amounted to about half a million pounds a year. Of this sum much more than one-third was spent on objects of benevolence and much less than one-third upon their own entertainment.[215] The Trust income was, as the Charity Commissioners bore witness, impeccably administered. The Companies were seen to have been, from their very early days, remarkable innovators in various fields of education and their government was carried out in the spirit and even, where archaisms did not make it impossible, in the letter of their Charters and bye-laws.

All in all, the report should clearly have been a triumph for justice but as occurs in many a tribunal to which the public has apparent democratic recourse, the result was already decided by the composition of its membership. Even so it was significant that when the unfavourable report inevitably emerged there were left only two of the most rabid members to advocate a total abolition of the Companies: the remainder of those who signed the majority report were content to settle for some form of State control. It was the minority report that was of interest in restating concisely the historical evolution of the City Livery Companies and demonstrating that their contemporary condition was the result of an entirely natural and legal development.

As is so often the case with Royal Commissions, the report sank slowly and without trace into the political quagmire and a change of government in 1885 – the year for which some sort of action on the report had been promised – ensured that the immediate danger was ended.

And all the time that this cloud of anxiety had hung above them the Cutlers had been fighting a battle upon another front.

In 1880 a Bill was to be put before Parliament by which the Metropolitan and District Railway Companies would be allowed to tunnel beneath properties without having to purchase them. The Cutlers decided to oppose this 'prejudicial' scheme and it was, at last, thrown out of the Commons. But, in December that year, the railway companies announced that they were preparing to exercise their powers of compulsory purchase.

In April, the following year, the Company received notice to treat for an Estate which included premises in College Hill, Cloak Lane and part of the Hall itself. The Court had in mind the sum of £84,000 but, wisely, decided to demand £115,000. In a letter to the Metropolitan Railway Company they referred to 'the peculiar position of a City Company in having to make a claim for its Hall and to the great difficulty the Company will have in finding a convenient and adequate Freehold site on which to erect a new one. . . .'

If, said the Cutlers, the railway company would provide a site not less in extent or convenience, they would strike out all claims relating to the Hall though, of course, the railways would have to pay the costs of rebuilding. On 22 December 1882 the forces of progress achieved what centuries of civil strife had failed to do: the Cutlers were dispossessed of their historic site, their furniture – with certain exceptions – was sold and they accepted gratefully an offer of temporary accommodation at Salters' Hall. The site suggested by the railway company to replace their old home was quite impracticable and the Cutlers very properly insisted that their new Hall should have no less space in it than their old one and that there should be room, as before, for the Beadle's house and the offices. Their last meeting in their old home had taken place on 20 December and in January 1883 the Committee met for the first time in Salters' Hall to discuss their strategy for the arbitration which had been demanded and granted. Every effort was made to see that life continued in as normal a manner as possible. They actually held an Exhibition at Salters' Hall which was visited by more than eleven thousand spectators in June that year and their lectures in technical education were held at Ironmongers' Hall. It was noted, however, that the series of lectures was running into difficulties: it was not easy to obtain the services of speakers who combined theoretical and practical knowledge of their subject. The Cutlers decided to discontinue them and give – in addition to the hundred guineas that they already gave – £15 to the City &

Guilds of London Institute for prizes for those engaged in the cutlery trade.

Mr. Cheesewright, who had by now become official adviser to the Company on Technical Education, reported that the money they had already subscribed had not been applied to any purposes of the cutlery trade – although forges were to be built at the Institute when enough funds were available – but he had been told by the Director that it was not possible to divide proportionately all the subscriptions received: the cutlery trade was, in fact, being helped by subsidies for training, particularly at Sheffield.

Meanwhile, from their temporary headquarters, the Cutlers considered the problems of rebuilding. Would it be possible to erect their new Hall upon what was left to them of the old site? That way they would avoid having to apply for extended licences in mortmain 'which considering the recent agitation against City Companies might possibly not be granted'. Their surveyor had assured them that he could construct a Hall upon the Cloak Lane site even more spacious than of old but they were not convinced that this was possible. Building sites in Warwick Lane and St. Andrew's Hill were considered. Was it possible, they wondered doubtfully, that they might share for ever with the Salters? Eventually they chose the site in Warwick Lane and asked the Salters if a price could be put upon their tenancy. Their hosts replied that they had not looked very closely into the amount that the Cutlers cost them: they were unwilling to charge rent or to estimate for coals, gas, candles and service but looking at their accounts it seemed to them that, apart from wear and tear, their annual expenses had increased by about £100 since their guests had arrived. The Cutlers sent them a cheque for £200, for the two years of their occupancy, and the Court resolved that two pictures by Sir Joshua Reynolds – of George the Third and Queen Caroline – would make an acceptable present in recognition of the hospitality they had received.

Eventually they offered £14,000 for the Warwick Lane site, a sum that would be more than covered by what they could expect to receive from Cloak Lane after the long and tiresome arbitration that was dragging on should be ended. They would auction the ground rents on what remained of their former site. On 22 April 1886, for the price they had named, they acquired 6012 feet of land for the New Hall, and started out upon the long road of construction.

The first problem that confronted the Building Committee was that of the architect – should others beside the Company's salaried surveyor be asked to submit designs in a competition? The idea seemed acceptable but it prompted the further question: how much money was to be spent? If they were to receive their estimated £950 per annum from the Cloak Lane property that would give them no more than an extra £350 with which to cover both the new five per cent Corporation Tax and the expenses of maintaining a larger Hall. The greatest sum that they could reasonably expend on the Hall, its furnishings and the fees for its architect, was £15,000. If that was the outside figure then £10,000 would be the prudent sum to allocate for the new Hall.

Now such a sum as this is not more than would be expended by many private gentlemen in the erection of a house and it is certainly unusual to invite competition among Architects for the erection of a private house. Still, a Company's Hall to a certain extent is in the nature of a public building. . . .

Thus the committee mused in an agony of indecision. They had perfect confidence in T. Tayler Smith, their surveyor, but different minds brought to bear upon the subject might prove advantageous. On the other hand, architects, being what they were, tried – perhaps unconsciously – to gain such prizes regardless of cost. The more elaborate and enticing a design the more likelihood there was of it being chosen. This might involve the Company in extra cost. Finally the committee were 'of the opinion that the Company's Hall must be treated as a private gentleman, with limited means, would treat his own house': if £10,000 was all that was to be spent then £10,000 was all that must be spent.

These were brave but naive words. They had decided that they would treat the affair as a private gentleman would treat it. Like all private gentlemen – architects being what they are – they soon found that events began to erode the fine façade of their decisions.

The size of the Hall – to seat 110 diners in comfort and 120 if necessary – determined the use of the site: there would be no room for a Beadle's house but there would be quarters for a caretaker.

And by August it had emerged that the cost would be just above the very outside figure of £15,000 and even that did not include all the furniture that was necessary. To add to the financial problems the Cloak Lane site had not yet been let, the sale of the Irish Lands, although it produced a useful capital sum of £10,000, was likely to lead to an annual loss of £100 a year and the Houndsditch leases falling in might not be disposable at the same rents. However, the Committee considered – as private gentlemen will – that it would be a pity to spoil the Hall for a ha'porth of tar: the full estimate should be accepted even if this meant economizing on Dinners and Court Fees. To shew, however, that they were not to be imposed upon they pointed out that the contract gave 'the most unlimited powers to the Surveyor with regard to the important matter of "Extras" and other items without any reference whatever to the Company'. They instructed the Clerk to tell the surveyor that they would not be responsible for any extras that had not been approved by the building committee.

Tenders were sought from sub-contractors and estimates shewing unusually wide discrepancies were received and mulled over and choices made. The preparation of the site for the building work had already given rise to three writs against the Company but these were disposed of in a fairly satisfactory manner. But the amateurs of the committee were soon at grips with true professionals. Mr. Brass, the builder, was found to be installing oak woodwork of a different description to that in the contract; the surveyor suggested that this be accepted and a lower price paid; the committee demanded that the conditions of the contract be strictly observed: the specification had been for 'Wainscot' and the surveyor had told the Court that this meant 'English Oak'; Mr. Brass thought it would be most injudicious to use English oak – that would be positively asking for trouble later on – in any case, the cost in material and labour was at least twenty per cent more than a good Riga or Danish oak; Mr. Brass said that in the trade 'Wainscot' always meant 'Imported Oak' and that had been what he had estimated for; the quantity surveyor, Mr. Barnett, agreed with Mr. Brass – it always caused trouble did English oak – and Mr. Brass was quite correct in his interpretation of the trade description of 'Wainscot'; the committee said angrily that that was not what he had said previously; the quantity surveyor replied blandly that he could not remember ever having told anybody anything else. . . .

The situation was, in fact, entirely normal and, indeed, predictable. The gentlemen were, ultimately, helpless and all they could do, in the face of angry letters from Mr. Brass' solicitors, was to agree to arbitration. But the Great Hall, at any rate, was to be of English oak. All the time the costs, in small almost unnoticeable steps, were mounting. The surveyor one day, for example, recommended Taylors sanitary fittings as being most 'suitable'. Of course they would cost more. But only an extra £15. It was hardly possible for gentlemen to quibble over such small amounts but when in October – a month in which they asked Mr. Brass for an explanation why the work was progressing so slowly – the surveyor asked to spend an extra £50 on woodcarving the sum was sufficient to warrant a great firmness in their abrupt refusal. And they displayed a commendable worldly wisdom when the quantity surveyor, at the end of 1887, asked to be allowed to carry out measurements for determining variations: his fee of one per cent for additions to the specification would be raised to two per cent for omissions. In November the business was further complicated by the sudden bankruptcy of Mr. T. Tayler Smith who was forced to resign with only about one month's major work on the Hall to be completed. And although he brought evidence from trustees to shew his lack of personal blame in his failure and asked to be allowed to continue for perhaps three months to carry out all the minor work necessary to complete the project the Court was adamant: he must leave at the end of one month. In this decision they were no doubt influenced by a committee memorandum of the difficulties they had suffered through Mr. Smith's 'delay and want of attention'. They were suffering too from Mr. Brass and in the new year of 1888 they expressed themselves 'much dissatisfied with the progress made with the completion of the New Hall' to which Mr. Brass replied only that he was 'pushing on'.

At last the day arrived when they could foresee in the near future a meeting in the Hall. Coals were ordered and delivered. Carpets and decorations were ordered. There were all the excitements and all the pains of moving into a new home.

And on 7 March 1888 the first meeting of the Building Committee took place in the Hall. Almost the first item on the agenda was a letter from the Stereoscopic Company: it would be necessary, they said, to erect scaffolding to take pictures of the frieze – a lively work in terra cotta by Creswick – outside the Hall. The Clerk was requested to reply that 'as the Company did not require any photographs and had not ordered any, they declined to erect the staging mentioned'.

The Cutlers settled down to count the cost.

The property in Cloak Lane had at last been let. But it was still a source of seemingly endless trouble and dissension among tenants, sub-tenants and their various solicitors.

The gas bill, too – more than £24 for the March quarter – was a source of worry: 250,600 feet of gas seemed a somewhat excessive consumption and, perhaps, some of it might be attributed to the building contractors. The Court still found it impossible to obtain any figures upon which they could make an estimate of the total cost of the new Hall. To complicate matters a considerable amount of work had been taken away from Brass, the builder, and allocated to other firms by the architect without any reference to the Court and this caused further delays in accountancy. The quantity surveyor, was, in June, still working away at the variation figures which he admitted 'are *very* considerable'; in August, when pressed, he still had nothing to report but hoped 'shortly to be able to place the account before the Committee'; in October he could say no more than that it was a 'very tedious and complicated measurement'. It was not until November that the final figures for Brass' account of some £17,000 were available. 'The extras on this portion of the work alone amounts to the large sum of £4468. 11s. 8d.; this sum does not, however, in any way adequately represent the total amount of the extra expenditure on the building and other matters connected therewith. . . .' It was also stated that the quantities had been prepared upon most imperfect plans submitted by Mr. Smith, the architect, and that the specification had not been prepared 'as is inevitably usually [*sic*] done by the Architect by Mr. Barnett at Mr. Smith's request'.

The committee decided to ask Mr. Smith for an explanation – especially in the light of the fact that they had expressly warned him in writing that he would be held responsible for any extras incurred without the authority of the committee.

It would be unprofitable to recount in detail the ensuing dispute: the broad outline will be familiar to anyone who at any time has had dealings with architects, quantity surveyors, builders and their various legal advisers. Suffice it to say that virtually the whole of 1889 was occupied in the tiresome and, inevitably, unsuccessful struggle. Solicitors' letters containing accusations, denials, and counter accusations shuttled back and forth. Arbitrators were consulted; even the President of the Society of British Architects was appealed to. In the event the only scrap of satisfaction that could be grasped was that Mr. Brass eventually reduced the sum of his bill by about £1500 and the Committee with a fine disregard for the conventions of modesty had 'much pleasure in congratulating the Court upon the very successful negotiations of the Committee. . . .'

Their installation in their new and palatial home provided the Cutlers with an opportune moment for taking stock of a number of aspects of their situation. They owned £15,000 in Consols which contributed £450 in dividends to their yearly income of £5400, and they were able to expend more than £1000 a year on various good causes including the now firmly-established City and Guilds of London Institute.

On a more prosaic note of stock-taking their wine inventory shewed that their cellars contained 5239 bottles of which four-fifths were port, champagne and sherry: the mere thirty-one bottles of Burgundy were clearly not greatly esteemed. With the sale of the Irish Estates came the opportunity to review that branch of their investment historically. In 1615 the Cutlers had invested £225: they had received back nearly £16,000 in income – roughly twenty-five per cent per annum 'but this rough calculation does not take into account the fact that for many years no income whatever was received nor does it take into account the question of compound interest – or the fact that, at the date of the advance, money was four or five times dearer than at the present time. In addition to the *Interest* it will be seen that the Company have received £11,272. 10s. 0d. in lieu of the £225 originally advanced by them.'

Even taking the higher figure for the dearness of money it meant that the Company had received more than ten times their original investment – a result that would have seemed highly improbable in the days of their first adventuring in the Plantation.

The Company were, in fact, in that last decade of the nineteenth century, fairly prosperously placed.

Yet, in spite of this, the suggestion was put forward that the fees for taking up both the Freedom and the Livery be increased and, at the same time, the numbers of the Livery be restricted. A committee surveyed the problem.

The number of the Livery was now fairly stable. There had been in 1829 one hundred and nine members: there were, in 1893, only three less. The problem was one of space. The Dining Hall could seat 90 in comfort whereas 109 invitations – including the Chaplain and one 'Vocal' – had to be sent out. Of course, not everyone would or could accept but it was still a tight squeeze. Some statistics that may seem surprising emerged: in the old days it had taken thirty-seven years to get on to the Court, now it was taking no more than twenty-six or twenty-seven years. This must imply that the Court were dying or retiring more quickly than of old – a state of affairs that seems to run contrary to the general increase in longevity in the nation. It also meant that more members of the Court than hitherto were likely to be spry enough to attend the dinners and that factor, too, would add to the difficulties of accommodation.

In spite of this, the Committee were opposed to any restrictions upon entry. On the subject of fees they were less conservative. The fees in many other Companies were much higher and, in the Cutlers, they therefore represented particularly good value for money: for only £27. 10s. both the Freedom and the Livery could be acquired by Patrimony or Servitude (the combined fee was £80 if entry was by Redemption) and for that trifling sum the privileges were disproportionately large. The Committee listed them: a vote for a London Member of Parliament; a vote for Lord Mayor and Sheriffs; the likelihood of election to the Court with its subsequent emoluments such as they were; and invitations to Dinners, both personal and for guests, which cost the Company £10 a head. It was suggested that the joint fees be increased to £50 for admission by Patrimony or by Servitude to a Cutler, to £100 by Servitude to others and to £150 for admission by Redemption. For many years apprentices had been entitled to come on to the Livery at reduced rates – the Committee had no objection to this state of affairs continuing provided that they were bona-fide apprenticeships to genuine working cutlers, surgical instrument makers and the like.

The apprenticeship scheme that had been launched with the drive for technical education was still flourishing: at the end of each year the boys met together at the Hall and were presented – if they had been virtuous – with five-shilling Christmas boxes which were withheld for such offences as failing to work on Saturday afternoons. It was over apprentices that, to all intents and purposes, the last trade control was exercised by the Cutlers although in 1898 they refused to approve a proposal by Messrs Mappin & Webb that their plate might be stamped 'London and Sheffield'. By the end of the century the Court minutes had become of little general historical interest being concerned, almost exclusively, with the routine of admissions, with Exhibitions at the Universities and with notes of an increasing number of charitable disbursements.

It was in the Committee records that all the great business of property management was recorded.

The age of steam was still making its inroads upon the Cutlers' properties; the Balls Pond Estate had been threatened by the London, Tottenham and Epping Forest Railway and in Houndsditch the Metropolitan line had taken its toll. This property now consisted of fifty-one houses together with the former Clothes Exchange and the Synagogue. The rent roll was almost £1500 but, although the tenants had done their best, the properties were now in a sorry state and greatly in need of modernization. The Company decided to do what they could but they recognized that nothing but demolition and total reconstruction could make the estate a credit to the Company. Unfortunately there were two houses in Cutler Street belonging to other landlords which stood in the way and, eventually, patching up the Company properties – a step that, they anticipated, would create goodwill – was all that could be carried out.

In their own Hall, which in 1891 had been damaged by water from the hoses of firemen fighting a blaze in a property at the rear of the building and on which the Phoenix Fire Office had shewn less than generosity in dealing with the Cutlers' claim, the great pre-occupation was now with electricity: should it be installed?; how could the gas fittings be utilized?; would it be more efficacious than installing the incandescent gas lighting system? By 1897 they had taken the plunge and voted for electricity but they were for many years to treat it with both suspicion and unease. The committee, right from the start, recommended 'that on the occasion of Dinners at the Hall, Messrs Laing, Wharton and Down should be requested to send some competent workmen to attend to the electrical installation'.

And when that year they celebrated the Diamond Jubilee of Queen Victoria it was with gas that the outside of the Hall was illuminated at a cost of £24. 10s. with 'festoons with bows about 25 ft. in length and two dates 1837 & 1897 in 12-inch double-line figures surmounted by a 5ft. 3 inch crown – the whole forming an effective device with all necessary Iron service pipes, and regulating cocks fitted down to the pavement level ready for the Gas Company to connect to its service. . . .'

With the end of the century old-fashioned ideas were everywhere in retreat. At his own expense the Clerk was allowed to connect a private telephone to his two offices. And the last of the old-fashioned wars, in which it was possible for the populace to send out fighting teams to a foreign land – in this case to South Africa – without themselves becoming actively involved, other than financially, was fought. At the end of 1899 the Committee recommended a gift of 100 guineas to the Mansion House Fund for the wives and families of soldiers in the Transvaal and South Africa and early in 1900 a special Court was called to consider an appeal, from the Lord Mayor, for the City of London Imperial Volunteer Fund. The Corporation, it was pointed out, had subscribed £25,000 'with unanimity and enthusiasm' towards a patriotic movement which was a matter of some urgency since the contingent for which the fund was being raised was expected to leave in two weeks' time. The Court Minutes failed to reflect the same note of enthusiasm and the word 'unanimously' was not mentioned but, nonetheless, they voted 200 guineas towards the fund. By the end of the year they had decided to present the Freedom and Livery in addition to 'a Sword or an Ornamental Casket to one of the distinguished Generals who have been, or are, engaged in the South African War'. General French was the officer selected and the presentation sword was to be made, at a cost of not more than £150, by Wilkinson or some other well-known firm.

The Cutlers, in return for their subscription, were presented with the South African Medal with clasps and, then, on 22 January 1901, Queen Victoria died. Even the oldest member of the Company could scarcely remember living in another reign. The psychological effect of the ending of the life of a monarch who had seemed virtually immortal, of the passing of an era of great deeds and ever-increasing Empire, was recognized as being severe.

Mercifully hidden from even the most far-sighted were the events which the new century were to bring: it was, perhaps, twenty years before anyone was to realize that, with the death of the old Queen, nothing would ever again be the same.

18

The Old World Ends

1901-1939

JUST for a little while, however, the old splendours continued. The change from the unbendingly upright Queen to her elderly and none-too-scrupulous son, from a Court of ageing aristocrats to a Court circle of recently ennobled nouveaux-riches, was accomplished without any complications. The expressions of regret and esteem, traditional on such occasions, were entered in the transactions of institutions everywhere. In the Cutlers' Company it was the wine warden, old Mr. R. J. Cheesewright, who proposed that the Company 'desire to record their profound sense of the great loss that the Empire has sustained by the death of its beloved Sovereign . . . and their admiration of her conspicuous virtues and the benificent and glorious character of her illustrious Reign'. They congratulated King Edward VII and assured him of their 'loyalty and devotion'. They prepared to celebrate the coronation and considered various festive suggestions. The motion that the Ceylon Mounted Infantry should be entertained at the Hall was rejected and so, eventually, was the idea of a coronation banquet. Instead every Member was to be presented with a present valued at 25/- and the Company were to spend £200 on commemorative Plate. The Hall was to be illuminated for two nights at a cost of not more than £30, exclusive of electricity or gas – eventually they chose gas for they still exhibited considerable suspicions of electricity. Eventually they decided to have, too, a coronation ball in the Christmas season and Mr. J. U. Morton presented the Company with a specimen pair of old carvers which had, in addition to their technical interest, the distinction of having 'been used for cutting up a Roasted Ox, i.e. Baron of Beef, at the Coming of Age of a Peer of the Realm'.

The Company's financial position in 1903 was sufficiently comfortable: their credit balance for the previous year had been nearly £700, and after spending some £11,000 (which they had received from the Irish Estates) upon property in Charing Cross Road they still had £5000 remaining in the Funds.

They could afford to hold the Ladies' Dinner in July at what they called with a fine accuracy the 'Hôtel Métropole' and, when they became dissatisfied with the fare provided, at the Savoy. But, nonetheless, by 1904 they were again worrying about money; it was 'in the knowledge of the Court that during the last few years the expenditure of the Company has been exceptionally heavy' and that, for the next two years there was to be a reduction of income of about £300 on the Houndsditch Estate. It was suggested that 'all Court Dinners at which guests are not invited be abolished'.

The following year they were once more feeling optimistic: 'the financial position of the Company is excellent and indeed stronger than it has ever been before and its present normal income is sufficient for its present normal expenditure'. But, none the less, they determined not only to maintain the economies of 1904 but to do away with the February Dinner and the five ordinary dinners of the committee. In this way they could save £200 a year. The need for what might appear, under the circumstances, rather trifling economies was due to the fact that many years previously 'it was considered that there was no reason to continue to accumulate Savings. As long as Savings existed resort has been made to them on the Capital account and during the last few years, by the increase of Charitable Donations Exhibitions and Salaries, the expenditure of the Company has permanently increased by £530 a year.' And the savings account had been finally exhausted by paying both tithe and land tax redemptions. It was thus necessary once again to accumulate reserves to meet any extraordinary costs that might arise – such as the purchase of wine, the stocks of which had fallen to a dangerously low level and for which at least £250 a year ought to be set aside. And there were all the expenses, too, of a Cutler Mayoralty with carriages and banners and a band to accompany him.

Their attitude towards their finances was, in fact, volatile: soon they felt able, for a little while at least, to talk about 'the improved financial position of the Company' and recommend that the Court dinners without guests be resumed.

They were still fortunate in their benefactors. Part of Mr. H. R. Boot's timely legacy was spent on having some four dozen reproductions made to match the old chairs with which the Hall was furnished.

But there were some doubts about how secure a place the Hall really was to house their treasures: the Master called there on the Wednesday before Christmas and found the place in charge of a charwoman only. The Police were consulted and recommended that electric bells be attached to windows and doors. For £135 a year they could have a night policeman, supervised by a sergeant, permanently on duty and in telephonic communication with the police station. For about 24/- a week they could have the services of a retired policeman as caretaker. Eventually they, more economically, bricked-up a strongroom window and bought a watchdog.

But, at the Hall, it was the electricity system that was their preoccupation. Was it really safe? Mr. Horace Boot, a Liveryman, offered his services as electrical engineer. It seemed very expensive. Was the meter accurate? They had it checked and found, disconcertingly, that it operated slightly in the Company's favour. Could the gas element be removed from the dual lighting fixtures? If so Mr. Boot might make provision for artistic improvement of the fixtures. It was many years before they could bring themselves to feel entirely at ease with this somewhat alarming invention.

Meanwhile they were from time to time diverted from such considerations by vestigial and sometimes agreeable reminders of their old trade functions: it emerged that employers found that the Cutlers' apprentices – who now numbered twenty-one – were better than any others and this they attributed to the system by which the Company held a yearly inspection of their work: 'the lads always look forward to this yearly exhibition and we can

D2

hold it out before them as something to strive for. Further we have no doubt that the very liberal gift which we understand is made at the end of the term is a great incentive to earn a good report.'

The Company, in fact, paid their apprentices £10 at the end of their articles in addition to the 5/- that they each received, if they were sufficiently well-behaved, as a Christmas box.

The apprentices were all that remained to them of their industrial responsibilities and they were not anxious to become involved in trade disputes. When, in 1911, Italian manufacturers in Milan falsely stamped their goods with a London mark, the Master Cutler and the Lord Mayor of Sheffield suggested that the Cutlers' Company should bring an action against the foreigners. The offence was against the London trade and Sheffield did not, therefore, think that the trade protection funds of that City should be used for fighting the case. It would be fairly straightforward: Mappin and Webb, who had business premises in Italy, were prepared to act as nominal prosecutors – provided they were indemnified against the costs. The Board of Trade promised £100 and the London Chamber of Commerce were prepared to support the Cutlers' Company by means of a guarantee fund to be raised among members of the trade. But the Cutlers' committee recommended that the matter be adjourned and, of course, nothing came of it. Yet they were not unmindful of their great past for, apparently spurred by emulation of the Cutlers of Hallamshire with whose history they had recently been presented, they had commissioned from Mr. Charles Welch a monumental history, the expense and extent of which was already beginning to cause embarrassment. For they were again worried about their finances. In that same year of 1911 a special sub-committee was appointed to consider the ever engrossing subject. They reported that, in the previous three years, the Company had overspent in all about £1200. There were several reasons for this: they had made capital expenditure out of income; they were suffering a temporary reduction of income from the Houndsditch Estate; they had spent an increased amount upon dinners; the history and the repair of their old records were disproportionately expensive – already Mr. Welch had cost them £616. 12s. 6d. which must be paid for out of capital and the capital made up again gradually out of income. Although the committee thought it was not necessary, normally, to accumulate any reserve from the income it was 'very desirable' to turn the annual deficit of £500 into a surplus of £100. It was at this moment that the Painter-Stainers asked them what, if anything, they intended to do about the coronation. The Cutlers, beset by expenses, replied that they had not yet decided.

Edward VII long-awaited and brief reign was over and his son, George V upon the throne. Reform was again in the air: a Franchise Bill affecting the rights of the Livery was before Parliament and the City of London Conservative Association planned, for the Autumn of 1912, a great demonstration against it. Before they committed themselves, the Cutlers cautiously decided first to discover what action other Companies were taking and then to leave the matter to the Master's discretion. In the end they did nothing. The times were against them and already there were ominous events overseas to distract their attentions and make them look uneasily to the more important future. And at home the assaults of railway age upon the Company had still not come to an end: now it was the miniature Post Office Railway that threatened to interfere with their lands in Aldersgate.

For the better regulation of their internal affairs they contemplated alterations to their bye-laws but by August 1914 it was possible to write that such alterations should be postponed because of the 'International Position'. By September the Position had been elevated to a Crisis in view of which, and because of 'the impossibility of fore-casting what questions of extreme urgency may arise, it is resolved that in the event of a question which, in the opinion of the Master, is of serious and urgent importance, the Committee shall have the full powers of the Court to deal with such a question'. Their first action was to recommend that all dinners be cancelled and that the Livery be so informed.

By December the word 'War' was, for the first time, mentioned – but only in connection with a group of charities – a gift of £300 to the Young Men's Christian Association for a recreation-hut for troops in camp and small cash offerings, some of £10 and others of £20, to amongst others the City of London Territorial Force, the Indian Soldiers Fund, the Women's Emergency Corps and the Servian Relief Expedition. The formation of a National Guard for the City was proposed but the Clerk could get no information about it: on the other hand, the Adjutant of the Corps of Citizens sent them details of his organization – which was 'to enable Livery-men and Freemen who could not enlist owing to age etc. to learn the elements of Musketry in their spare time' – and invited the Cutlers both to enrol men and to subscribe money.

The Court Minutes shrank in size to six or seven lines. Business was at a standstill. The motion by Mr. Welch 'that it is desireable that women shall have some share in the educational advantages provided by the Company in connection with the Universities of Oxford, Cambridge and London . . .' was withdrawn: in 1915 the Committee agreed in principle to this revolutionary idea but recommended that no scheme be prepared until the end of the war. In the meantime a grant of up to £25 was made to a Liveryman who intended to run a motor ambulance and who asked for a contribution towards the body-work; insurance of their estates against action by enemy aircraft was effected in cases where the tenants were prepared to pay half the premiums; Christmas presents were sent to Liverymen on service overseas.

In 1916 the Y.M.C.A. wrote very civilly and encouragingly, on the first anniversary of the opening of the Cutlers' Recreation Hut at Purfleet Camp, that 'the same was packed with men and that most glowing tributes were paid by Officers and Chaplains to the work accomplished'; the Chamberlain of the City also wrote to say that, in future, naturalized Germans would not be admitted to the Freedom of the City and that, therefore, birth certificates must now accompany any applications.

It was not a very cheerful year in which to celebrate the quin-centenary of the Company. The committee thought that the Livery should certainly be summoned to the Hall on such an important occasion to be entertained inexpensively to supper in morning dress and with medals and music but without guests. Luncheon –

it was felt – would be inconvenient because of business hours and dinner would prove insufficiently inexpensive. The meal was provided by Messrs Ring and Brymer: other firms were unable to find waiters.

In addition to such personal celebrations it was decided that the sum of £500 should be spent on some such object of public utility as a hospital bed or cot. On enquiry, however, it was found that at least £1000 was demanded for the endowment of a bed and that some hospitals even demanded that amount for a children's cot. Eventually for the stipulated sum of £500 they were able to name a cot in the Victoria Hospital for Children.

The final act of celebration was to present every member of the Company with the first volume of Mr. Welch's history.

The history was, in fact, running into considerable difficulties and occupying in the scanty Minutes an amount of space that was altogether disproportionate.

By 1917 the cost had increased enormously and the printers reported that they could not match in the second volume the colour of the paper used in the first. To this news Mr. Welch reacted with the opinion that a third volume would certainly be necessary if he were not to have to write a foreword to say that the history was *abridged* – a highly undesirable action.

The apprenticeship scheme was also meeting difficulties: when Messrs Allen and Hanbury expressed their readiness to employ a youth whose masters had refused to pay the scale of wages demanded by the Cutlers they ran into trouble with the appropriate trade union which not only refused to permit any new apprenticeships but would not even allow vacancies to be filled. It provided a disappointing set-back at the end of the year to a scheme that had, so far, worked well, and in which seventeen apprentices were still involved.

The war-time finances of the Company were being carefully husbanded: in February 1917 they borrowed £20,000 from the Bank of England with which to invest in War Loan. It was, under the circumstances, an unusually short-lived investment for within about three months the War Loan had been disposed of and the Bank of England repaid.

In the same way that they manipulated their finances they watched over such assets as their stocks of wine. They anticipated that in the forthcoming Budget there would be an increase in the excise duty, and considered what action they should take: they found that they had no less than 2400 bottles of champagne and, in spite of the prospect of the Budget, sold 135 dozen at a reasonable profit – its condition was nearly past its best and would soon deteriorate at their war-time rate of consumption. Of port they had nearly 1750 bottles and to provide for the future they decided to lay down a pipe of Cockburn and a hogshead of Butler & Nephew. Though the total cost would be £150 the sale of the champagne would bring in £865.

With such sound financing they were well able to afford the entertainment they provided for wounded soldiers at Christmas and the hampers they sent to Liverymen on active service.

So, with 1918, the War came to an end. The history of the Company was still an affair of much concern yet the historical sentiments of the Court seem to have been singularly unmoved. A motion to revive the ancient custom of attending the Parish Church on election day, led by the Beadle with his staff of office, was rejected. Rejected, too, was the motion that

viewing with satisfaction the efforts that were made in the past to restore the ancient connections between the Company and the Trade, with its branches, and being informed of the practices of unscrupulous foreign competitors in copying and falsifying names and marks of well-known and esteemed members of the said allied trades which has obtained for many years to the great loss of business and reputation of English Manufacturers, the Worshipful Company of Cutlers do hereby agree to take such steps as may be thought reasonable to draw public attention to these conditions. And, in order that the opinion of those most concerned may be ascertained, resolve to summon a conference to be held at this Hall at an early date to discuss the subject.

The whole tone of the rejected motion was reminiscent of the earlier days of the Company, for the recounting of which Mr. Welch now demanded two further volumes of 500 pages each. But the cost of paper had increased by fifty per cent and, under the circumstances, the committee decided that there had 'been already a certain amount of over-elaboration' and that the work should be compressed: they had not enough money to justify such expense.

The cost of celebrating the peace was their immediate concern: the Clerk outlined to the Court the amount that was available for the occasion out of income. But he suggested that, as the celebration was so especially noteworthy, it might be permissible this year to over-expend the Company income. Eventually they decided to hold a Livery Dinner in October, with guests, and as souvenirs of the occasion 150 silver cigarette boxes, suitably engraved and costing 57/6d. each.

They still possessed some £5000 in the funds and their annual balance was nearly £1500. But increased taxation was to be feared and they would have to exercise restraint: in the meantime they decided that 'the principle of hospitality should be exercised as far as possible, subject to a provision that 25% of the Company's net income be set aside for charitable purposes'. With the presentation by the Cutlers of Lord French to the Lord Mayor to receive the Freedom of the City the final curtain was drawn upon the First World War and the Company settled back to enjoy the fruits of victory and peace.

The England to which the victorious warriors returned proved to be something less than they had been led to expect. As far as the Cutlers' Company were concerned the internal scene was, if the Minutes reflect the image truthfully, one of a monumental dullness. The return to normality was marked by such events as making a contract with the Gas Light and Coke Company for lighting the archway of Belle Sauvage Yard which saved the Company six shillings a year.

View Days, on which the whole Court visited the properties, were still held; Rent Days in which tenants, in decreasing numbers, turned up, cash in hand, to pay their dues personally at the Hall still took place – although the majority clearly preferred to pay their rents in the more normal commercial manner; Court and

Livery Dinners were resumed; the Company properties and their trusts and charities were skilfully administered without dispute or difficulty.

In 1921 their responsibilities were agreeably increased by a legacy from Captain F. G. Boot, one of a family whose benefactions to the Company had already been considerable. The property was bequeathed unconditionally but the known wishes of the Captain were observed. There was to be an annual dinner, a scheme for assisting boys to learn foreign languages, and a fund for such purposes as the Court might decide.

It was agreed that the boys should be selected from those in secondary, or similar, schools who wished to make Commerce or Engineering their vocation and the Company consulted with various educational authorities. Eventually they founded a number of Cutlers' Scholarships in Modern Languages – there were to be five in London of £90 a year and one in Sheffield of £100, all tenable for two years. As an afterthought it was agreed that women could be eligible for the benefits. Yet there proved to be a strange and disappointing difficulty in getting the scheme to function properly. The Company, and the University too, were surprised to find that there seemed to be little interest among students and it was not until the end of 1924, when conditions were varied to cater for boys, aged between fifteen and nineteen and training for Commerce, who wished to study languages on the Continent, that the benefaction was successfully applied. Although in practice the proviso made little difference, there was a stipulation that preference should be given to the relatives of Cutlers. The Company was, in many ways, a family concern. There were names that sounded a recurring litany in their affairs: Beaumont and Boot, Herbert, Perkins, Pocock and Welch – the representatives of each family, often three or four of them at a time, seemed always to be upon the Court, with others of the same name among the Livery waiting their turn. The very nature of the old gilds in which members had pursued the only trade they were by law allowed to practice led to this situation of a family continuity. And in 1922 when the retiring Master, Macdonald Beaumont, endowed a scholarship of £50 a year he was able to point out with manifest and justifiable pride that three members of his family in succession had now for nearly a century held the office of Clerk.

By this year they had accumulated in the funds and trusts no less than £19,000 and in 1925 they decided to spend £11,000 of this upon the purchase of property in Friday Street. Their properties were of ever-increasing importance and in 1926 there was a suggestion by Mr. Welch that the office of Renter Warden – which had been abolished in 1858 – should be revived. The suggestion was not well received by the rest of the Court: they felt that it stemmed less from a desire to revive the office than from the sentiment, in certain quarters, that the Livery were not sufficiently in touch with the administration of the Company affairs and that, to correct this state of ignorance, they should have some representative, appointed annually, to attend the meetings of the Court.

The predictable cries of outraged protest were more dignified than they would have been in earlier days but they were nonetheless effective. Such a revival was 'unnecessary and undesirable'; it was 'not in the interests of the Company' and, moreover, a situation in which 'a Livery delegate on the Governing Body would have no responsibility and no powers of voting but would at the same time have power of criticism, could not work satisfactorily'.

But, of course, the Livery should be kept informed: the Clerk was instructed to answer any question which any Liveryman might care to put to him.

Another proposal that was equally unacceptable – though on a different level – came from the trustees of the Polish Synagogue who announced that they wished to buy their premises under the terms of the Places of Worship Act and offered the Company £50. The Court considered, as well they might, that such a figure was 'entirely inadequate' and even when the offer was increased to £375 they were still insufficiently tempted to sell.

They were still, however, tempted to buy and in 1930 they raised a mortgage of £15,000 and bought for £25,000 two houses in Ludgate Hill. The annual survey now took those members of the Court who attended to such widely spread and mixed properties as Watling Street, Bow Lane, Houndsditch, Ludgate Hill, Peckham, Cloak Lane, Aldersgate Street and Charing Cross Road.

Their charities, which would ultimately benefit from such property speculation, were also very much in their minds that year. For several years past the charitable fund which they had set up had proved insufficient to discharge the grants they wished to make: now they drew up a supplementary deed increasing the income to £2000 a year.

In such worthy and undramatic pursuits the years between the German Wars slipped by. Their apprenticeship scheme – the sole vestige of their Trade activities – waxed and waned. Sometimes the number of boys fell as low as three and then, just when it seemed as if the scheme would altogether fail, there would be a revival of interest and the number would rise again to twenty.

In 1932 – a year in which the Pewterers, whose Hall was to be demolished, sought and were granted asylum – admissions to the Cutlers' Livery were restricted with the intention of limiting the numbers to ninety but by 1935 it was decided that, at the discretion of the Court, that number might be raised.

Members were still happy to present the Company with gifts which expressed, in their individual fashion, the old loyalty to the gild: the Clerk presented a loving cup to celebrate one hundred years of continuous Beaumont Clerkship and Mr. A. Goodwin, a Liveryman, gave 'a pair of splendid Elephant Tusks which he had obtained as the result of a shooting expedition in Uganda'.

But, as the fears of an even greater shooting expedition in Europe began to grow, the atmosphere of agreeable but uninteresting prosperity began to change.

Property became suddenly less desirable. There was considerable difficulty in letting the Company premises in Watling Street and Friday Street. It might be a good idea, the surveyor thought, to give them a lick of paint in the Spring and brighten them up a little. In spite of such set-backs the Company rejected the idea of budgetary control of their finances and they held out until 1937 against proposals to employ professional auditors for their accounts.

Even then, in that coronation year, there seemed no need for any great alarm: the country had enjoyed many years in which to re-arm and the Government assured the people that Britain was fully prepared. The Coronation Dinner was held and small gifts were presented to the Livery. The Company had insufficient liquidity to adopt a Territorial Unit and the proposal was reluctantly turned down. As a matter of policy and becoming tired of the difficulty, in spite of the repainting, that they experienced in disposing of the leases in Friday Street and Watling Street, they sold these properties for about £11,000, the greater part of which was applied to paying off their mortgage.

By October 1938 they were thinking hard, in spite of the assurances of peace in our time, about ensuring the safety of the Hall against air-raids and in the Spring of 1939 the country, as a whole, was in a fever of preparation for war. Territorial soldiers returning from their camps, the previous summer, had disclosed the fantastic disarray in which they had found the defences, largely unequipped, to be standing. The Cutlers' Company were now, like everybody else, seeking every possible means for protecting their property. They were represented, that May, at a meeting at the Mansion House at which national defence was discussed and in the same month past-Master Perkins, Senior Warden Jeffkins and the clerk took the most valuable plate and the early records of the Company to Barclay's Bank in Barnstaple for safe-keeping. It was decided that no action should be taken about removing and storing the stained-glass windows of the Hall, although this was the only way, so it was said, to protect them: instead they were boarded-up from outside.

The Court decided to construct air-raid shelters at the Belle Sauvage but not, for the moment, at the Hall. There the Beadle and his family had selected an already reasonably safe position, near the wine cellar, for which no further constructional work was deemed necessary.

On 1 September the movable objects of value, such as clocks, pictures and ornaments, were collected from around the Hall and removed to a safer position underground and the Court ordered that the current records be photocopied. Two days later war was declared.

19

A New Age Begins

1939–1975

AFTER the initial shaming moment of panic that greeted the first false alert that sounded shortly after the declaration of war against Germany – a panic in which fear of the unknown surely played an important part – London settled down to the unreal months of the 'phoney War'.

In December it was even found possible to arrange a Ladies' Lunch at Cutlers' Hall, at which no doubt the guests discussed the proposal made by the Lady Mayoress in October that the Court and Livery should persuade their womenfolk to become members of the rather grandiloquently titled *War Emergency Council of the City of London Branch of the Red Cross Society* 'for making various garments for the wounded'.

In the meantime the records and such small valuables as had not been 'evacuated' were placed in the strong-room in a safe sealed against flooding.

The unnatural state of inaction on the war front continued: on 1 May 1940 it was decided to hold the Captain F. G. Boot Dinner for the Livery – with a lady or gentleman guest – under the usual terms of the will.

But by June the matter was, not unnaturally, deferred. After the swingeing defeat of the Allies and the seemingly almost miraculous escape of the British through Dunkirk Great Britain had become a beleaguered island, in which, apart from any such considerations as that of the rationing of food, the physical assaults of the enemy upon the City made such occasions as the Boot Dinner highly unattractive. For this reason in July, the commemoration was a

simple one: the Court, after an adjournment to inspect the basement refuge, returned to the Court Room and there 'drank to the
memory of Captain Francis George Boot and the Clerk read the
relevant extract from Captain Boot's Will'.

There were many ingenious propaganda devices to involve the
citizen in a personal commitment to the war effort. It is now hardly
to be doubted that the country would, in any case, have manufactured all the weapons of war that it was possible to manufacture
and that cost was not a matter for consideration in the face of
survival. But the civilian was made to feel that his personal out-of-
pocket contribution towards the purchase of an aircraft or a tank
or a battleship was no less vitally necessary than it had been in the
old days when the City and the citizens had paid for the *Loyal
London*.

In September the Cutlers received the first of such appeals in the
form of a letter from the *Provisional Committee of the National War Effort
Fund of the Jewellery, Watch, Clock & Metal Trades* inviting them to join
in the effort to give the Government two presents – a fighter
aircraft and a Red Cross mobile X-ray unit. They were not impressed by this weighty title and took no action. Nor did they have
any money to spare for the London Area Home Guard Welfare
Fund. They were greatly concerned with financial survival in so
uncertain and dangerous a world. The payments by their smaller
tenants had been reduced because of the decay of trade and the
rent paid by the Pewterers had been similarly reduced 'under the
present circumstances of rising expenses and that they do not use
the Hall as much as they used to'. And although the remains of the
Irish Estates were to be sold and the assets distributed among the
Salters, the Cutlers and the Joiners, there was little cash immediately available.

The raids upon the country in general and the City in particular
were increasing. On the night of 15–16 November damage was done
to the Cutlers' Belle Sauvage property which had already suffered
during raids in August. It became clear that fire was to become as
dangerous a weapon as explosives and in December the Court
contrived plans to protect the Hall against incendiary bombs.

Night-watchmen were urgently required but 'the main difficulty was the dearth of suitable men for the job'. It was suggested that a system of mutual aid with local firms be organized: the Clerk was to enquire whether it might be possible to compile a rota of watchers among the Livery. At last the Court discovered a fire-watcher. For £1 a week and the provision of bed and breakfast he was to attend at the Hall during the hours of black-out, to sleep there, to go on duty whenever there was an 'alert' and to help the Beadle to fight any fires that might break out.

Sand and water were to be provided on all floors.

But on 29 December 1940 a fire-raid was launched against the City on a scale that utterly dwarfed the Cutlers' modest defences.

It was Fred Hall, the Beadle and Hall-keeper, who described to the Clerk, Mr. Champness, what happened on that dreadful night. The Clerk's subsequent report to the Court may be quoted in some detail.

Soon after 6.30 p.m. the 'Alert' sirens sounded and almost at once incendiary bombs rained down thickly from the sky. The noise of enemy aircraft overhead was loud and continuous and very quickly ugly-looking fires began to spring up on all sides. Towards the Cathedral a great blaze commenced to light up the sky. The buildings on the North side of St. Paul's churchyard . . . were alight and Paternoster Row, with its houses of well-known publishers, was soon in flames.

Then buildings at the end of Ave Maria Lane were seized by the flames and a huge fire began to creep northwards towards Warwick Lane and Cutlers' Hall.

There was a fresh light wind to fan the flames and for some reason the water-pressure failed so that no hoses could be used and the firemen stood by, powerless. It is said that, although water was subsequently obtained from the Thames, the tide was for this purpose too low during the earlier stages of the fire. So for two hours the great fire raged, eating up building after building in its greedy fury and every minute creeping nearer to our Hall.

It must indeed have been an awful and terrifying spectacle to the Halls, standing at their side-door, to see the flames coming closer, with two great fires bearing down on them – one raging up Warwick Lane and the other along Newgate Street. When the flames reached Warwick Square the Halls were ordered to leave Cutlers' Hall and, with a few clothes and belongings hastily got together, Hall and a [A.R.P.] Warden took Mrs. Hall to a place of greater safety in Old Bailey. But Fred Hall refused to quit his post and took up his stand on the steps of the old General Post Office building in Newgate Street, whence he could watch the progress of the fire as it approached the hall.

Two thoughts were uppermost in his mind at this dramatic moment – first 'to see what was going to happen to the hall' and second 'to keep an eye on the wine-cellar'. As he stood there, watching, he saw the flames cross the opening to Warwick Square on the West side of Warwick Lane and attack . . . premises next door but one to the hall; while on the east side of the Lane the fire swept on and engulfed the tall building facing the hall on the opposite side of the narrow street.

It now seemed that nothing could save the hall from the fate suffered by the rest of Warwick Lane; when suddenly, after what was literally hours but must have seemed like days to those who stood anxiously by, the waiting firemen heard the glad sound of water in the hoses, the pressure came on and the hungry flames were checked and finally beaten back. The firemen got up on to the roof of the hall and flooded it with water to stop flying sparks from the buildings getting a hold.

Thus was Cutlers' Hall saved at the eleventh hour, suffering no damage but some comparatively unimportant glass cracked by the intense heat of the surrounding inferno. Practically the whole of the rest of Warwick Lane was left a desolate waste of smouldering ruins.

In 1924 the Company had commissioned from a Mr. Thomas a wrought iron sign, incorporating the Cutlers' elephant, to hang outside the front door of the Hall. Now, in the smoking aftermath of the holocaust, it provided a note of anthropomorphically sentimental symbolism.

What, asked the Clerk rhetorically, were the Beadle's feelings as he witnessed the almost miraculous escape of Cutlers' Hall?

Let this account conclude with his own simply picturesque and dramatic words as he told the story to the Master: 'I looked down the Lane' (he said) 'at the old Jumbo to see whether he'd stand up to it – and, Master, he did!'

The Cutlers' Hall had escaped. Others, that night, were less fortunate. Eight City Companies lost their Halls, nine Wren churches were wrecked and Guildhall was damaged. The Cutlers, in common with other Companies, provided accommodation for those whose premises had become unusable: the Turners, Plumbers and Spectacle-makers all held their meetings at Cutlers' Hall.

And the Company, in addition to working out neighbourhood schemes for mutual aid, continued to hire a full time fire-watcher.

Some of the war-time problems were of an unusual kind and led to unexpected bonuses. What, for example, was to happen to the large stocks of port in the Hall cellars? There were no dinners and all might at any moment be destroyed: the Court decided that each Member should be given six bottles of the Taylor '27 – provided he collected it himself. Another 40 dozen of Croft '20 were sold at 95/- a dozen.

Quite soon, their caution was seen to be justified: on the night of 10/11 May 1941 – a night on which six more Companies lost their Halls – Cutlers' Hall was extensively damaged when a high-explosive bomb demolished their neighbours on the corner of Warwick Lane and Newgate Street. Those on the staff escaped, shaken but unhurt. The north main wall had been demolished, the north-west party-wall badly cracked; one end of the Livery Hall had been left exposed and part of the floor torn away. This much could be immediately seen but it was impossible to judge the full extent of the damage as the property was 'encumbered at the North End by a great mass of debris of this building and of the adjoining, totally demolished, building'.

Things might well have been worse and at the next Court meeting 'on the suggestion of Past Master Perkins, the Master moved a resolution of thankfulness that the harm to the Company had not been greater and for the preservation that had been vouchsafed, with all present standing in silence'.

Advice was taken about providing first-aid for the premises; the cost, it was estimated, would be something in the region of £1750, a calculation which raised certain further problems under a system in which, by Government decree, no more than £500 might be spent on such repairs.

In that great raid upon London other of the Company's properties had suffered damage or destruction: the whole of the estate on Ludgate Hill was badly hit and some of Belle Sauvage Yard totally wiped out. These, with the Watling Street Estates which had also been destroyed, involved a considerable loss of rental income which was likely to cause a probable deficit of £3000 a year. Drastic economies were necessary: although the Committee were still to meet when necessary the Court was to meet quarterly instead of monthly and the services of a professional accountant for their audits were dispensed with. There were to be no black-out curtains at the Hall but instead the windows were to be covered with brown paper. The Clerk, whose salary had been increased by £100 a year in view of the extra work that war-conditions imposed, nobly insisted that the decision be rescinded until such time as the state of the financial resources of the Company should be more clearly seen.

Salvage work at the Hall began. Some objects of value were removed to areas thought to be less unsafe: a tall-case clock was stored with Past Master Perkins at Bushey; the Company streamer was taken from the Victoria and Albert Museum, where it had been deposited immediately after the Hall had been torn open, and stored in the most secure part of Sheriff Boot's house in Maidenhead; one copy of the Minutes was to be lodged in a bank at Sevenoaks.

And, although all these items successfully weathered the storms of explosive and fire the suburbs were by no means entirely safe: in June that year there was severe damage to the Company's properties, recently bequeathed to them by Macdonald Beaumont, in Thornton Heath. The difficulties of day to day administration were increased by the appointment of the Clerk to join a branch of the Ministry of Food at Colwyn Bay – but his place was taken by his father and his personal clerk, and by September when the gas supply was reconnected something approaching a war-time normality had been restored to the Hall.

As far as the City was concerned the very worst was over and with 1942 the gradual recovery began.

Once again the Minutes contracted in size and diminished in interest. The Court made only two major decisions in 1942 and they both concerned temporary matters: in order to maintain a continuity of expertize in negotiations concerning the damaged Hall, the Master and wardens were re-elected for a second year, and, because of the fall in their income the charitable grants made by the Company were to be limited for the next seven years to an annual £1000.

But there were tiny signs for those who cared to see them of a stirring of hope. An order was placed for wines and spirits; it was for a miniscule amount – barely fifty guineas' worth – but it was something. A member who had been refused invitations to the Company's functions since 1929 was reinstated. The Company decided to send representatives to the Royal Courts of Justice on Lord Mayor's Day – though that was, no doubt, because the Mayor and one of his Sheriffs were Cutlers.

By 1943 the signs of future recovery were increasing. At St. Paul's Cathedral the first United Guilds Service was held. The normal monthly Court Meetings were renewed: after one of them some members of the American Forces were entertained to luncheon.

Members of the Company were again shewing their affection and loyalty by gifts and bequests: Captain Potts, a prisoner-of-war in Japan, gave a grand pianoforte to the Hall; past-Master Howard G. Potts first caused the Committee Room to be panelled with Jacobean oak removed from Lady Carnarvon's house in Regent's Park and then furnished it appropriately with items which included, if the Minutes are to be believed, 'an antique Refractory Table'. Horace Boot bequeathed £3000 to be spent upon an annual 'Sir Horace Boot Luncheon'. The feeling that the Company was a family affair was never very far distant.

The Company were also pleased to receive a letter from the Senior Warden's son-in-law who was serving as a surgeon with the North East African Forces: 'You may be interested to know that, of all the Instruments we use, "Down Bros" are quite easily the best. I suppose I've done about 650 fairly biggish cases since being out. . . .'

The Cutlers passed on this handsome and unsolicited testimonial to the firm concerned and received an appropriately gratifying reply:

It has always been our great desire to gain a reputation for excellent work, rather than the realization of profit, and although we can justly claim to have taken great care in the training of our apprentices, we wish to acknowledge how great a share is due to the interest taken by your Company in the encouragement of apprentices and the emulation caused by the yearly inspection of their work . . .

To the Cutlers, in fact, the War was now more of a nuisance than an immediate physical danger. There were the propagandist 'Wings for Victory' Weeks – 'an aeroplane and other exhibits' were exposed upon the Company's bombed site in Ludgate Hill to encourage the public to present themselves, through their Government, with such warlike gifts.

Already the War Damage Commission was dealing with the Company claims: they agreed that seven properties in Belle Sauvage Yard, four houses in Ludgate Hill and one in Poplar would come into the category of buildings involving 'total loss'.

By 1944 it was possible again to enjoy the luxury of indulging in purely internal politics and the Company's eminent lawyer, Sir John Beaumont, requested that a formal record be made of his objection to being passed over in the election of Junior Warden without having first been consulted: it was clear that the failure of communication was more important than the act of exclusion. Of course, there were still a few last dangers to be survived as the enemy's secret weapons, the flying bombs and the rockets, briefly bombarded the City before the advancing Allies over-ran their launching sites. The Cutlers' property in Balls Pond Road was among others damaged in the closing aerial attacks of the War. But already the advance plans for peace and reconstruction could be discussed without the feeling that they were indulging in *hubris* to a dangerous degree. And the Georgian Society made what might be considered an uncharacteristically bizarre suggestion that, in the restoration of Cutlers' Hall, it might be possible to incorporate the façade of the Pantheon from Oxford Street – a suggestion that the Court found 'unsuitable'.

1945 was the year of victory in Europe, and, in spite of rationing, it was possible once again to hold a Court and Ladies' Dinner and to plan for a similar function for the Livery in the following year, when hostilities finally ended and the processes of demobilization of the Forces began to accelerate. Plans were now prepared for rebuilding the Hall and the plate came back in good condition from the vaults in Barnstaple to its old setting.

From Warwick Lane, on the other hand, went 'a piece of carved oak salvaged from the roof of Cutlers' Hall'. It was a Masonic gift to the 'Master of the Ancient St. John's Lodge No. 3 of Kingston, Ontario . . . for the purpose of making working tools for his Lodge. The worshipful Master had expressed a wish to procure timber with some history attaching to it' and it was thought that 'a piece from the damaged Cutlers' Hall would be suitable'.

With this return to normality the Company were able to settle down to the serious business of managing their properties. As war damage payments began to flow in the great question arose as to how the money was to be invested: there was, for example, in 1948 some £30,000 available from four houses in Belle Sauvage Yard and £11,000 in 'Value Payments' on two Ludgate Hill properties. And there were other amounts pending. Wisely the Court decided to reinvest in property. In order to do this they had to apply for increases in the value of land they were permitted to hold in mortmain. Eventually they decided to obtain a supplementary Charter under which they would not only be allowed to hold lands to an unlimited value but would also be absolved from any forfeitures which might have arisen from accidentally infringing the Statute of Mortmain. By 1949, when another £15,000 was obtained from Belle Sauvage Yard, they had received what was by now a very necessary authorization for their property holdings although they were, in fact, limited to an annual value of £30,000.

The Belle Sauvage Estate brought, with its profits, a number of problems. First of all it was learned that the Corporation were contemplating the compulsory purchase of the Yard and of property in Ludgate Hill. The Company, therefore, to protect their interests decided to put forward their own plans for developing the site upon a building lease although there was little likelihood of such schemes being accepted. The position was further complicated by the fact that the Electricity Board wanted part of the property and there were other official claimants for other parcels of land: it was hard for the Cutlers to avoid the fate of being finally left with a number of tiny, unusable and indisposable fragments of the land. The problem was crystallized the following year when it became apparent that the City Planning Authority would want 12,000 square feet for widening Seacoal Lane – midway through the site from North to South – and that the London Electricity Board would need 9750 square feet for their installations: this would leave no more than a long narrow strip of land along Ludgate Hill. The Company Surveyor, therefore, recommended that application be made to develop the whole site. This would certainly be refused and the Company could then serve a notice requiring the Corporation compulsorily to purchase the whole site.

In the meantime, although considerable capital sums were becoming available, the Company accounts were causing alarm in certain quarters. The Clerk, in 1950, pointed out that 'the Company was continuing to spend very considerably more than its total income and that this could not go on indefinitely without the Company's capital investments being ultimately exhausted. He suggested that the day would inevitably come when a drastic reduction in expenditure in certain directions would have to be considered'.

And one member of the Committee refused to approve the acceptance of the audited accounts until the Court had been alerted.

Eventually, however, it was decided that there was no need at that time to recommend any action. And certainly it might be thought that the investment income from the capital sums received would be for the moment sufficient.

Now their Minutes were occupied, almost entirely, with the problems arising from their property holdings.

Yet there were occasional entries of a less specialized nature: there were, now and again, faint stirrings of what had once been Company matters of greater import. A Liveryman, for instance, wished to resign and was told 'it did not appear possible to resign from the Livery' – a judgement that was, perhaps, mistaken, for in earlier days there had been instances in which members had been compelled to resign from the Livery. However, the request was noted and a form of Limbo created in which no more communications would be made with the Liveryman concerned until he notified the Court that he had changed his mind.

And the Cutlers still interested themselves in apprenticeships, although it appears that by 1951 they had given up paying all – or, in some cases, even part – of the indentures. There were now about forty young men in training who still received the 10/- gift that had become a somewhat nominal Christmas box.

There were also signs, after the years of austerity and although there were still several years of rationing to be endured, of a return to the lighter social side of Company life.

The Dining Hall had, by 1949, been sufficiently repaired for dinners to be once more held in it: the Boar's Head Feast – a ceremony of great antiquity but not a part of the Cutlers' celebrations until some time in the third decade of the twentieth century – again took place there that year.

In 1951 the stocks of wine were to be replenished and there were all the preparations for celebrating the Festival of Britain – an attempt to disperse the post-war inertia with an inspired Exhibition that attracted the same sort of attack from Lord Beaverbrook as had been launched, no less unreasonably, one hundred years earlier by the ineffable Colonel Sibthorpe against the Crystal Palace. Undeterred by the *Daily Express*, the City planned its modest contributions to the Festival: an exhibition of plate at Goldsmiths' Hall, 'popular accounts of City Companies', the opening to the public of Livery Halls and flagstaffs in St. Paul's Churchyard.

The Cutlers agreed to furnish details for publication in the pamphlet of what their Company was doing in the fields of technical education, the encouragement of craftsmanship, and so on: they would guarantee, too, a maximum purchase of pamphlets to the value of £10 in case the publishers found themselves facing a loss.

Towards their own private celebration Mr. John Wilkinson Latham presented them with a ceremonial sword made by himself: 'an example of contemporary craftsmanship embodying the ancient crafts of the bladesmith, the forger, the sheather, the haftmaker, the silversmith and the cutler'. He suggested that it might be used ceremonially on certain occasions at the Hall.

The Court expressed their gratification that such a splendid piece of contemporary craftsmanship should have been made by a Liveryman – in the old days such a comment would hardly have been necessary – and considered the idea that the sword should be carried before the Master at the Company's dinners. They consulted Sir Gerald Woolaston, the Norroy King of Arms, upon the suitability of such a ceremony. His reply was discouraging:

the Sword carried before the Lord Mayor in the City was emblematic of the King's Justice in the City and that was why the Lord Mayor surrendered it whenever the King came to the City. It seemed to Sir Gerald that a sword is altogether inappropriate to a City Company for ceremonial purposes and he could not see what meaning it would have carried in procession before the Master of the Company. Sir Gerald went on to say that no doubt the Master and Wardens of the Company have or had authority to punish wrongdoers in their Company but it seemed to be stretching this rather far to carry the sword of justice before the Master. . . .

The committee, therefore, decided that the sword should not be carried but should be placed 'in a prominent position'.

The Festival of Britain was followed by the coronation of a new monarch: the accession of Elizabeth II to the throne recalled nostalgically to those who knew little about them the days of the first Elizabeth. Hopes for a revival of Britain's greatness were everywhere expressed in terms that owed more to sentiment than to practicality: it was ironical that the less desirable attributes of the first Elizabethan age were those that were the first to become apparent.

In the meantime, preparations for a Merrie-England-style river pageant, from Greenwich to Westminster, were afoot. The organizers envisaged the state barges of the Companies, headed by the Lord Mayor and by Naval and Merchant vessels. In view of the cost of hiring such a craft and of fitting it out, and because insufficient time had been allowed for the preparations, the Cutlers elected to take no part. And the splendid turn-out expected from the twelve great Companies was, in the event, reduced to a single water-bus hired – and decorated at a cost of £600 – between them all. Could not – the organizers pleaded – the minor Companies at any rate do likewise? The Clerk considered that, because of the paucity of information or advice from the organizers, few would join in such a venture. They, therefore, took no action.

They shewed less reluctance when Field-Marshal Earl Alexander wished to revive, in that coronation year, the custom whereby, from Elizabethan days, the Livery Companies were linked with the Auxiliary Forces. The Lord Mayor, in forwarding the scheme, considered that it was important for the City's prestige that the fostering of units by the City Companies should be encouraged: the Cutlers agreed to adopt a unit of the Territorial Army. For the Cutlers' Company the immediate necessity was to formulate an investment policy that would take into consideration the very real dangers which, although currency inflation was still within acceptable bounds, were to be anticipated. Eventually they decided upon a policy that would divide their investments: two-thirds of their resources should be placed in freehold ground-rents; the remaining third in 'Gilt-edge (long or non-dated), first class debentures or good class insurance ordinary shares'.

Although, with hindsight, it is possible to fault the investment in gilt-edge, the policy was adopted: £35,000 was immediately transferred to a 'portfolio' yielding a gross percentage of £3. 14s. 6d. and when further sums were received from the City for the compulsory purchases of their lands, £50,000 was to be immediately invested in insurance shares.

The value of capital was already beginning to decline: the income from the Sir Horace Boot Fund, instead of providing a luncheon, was now sufficient only for a cocktail party. But property was still a safe investment. Through a commercial agent the Cutlers set about negotiating for small properties on a wide scale: at Aldershot, Hove, King's Lynn and Swindon. In 1954 properties were bought at Watford and Hounslow: when they viewed the latter premises it is permissible to wonder whether any race memories stirred within the Committee – memories of Benjamin Stone and the Hounslow sword manufactory 'of unexampled perfection' and the fiasco that it had all turned out to be.

Some of the small properties they already held in such places as Poplar were with their weekly rents fixed at 12/-, or thereabouts, and with many essential repairs to be carried out, proving to be rather indifferent investments. Nor, if they were to be sold – as sold they eventually were to a Poplar dealer – could the Company expect more than about £50 for each house.

By 1955 the Court were able to assess the working of their policies: the insurance shares had gone up; the gilt-edge had gone down. There was a total capital appreciation of some £8500 but there were still those who were worried by the financial situation: Sir John Beaumont, for one, 'expressed the opinion that the Company should now live on its income'. There was, in fact, a change in the presentation of the accounts: the Court recorded, genially enough, that the wine stock had now been included in liquid assets.

Thus the new Elizabethan age proceeded, apparently, into post-war normality but, in fact, towards perils that were entirely new and unforeseen.

But for the moment it was the normality that prevailed. The Cutlers, in their Hall, were able to act as hosts to other City Companies still, for one reason or another, dispossessed. From time to time they made accommodation available to the Butchers, Carmen, Fletchers, Glaziers, Glovers, Joiners, Pewterers, Plaisterers, Plumbers, Upholders and Wax Chandlers. But, at the same time, the repairs to the war damage at the Hall were still being carried out. The restoration that had continued throughout the whole of 1955 was still unfinished in 1958: the difficulty, it appeared, was in obtaining the great blocks of Mansfield stone without which the work could not be completed. And, although there were hopes that supplies might soon be procured, the Company encountered the usual disappointments attendant on any building scheme: when the undamaged stones were taken down many of them were found to be incapable of further use. The frontage provided many difficult and irreconcilable angles: as the report put it, 'no one surface squares up to another'.

While the work was still going on there suddenly arose a serious incident that might well have resulted in the already damaged Hall being destroyed to an extent unachieved by the Germans. For on 30 June 1959 while the Inventory Dinner was being held, a serious fire broke out only two doors away from the Hall, at 5 Warwick Lane. 'Within half an hour the fire assumed serious

proportions and some 30 appliances and a considerable number of
firemen and policemen were at work. Clouds of choking smoke
made the firemen's task very difficult and several were overcome.
Beginning in the basement the fire ascended the lift-shaft and at
9 p.m., despite the efforts of the firemen, the roof caught fire and
flames roared high above the top of the building. . . .'

Only one narrow building stood between the fire and the Hall
and there was an obvious danger that the flames might jump the
intervening roof at the rear of the properties where the premises
were crowded together and difficult of access.

Firemen, policemen, journalists – all ran in and out of the Hall
to make telephone calls or to observe the progress of the fire. In
the face of this invasion the staff achieved prodigies in hastily
removing objects of value to the strong room.

The Senior Warden was subsequently to comment, on behalf of
all who attended the dinner, on 'the admirable bearing and attitude
of the Beadle under the difficult conditions imposed. . . . The fact
that the Beadle was able to regulate the comings and goings of a
large number of strangers in the Hall, to make sure that all the
valuables were looked after and that no damage was occasioned
and yet to keep the dinner arrangements running smoothly was observed by
guests and members alike. . . .' The italics are ours for the phrase
sums up the extraordinary skills generally exhibited by the most
ancient officers of the Livery Companies. On this occasion 'the
Master was at pains not to introduce any alarm to the proceedings
and the Inventory Dinner was completed, toasts drunk and
speeches made, but when the lights failed the company broke up
and began marshalling cars, some of which had been removed
from nearby to make room for fire appliances. The Hall suffered
but one broken pane of glass and there was some flooding of the
basement which was soon cleared up with no ill effect. . . .'

A splendid picture may be conjured up by this account: the
crackle of the flames, the smoke, the roar of pumps, the cries and
shouts, the trample of strangers rushing in and out of the building,
to telephone and observe – and, all the while, the toasting and the
speeches continuing until, with the failure of the lights, all, listeners
and speakers alike, were plunged into darkness.

It is impossible not to admire such imperturbability. Six months later, when the lights again failed, at a Ladies' Dinner, the Court decided to investigate a simple system of emergency lighting.

A crisis of another kind was now upon the Court. They were faced, suddenly, with the difficulty of filling the office of Junior Warden. The number of the Court was restricted and if there were no vacancy then no member of the Livery could be elevated and there was none to serve as Junior Warden. It was a predicament that had not previously arisen: there was, in fact, in times of such difficulty, ample precedent for those who had filled the various offices to repeat the cycle eight or ten years later.

But now in 1960 it seemed that this solution was not available and Sir John Beaumont proposed that a supplemental Charter be obtained in which the Court members could be varied between twenty and thirty according to need. As it happened an assistant resigned that year, causing a vacancy, and so the matter was held in abeyance. But the thought of what was to happen in future years was naturally ever-present. In 1962 past-Master W. A. Herbert resigned 'owing to the increasing difficulty of attendance and in order to facilitate the election of a younger man' – a gesture which was much appreciated by the Court who expressed the hope that he would continue to attend the Company functions 'as Past Master Emeritus'. And then past-Master Jeffkins died, which made the succession of warden secure for yet another year. But it was clearly an uneasy and not altogether satisfactory situation.

Another situation that caused some misgivings was raised, in 1965, by that tireless old lawyer Sir John Beaumont who was by now the Father of the Company. A special sub-committee was appointed to report upon the vexed question of 'Contracts with Assistants'. It was the opinion of their Counsel that

in law any contracts entered into by the Company with any member of the Court of Assistants, or with any firm or company of which a member of the Court of Assistants was a partner, director or even a shareholder, is not legally binding and can be avoided at the instance of the Company.

Their counsel recognized that this was most inconvenient and could lead to absurd conclusions; he regretted the position in which they found themselves and suggested that they might seek an amending Charter to cover any such situations as might arise.

It was Sir John who 'forcibly' pointed out the adverse publicity that must inevitably arise from any such public application and he was, undoubtedly, right: one of the many untrue assertions against the City in the evidence to the Royal Commission of 1874 had been of the 'jobbing' of contracts to members of the Courts of the Livery Companies. To revive any such conceit could now hardly fail to attract the unfavourable attention of 'the media'. Instead the Committee recommended a new Standing Order to lay down the general principle that contracts should not be entered into with Assistants of their Companies. But should the Court be satisfied that such a contract was, in the best interests of the Company either by reason of difficulties of placing it elsewhere, or because price or convenience made it desirable, then they should go as far as the law allowed them to grant such a Contract. The Order naturally included stringent stipulations for the declaration of interest by those involved and for their exclusion both from voting or even from forming a quorum.

Thus when, in the nineteen seventies, there came to light a growing spate of instances of corruption amongst politicians and local government officers and professional men throughout the country it could reasonably be supposed that the Cutlers' Company were utterly unlikely to be involved in any such dubious activities.

Their internal activities and problems were, indeed, all of a very minor nature. It was now the declared policy of the Court that the Livery should be 'well-informed', and, to this desirable end, a talk was arranged in 1966 in which the Comptroller and City Solicitor explained 'The Government and functions of the City and the part available therein to the Liveryman'. The number of such members of the Company was increased first to ninety-five and later to a hundred – those taking up the Livery after the previous limit of ninety had been reached were to be warned as they did so that the seating accommodation in the Dining Hall was limited. One application for Membership, received from a Freeman living on the Continent, caused great discussion. Could he really swear allegiance to the Queen?; could he attend Livery functions?; would he not be taking the place of a Freeman resident in the United Kingdom?

'The Court were reminded that the country might soon be part of the European Community when it might become commonplace for members to be drawn from abroad.' Although this may seem to be slightly over-stating the case, the Clerk was instructed to find out if he really intended to remain British and how he would carry out his Livery duties.

There came, from time to time, reminders of their nominal trade. The apprenticeship scheme was still active and was extended to include those in the polishing trade; means of securing the retention in the trade of surgical instrument apprentices when they qualified was explored; the Company acquired a collection of antique cutlery to add to the historic specimens they already possessed; to this purchase were joined gifts – a seventeenth-century knife from an American collector and a ceremonial sword from Messrs Wilkinson who, celebrating their bi-centenary, wished to mark their long association with the Cutlers' Company.

So the darkening years went hurrying by. And as they did so the Cutlers began to demonstrate that *zeitgeist* by which, in times of present unpleasantness, there is a tendency to pre-occupation with the past: they considered the suggestion that a dagger and scabbard should be introduced into the ceremony of the loving cup but decided that the problems involved outweighed the attractiveness of the idea; they entrenched the tradition of the Boar's Head Feast; they decided to have compiled an account of their own very considerable history. . . .

But, all this while, it was the Cutlers' real estate that continued to provide the greatest and most vitally important part of their activities. Their property in College Hill they sold to the Skinners who were consolidating their own estates in that area; some buildings that they owned in Watford were also sold. More and more funds were thus becoming available for re-investment: the proposal was made to acquire properties in Newgate Street, next to the Hall, and lease them – with certain options to purchase the lease – to a developer for 125 years at a premium equal to the purchase price and five per cent of the rack rents. And although the first developer withdrew from the scheme others were soon found. In the building that was subsequently erected – in its name it perpetuated their great benefactor Craythorne – the Cutlers rented a small portion to make such additions to the Hall as a flat for the Master.

In 1963 they sold their Charing Cross Road Estate for £155,000 and invested the money in short-term loans in order to have cash instantly available for further property deals. The following year the Balls Pond properties were sold. By the time of the 550th anniversary of their original Charter they had already built up very considerable reserves and by 1968 they had accumulated some £235,000 which they maintained on deposit. In spite of the objections of Sir John Beaumont the Committee recommended no permanent investments – the money might be needed suddenly for the purchase of real property. To this respectable sum they were able to add other amounts raised by the sale both of stocks and of the valuable options that they held to repurchase the lease of Craythorne House.

In 1972 the man who was perhaps most responsible for the Cutlers' advance to prosperity – Howard Potts, who had been Master eighteen years earlier – died. He it was who had modernized the Company's system of keeping accounts; he had initiated the breakaway from the dead-hand of gilt-edge 'securities'; he had diversified the Company's investments and had thereby transformed their finances. He had also done much to transform their Hall: among other notable activities he had panelled the committee-room, designed the heraldic wall-paper, rebuilt the minstrels' gallery, restored the roof of the banqueting hall, furnished the Craythorne Master's suite. And, at the time of his death, it was clear that the Company had been well-advised to keep their funds 'liquid': with interest rates at a level that to their ancestors would have seemed unbelievable and in a stock market that was to decline in value by more than fifty per cent in eighteen months they were, by 1974, most enviably placed to take advantage of any opportunities that might arise.

The opportunities, as the Cutlers entered the last quarter of the twentieth century, were to be snatched as they occurred. For perhaps never in the whole of their history had the problems of planning for the future been more obscure or more difficult to assess. Certainly the potential dangers that faced the nation were as great as any as had yet been borne.

There were, of course, certain familiar features that they had encountered – sometimes repeatedly – before. There was, for example, inflation: they had already survived several severe attacks when, as we have seen, the groat in their pockets had been reduced at a stroke to half its face value. There was violence: to the Cutlers there was nothing new about that – the greater part of their story had taken place against a frightening background of violence and cruelty. They had already faced the problems of the Mob learning, as it descended on to the streets, the meaning of power. There was Ireland: that problem had been with them for ever. There might be civil war: it was an event that was by now by no means impossible to envisage and this they had experienced on at least two occasions. Dictatorship – another eventuality that had become by no means unthinkable – they knew all about: they had suffered too often the tyranny of Kings and Parliaments. There was the familiar face of crippling taxation to which the Stuarts, in particular, had accustomed them. There was State interference which they had already fully experienced under the writ of Quo Warranto and which had again been attempted in the nineteenth century: if now they were to suffer at the hands of the Orwellian 'shiny-bottomed bureaucrats' there was nothing intrinsically new about that.

It is tempting to draw from these historical precedents the facile deduction that there was nothing that could not, once again, be cured – or endured. But now there was an additional complication: many of the dangers arose from circumstances which were impossible for the nation, of itself, to control. The world had shrunk to the concept of a 'Global Village' in which the peasants, in the guise of the 'Third World' or the 'Emergent Nations', were able to impoverish the squirearchy who depended upon them for their raw materials – oil and copper and, indeed, all the necessities that were not found upon the squires' land, necessities which, at the same time, were being consumed and wasted at a terrifying rate by an explosively expanding world population. The so-called 'energy crisis' affecting supplies of oil was the first manifestation of the new problems.

Moreover, in the global village, news spread as rapidly as in any old-fashioned country hamlet: within minutes of some act of revolt or anarchy being committed the whole world knew the facts and everywhere there were many men of ill-will who were only too ready and anxious everywhere to imitate and emulate. The old truism was reversed: it was now good communications that corrupted manners. And in a world of such civilized complexity, in which the inhabitants were so interdependent one upon the other, it was possible for almost any minority group, however small, to use the power of its own little sector utterly to disrupt the rest in order to obtain a temporary and often illusory advantage. Loyalties seemed to be reverting from the Nation to the Tribe.

Under the stress of such a situation, many of the old values were no longer to be sustained: the exhortation, for example, that to work hard was a prescription for success could be instantly refuted: a man might work hard all his life and at the moment of his success be plunged overnight into unemployment by a merger for the sake of 'rationalization' or by the 'take-over' of his business. And, however unreasonably the young might appear to behave, it had now become increasingly difficult to maintain with any credibility that their elders knew better – a sure recipe for instability.

Yet in such a situation of uncertainty there did remain one remarkable constant. The Cutlers, in common with the other Livery Companies, still operated as a voluntary organization. Of course there were salaried staffs of experts without whom the day-to-day burden of administration would have been impossible to bear but the ethos, the strategy, the will to survive and prosper and fight on behalf of those charitable causes that they had made particularly their own were all the responsibility of the unpaid volunteer. It was almost incredible to realize that this system of dedicated and disinterested amateurism had survived for much more than a thousand years. From the small groups banded together for self-protection, with the headman responsible for the good behaviour of the individuals in his group, to the great charitable property-owning empires that the Livery Companies had become, all had survived and had grown and had been sustained through voluntary effort. Kings had been made and unmade; governments had been elected and unseated; the country's wealth had been built-up and, often, its financial survival secured – all the time by amateurs.

To the tidy and rationally minded it was undoubtedly outrageous. But it was a fact. And as long as the volunteers did not tire – or were not too discouraged – in doing good, as long as there remained those who were able and willing to devote their time and their talents and their energies to such causes, then the future of the Cutlers – and, perhaps, the future of the nation too – might still be faced with a guarded optimism.

Glossary

ALLOWE a hired servant

AMBODEXTER (or ambidexter): able to use both hands equally well. Thus, by extension, a double-dealer; one taking money from both sides.

ARQUEBUS (or harquebus): An early type of portable gun, sometimes supported on a forked rest.

BASELARD: a dagger or hanger, worn at the girdle.

BRIMIGER (or Bromedgham or Brummagem): Birmingham.

BUCELLAS: a Portuguese white wine.

BUDGE: a kind of fur; lambskin with the wool dressed outwards.

CALIVER: a light kind of *arquebus* (q.v.) fired without a rest.

CHANTRY: an endowment for the maintenance of priests to sing masses.

CHAPE: the metal plate of a scabbard – especially that covering the point.

CHAPMAN: a trader or dealer.

CHEAP: a market place (as in Cheapside or East Cheap).

CULINE: not in O.E.D. Obviously derogatory, various derivations suggest themselves. The most probable may be Culhon – a base despicable fellow.

EVECHEPYNGS: trading after dark.

FIFTEEN (properly fifteenth): a tax on personal property.

FLUX: an abnormal discharge; an early name for dysentery.

FOLIAT: gold or silver leaf.

FOREIGN: belonging to, or coming from, another district or society. Not to be confused with *Alien*. It is thus permissible to speak of 'English foreigns'.

FOYNES (or Foins): the fur of the beech-marten.

FURBING: burnishing. By extension, cleaning or renovating.

GALLISLOPS: not in O.E.D. Cheap ready-made clothing – especially the loose trousers worn by sailors. Here, perhaps, a loose tunic or smock.

GLASING: the act of polishing knives, etc.

HAGBUTTER: a soldier armed with a hackbut, a weapon similar to an *arquebus* (q.v.).

INSPEXIMUS: a Charter reciting and confirming an earlier Grant.

KERSEY: a kind of coarse, narrow, woollen cloth, usually ribbed.

LARRYMEN: see *Lorimers*.

LIRIPIPE (or Liripoop): the tippet of an (academical) hood.

LORIMER (or Loriner): a maker of horses' bits, etc.; a spurrier; a maker of small iron ware.

MANDAMUS: a writ commanding the performance of a specified act.

MARTENER: the skin or fur of the marten.

MILL: an engine; part of a horse's harness.

MORION: a kind of vizorless helmet.

OLLIFAN: elephant.

PARTING FELLOWS: partners.

PATRIMONY, admission by: acquiring membership of a society by means of a family connection.

PLANTATION: settlement in a new or conquered country.

POMPOUS: magnificent.

POWTS: not in O.E.D.? Pelts; skins with short wool on.

PRESENTLY: immediately.

PRINCE: a monarch.

QUILLION: one or other of the two arms forming the cross guard of a sword.

QUO WARRANTO: a writ demanding evidence to show by what right an office or franchise is held.

RANDYVOUSE: rendezvous.

REDEMPTION, admission by: acquiring membership of a society by means of purchase.

SERVITUDE, admission by: Acquiring membership of a society by means of Apprenticeship.

SPARAGOS: asparagus.

SIMPLICITY: want of ordinary knowledge or judgement; ignorance.

STRANGER: foreigner or alien. Not to be confused with *Foreign* (q.v.).

STYCHE: a stabbing pain.

TOUCH-BOX: a box for holding priming-powder – formerly part of a musketeer's equipment.

WHIFFLER: an attendant, carrying a staff and wearing a chain, to clear the way at processions, etc.

Past Masters of the Cutlers' Company

(as recorded in the Company archives)

1416-17	Richard Wellom.		1492-3	Symon Newenton.
1417	John Chadde.		1494-5	William Hartwell.
1420	John Munt.		1496-7	William Seton.
1420	William Multone.		1498-9	Symon Newenton.
1428	William Brown.		1522	William Patrick.
1433	Richard Asser.		1540	Hugh Holmes.
1442-3	William Brown.		1541	John Ayland.
1444-5	Thomas Trylle.		1547	Thomas Atkynson.
1449-50	William Brown.		1548	Richard Carter.
1451-2	Thomas Trille.		1550-1-2	John Smyth.
1453-4	William Brynkill.		1558	John Leycester.
1455-6	Thomas Otehill.		1559	John Craythorne.
1457-8	John Catour.		1563-4	Laurans Grene.
1459-60	John Arnell.		1571	Laurans Grene.
1461-2	William Brynkill.		1572	John Iland.
1463-4	John Wakeman.		1576	Richard Atkinson.
1465	John Catour		1584	Roger Knowlls.
1467	John Deye.		1585	Richard Mathew.
1468-9	Robert Pykmere.		1586-7	Richard Vale.
1470-1	William Seton.		1588-9	Richard Mathew.
1472-3	Henry Penharger.		1590-1	Richard Hawes.
1474-5	John Dey.		1592-3	Thomas Porter.
1476-7	Robert Pykmere.		1594-5	Thomas Greene.
1478-9	William Seton.		1596-7	John Gardiner.
1480-1	William Vale.		1598	Thomas Asshott.
1482-3	Robert Pykmere.		1599	Thomas Assher.
1484-5	William Seton		1600-1	Henry Siddon.
1486-7	William Vale.		1602-3	Oliver Pluckett.
1488-9	William Hertwell.		1604-5	George Ellis.
1490-1	William Vale.		1606-7	Thomas Porter.

1608	Oliver Pluckett.	1652	George Sanders.
1609-10	Christopher Hatfield.	1653	Henry Beale.
1611-12	Reynold Greene.	1654	Richard Batson.
1613-14	Henry Adams.	1655	Thomas Hopkins.
1615-16	Thomas Chessheire.	1656	Jacob Ash.
1617-18	Miles Bancks.	1657	Walter Gibbons.
1610-20	John Porter.	1658	Ald. John Maniford.
	(James Tackley fined.)	1659	Robert Carrington.
1621	John Porter.		(John Partridge fined.)
	(By Order of Court of	1660	Tobie Berrey.
	Aldermen.)	1661	William Fulwell.
1622-3-4	George Harberd.	1662	William Carter.
1625-6	William Davis.	1663	Thomas Bywater.
1627	Thomas Tuck.	1664	Richard Tredwell.
1628	Henry Withers.	1665	Thomas Smyth.
1629	Robert South.	1666	Jeremiah Greene.
1630	Edmund Hutchenson.	1667	John Flampstead.
1631	John Berrey.	1668	Capt. Edward Ball.
1632	Adam Ward.	1669	Robert Saywell.
1633	Francis Fulwell.	1670	Robert Rastrick.
1634	Francis Cob.	1671	Richard Hopkins.
1635	Thomas Taylor.	1672	Thomas Birtwhistell.
1636	Joseph Rogers.	1673	Henry Whittaker.
1637	George Moore.	1674	Thomas Dermer.
1638	Edward Hynson.		(Capt. Thomas Powell
1639	Thomas Byewater.		fined.)
1640	William Cave.	1675	William Paxton.
1641	Thomas Hart.	1676	Thomas Bradford.
1642	Gabriel Partridge.	1677	Thomas Hooker.
1643	Thomas Beedham.	1678	Simon Weaver.
1644	Robert Fowlzer.	1679	Capt. Richard Blaney.
1645	William Tooley.	1680	Robert Grymes.
	(Richard Bates fined.)	1681	John Howes.
1646	Isaac Ash.	1682	Adam Ball.
1647	Thomas Cheshire.	1683	Edward Faulkingham
1648	Percival Moore.	1684	Thomas Pennington.
1649	Edmund King.	1685	William Chiffinch.
1650	Thomas Parsons.	1686	Francis Browne.
	(Col. Lawrence Bromfield	1687	John Hawgood.
	fined.)	1688	Daniel Wilson.
1651	Thomas Freeman.	1689	Anthony Clapham.
	(Edward Warnett fined.)	1690	Thomas Tunn.
	(Richard Evans fined.)	1691	Samuel James.

1692	John Kettlebuter.	1737	Jarvis (Gervase) Boswell.
1693	John Godman.	1738	Thomas Bibb.
1694	Abraham Smith.	1739	William Falkener.
1695	John Wilcox.	1740	Thomas Yelloley.
1696	William Mereden.		Edward Holden.
1697	Richard Wise.	1741	William Chambers.
1698	Henry Benson.	1742	William Loxham.
1699	Richard Geast.	1743	Samuel Smyth.
1700	Clement Tookey.	1744	Benjamin Cox.
1701	Richard Hopkins.	1745	Henry Collett.
1702	John Woodcraft.	1746	Thomas Geary.
1703	Capt. John Frith.	1747	George Fisher.
1704	Humphrey Bellamy.	1748	Charles Cotton.
1705	Nicolas Levett.	1749	William John Andrews.
1706	Ephraim How.	1750	John Bennett.
1707	Anthony Ball.	1751	William Collins.
1708	John Merreden.	1752	William Hardy.
1710	Philip Mist.	1753	Joseph Hatton.
1711	Joseph Shepheard.	1754	Thomas Crouch.
1712	Edward Patteson.	1755	James Cullum.
1713	Richard Piggott.	1756	Thomas Cross.
1714	Richard Kay.	1757	Robert Perry.
1715	Job Worrall.		(John Baldwin excused.)
1716	Edward Williams.	1758	Edward Loxham.
1717	William Powell.	1759	John Chambers.
1718	Edward Tomkins.	1760	George Gibson.
1719	Guy Stone.	1761	John Carman.
1720	Anthony Russell.	1762	Joseph Miller.
1721	Charles Thompson.	1763	James Richardson.
1722	William Smith.	1764	Thomas Dunnage.
1723	Sir Richard Hopkins.	1765	Thomas Reid.
1724	John Bully.	1766	Francis Thurkle.
1725	Peter Spitzer.		(George Watson fined.)
1726	Thomas Braugh.	1767	Joseph Bayzand.
1727	Richard Chapman.	1768	John Beaumont.
1728	Thomas Cox.	1769-70	Joseph Hatton.
1729	John Bully.	1771	Thomas Dealtry.
1730-1	John Fisher.	1772	Joseph Fisher.
1732	Thomas Horne.	1773	Peter Cargill.
1733	Amos White.	1774	Thomas Squire.
1734	Francis Hyde.	1775	William Ayres.
1735	Thomas Alcroft.	1776	Joseph Miller.
1736	Charles Cotton.	1777	John Beaumont.

1778	Thomas Copous.	1819	Yeeling Underwood.
1779	John Bennett.	1820	Stephen Boyce.
1780	Henry Allen.	1821	Richard Johnston.
1781	John Bell.	1822	William Hasledine Pepys.
1782	James Scott.	1823	William Ayres.
1783	James Looker.	1824	Abraham Skynner.
1784	Robert Lepper.		George Moses Thurkle.
1785	James Beavan.	1825	William Squire.
1786	John Copous.	1826	Richard Rees.
1787	Yeeling Charlwood.	1827	Walter Allen Meriton.
1788-9	Thomas Patrick.	1828	William Hasledine Pepys.
1790	John Phipps.		(Walter Allen Meriton
1791	John Dunnage.		fined.)
1792	William Pepys.	1829	Ald. Henry Winchester.
1793	John Bennett.	1830	William Pryor.
1794	Edward Dowling.	1831	James Johnston.
1795	Francis Thurkle.		(Zachariah Uwins fined.)
1796	George Jeffries.	1832	William Johnston.
1797	Robert Loxham.	1833	Henry William Looker.
1798	James Looker.	1834-5	John Wort.
1799	Robert Huddy.		(Thomas Johnston fined.)
1800	Charles Biggs.	1836	Henry Verinder.
1801	John Foulds.	1837	Henry Thomas Under-
1802	Edward Parry.		wood.
1803	John Gent.	1838	Zachariah Uwins.
1804	Thomas Squire, Jun.	1839	William Squire.
1805	George Skelton.	1840	Thomas Higgs.
1806	John Dowling.	1841	James Copous.
1807	Charles Biggs.	1842	Joseph Hoppe.
	(Joseph Thomas Rolph	1843	Walter Allen Meriton.
	fined.)	1844	Henry Verinder.
1808	Robert Taber.	1845	John Evans.
1809	James Dunnage.		(Sir John Hall fined.)
1810	George Skelton.	1846	Edward Stammers.
1811	Robert Loxham.	1847	Thomas Boot.
1812	John Greer.		(William Scott fined.)
1813	William Ayres.	1848	Peter Paterson.
	(John Beaumont fined.)	1849	William Hallett Hughes.
1814	George Moses Thurkle.	1850	Thomas Pocock.
1815	Henry William Looker.		(James Lee fined.)
1816	William Pryor.	1851	Thomas Barnjum.
1817	James Carden.		Thomas Pocock.
1818	James Priest.	1852	Charles Greer.

1853	Ald. Sir Robert Walter Carden.	1886	Ebenezer Pocock.
1854	Robert Burra.	1887	Robert Greer. (Charles Welch fined.)
1855	George Frederick Davis.		
1856	Richard Lloyd.	1888	James Greer.
1857	William Squire Pryor.	1889	Horace Charles Lloyd.
1858	Thomas Hammant.	1890-1	Richard James Cheeswright.
1859	Thomas Boot. (John Pryor fined.)	1892	Joseph Morton.
		1893	Ebenezer William. Joseph Morton.
1860	Joseph Fisher.	1894	Francis George Boot.
1861	William Liveing.	1895	Robert Perkins.
1862	George Frederick Carden.	1896	Joseph Underwood Morton.
1863	Thomas Dunnage.	1897	Henry William Ashmole.
1864	James Rhodes.	1898	William Cumin Scott.
1865	Ald. Sir Robert Walter Carden. (Richard James Rees fined.)	1899	James Alfred Rhodes.
		1900	Edward Beaumont.
		1901	Henry Ross Boot.
1866-7	William Anderson.	1902	Algernon Graves.
1868	Henry Graves. James Rhodes.	1903	Thomas Alfred Dunnage.
		1904	Benjamin Pratt.
1869	Frederick Smith	1905	James Beaumont Waller.
1870	Thomas Gotch Pocock.	1906	Charles James Scott.
1871	William Grenville Johnston.	1907	Charles Welch.
1872	William Adam Oldaker.	1908	Edmund Walter Rushworth.
1873	Richard Tress.	1909	Alfred Pocock.
1874	John Llewellyn Evans. Henry Graves.	1910	Francis William Williams.
		1911	Ald. Sir Walter Vaughan Morgan, Bart.
1875	James Nairne Scott.		
1876	Ald. Sir Robert Walter Carden. (James Beaumont fined.) (Henry Carnegie Carden fined.)	1912	William Alfred Herbert.
		1913	George Pocock.
		1914	William Price Pepys.
		1915	Alfred James Thomas.
		1916	William Coppard Beaumont.
1877	Henry Graves.	1917	Charles George Beaumont.
1878	Thomas Gotch Pocock.	1918	Samuel Welch.
1879	William Adam Oldaker.	1919	Percy Rogers Pocock.
1880	Alfred Pocock.	1920	Frederick Richard Cheeswright.
1881	John Parry Edkins. (George Tyler fined.)		
		1921	Macdonald Beaumont.
1882	Joseph Thorne.	1922	Edwin Hedley Williams.
1883	Richard Gore Lloyd.	1923	Sir Thomas Cato Worsfold, Bart.
1884	Samuel Poynton Boot.		
1885	Robert Balls Hughes.	1924	Thomas Henry McLean.

1925	James Arthur Gregory Beaumont.
1926-7	Atwood Thorne.
1928	Francis Weston.
1929	Alfred Squire.
1930	Arthur Elliot Rhodes.
1931	Henry Graves.
1932	John Paynter Hamilton.
1933	George Herbert.
1934	Herbert Charles Welch.
1935	William Alfred Herbert.
1936	Sir Horace Louis Petit Boot.
1937	Percy Tennyson Perkins.
1938	Thomas James Herbert.
1939	Arthur Jeffkins.
1940	Sydney Elsdon Pocock.
1941-2	Walter Joel.
1943	Percy Laurence Pocock.
1944	Samiel Horace Rexford Welch.
1945	Cuthbert Gerald Welch.
1946	Cyril Howard Welch.
1947	Kenneth Macdonald Beaumont.
1948	Richard Donald Cheeswright. (Died 18.9.48.) Sydney Elsdon Pocock.
1949	Leslie Gordon Welch.
1950	Dudley Pocock.
1951	The Rt. Hon. Sir John Beaumont.
1952	Robert McVitie Weston.
1953	Kenneth Percival Strohmenger.
1954	Howard George Potts.
1955	George Traill.
1956	Herbert Sutton Syrett.
1957	Bertram Humphreys Jones.
1958	Alan Lile Llewellyn Evans.
1959	George Vert Thomson.
1960	Dennis Charles Corfield Roberts.
1961	Arthur Charles Jeffkins.
1962	Charles Victor Jacobs.
1963	Walter Edward James McDonnell.
1964	Joseph Wilfred Pocock.
1965	Ernest Gordon Welch Roberts.
1966	Kenneth St. John Beaumont.
1967	John Marten Llewellyn Evans.
1968	Ald. The Rt. Hon. Lord Mais of Walbrook.
1969	Norman Wilson Iorns.
1970	Roland Francis Champness.
1971	Eric Lawrence Northover.
1972	Edward Buchanan Young.
1973	Anthony David Allen Kelly.
1974	Canon Douglas Webster.

Source Notes

1. Various Hands, *Cambridge Mediaeval History*, 1966–67.
2. George Unwin, *The Gilds and Companies of London*, 1908.
3. A. P. Usher, *An Introduction to the Industrial History of England*, 1921.
4. Ibid.
5. Unwin.
6. Ibid.
7. Usher.
8. Ibid.
9. Cutlers' Company, *Book of Precepts*.
10. J. B. Himsworth, *The Story of Cutlery*, 1953.
11. *Chronicle of London*.
12. H. T. Riley(ed), *Memorials of the Mayors and Sheriffs of London 1188–1274*.
13. Unwin.
14. *Inquisitiones post mortem*, Ed. I, file 42, No. 12 (cited by Welch).
15. Sylvia L. Thrupp, *The Merchant Class of Mediaeval London*, 1948.
16. Ibid.
17. P. H. Ditchfield, *Memorials of Old London*, 1908.
18. Charles Welch, *History of the Cutlers' Company of London. Vol. I*, 1916.
19. Fabyan, *The New Chronicles of England and France*, edn 1811.
20. Ancient Petitions, file 260, No. 12975 (cited by Welch).
21. Fabyan.
22. Unwin.
23. Letter Book E.
24. A. R. Myers, *England in the late Middle Ages*, 1952.
25. Unwin.
26. *Chronicle of London*.
27. Unwin.
28. *The French Chronicle*.
29. Letter Book E.
30. Thrupp.
31. *Chronicle of London*.
32. Himsworth.
33. W. Herbert, *The Twelve Great Livery Companies*, 1836.
34. Ibid.
35. Welch.
36. *Chronicle of London*.
37. Thrupp.
38. C. T. P. Bailey, *Knives and Forks*, 1927.
39. Letter Book G.
40. J. D. Aylward, *The Small-Sword in England*, 1946.
41. Letter Book G.
42. Ibid.

43. *Chronicle of London.*
44. Thrupp.
45. Unwin.
46. Thrupp.
47. Riley.
48. *Chronicle of London.*
49. Thrupp.
50. Unwin.
51. Thrupp.
52. *Petition of the Cutlers, Bowyers and Other Crafts against Nicholas Brembre,* Ancient Petitions, file 21, No. 1006.
53. Tom Girtin, *The Triple Crowns,* 1964.
54. Riley.
55. Kremer, *The English Craft Gilds.*
56. Unwin.
57. Ibid.
58. Welch.
59. *Chronicle of London.*
60. Thrupp.
61. Myers.
62. *Chronicle of London.*
63. Froissart,
64. *Rolls of Parliament: vol. 3,* p. 536a (cited by Welch).
65. Ancient Petitions, file 198, No. 9889 (ditto).
66. Ibid, file 102, No. 5070 (ditto).
67. Letter Book I.
68. *Chronicle of London.*
69. Ibid.
70. Thrupp.
71. Welch.
72. Letter Book I.
73. Thrupp.
74. Letter Book K, ff 93–4.
75. Unwin.
76. Sir Ernest Pooley, *The Guilds of the City of London,* 1945.
77. Unwin.
78. Welch.

79. Cutlers' Company: Wardens' Accounts 1442–3.
80. Myers.
81. Fabyan.
82. *Gregory's Chronicle,* Camden Soc. NS Vol. 17.
83. Ibid.
84. G. M. Trevelyan, *English Social History,* 1946.
85. Gregory.
86. Fabyan.
87. Gregory.
88. Ibid.
89. Charles Welch, *History of Pewterers' Company,* 1902.
90. Thrupp.
91. Letter Book I.
93. Jan Huizinga.
94. Fabyan.
95. *History of the Mercers' Company.*
96. Thrupp.
97. Charles Welch, *History of Cutlers' Company,* 1916.
98. Journal 9, f. 282. (cited by Welch).
99. Welch.
100. Tom Girtin, *The Triple Crowns,* 1964.
101. Fabyan.
102. Journal 10, ff. 367b, 370b (cited by Welch).
103. G. I. H. Lloyd, *The Cutlery Trades* (etc), 1913.
104. Welch.
105. Girtin.
106. Ibid.
107. Myers.
108. Girtin, *Golden Ram.*
109. Fabyan.
110. Girtin, *Triple Crowns.*
111. J. F. Hayward, *English Cutlery,* 1956.
112. Unwin.

113. Fabyan.
114. Himsworth.
115. Myers.
116. S. T. Bindoff, *Tudor England*, 1949.
117. Fabyan.
118. Ibid.
119. Lloyd.
120. Welch.
121. Letter Book S, f. 121 (cited by Welch).
122. Drapers' Company: Minute Books.
123. Usher.
124. Ibid.
125. Rep. 15, f. 74b (cited by Welch).
126. Welch.
129. State Papers Domestic, Eliz 5.
130. J. Stow, *A Survey of London*.
131. Sir William St. John Hope (cited by Welch).
132. C. M. Clode, *Early History of the Merchant Taylors' Co*, 1888.
133. Girtin, *Golden Ram*.
134. Girtin, *Triple Crowns*.
135. Stow.
136. J. Strype, *Stow's Survey of London, corrected*.
137. Welch.
138. Drapers' Company: Minute Books.
139. P. Stubbes, *Anatomy of Abuses*, 1585.
140. Rep. 22, f. 106b (cited by Welch).
141. Welch.
142. Ibid.
143. Greene, *A Quip for an Upstart Courtier*, 1592.
144. Welch.
145. R. E. Leader, *The History of the Cutlers of Hallamshire*, 1905.
146. Bindoff.
147. Ibid.
148. Rep. 27, f. 207b (cited by Welch).
149. Letter Book CC, f. 162.
150. Rep. 27, f. 225b.
151. *Remembrancia*, p. 93 (cited by Welch).
152. W. C. Hazlitt, *Livery Companies of the City of London*, 1892.
153. W. A. D. Englefield, *History of the Painter Stainers' Co*, 1950.
154. Welch.
155. State Papers Domestic.
156. Rep. 35, f. 198b (cited by Welch).
157. Welch.
160. State Papers Domestic.
161. Ibid.
165. Aylward.
166. M. Ashley, *England in the Seventeenth Century*, 1952.
167. Ibid.
168. Rep. 53, f. 68b.
169. Sir J. Finch, Ld Keeper, cited in *Parlty History of England*, 1751.
170. *Parliamentary History of England*, 1751.
171. Ashley
172. *Parlty History*.
173. Girtin, *Triple Crowns*
174. Ashley.
175. *Parlty History*.
176. Ibid.
177. Ibid.
178. Ashley.
179. *Parlty History*.
180. Ibid.
181. Ashley.
182. *Parlty History*.
183. Ashley.
184. *Parlty History*.
185. Girtin, *Triple Crowns*.
186. R. J. Cheesewright.
187. Englefield.
188. Aylward.

189. R. Stephens, *Information about Non-conformists*, PC Papers, 1678.

190. W. Badcock, *A New Touch-stone for Gold and Silver Wares* (etc), 1679.

191. Girtin, *Triple Crowns* (citing W. Herbert & State Papers Domestic).

192. Welch.

193. Herbert.

194. Hazlitt.

195. Welch.

196. Rep. 106, f. 554 (cited by Welch).

197. J. H. Plumb, *England in the Eighteenth Century*, 1950.

198. Ibid.

199. Anon, *General Description of All Trades*, London 1747 (cited by Lloyd).

200. St James's Chronicle: 27–29 October 1763 (cited by Welch).

201. Aylward.

202. Welch.

203. Lloyd.

204. Ibid.

205. C. Blagden, *History of the Stationers Co.*, 1960.

206. Unwin.

207. Hazlitt.

208. Himsworth.

209. Lloyd.

210. Hazlitt.

211. Ibid.

212. Ibid.

213. Ibid.

214. Ibid.

215. R. J. Blackham, *The Soul of the City*, 1931.

Bibliography

Internal Sources

The greater part of the material in this volume has been compiled from the original records of the Cutlers' Company deposited in the Library of Guildhall. These records consist of Account Rolls for thirty-six years between 1442 and 1498 and Minute (and other) Books which – apart from certain notable lacunae – form a very comprehensive record from 1602 to the present day.

Much of the material has been published in fragmented form in the two monumental volumes of the *History of the Cutlers' Company of London*, the first of which, by Charles Welch, was published privately in 1916 and the second of which, completed by his son, was published privately in 1923.

The present work, containing much new material and further continuing the history of the Company, forms a narrative to which the previous volumes may provide, with their extensive documentation and wide range of scholarship, some useful footnotes.

Material has also been taken from R. J. Cheesewright's short chronicle of the Cutlers' Company.

External Sources

Letter Books of the City of London.
State Papers Domestic.
Remembrancia.
Chronicles of London.
London Chronicle.
New Chronicle of England and France.

General Reading

ASHLEY, M. *England in the Seventeenth Century*, 1952.
AYLWARD, J. D. *The Small-Sword in England*, 1946.

BADCOCK, W. *A new Touchstone for Gold and Silver Wares* (etc) 2nd edn., 1679.

BAILEY, C. T. P. *Knives and Forks*, 1927.

BINDOFF, S. T. *Tudor England*, 1949.

BLACKHAM, R. J. *The Soul of the City*, 1931.

BLAGDEN, C. *History of the Stationers' Company*, 1960.

CLODE, C. M. *Early History of the Merchant Taylors' Company*, 1888.

DITCHFIELD, P. H. *Memorials of Old London*, 1908.

ENGLEFIELD, W. A. D. *History of the Painter Stainers' Co.*, 1950.

FABYAN, R. *The New Chronicles of England and France* (ed. H. Ellis), 1811.

GIRTIN, T. *The Golden Ram*, 1958, *The Triple Crowns*, 1964.

GREENE, —. *A Quip for an Upstart Courtier*, 1592.

HAYWARD, J. F. *English Cutlery*, 1956.

HAZLITT, W. C. *Livery Companies of the City of London*, 1892.

HERBERT, W. *The Twelve Great Livery Companies*, 1836.

HIMSWORTH, J. B. *The Story of Cutlery*, 1953.

LEADER, R. E. *The History of the Cutlers of Hallamshire*, 1905.

LLOYD, G. I. H. *The Cutlery Trades* (etc), 1913.

MYERS, A. R. *England in the Late Middle Ages*, 1952.

PLUMB, J. H. *England in the Eighteenth Century*, 1950.

POOLEY, Sir E. *The Guilds of the City of London*, 1945.

RILEY, H. T. (ed.). *Chronicles of the Mayors and Sheriffs of London 1188–1274*.

STOW, J. *A Survey of London* (repr.), 1933.

STRYPE, J. *Stow's Survey of London, corrected* (etc), 1893.

STUBBES, P. *Anatomy of Abuses*, 1585.

THOMPSON, D. *England in the Nineteenth Century*, 1950.

THRUPP, S. L. *The Merchant Class of Mediaeval London*, 1948.

TREVELYAN, G. M. *English Social History*, 1946.

UNWIN, G. *The Gilds and Companies of London*, 1908, *Studies in Economic History*, 1927.

USHER, A. P. *An Introduction to the Industrial History of England*, 1921.

VARIOUS HANDS. *Cambridge Mediaeval History*, 1966–67, *Parliamentary History of England*, 1751, *Middlesex Chronicle*, 8, iii, 1974.

WELCH, C. *History of the Pewterers' Company*, 1902.

Index